LETTERS FROM OLE ROCKSVOLD

LETTERS FROM OLE ROCKSVOLD

By

SHARON SMITH BOWEN

Book layout and design:
Erik Anundsen
Anundsen Publishing Company
Decorah, Iowa

Dedication

This book is dedicated to my husband, Max Bowen, my son, Nathan Kalmoe, his wife, Katie Will, my mother, Florence Ohnstad Smith, my stepdaughters, Joy Ochs, Anna Bowen, Sara Bowen, their spouses, and to all those like Ole Rocksvold who have the courage and compassion to make a positive difference in their communities and world.

Preface

$\mathcal{L}$etter writing has almost become a lost art. Few people take the time to sit down and write out in longhand their thoughts, feelings, and experiences, using careful reflection in the process. Instead, we tend to use shorter means of communication- a brief phone call, text message, or a social media posting-often with little editing.

Ole Rocksvold was my great grandfather and a gifted letter writer. He didn't have all the modern options we have for communicating, and I am thankful he put much time and thought into his writing. His letters help us get to know him and draw back the curtain into the world in which he lived. We are the richer for it. Fortunately Ole's great granddaughter, Bev Anderson Swenson, discovered dozens of letters in storage and together we hired a translator to turn the Norwegian into English to share with all of you. Although I never met him, he is very alive to me after spending four years of researching my ancestors and learning what an admirable, accomplished person he was. Respected by his family, his comrades in the Civil War, the community, and state, Ole's life story deserved a book. I have a strong desire to preserve and learn from history, and hope you will be as inspired as I was by Ole's life.

Acknowledgements

Many people have helped me learn about Ole and his family and I am extremely grateful for their help. My husband, Max Bowen, taught me much as I observed him write two books on his ancestors upon retirement. He encouraged me and shared many problem-solving suggestions and proofing and editing ideas. My son, Nathan Kalmoe, a political scientist and Civil War buff, has inspired me with his love of history, research skills and publications, and has recommended many books to further my background knowledge on the Civil War and history from the 1800's. Nathan provided information about Ole's company G in Iowa's 12th regiment, as well as valuable editing help. A special thrill was a trip Nathan and I took together in April of 2012 to some of the Civil War National Battlefields where Ole fought. At Shiloh/ Pittsburg Landing, in Tennessee, we went on 15 miles of docent-led hikes on the exact 150th anniversary to the day of Ole fighting there. We stood at the site April 6, where 150 years earlier Ole fought for many hours before ultimately being captured and taken as a prisoner of war for almost seven months. Additional help was offered by Nathan's wife, Katie Will, a Shakespeare and English scholar, who shared information about her writing process and editing suggestions as well.

Some genealogists who helped find information about Ole Rocksvold and Anne Guldbrandsdatter Standbakken's families, their ancestors, and the lands where they lived were Millie Andorfer and Mette Engeskog Nordengen of Totenlag and Sharon Babcock of Hadelandlag. Totenlag and Hadelandlag are two of the four Norwegian-American genealogical organizations to which I belong. Millie and Sharon found maps of the Roksvold, Strandbakken and Egge farms. Mette worked with people in the historical society in Toten, Norway, to research far back into Ole's ancestors using the old bygeboks and other documents there. Mette also helped locate the Raddum cousins to arrange for my husband and I to meet them in June, 2014, and she and Rune Nedrud accompanied us on part of the touring of the farms and schools of my ancestors in the area.

Many cousins generously shared information with me and provided encouragement in my research and writing process. Those who provided the most information by far were Bev Anderson Swenson and Dorothy (Dot) Rocksvold Pulliam, second cousins of mine. Dot provided much encouragement and support, as well as many photographs and documents and helped with picture identification. Even more importantly, Dot was the connection through Ancestry to introduce me to cousin Bev Swenson. Not only did Bev provide many pictures, picture identification, dates, and much information about ancestors, but she discovered in her home dozens of very informative letters, over 600 pages worth, written by Ole and other relatives and friends which tell the story of their lives and times. Among those letters are 14 priceless letters of both historical significance and family interest written by Ole as a Civil War soldier to his future wife, Anne! His writing is both informative and poignant. I still marvel at such a find that she has shared! I am so very thankful to Bev's ancestors- Ole, his daughter, Matilda Rocksvold Anderson; and her daughter, Irene Anderson; and Irene's brother, Ernest Anderson (Bev's father); who all kept these letters safe. Many of these letters were written in the old style of Danish-influenced Norwegian of the 1800's, which is very challenging to read. The style of handwriting, vocabulary, and figures of speech have changed since when the letters were written, so we knew it would be a difficult challenge to translate. Bev also very generously offered to split the costs of the translating with me.

I would like to thank these translators: Jim Skurdall, Rune Nedrud, Liv Arafat, Marit Barkvema, and Tove Tobiassen. Jim Skurdall did the lion's share of initial translating of most letters, and in some cases provided a second version for some of these letters already translated by others. Jim also provided some historical context because of his familiarity with the Decorah, Iowa area where Ole Rocksvold and some of Jim's ancestors coincidentally also lived. Jim's career in education, genealogical and historical writings, and translating experience in English, Norwegian, and German made him uniquely qualified to do a wonderful job. We discovered that Jim happens to be related to my cousin, Bev Swenson, through her mother's side. Rune Nedrud also has much expertise with genealogy and translating, having been the president of the Norwegian Genealogical Society, and is from the Toten area where Ole was born and raised.

Other relatives who shared valuable ancestor pictures, books, and information include: my mother, Florence Ohnstad Smith, brothers Stan and Sherman Smith, and cousins: Steve Timmer, Håkon and Sveingung Raddum, Inger Guro Melby and Hans Grefsrud, Dee Randash Seay, Dorothy Randash Forder, Dean Randash, Peter and DiAnn Rocksvold, Iona Rocksvold Crawford, Darrel and Mary Crawford, Craig and Connie Rocksvold, Kert and Karen Rocksvold, Loraine Dennis Trollope, Marlene Amunrud Welliever, Donie Ueckert and Don Erstad, Fred Hagen, Robert Rosseth, Rome Mickelson and Rhude Thompson. While my husband, Max, and I were in Norway in June, 2014, Inger Guro Melby and Hans Grefsrud graciously welcomed us to their home in the Brandbu area of Norway, and guided us on a tour of the Egge, Sønsteby, Sivesind, and Strandbakken farms. Sveinung and Håkon Raddum guided us on touring the Toten areas of the

Roksvold farm, churches and cemeteries, and Håkon and his wife Liv lavishly hosted a dinner party at their home for both sides- our Rocksvold and Strandbakken cousins. Reading E.Palmer Rockswold's novel, *Per*, helped me learn more about the immigrant experience as well. I interviewed him by phone upon learning his relative was the wife of Anton Rocksvold, Ole's brother. *Developing Character and Creating Characters* by Dennis Loraine Trollope provided insight into the western ND and eastern MT pioneering experience of some of our ancestors as well. Sveinung Raddum also wrote a book, *Norges Jernalder*, a very early history of Norway, in Norwegian. So there are quite a few authors among our relatives. Thank you also to Rev. Stacey Nalean-Carlson of Glenwood Lutheran Church near Decorah, IA, for sending me the minutes of the Glenwood Church.

The process of researching and writing family history is challenging and fascinating. I love being a detective. I learned to not trust one piece of information or document as necessarily accurate unless I can locate one or more corroborating documents or sources. Many sources have errors, some due to inadvertent mistakes, such as difficulty reading handwriting, poor condition of documents, lost records, or the person originally asked didn't have the correct information. I learned that for census records long ago, for example, if the head(s) of the household wasn't home when the census taker came, they sometimes just asked other people who lived there or neighbors for information. Also, when someone died, they asked whoever was conveniently available to supply information for the gravestone, obituary, etc., sometimes resulting in mistakes. Occasionally people purposely gave out wrong information to mislead, preserve privacy, or avoid embarrassment, such as if someone wanted to seem younger at age of marriage or wanted to make it look like a baby was born later after the wedding date.

A special challenge for Scandinavian research is that up until the early 1900's the last name changed each generation with parents usually giving the father's first name and adding the Scandinavian word for "son" or "daughter" to form the children's last names. Since there weren't very many name choices, several people in a community may have had the same name, so getting accurate dates for birth, marriage, death, and locations was imperative to make sure you have the right person. Sometimes a last name changed multiple times during someone's life- for example with each move to a different farm, some people took the name of that farm/farm owner. This often happened regarding people who were workers on the farm or rented some farmland, rather than people who owned of the farm.

For example, Ole's wife, Anne, was first known as Anne Guldbrandsdatter, (Anne, the daughter of Guldbrand). Her family first lived at the Egge/Eggebraaten farm, so her parents and older siblings added Egge or Eggebraaten to their last name. By the time Anne was born, her family had moved to the Strandbakken farm and exchanged Egge for Strandbakken as their last name. So Anne was then known as Anne Guldbrandsdatter Strandbakken.

Some people also changed their last name upon coming to the U.S. or within a year or two of arriving. Various reasons included people having trouble pronouncing it or spelling it, or too many people with the same name in a community caused confusion. Others just wanting the fresh start of a new name in a new land. Anne changed her name to Gilbertson instead of Guldbrandsdatter, as did many in the Midwest with that last name, perhaps thinking Gilbert sounded more American or easier to pronounce than Guldbrand. Also, by that time some had started just putting "son" at the end of the father's name for both sexes, instead of "datter" for daughters. Upon marriage, Anne took Ole's last name of Rockswold, and later spelled Rocksvold. Ole changed the spelling of his last name after the Civil War since so many people were already spelling the w" with a "v" since the "w" sounds like the "v" sound when pronounced in Norwegian.

Interestingly, in June, 2014, when I saw the road running along Ole's ancestral farm in Vestre Toten, Norway, the sign was spelled Roksvoll. Sometimes final "d's" are silent in Norwegian so perhaps they didn't bother to put a "d" at the end of Roksvold for the sign. Also, historically in the absence of a dictionary and with many people illiterate, most people just knew a word or name by its sound. Thus, there were often multiple spellings used for a given word or name. So in researching Anne, ultimately I had to look up the following last names: Guldbrandsdatter, Gulbrandson, (plus her other family members with last names of Egge and Eggebraaten), Strandbakken, Gilbertson, Rockswold, Rockvold. Whew!

If you find any errors in this book that I may have made, or you have access to more sources that dispute any information I found, please let me know so. My contact information is:

Sharon Bowen
sharonraesmithbowen@gmail.com
Copyright © 2017

Table of Contents

Guide to Key People in the Book

Ole Rocksvold-husband of Anne Strandbakken, son of Peder Rocksvold and Kjersti Kjøs.

Siblings of Ole: Helene Rocksvold Dahl, Anne Mathea "Mathea" Thorstenson Evenrud, Anton Rocksvold.

Anne Guldbrandsdatter (Gilbertson) Strandbakken- wife of Ole Rocksvold, daughter Guldbrand Egge Strandbakken and Marte Eggebraaten.

Siblings of Anne: Maria, Ingeborg, Hans, Elena, Anders, Hans O., Berthe.

Ole and Anne's Children (spouse in parentheses)**:**

 George
 Matilda (Andrew Anderson) "A.O."
 Carl
 Theodor Victor
 Emma (Oscar Amunrud)
 Manda
 Theodor Olaf
 Hilda (Edward Ohnstad)
 Anton Norman "Norman" (Tilda Foss)
 Peter William "Willie" (Helen Bengtsen)

Other Relatives:

Ernest Anderson - son of Matilda and A.O. Anderson, grandson of Ole and Anne

Peter and Albert Rocksvold- sons of Anton and Anne Elvestuen Rocksvold, nephews of Ole and Anne.

Helene Marie Dahl Øistad - daughter of Helene Rocksvold and Lars Dahl, niece of Ole and Anne.

Lars Dahl, spouse of Helene Rocksvold Dahl, married to Ole's sister.

Hilda Øistad Garaas - daughter of Helene Marie and Bernt Øistad, great niece of Ole and Anne.

Pauline Evenrud Mickelson - daughter of Anne Mathea and Paul Mickelson, granddaughter of Ole, Anne.

Non-Family Member:

Ole Kjørlien- Person Ole traveled back to Norway with him in 1902.

Ole Rocksvold Timeline

- March 30, 1832 Ole Pedersen Roksvold (later spelled Rockswold, Rocksvold) born with twin sister, Anne Mathea, to Peder Roksvold and Kjersti Kjos and at Roksvold(en) farm, Vestre Toten, Norway

- 1846 confirmed at Ås Lutheran Church, Vestre Toten, Norway

- April 26 (27), 1853 left Christiania (Oslo), Norway on the "Deodata" ship to emigrate with family, but sister, Helene Roksvold Dahl, remained to farm with her husband

- June 15, 1853 arrived in Quebec, Canada, traveled through the St. Lawrence River to Yorkville, WI (Milwaukee area), staying about two months

- Aug., 1853 arrived in Glenwood, IA to start farming

- Fall of 1853, Vilhelm Koren was called to start a new congregation in the area. Ole and his family are among those helping to get the church started.

- Oct. 18, 1861 enlisted in the army in the Civil War, 12th Infantry, company G, Iowa

- Nov. 5, 1861 mustered into the army as private

- Winter of 1861-2 camped at Benton Barracks, MO

- Feb. 6, 1861 fought in battle of Fort Henry

- Feb. 14-15, 1862 fought in battle of Fort Donelson, TN

- March 25, 1862 promoted to corporal

- April 6, 1862 fought in the battle of Shiloh/Pittsburg Landing, was part of the "Hornets' Nest"

- April 6, 1862 Ole suffered a ramrod through the hand when reloading gun, later taken prisoner of war at Shiloh/Pittsburg Landing, TN, were marched to Corinth, MS, then transported to Memphis, TN, Cahaba Prison near Selma, AL, Camp Oglethorpe, Macon, GA, Libby Prison, Aikens Landing, VA, spending 7 months in captivity

- Oct. 26, 1862 paroled (released from being in captivity)

- Nov. 10, 1862 Union and Rebels exchanged prisoners and Ole was transported to Annapolis, MD, then to St. Louis, MO, where the regiment reorganized April 1, 1863

- May-July, 1863 Ole fought, did guard duty, and other military action in the battle of Vicksburg, MS, Jackson, MS, and surrounding area

- April 9, 1864 Ole was wounded in thigh at Pleasant Hill, LA, in the Red River Campaign, plus marched hundred of miles that spring through fall in a variety of military actions in multiple states

- Nov. 30, 1864 (Dec. 7) mustered out of the army at Nashville, TN

- Feb. 12, 1865 married Anne Guldbrandsdatter (Gilbertson) Strandbakken at Decorah, IA. Anne was born Nov. 16, 1839, Strandbakken farm, Hadeland, Norway

- Nov. 14, 1865 son, George Paulus, was born at Glenwood township, IA

- Feb. 17, 1867 daughter, Mathilda (Matilda), was born at Glenwood township, IA

- Oct. 9, 1868 son, Carl Oscar, was born at Glenwood township, IA

- Oct. 17, 1870 son, Theodor Victor, was born at Glenwood township, IA, died March 7, 1871

- March 31, 1872 daughter, Emma Theodora, was born at Glenwood township, IA

- April 1, 1874 daughter, Manda Augusta, was born at Glenwood township, IA

- Feb. 27, 1876 son, Theodor Olaf, was born at Glenwood township, IA

- Dec. 5, 1878 daughter, Hilda Oleana, was born at Glenwood township, IA

- Aug., 31, 1880 son, Anthon (Anton) Norman, was born at Glenwood township, IA

- Dec. 13, 1882 son, Peder Wilhelm (Peter William), was born at Glenwood township, IA

- Mar. 12, 1885 death of father, Peder

- Sometime after April 3, 1896, Ole left the Glenwood Lutheran congregation to become a member at St. John's Lutheran, Waukon, IA.

- June 29, 1886 death of brother, Anton

- March 3, 1890 death of son, George

- Fall of 1893, after changing parties, Ole ran for Iowa assembly on the Democratic ticket, did not win

- March 17, 1894 death of son, Theodor Olaf

- March 9, 1895 death of mother, Kjersti

- July 4, 1895 death of wife, Anne

- June 4, 1902 Ole wrote a postcard from Washington, D.C. As he traveled with Ole Kjørlien, visiting monuments, museums, Gilbert Haugen, his 57th dist. IA representative in Congress, the White House and saw Theodore Roosevelt, but did not meet him. They were on their return trip to Norway after 49 years.

- June 18, 1902 Ole arrived in Gothenburg, Sweden, having traveled by way of Hull, England, then took the train from Gothenburg to Oslo, and started an extensive trip around Norway, visiting relatives and sightseeing

- Aug. 17, 1902 Ole left from Oslo, Norway, to return home by way of Liverpool, England

- July 1, 1903 Ole retired as postmaster of the Thoten Post Office after 25 years

- April 12, 1906 death of sister, Anne Mathea

- March 20, 1908, moves to a newly-purchased farm near Beach, ND, with son, Peter William, and daughter, Hilda

- Dec. 19, 1910 death of sister, Helene

- June 18, 1912 death of daughter, Emma

- Sometime between Dec. 14, 1913-April 4, 1914, Ole moved back to Decorah, IA, to a "nursing home"/senior housing, but still traveled

- May 12, 1922 death of son, Anton Norman

- June, 1922 Ole traveled to Madison, SD, with daughter, Matilda, for a failed surgery to restore his sight, kidneys started to fail

- Aug. 20, 1922 death of Ole Rocksvold at Inwood, IA, home of daughter, Matilda. Buried at Glenwood Church cemetery, IA, in Rocksvold family plot

Ole Rocksvold, in Decorah, IA,
probably taken 1905-1910, in his seventies.

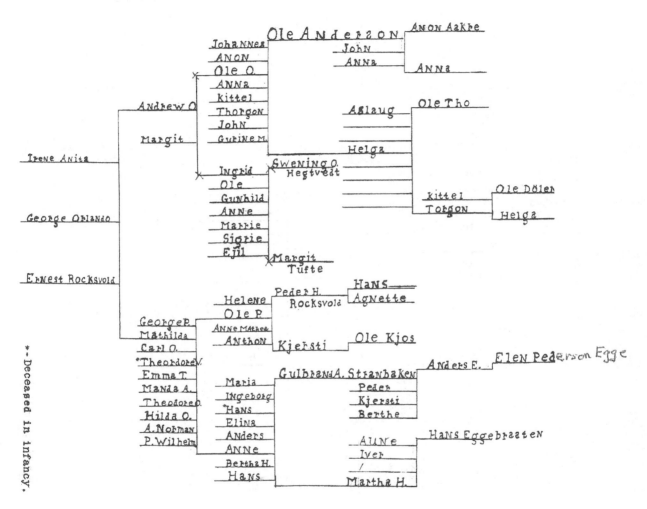

Family Tree of Ernest Anderson, son of Matilda Rocksvold, A.O Anderson

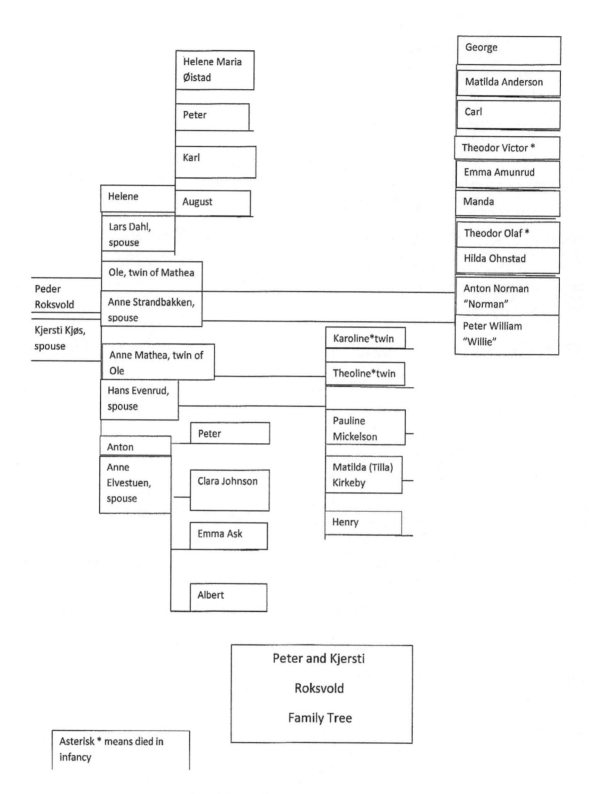

Family Tree of Peder Roksvold Family

∿ Chapter 1 ∾
Introduction to Ole Rocksvold

"Benton Barracks, St. Louis, Mo.
Feb 15, 1863

Unforgettable special friend, Miss Anne:

Your most welcome letter dated the 8th of this month arrived today and was read with greatest pleasure. Slowly but surely your first letter arrived, and it was likewise the first letter I have ever received from a young lady.

I cannot properly express nor thank you for your encouraging and honest words articulated in the letter. You also say that you are happy to see from my letter that I have not forgotten you. Oh no, dear Anne, I would be more likely to forget my own existence than forget you..."

Ole Rockvold
Translated from Norwegian by Jim Skurdall.

So begins one of 14 poignant and informative letters written by Ole Rocksvold, my maternal great grandfather, to his future wife Anne, during the Civil War. His great granddaughter, Bev Anderson Swenson, found these treasured documents in boxes in her home, and kindly shared copies with me, along with several dozen more letters written by Ole and others after he had completed his military service. The love between Ole and Anne helped sustain him during the war through many hardships, multiple battles, and almost seven months of suffering and near-fatal illness as a prisoner of war after being captured in the Battle of Shiloh/Pittsburg Landing. Translations of these Civil War letters appear within chapters 3 and 4, and other letters written by Ole and his relatives and friends are in the appendices of this book.

Ole in His Own Words

Who was Ole Rocksvold? A Norwegian immigrant and Civil War veteran, he was also an active parishioner at the church he helped establish, husband, father of 10, successful farmer, postmaster, and community leader. In 1905 at age 73, he was asked to write a chapter about Glenwood township for the book, *Standard Historical Atlas of Winneshiek County 1905*, published by Anderson and Goodwin. Toward the end of the chapter, Ole added a one-paragraph autobiography, and as far as we know, is the only "autobiography" written by Ole. I quote that last, long paragraph here:

"It may not be out of place to mention the writer as being an old settler, as my name has not been mentioned among the old settlers. I came to Glenwood township direct from Norway in 1853, and have resided here ever since with the exception of three years when I served in the army. My first occupation was to build houses, clear land and break, was known as an expert shingle maker, making at least 100,000 in one single summer splitting and shaving them by hand. In the fall of 1861 I enlisted in Company G, Twelfth Iowa Infantry, and served three years and two months. I participated in the following battles: Fort Henry, Fort Donelson, Shiloh, where on April 6, 1862, our regiment was captured at what is known as the Hornet's Nest and we were kept in prison for six and one-half months. We were kept at the following places: Memphis, Tenn., Mobile, Ala., Cahaba, Montgomery and Macon, Ga., where we were kept for five months, then sent to Libbey Prison and exchanged on James River above Fort Monroe; were then sent to Annapolis, Md., and from there to St. Louis; when the regiment was reorganized and in the spring of 1863 went to Vicksburg, and from there to Jackson, Mississippi, where we had a hard time to capture the city, then back to Vicksburg, participating in the siege until July 4, 1863, when the Fort surrendered, then turned around and went with General Sherman's army and drove the rebels back to Jackson and captured the city again. In 1864 we were sent (6,000 men) up the Red River under General Smith to assist General Banks on his raid to Shreveport, La. We captured Alexandria, taking some three or four cannons there, and twenty-two miles above we captured Henderson's Hill, took four cannons there and two regiments of rebels, one cavalry, the other infantry; then further up we captured a fort and garrison with ten cannons, the name of the fort I have forgotten. At a place called Pleasant Hill where General Banks had been defeated we met the rebels and drove them back, covering his retreat to the Mississippi river, a distance of over one hundred miles, having a rebel fence around us of about 18,000 men, which we had to fight every day for two weeks.

In the fall of 1864, I was mustered out at Nashville, Tenn., went home, got married the following spring, resumed farming and have been at it ever since. I am now seventy-three years old and feel played out."

I found this mini-autobiography interesting in what it includes as well as what it doesn't. For whatever reason, Ole did not mention a hand injury at Shiloh, a bullet wound to his thigh at Pleasant Hill, nor that he was very ill during imprisonment and almost died. He didn't mention his run for Iowa state assembly in 1893, nor much other community service like his postmaster role for 25 years. It is significant that he spent almost all of this long paragraph on his Civil War service, with a just short mention of his marriage and farming life and his prowess in shingle-making. This shingle-making skill was a money-maker for Ole, as he sold shingles to others in the area as a sideline to his farming. The 51 letters and postcards Ole wrote, plus the 49 letters written by others, show he was very close to his wife and family, but he apparently decided it wasn't something he wanted to share in a book of this sort.

I found it interesting that Ole was so respected that he was asked to write this Glenwood history chapter. It is also apparent that Ole developed his English writing skills to the point where others considered him capable of doing well as an author. Our translators have noted that his letters in Norwegian are very fluent, informative, and emotionally expressive, so he probably had quite a bit of education before coming over to the U.S. at age 21.

After researching Ole's whole life, I marvel at his resiliency and accomplishments. I believe he deserves a biography. So here is his story.

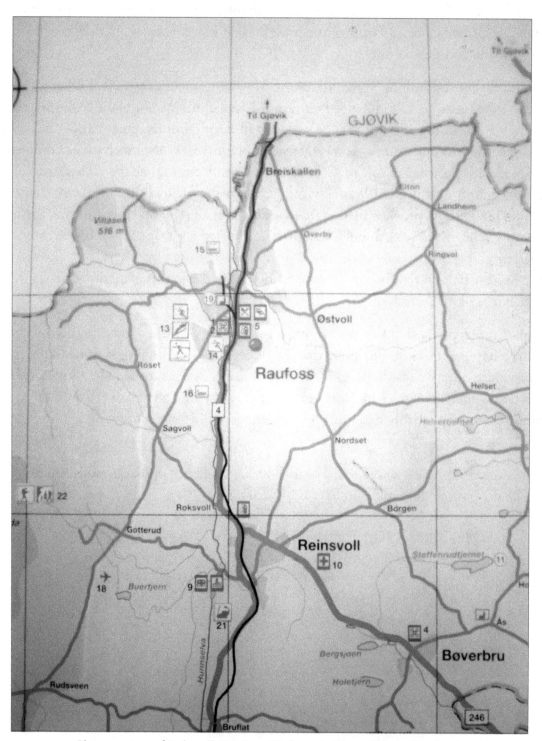

Close up view of Roksvoll (Rocksvold) farm, in Vestre Toten, Oppland,
Norway, where Ole Rocksvold grew up.

~ CHAPTER 2 ~

OLE'S EARLY LIFE AND TIMES

Ole Rocksvold was born as a twin with Anne Mathea on March 30, 1832, at Vestre Toten, in the beautiful, rolling hills of Oppland, Norway, on the "Roksvoll" farm, 2830 Raufoss, Vestre Toten, 66 miles north of Oslo, according to bygdebok (church records) and gardsbruk (farm records) in Norway. The "Roksvoll" farm had clay and humus soil with about seven and a half acres of farmland and 25 acres of timberland. The original farmhouse and barn were built in 1818 and still stand in 2017, with additions to the house made after it was built. Ole's parents, Peder Roksvold and Kjersti Kjøs, lived in this farmhouse when Ole was born, but I found no evidence of who actually built it. The Rocksvolds used to have a grist mill for grinding wheat on the property, but it no longer exists. According to Anne Gesme in

Roksvoll Farm with Sharon Bowen, 2014, Vestre Toten, Oppland, Norway

Between Rocks and Hard Places, most farms had a few cows, goats, or sheep. Crops common at that time included barley, rye, occasionally wheat in some locations, turnips, onions, and peas. Potatoes weren't imported until about 1850. So there couldn't have been any lefse (Norwegian potato bread) for Ole until he was about 18 years old! Children

The barn on the Roksvoll farm where Ole Rocksvold grew up, Vestre Toten, Oppland, Norway. Photo taken 2014.

helped with the farming and other chores as soon as they were capable.

Ole had blue eyes and pictures vary on the color of his hair. The earliest picture we have, Ole in his Civil War uniform, appears to show dark blond/light brown hair, but the picture is somewhat blurry. Other early black and white pictures look like he had dark hair. While Ole was applying for U.S. military pension benefits in 1890 and 1907, at ages 57 and 75 respectively, the records described his hair as sandy and later white. They also described his complexion as light. Ernest Anderson, Ole's grandson, wrote an autobiography-family history in 1924 for an assignment at St. Olaf College, with his mother, Matilda, and other relatives as sources. In that document Anderson described Ole as large-boned, with lots of white hair "which had been black." He had a Roman nose, and a dignified, "stern, yet kind" expression. Ole was very kind-hearted to those in need, but had a certain "stern relentlessness in seeing that what he willed was carried out." He had broad shoulders, sat and stood very erectly, and had an amazing memory. His adult height, recorded in pension records, was five feet ten and a half inches in 1893, age 61, and five feet and eight and three-fourth inches, 176 pounds in 1907, age 75.

Ole's parents, Peder Hansen Drager Stenberg Roksvold(en) (1798-1885), and Kjersti Olsdatter Drager Kjøs (1799-1895), married on Oct. 7, 1825, at Naess Church, Gran, Hadeland, about 29 miles south of the Roksvoll farm. By the time Ole and Anne Mathea were born, Peder and Kjersti already had one daughter, Helene, born June 21, 1829. They would gain one more son, Anton (Anthon), on Mar. 17, 1839. The children were all baptized and confirmed at Ås Church, 155 Gimlevegen, Bøverbru, 4.2 miles from the Roksvoll farm. Ole and Anne Mathea were confirmed in 1846.

Ole's Parents and Grandparents

Ole's father, Peder Hanson Rocksvold, was born May 1, 1798, to parents Hans Drager Paulson (1764-1815) and Agnette Tonette Olsdatter (1770-1809). Anderson wrote that Tonette was known for being a fast worker, twice as fast as others in rolling out her flatbrod (flat bread) and doing her knitting and handwork. Her son Peder's hair was almost black and very thick. He had blue eyes, a small straight nose, long thin fingers, and was medium height. Peder spoke slowly, was an avid reader, and had a dry sense of humor, and served in the Norwegian Cavalry as a young person. He must have been very strong since he still chopped his own wood until a month before he died at 86.

Unfortunately, Peder had a weakness for alcohol. He wasn't a regular drinker, but tended to imbibe at parties, Anderson wrote. If he had too much to drink, his wife would tell him to go to bed and stay there until he recov-

From left in front: Kjersti Kjøs Rocksvold (Ole's mother), Anne Mathea Rocksvold Evenrud (Kjersti's daughter and Ole's twin sister)
From left in back - Matilda (Tilla) Evenrud Kirkeby (daughter of Mathea), Ida Kirkeby (daughter of Tilla) Picture Circa 1888-1895, location unknown, likely near Decorah IA.

ered. He grew tobacco for his own use. Peder was generous and kind, and loved being with children. He regularly attended church, but by the time he was elderly had trouble hearing the sermon when his ears began to fail. Peder liked to retire early so he could pray and read hymns in his bedroom. He was a gifted carpenter and gave away some of his creations to relatives. Common items made of wood at that time were skis, containers, drinking vessels, cabinets, trunks, and cooking implements. The tradition was to carve wooden items ornately and/or paint them with Norwegian rosmaling technique to decorate. We do not know whether Peder added these decorative touches.

Peder Roksvold's wife, Kjersti Olsdatter Kjøs, as being born July 11, 1799, was medium height, large boned, and had long, thin fingers like Peder. Anderson described Kjersti as having light hair, light complexion, and dark blue eyes. She was also an excellent singer. She was very strong and lived to be 95. Kjersti loved playing with children, telling them fairy tales from Norway, and teaching them songs. She sang around the house while she worked. When she was 75 she was run over by a colt that hurt her hip. She needed a crutch to walk the rest of her life. Nevertheless, she could still walk faster than many people her age. She got glasses at age 40, but around ninety she didn't need them anymore for reasons unknown.

Life in Norway

What was life like for the Rocksvolds, their ancestors, and their neighbors in Norway so long ago? Norway is mountainous with little good farmland. So farms tended to be small and isolated, especially on the west coast and far north where it is especially mountainous. Since Ole's family lived north of Oslo, it was more hilly than mountainous and so somewhat easier to farm.

According to www.sciencenordic.com, the potato made its way from South America to Portugal in 1567, but priests, soldiers, and sailors didn't bring potatoes to Norway until around 1850. The potato helped to prevent starvation, and it was soon used to make alcohol as well. In 1816 the Storting (parliament) made it illegal to distill alcohol unless it was grain-based. So Norwegian lefse, a potato-based flatbread, wouldn't have been made prior to 1850.

Common foods were potatoes, flat bread, mush, sour milk, dried meat, fish, ham, cheese, cabbage, porridge, lefse, peas, nuts, and berries. Lefse is a potato bread, rolled thin and cooked in a pan, similar- looking to tortillas. If a family was very poor, they ate mostly potatoes and even added bark or moss ground into flour to make it stretch further. They drank water, beer, ale, buttermilk, and by the early 1800's, coffee, which quickly started to replace other drinks once it was available. We have no evidence that Ole's family was starving, so it is likely they had a variety of foods to eat while he was growing up, which of course helped the children's mental and physical development. At Christmas, the traditional entrees were pork or mutton and sometimes lutefisk. Lutefisk is dried whitefish, usually cod, treated with lye. In the United States, Norwegian immigrants gradually started to eat more lutefisk for Christmas, when available. Popular desserts for Christmas were rice pudding and many kinds of cookies. Another popular food eaten at Christmas by the descendants of Norwegian immigrants in the U.S. is lefse.

What did people wear at that time? In *Between Rocks and Hard Places* Gesme noted that clothing tended to be distinctive to the region, so one could identify where someone was from in Norway by the design and decoration of their clothing. Clothing tended to be of wool or linen and made at home, as well as shoes of leather. Men tended to wear dark pants, light shirt and red caps. Women often wore a light colored blouse, with dark colored jumper over the blouse and long skirt. Women also wore a cap, kerchief, or bonnet, with different colors/designs for their region. Metal hooks were often used to close bodices or pants. The sturdy wool bunad folk costume for men and women was usually obtained at confirmation, and then used for special occasions. An example of such a holiday would be Syttende Mai (May 17th), Norwegian Independence Day, starting in 1814. Parades are still popular on that day, with many wearing their colorful bunads and carrying flags. The bunads had elaborate embroidery and were usually designed to be adjustable so it could be let out or taken in for the rest of one's life. Clothes washing was only done 3-6 times per year and never in winter, so hygiene habits were quite different from today. Soap was made at home with left over fat, water, and lye.

Gesme said people remaining unmarried were very rare prior to the 1900's since having help to take care of a farm was essential. If a spouse died, the widow or widower quickly looked for a new spouse. It was often a matter of survival. Young people tended to select their own spouses, but parents sometimes voiced their opinions. It was not uncommon for babies to be born – or at least pregnancies to occur – before marriages. For some it was seen as a way to make sure a woman was fertile before committing to marriage. There usually was only some voiced disapproval, but sometimes punishment if the couple didn't follow through with a wedding after the baby was born.

According to *Between Rocks and Hard Places,* people living in what is now Norway held pagan beliefs until about 1,000 years ago. The conversion to Christianity began with missionaries, but St. Olav is mainly credited with achieving the conversion, under threat of death. By the 1100's most places had a Catholic priest and a place of worship built. Some buildings were made of stone, but many of wood, including those in the famous stave style of Norwegian churches, distinctive with their decorative dragon heads on the roofs. There was a halt to building churches during the Black Death (bubonic plague), but was resumed after the Reformation, when there was a division between the Catholic Church and the newly created Protestant denomination. According to Ole Benedictow in *The Black Death: The Greatest Catastrophe Ever*, the Black Death killed between 30-50% of Norwegians in 1349-50 when it is believed to have arrived in grain cargo from a ship from England, initially spread by rats and fleas.

In 1537 Denmark established the Lutheran Church, distinct from the Catholic Church, and since Norway was under Denmark's control at the time, Norway converted to Lutheranism as well by 1539. The government took over all the churches at that time, and all priests had to agree to convert or lose their jobs. Most new pastors were from Denmark, and people found it difficult to accept their authority, as their country had taken Norway over. It took a few generations to do the conversion. By the time the University of Christiania (Oslo) was established in 1811, Norway was able to train its own pastors and the profession became more respected. Back at that time, pastors served as spiritual leaders, teachers, and also served as quasi governmental authorities. They were in charge of recording births, baptisms, marriages, and deaths for the government. After the Great Northern War of 1720, Denmark could no longer afford to maintain the Norway churches and so sold them to wealthy families in Norway to take care of. This ownership continued until the late 1800's. In 1736 people were required to be members of the Lutheran Church upon birth and get confirmed. This necessitated universal education. Since there were no public schools at this time, education was provided by pastors at first, who were usually the most educated people of the area. In the absence of many books, hymns and rote learning of the catechism and Bible were the primary resources used for teaching.

According to Gesme, by 1739 elementary schools were paid for by general taxes, and it became the job of pastors to locate teachers and train them, especially if they weren't near a large city. Before there were school houses, people's homes served as schools which helped the parents learn to read and recognize the importance of education. Because of farming needs and lack of trained teachers, schooling was done in segments of 3 months, with the teacher traveling from region to region to provide the education. Ole was fortunate to have had a good teacher because his letters during the Civil War showed he was a skilled and fluent writer of Norwegian.

Parents and Grandparents of Anne Strandbakken, Ole's Future Wife

What do we know about Ole's future wife, Anne, and her family and their life in Norway before immigration? According to Lyla Ruen's book, *Kjøs-Eggebraaten Family History,* Anne was born to Guldbrand and Marthe Eggebraaten Strandbakken on the Strandbakken farm on the western shore of Lake Einavatnet, in Vestre Toten, Norway, Nov. 15 (or 16, records differ), 1839, so she was about 7 years younger than Ole. This farm was about 58 miles north of Oslo. Her nuclear family was originally at the Egge/Eggebraaten farms near Brandbu, in Hadeland, but they moved 13 miles northeast to the Strandbakken farm before her birth, hence the last name change, which was a common custom in Norway at the time. Anne, while in the U.S., was also known by the last name of Guldbrandson and Gilbertson, Americanizations of her original name, so documents differ on which name is listed. Anne changed her last name to Rockswold when she married Ole.

Ernest Anderson's autobiography-family history stated that Anne's father, Guldbrand Anderson Egge and his siblings were tall and quite slender, with black hair and brown or black eyes. Not the usual coloring that comes to mind when one thinks of Scandinavians. Anne herself was five feet six inches, large boned but slender as a child, walked with a "queenly carriage," had black hair and large brown eyes. She was very active and healthy.

Marthe Eggebraaten Strandbakken, mother of Anne Strandbakken, Ole Rocksvold's wife. Likely taken around 1850-52 in Norway.

According to a combination of information from Ernest Anderson's autobiography and the Kjos-Eggebraaten Book, Guldbrand's parents were Anders Egge and Marte Larsdatter Daelen, from Ovre Egge, Hadeland, Norway. They had four children: Peder, Kjersti, Guldbrand, and Berthe. Anders' father's name was Ellen Pederson Egge, but his wife is unknown. Guldbrand's wife, Marthe Eggebraaten, was born to Pernille Pedersdatter and Hans Eriksen Eggebraaten. Marthe was one of 6 children: Peder Ruen, Iver Sonsteby, Espen Ruen, Ole Eggebraaten, Anne Eggebraaten, and Marthe. The differing last names probably reflected the farms they lived on.

Childhood home of Anne Strandbakken, Ole Rocksvold's wife, taken in 2014 by author. Strandbakken farm in Vestre Toten, Oppland, beside Lake Einavatnet. Before Anne was born, Anne's family lived at the Eggebraaten/Egge farmland in Hadeland.

In Lyla Ruen's book it said Anne Guldbrandsdatter Strandbakken had 7 siblings, Maria, Ingeborg, Hans who died in infancy, Elena, Anders, Berthe Helene, and Hans (2). Anne's father made cabinets, chests, and other furniture. An interesting anecdote about Anne's parents was that Guldbrand made hooks and eyes for his wife, Marthe, for closing garments when sewing. One day a hen was caught in the act of eating the hooks and eyes. Marthe caught the hen, cut open the gullet, removed those very needed hooks and eyes, sewed up the gullet, and the hen was fine after that!

Lyla mentioned that Strandbakken (beach hill) on Lake Einavatnet in Hadeland, was a mile long and the children had fun sliding down the hill in the winter on sleds. They loved to ride Mountain Pony, their horse. Ingeborg told the story of one day riding the horse to go visit Rev. Magellson. The horse was running around a building and found little brother Anders playing in its path. The horse leaped over him, leaving him unhurt.

According to Lyla Ruen and Ernest Anderson's autobiography-family history, Anne's father, Guldbrand, was described as soft-spoken, modest, careful, and devout. He was a cabinet maker and farmer, and was literate. When there wasn't to be a church service on a given Sunday, he called the family together for devotions in place of the service at church. Guldbrand died age 50 of typhoid fever in 1847, leaving Marthe with 7 children, ages 2-19 to raise. The older children left home to work, with daughter Ingeborg emigrating in 1850 with the Hans Eggebraaten family and uncles Peter Ruen, Iver Sonsteby, their families, and Aunt Svensrud, a widow. Anne was sent at 8 years old to the home of a relative in Hadeland to herd cattle during the day and help care for children the rest of the time.

Anne Strandbakken's Family Emigrates

In 1852, when Anne was 12, her mother Marthe decided to emigrate with the rest of the children, but we don't know the specific reasons. Some common causes for emigration at the time included: many crop failures in Norway in the mid-1800's, religious freedom, growing population due to arrival of the small pox vaccine and importation of potatoes, and the dividing up of farmland due to sharing the land with siblings upon the death of parents. Another common reason was hope for a better, more successful future for their children. People in Norway gradually started to hear accounts of people successfully emigrating to the U.S. and many decided it was worth the risks. The first Norwegian emigrants left in 1825. Emigrants sent letters and newspapers back home, many telling positive stories about their experiences and encouraging others to join them. According to Gesme's *Between Rocks and Hard Places*, Ole Rynning, a Norwegian Immigrant in Illinois, wrote a book called *A True Account of America*, in 1838 which was widely circulated in Norway, influencing many to come. However, some immigrants told of people who cheated them when buying tickets for transportation or purchasing land. Other hardships of emigration included illnesses and deaths during the many weeks crossing the ocean, and the challenges of clearing land, getting used to a new culture, and missing their loved ones back in Norway. Many officials and pastors actively discouraged people from leaving.

Nevertheless, Marthe and her family decided to leave anyway, and first went to Kilbourn, WI, Columbia County, near Portage, where Anne worked for various families. An anecdote Lyla Ruen related in her book was that one night Anne had a great scare when she was alone and heard Indians shouting and saw them dancing around a fire, but they did not come near Anne. Perhaps this was her first exposure to this unfamiliar Native American cultural activity.

In 1856 Marthe moved with the unmarried children to Glenwood Township, IA, to live near the Eggebraatens and Ruens. As an adult, son Anders became owner of the farm and raised his family there. By then Ingeborg had married Hans Ruen. Elena had married Gulbrand Gorgen, with Berthe moving with them to New Richmond, MN. Berthe married Joseph Babcock. Maria married Hans Sandbeck.

As the children grew up and married, Marthe lived with son Hans, who had been sickly. He died at almost 18 years old, in 1863. Marthe then lived with daughter Ingeborg and her husband, Hans Ruen, who was also her cousin. When Marthe's son, Anders, got married, she went to live with him and his wife, Berthe Sivisind, and their children.

Anne's mother, Marthe Eggebraaten Strandbakken, was quite tall, slender, and had blue eyes and brown hair. Marthe worked very hard, and was kind. Ernest's book said she had three brothers and a half sister, but Lyla Ruen's book indicated four brothers. The brothers were in Norway's war with Sweden in 1814 which resulted in Norway becoming an independent country. Peder and Iver came over to the U.S. in 1850. Coincidentally, they died the same day, Oct. 15, 1879, when elderly. Anne, Marthe's sibling, was blind several years before she died. According to Ernest Anderson, Marthe died at age 65 of a hemorrhage caused by a cancer under her left arm, but Lyla Ruen listed an age of 68 at death. The discrepancy is perhaps due to different sources for the information or clerical error.

According to Ernest Anderson, Anne Strandbakken was five feet six inches, large boned but slender, and had an "aristocratic, queenly bearing expression" by the time she reached adulthood. Anne was a very active and healthy person, with thick, silky black hair, large brown eyes. Both Lyla Ruen and Ernest Anderson noted that she was confirmed by Rev. Koren at Washington Prairie Church, in Glenwood township and worked for a while at a hotel and later a millinery shop at Lansing, IA. Ruen reported that Anne learned a lot from these work experiences, and the people for whom she worked were very kind to her. They brought her to church and Sunday School and one family even gave her a leather Bible in English, which she greatly valued.

Ole Rocksvold's Family Emigrates

We do not have any specific documentation of the Rocksvold family's reasons for emigrating.

On April 26/27, 1853, Ole departed with his parents, twin sister Anne Mathea, and younger brother, Anton, on the ship, *Deodata*, with Captain F.T. Schroeder/Skoder from Christiania (Oslo) to Quebec, Canada, a trip lasting 7 weeks, arriving June 15. The *Deodata* was a bark with three masts, built in 1851 in Drammen, Norway.

According to www.norwayheritage.com, in the early days of emigration, people usually traveled on boats designed for transporting cargo, so accommodations tended to be primitive. I have not found specific information on whether the Rocksvold family traveled in steerage, which was the cheapest accommodations, or had a cabin, which cost more. Steerage passengers slept between decks, in a space with a height of 6-8 feet. Bunks were made of rough boards with mattresses of straw, and one bunk usually held 3-4 people, with passengers providing their own blankets and pillows. For those bringing trunks for their few possessions, some emigrants designed a curved cover in an attempt to avoid heavy things being stacked on top of them. It was quite common for people to get sick or die traveling across the ocean for these long trips of 6-16 weeks on sailing ships due to the density of people and primitive hygiene and ventilation. Diet tended to be quite limited since the food they brought needed to keep for a long time.

The bark on which the Rocksvold family crossed the Atlantic as they emigrated to the U.S. in 1853.

Dried, salted meats, wheat, cheese, and flatbread were commonly packed in their trunks. Cooking could be done in good weather on deck. According to Gesme, fares from Norway to New York were up to $40 in the 1850's, while traveling to Quebec cost $12-30 dollars, with children under 14 half-price, and babies under age 1 traveled for free. The Canadian ships brought emigrants going west and then returned east with timber for England. By the 1860's steam ships were available, reducing the length of the trip to America to 2 weeks, costing about $44.

After arriving in Quebec June 15, the Rocksvolds and fellow passengers traveled down the St. Lawrence River through the Great Lakes to Wisconsin. The Rocksvolds stayed in Yorkville, Racine County, in southeast Wisconsin, for about 1-2 months, according to two obituaries, one in the *Decorah Journal*, one in the *Decorah Posten*. While there Ole worked on the railroad. The Rocksvolds then traveled to Winneshiek County, IA, and lived in a small log house with the Han Sivisind family the first winter, according to Ernest Anderson. The children had to sleep on the floor. That winter Ole and Carl Sivisind worked on a farm at Pine Creek, east of Waukon, IA, splitting rails at fifty cents per hundred. The Rockvolds bought farmland in Glenwood Township east of Decorah in 1854 where Ole remained for most of his life. They started farming and also helped to start a Norwegian Lutheran church in the area. The Rocksvolds and other immigrants felt it was essential to get a church established soon upon arriving and worked hard to accomplish that goal.

Glenwood Church is Established

Pastor Don Berg, in *Glenwood-Hadeland*, an unpublished document furnished by Winneshiek County History Society, gave a short description of the settling of Glenwood Township that focused quite a bit on church history. Since Ole was so involved in the church, I thought it pertinent to include some of that history here. It is also fascinating to learn how they obtained pastors and their challenging transition to life and church leadership in the U.S. A deeper look at Glenwood Church history, Ole's very active role in it, plus summaries of church meeting minutes come later in this book.

Berg said Pastor C. L. Clausen, a Dane, served the surrounding areas as the first pastor among the Norwegians in Iowa and Minnesota, and established the St. Ansgar settlement in 1853. He visited Glenwood in 1851, and Pastor Nils Brandt from Valdres, Norway, came a year later, continuing to serve a large area. As the population grew, there was a greater need for pastors and in 1853 Ulrik Vilhelm Koren was called from Bergen, Norway, to serve this particular area. Rev. and Mrs. Koren came from the upperclass and so had been assured they would have a parsonage upon arrival. However upon arriving, there were only logs lying on the ground at the spot where they were to live at Christmas, 1853. According to Berg, Rev. and Mrs. Koren stayed with Ole Knatterud for two days, then with Erik and Helene Egge in their 14 x 16 feet cabin at Frankville Township until March 10, 1854.

Rev. Koren's wife, Elisabeth Hysing Koren, kept a diary about her experiences of emigrating and adjusting to primitive life in these pioneer days. Her father was a high school teacher of theology, eventually becoming headmaster, was a member of Norwegian parliament, and was mayor of the town of Larvik, Norway, for many years. Elisabeth grew up in a very large manor house. She had been taught to read and write English prior to coming to the U.S., but not to speak it, possibly because some may have thought she wouldn't be able to learn to speak it due to her significant hearing loss. In the *Diary of Elisabeth Koren 1853-1855,* she described the challenges of living with a lack of privacy from living in small homes of various families from Dec. 21, 1853 to finally getting a separate parsonage Oct. 1, 1854. People who hosted them were Nils Knatterud, Erik and Helen Egge, Ingebret Sørlands, and the Skaarlias.

Berg's article stated that Rev. Koren conducted the first service for Little Iowa Congregation in the largest room they could find, the Thorgrim home, Christmas, 1853. His first service in the Glenwood township was Jan. 1854, at Hans Lovbraaten's home, section 36. The first church building was erected at the Washington Prairie site in 1854, which was a little wooden shack with no floor or pews. People brought rails from fences to sit on. In summer it was very hot, and winter very cold. The first confirmation classes were held at the first parochial school house near the Pioneer Cemetery where Decorah, Glenwood, Frankville, and Springfield Townships all meet. The Glenwood cemetery land was given by Hans Blegen. (The nearby Pontoppidan cemetery was established after the split in the congregation in 1888.) The Little Iowa Congregation was "amicably" split into 7 congregations in 1863-4 due to growth, with Koren serving four, and the other three served by pastors at Luther College. The first Glenwood church was built of wood in 1856 on land donated by Christopher Evenrud.

In 1860 Ole sold 160 acres of farmland to his brother Anton Peter, and bought 100 acres on a nearby plot. By the next year their lives would change as the country was ripped in two by the Civil War.

VESTRE TOTEN HERRED   1143

Riber
Gnr. 6, bnr. 1. P.adr. Raufoss. Tlf. 112 b.

Sk.mk. 2,94. D. jord 85 da (leirbl. mold), annet jbr.-
areal 20 da, prod. skog 200 da. – Våningshus bygd 1800,
omb. 1911 og 1941, låve m. fjøs og stall bygd 1914 og
1924, garasje 1936. Brt. kr. 75 700. – Alm.rett. – 2 hester,
8 kyr, 1 okse, 3 ungdyr, 2 griser. – Ove W. Berge, beste-
far til eieren, kjøpte garden 1896 av Andreas Aastuen.
Eieren tok over 1931 etter moren.
  Eier: Gunnar W. Berge f. 1904 – sønn av Bøie W.
Berge og Marie f. Tollefsrud – g. 1935 m. Johanne Rote-
rud. Barn: Bjørn f. 1936.

Ringeli
Gnr. 39, bnr. 25. P.adr. Reinsvoll.

Sk.mk. 0,53. D. jord 30 da (leirbl. mold), annet jbr.-
areal 25 da, prod. skog 25 da. – Våningshus gml., vølt
1946, låve m. fjøs og stall m. m. bygd 1937, hønsehus,
skåle og stabbur. Brt. kr. 35 000. – Alm.rett. – 1 hest, 5
kyr, 2 ungdyr, 2 griser, 40 høner. – Mann til eieren kjøpte
garden 1932 av Tåle Ringeli, og dyrket opp 15 dekar.
  Eier: Anne Kyseth f. 1903 – datter av Ole og Anna
Amlien – g. 1930 m. Ole Kyseth f. 1903 (d. 1947). Barn:
Anna f. 1930, Solveig 1934, Hans Olav 1946.

Ringvold
Gnr. 17, bnr. 1. P.adr. Raufoss. Tlf. 31 a.

Sk.mk. 4,89. D. jord 130 da (morenejord på leirgrunn),
annet jbr.areal 40 da, prod. skog 65 da, annen utm. 55
da. – Våningshus og kårbygn. gml., uthus bygd 1821,
påb., vognskjul bygd 1951, smie 1953. Brt. kr. 85 000. –
Alm.rett. – 2 hester, 11 kyr, 2 okser, 8 ungdyr, 2 griser,
20 høner. – Eieren kjøpte garden 1924 av Aksel Thorstad.
  Eier: Peder Myhren f. 1883 – sønn av Johannes Myhren og Berthe Helene f. Markestad – g. 1914 m. Helene
Augusta Grøtthaug. Barn: Lovise Bergljot f. 1915, Paul
1917, Arne 1919, Johannes 1921.
  Bruker: Paul Myhren, sønn av eieren, g. 1953 m. Edith
Andersen. Barn: Per Arne f. 1953.

Roksvold
Gnr. 40, bnr. 1. P.adr. Raufoss. Tlf. 129 b.

Sk.mk. 1,83. D. jord 60 da (leirbl. mold), annet jbr.-
areal 30 da, prod. skog 100 da. – Våningshus bygd 1818,
senere vølt, låve m. fjøs og stall m. m. bygd 1818. Brt. kr.
52 000. – Alm.rett. – 2 hester, 7 kyr, 4 ungdyr, 3 griser,
30 høner. – Far til eierne kjøpte garden 1915 av Nils
Voldengen. Eierne tok over 1941. Mølle i gammel tid.
  Eiere: Marit og Ragna Sælid, døtre av Anders Sælid og
Ragnhild f. Liekren.

Roksvold Farm from the Gardbruk, 1957

Farm no. 40, 1 ('gård' & 'bruk'); postal address: Raufoss; telephone: 129 b

Cultivated land, 15 acres (60 decares], clay & humus; other farmland, 7½ acres (30 decares);
productive timberland, 25 acres (100 decares) — Main farmhouse built in 1818, later repairs;
haybarn with animal barn & stables, with other buildings, built in 1818; gross value, 52,000
Norwegian crowns. — Farm has access to common lands. — 2 horses, 7 cows, 4 heifers, 3 pigs,
30 hens (chickens). — The father of the present owner purchased the farm in 1915 from Nils
Voldengen. The present owners took over the farm in 1941. The farm had a gristmill in former
times.
Present owners: Marit &Ragna Sælid, daughters of Anders Sælid and Ragnhild, née Liekren.

Håkon Raddum, Rune Nedrud, Sharon Bowen, Sveinung Raddum, Mette Nordengen at Roksvoll farm, 2014, where Ole Rocksvold grew up.
Rocksvold cousins touring Vestre Toten area. Rune and Mette's genealogical research made it possible for us to meet.

Aas Church where Ole Rocksvold's family belonged while he was growing up on the Roksvoll farm, Vestre Toten, Oppland, Norway. Photo taken 2014 with Raddum cousins in the background by the front door.

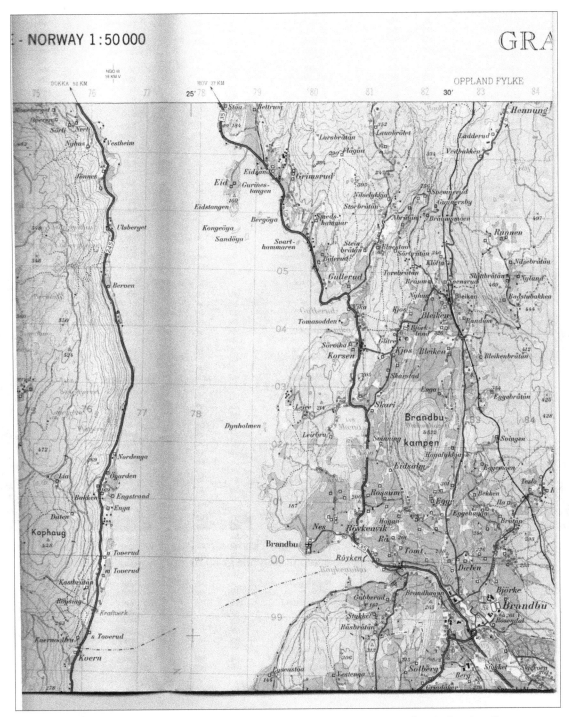

Egge Farm Map Section from Gran when Anne Strandbakken's family lived at first.

Lake Einavatnet, Vestre Toten, Oppland, Norway. This (insert) is the view from Strandbakken farm where Ole's wife, Anne Strandbakken lived while growing up. Photo taken 2014.

Valg Church where Anne Strandbakken Rocksvold's (Ole's wife) family were members while living on the Eggebraaten/Egge farmland. Cousin Sveinung Raddum, left, guiding our tour.

Glenwood Lutheran Church, Glenwood township, Winneshiek County, IA, 2013. Ole and his family helped to start the Glenwood congregation and was very active there. This building is not the original one.

~ CHAPTER 3 ~

CIVIL WAR

*H*ow difficult it must have been to be an immigrant, work hard to start a new life in the U.S., and a few short years later find oneself involved in a civil war! On Nov. 6, 1860, Abraham Lincoln was elected, followed by South Carolina voting to "secede" from the Union on Dec. 20. On March 4, 1861, Lincoln was sworn in as President. Rebels opened fire on Fort Sumter in Charleston, SC, on April 12 and thus the war began. The tiny Union garrison surrendered the fort the next day. That same month, Lincoln called on militiamen from states loyal to the Union and in July Congress authorized 500,000 volunteers to join the Union Army for three years of service. Many volunteered thinking the war would only last a few months, but they were sorely disappointed. The 12th Iowa Infantry Regiment was formed to answer Lincoln's call. Ole and many others from Winneshiek County volunteered.

Why Volunteer?

Why did these volunteers join the service and remain there despite the incredibly difficult hardships and horror they experienced? In *For Cause and Comrades*, James McPherson studied thousands of letters, diaries, and memoirs to learn about their motivations. Although towards the end of the war, inducements such as increased pay, bounties for joining or reenlisting, and other benefits increased, McPherson said for the vast majority of soldiers, pay was not the incentive. There were many reasons cited to volunteer on either the Union or Rebel sides. Some reasons specific to the Union side were: to eliminate slavery, to preserve the union, patriotism, and to prove to the world that this new form of representative government was viable. Some reasons specific to the Rebel side were: to preserve slavery (otherwise known as the "southern way of life"), and its economic benefit

Ole Rocksvold in Civil War uniform, probably
taken in IA, 1861, he served 1861 - 1864.

to the south (unpaid labor), to protect homeland/family's way of life, freedom/indepen-
dence, and states' rights.

Many more reasons to volunteer were common to both sides: duty, honor, peer pressure,
adventure and excitement, immortalize oneself, as an example to one's children, support and encouragement by the public and from those at home, and to escape difficult
circumstances at home (such as abuse, starvation), to prove manhood/courage, fear of
what their life and the country would be like if their side lost, and to resolve these conflicts so that there could be peace for their children and grandchildren. Still more reasons
included: sense of camaraderie and loyalty to the people in their unit (who usually were
people from their county or area), to follow what they perceived to be God's will, and for
self-preservation to be sure their side won. Later in the war additional reasons included
seeking revenge for what the other side had already done, hate, being drafted from 1863
on, being hired to substitute for someone who was drafted and didn't want to serve, and
to make sure those who had already died didn't die in vain.

Many Oles Go to War

According to Jerry Rosholt in *Ole Goes to War*, at least 6,500 Civil War soldiers were born in Norway, with virtually all serving in the U.S. forces. Half of all Norwegian-born soldiers served in Wisconsin companies (at least 3,609). Minnesota had at least 1,200 Norwegian-born men entering to serve. From Iowa units, 677 were Norwegian-born, with 231 coming from Winneshiek County. Norwegian-born men in the service included 146 John Johnsons, 46 Hans Hansons, 42 Tom Thompsons, 966 who were Olsons, with 199 Ole Olsons. There were 1,000 Oles. One out of every six Norwegian-born soldiers was named Ole, hence the name of Rosholt's book, *Ole Goes to War*.

The Life of a Civil War Soldier

Before I give the details of Ole's service and the specific action he saw, I will describe what his and other Civil War soldiers' lives were like, based on the book, *Hard Tack and Coffee: The Unwritten Story of a Soldier's Life* by John Billings. Upon entry into the service, soldiers were issued blouses (shirts), dark blue coats, sky blue pants, and a cap. There were variations of coats and hats, with a floppy kepi (cap) for fatigue and campaign wear and a more substantial hat for dress. Some soldiers bought a havelock hat which had cloth that hung down to shield the neck from the

Typical items often found among a Civil War soldier's supplies. Photo taken at the museum display at Fort Donelson National Military Park, Tennessee, 2012. Ole Rocksvold fought there in Feb., 1862. Upper left are hard tack biscuits.

sun. The overcoat was single breasted for infantry, double breasted for cavalry. A sack coat was issued for fatigue wear, a heavy lined one for dress. They were also issued leather boots.

The name of the book, *Hard Tack and Coffee*, is significant because those foods were commonly consumed. Hard tack was a biscuit made from flour and water and was often eaten for breakfast or any time of day for a snack. Sometimes they were so hard that soldiers couldn't bite into them. The creative soldiers came up with many ways to make hard tack more palatable and used them in cooking. Soldiers would dunk hard tack in coffee, milk, condensed milk, etc., to soften it. They would break it into pieces and put it in stew or soup, toast it on a stick, fry it in juice and meat fat, or put sugar on it. Soldiers got so tired of hard tack that they even wrote a few songs about it.

Humor Helps Soldiers Survive the Stress of War

To the tune of the song "Hard Times" they created these words (p. 118, *Hard Tack and Coffee*):

"'Tis the song of the soldier, the weary, hungry, and faint,

Hard tack, hard tack, come again no more.

Many days have I chewed you and uttered no complaint,

O Greenbacks come again once more."

(Greenbacks were a nickname for money, presumably desired to buy other food.)

An amusing tale was described in *Hard Tack and Coffee* by Billings in the 10th battalion Massachusetts when Gen. Lyon heard them singing and decided to tell the cook to make something else. The cook made cornmeal mush. Apparently they liked that even less than the hard tack and created yet another verse to the "Hard Times" melody on p. 118-9:

"But to groans and to murmurs, there has come a sudden hush.

Our frail forms are fainting at the door,

We are starving now on horse feed

That the cooks call mush,

O hard crackers, come again once more.

It is the dying wail of the starving.

Hard crackers, hard crackers, come again once more,

You were old and very wormy, but we pass your failings o'er,

O hard crackers, come again once more."

Indeed, the hard tack was sometimes wormy or moldy. If they were boxed too soon after baking and had not completely cooled, the moisture would sometimes cause mold to grow.

So what else did soldiers usually get in their rations? Coffee, tea, salt pork, fresh beef, salt beef, occasionally ham or bacon, flour, cornmeal, soft bread, potatoes, beans, split peas, rice, dried apples, dried peaches, dried vegetables, sugar or molasses, vinegar, pepper, salt. Sometimes they also got pickles or cabbage to prevent scurvy. Sometimes the meat was rotting when it arrived to them. Billings said if the meat was especially bad, sometimes the men showed their senses of humor by enacting a fake funeral for it rather than eat it! Of course they had no refrigerators and if the soldiers were in transit, it was even harder to keep things fresh. Sometimes a cook made the food for all, and sometimes the soldiers individually cooked for themselves. Alcohol was rarely given out, unless for medical purposes, so soldiers usually obtained alcohol on their own, if at all.

According to *Hard Tack and Coffee*, a camp ration consisted of: 12 oz. of pork, bacon, or beef, 1 pound 6 oz. of soft bread or one pound of hard bread. Per every 100 rations, there was also a peck (2 gallons) of beans, ten pounds of rice, half a bushel of potatoes, 10 pounds of green coffee or 8 pounds of roasted coffee, 4 pounds of soap, 2 quarts of salt, 4 qt. of vinegar, 4 oz. of pepper. A marching ration consisted of: coffee, 1 pound of hard bread, three-fourths pound salt pork or one and a fourth pound meal, sugar, salt, and 9 or 10 pieces of hard tack. A biscuit of hard tack was 3 1/8 inches by 2 7/8 inches and half inch thick. Soldiers were given a tin dipper, tin plate, knife, fork, and spoon for eating.

What was a typical day in camp like? The bugle blew about 5 a.m. in the summer and 6 a.m. in the winter. There was roll call/reveille, then a 15 minute assembly. Hygiene wasn't very consistent during the Civil War, and water not always abundantly available, so the tents often didn't smell good. Soldiers usually washed in the morning by pouring out a little canteen water for a fellow soldier to splash on his face. Or, they sometimes put water in a hollowed log for a make-shift sink. Since they had to get ready quickly, some slept in their uniforms to save time dressing in the morning.

Lyrics were sometimes created to go along with the various songs the bugler played. For example, here are lyrics for the first thing in the morning, on p.168 of *Hard Tack and Coffee*:

> "I can't get 'em up, I can't get 'em up, I can't get 'em up, I tell you. (repeat)
>
> The corporal's worse than the private, the sergeant's worse than the corporal,
>
> The lieutenant's worse than the sergeant, but the captain's worst of all."

After their short assembly, there was breakfast call, sick call, water call (for horses), fatigue call (for cleaning the camp, building structures, washing equipment, etc.), drill call (for practicing formations and marching, following orders, etc.), battery drill, special drill, dinner call, battalion drill, water call, stable call, attention, assembly, retreat roll call (with lectures about how they could improve), guarding and mounting drill (which could also be in the morning for infantry), assembly, tattoo (military musical performance or military display of troops), roll call, and finally taps before bed.

Insects were often a problem during the war, partially due to the lack of hygienic conditions, and partly due to simply being out in the elements all the time. Lice, mosquitos, biting flies, and ticks added to the discomforts soldiers faced.

What did soldiers do during free time? According to *Hard Tack and Coffee* and *The Common Soldier of the Civil War*, the troops would write letters, play card games such as cribbage or euchre, and play games like checkers, backgammon, chess, and dominos. Some soldiers liked to gamble during their free time. They liked to wrestle, box, rest, talk, watch others play games, smoke a pipe, or walk. Creative soldiers would make pipes, decorating them with badges of various corps from wood or clay, sing, play instruments such as violin or banjo, and dance. If they ran out of playing cards, they made their own. Reading material included newspapers, magazines, some classic books of Milton, Hugo, Dumas, and Shakespeare. However, more common were "dime novels" such as *Bill Arp, Mr. Dooley*, and paperback comics such as *Phunny Fellow*, and *Budget of Fun*. Some troops even created skits to entertain each other.

When the army needed to relocate, it was a major operation, moving troops and big wagon trains loaded with equipment such as axes, kettles, pans, mess chests, tents, etc. It took 6 mules to pull each wagon and 4 horses to pull each ambulance.

Ole's Specific Service in the War

According to his pension records, Ole enlisted in Decorah, IA, on Oct. 18, 1861. He was mustered into company G, 12th Iowa Infantry, on Nov. 5, 1861, as a private, and reported to Camp Union on a bluff two miles north of Dubuque, IA, where they learned to drill. Major S.D. Brodtbeck was in charge of the camp, with Col. David Woods taking over the immediate supervision of the companies Oct. 23. The 12th Infantry Iowa's 926 men received their canteens, knapsacks, blankets, and uniforms Nov. 15, including dark blue blouses and sky blue pants. They never received full dress uniforms, nor white gloves. Ole's company G consisted of 90 men under Capt. C.C. Tupper initially. In a letter to Ole written 4-13-1906, John Steen, a comrade of Ole's, said the two of them were the first in their unit chosen for guard duty, 10-26-1861. They were also the first to make corporal, 3-25-1862, a week before the battle of Pittsburg Landing (the name the North initially used, but called Shiloh by the South).

We are extremely fortunate that such good records of the actions of the 12th Iowa Infantry were recorded by Major David Reed, who provide most of the information I used for this chapter.

Life at Training Camp - Introduction to Hardships

In *Campaigns and Battles of the 12th Regiment Iowa Veteran Volunteer Infantry*, Bvt. Major David Reed said new recruits reported to Camp Union on a sand bluff above the Mississippi River about two miles north of Dubuque, Iowa. The barracks were rough wooden sheds, 20 feet by 50 feet per company, housing approximately 90-100 people. There were two platforms on either side of the building so that half the men could sleep on the top level, and the other half below. There were no partitions between men to make a "bunk." Sleeping this close together during the cold weather helped them keep from freezing to death. The sheds had open entrances without doors, and lacked wooden floors, fireplaces, or other sources of heat. There was no place for cooking indoors, so soldiers had to cook over a fire outdoors and eat there as well, no matter what the weather. So in this cold season, there was considerable hardship as the soldiers became accustomed to military life. It was believed at the time that these hardships indeed helped them adjust to military life, so no opportunity was given to the men to work to create better accommodations there. A guard was placed outside each shed to prevent any extra supplies entering the buildings, and no additional construction was allowed to help improve their conditions. Reed did not remember any other time during the war when the soldiers lived in worse actual camp conditions, although during some campaigns they often slept outdoors without any shelter at all.

While in Camp Union, they were kept very busy with drilling-squad, company, and battalion. Since most leaders and soldiers were new to the military, lots of mistakes were made. Soldiers were often exhausted and had sore feet from so much drilling, but some leaders knew that rigorous preparation and conditioning could make the difference between life and death in the future.

When outfitted, a soldier would roll his blanket, tie the ends, and place it over his shoulder. He also carried his canteen and haversack (a pack with a long single shoulder strap) with three days' rations, plus a musket, 40 rounds of cartridges carried in a leather cartridge box hanging from a strap, with more ammunition in his pockets.

Hurry Up and Wait

On Nov. 25, 1861, 926 men were mustered into the U.S. Service in the 12th Iowa Volunteer Infantry, companies A-K. with Ole in company G. They were immediately ordered to prepare 5 days' rations and were up all night doing just that before leaving the next morning by boat to St. Louis. When the boat didn't arrive all day while they waited in the cold and snow, Col. Woods learned they were only sending boats for the officers, and the men would have to ride in open barges. Woods refused to ride in the separate boats for officers, out of care for his soldiers, and instead had them march to Dubuque to wait for boats rather than use open barges to transport them. After spending the day outdoors in the cold and snow, in the evening they were finally allowed to go indoors into public halls and other buildings to spend the night in warmth. In the morning ladies in the town made coffee and placed it in washing vats for the soldiers, which was much appreciated. This was the soldiers' first experience with long waits in their military service, something they would experience many times.

Recollecting his experience in the army during WW II, my father, Edward A. Smith, mentioned to me while I was growing up that soldiers often had to get ready to go somewhere and then wait for long periods of time, and even joked about it as the norm. Sometimes delays during wars are unavoidable due to various complications of moving so many people, or changing battle plans or weather conditions. Delays are also caused by inexperienced leaders or inadequate plans regarding accommodations, supplies, and transportation. Unfortunately, a few leaders during the Civil War didn't give much thought to the health and welfare of the soldiers. This deficiency in good planning by some contributed to illness and death of soldiers in the Civil War, as it has in many wars.

Benton Barracks, Missouri-Cold, Sickness, Death

After the long wait for boats, it was finally decided the 12th Iowa would travel by train instead. On Thanksgiving, Nov. 28, the 12th Iowa crossed the Mississippi River to Dunlieth township, IL, then went by the Illinois Central Railroad to East St. Louis, a two-day trip. Next they crossed the river from Illinois to Missouri and marched to Benton Barracks to report to Gen. Halleck, joining other infantries where they stayed for the winter. The recently constructed barracks placed two companies of men in a space designed for one. On Dec. 1 they had their first inspection and review as a larger army.

Reed stated that although these soldiers from Iowa were of "the very best soldier material," their lack of prior knowledge and training contributed to much tragedy. Many soldiers had never seen a musket before and had little/no practice with drill. They had little knowledge of the need for discipline. Also, both officers and soldiers, and the general public for that matter, knew very little about hygiene to prevent illness, due to the extent of medical knowledge at the time.

During this cold and rainy winter, the soldiers and officers spread germs quickly and experienced bouts of measles, pneumonia, typhoid, and mumps while at Benton Barracks, Missouri. Often half of the men were sick at any given time. For example, almost all of the soldiers in 12th Iowa Infantry were healthy when they arrived, yet within the first month, half were sick and 75 of the 926 had died! Some were so sick for so long they ultimately had to be sent home instead of continuing their military service. Capt. Tupper, a very popular and promising officer who was in charge of company G, died of sickness there. No other place during the war was more deadly for this unit than Benton Barracks that winter.

Getting Outfitted and Downsizing

On Dec. 26, due to the amazingly determined efforts of Col. Woods, the 12th Iowa Infantry received the best type of weapons available – new Enfield rifles, which were much better than the Harper's Ferry muskets altered from old flintlocks. The unit was also issued Sibley tents, axes, heavy mess chests, kettles, pans, spades, and picks. In addition, they obtained a huge wagon train consisting of 12 wagons, pulled by 6 mules each, two ambulances with 4 horses each. This was more and better quality equipment than the whole 16th Army Corps had three years later in the war.

On Jan. 6 they received their first pay, $13.00 per month for soldiers, this time in gold and silver, but subsequently in paper notes for the rest of the war. On Jan. 26 Col. Woods received orders to join Gen. Grant in Cairo, IL. The soldiers were delighted to finally be able to leave this place of so much disease and death. By foot, ferry, and train, and the steamer, *City of Memphis*, they arrived in Smithland, KY, Jan. 30, 1862. It took two days to unload all the equipment and another day to set up the tents, so at first they slept at halls and churches. The Sibley tents were cone-shaped, about 16 ft. across the base and were designed to hold 16 men. They slept with heads towards the outside with their feet all towards the center. There was an iron tripod in the center to hold the pole, which also allowed room to build a fire, when needed. There was a one foot space near the apex of the tent for ventilation. For warmth, they built a fire between the legs of the tripod that supported the center pole of their tents. These 16 men had a heavy mess chest with the equipment needed to do their own cooking for the people in their tent. This luxury of accommodations was not to last. The tents and mess chests proved to be too heavy for practical transport. So, soon after their time at Smithland, they started using lighter wedge tents, and finally pup tents, accommodating only 2 people each, for the rest of the war. The equipment and mess kits were then distributed among the soldiers so from then on each person kept his own plate, cup, knife, and spoon, and rations. That way, the army could move much more agilely.

Fort Henry

They were just getting used to their comfortable accommodations at Smithland, when they were ordered to join Gen. Ullysses S. Grant in a fight to capture Fort Henry Feb. 6, 1861. At that time, Grant had only a small regional command, the District of Cairo (IL). They took a steamer to Paducah, KY, found a large group of transports, and were then part of a very large army for the first time. The 2nd, 7th, 12th, and 14th Iowa Infantries were assigned to the first brigade with Col. Tuttle commanding, which was within the second division, C.F. Smith's commanding. They had no time to get to know each other, but immediately went up the Tennessee River, accompanied by gunboats. The next 6 days the Union used boats to destroy Confederate shipping and railroad bridges along the Tennessee River. Soldiers were sorely challenged when trying to walk in this swampy, water-logged area to reach the fort on foot. They successfully captured the ill-sited Fort Henry.

Since the weather was warm and pleasant and the marching orders said "light marching order," they left their coats and tents behind, only bringing their blankets, a decision they were soon to regret.

Fort Donelson- Suffering From Exposure

They then marched 12 miles east to Fort Donelson, TN. The land was very hilly and Cumberland River was at flood stage so it was challenging moving in this terrain. The fort itself was 100 feet above the water, and protected by guns, rifle pits and abatis, rows of tree branches placed side by side on the ground. On the 13th of February, the 12th Iowa Infantry first experienced the sound of artillery aimed at them, watched injured men being carried to the back of the line, and some witnessed the first death of someone in their infantry due to gunshot wound, Private E.C. Buckner, from company A, who was shot in the head and killed instantly.

It was a miserable night as Reed described it. That evening rain started to fall and it became cold. They had not been issued rubber blankets yet, so they started the night either standing with the cloth blankets getting soaked or trying to sleep lying down on the wet ground with no tent, no coat, and wet blankets. Snow started to fall, accumulating to 5-6 inches. In order to avoid freezing to death, they got up and marched in circles all night. They weren't allowed to start fires since the enemy would see where they were. At daybreak they finally were able to sit and lie down, making fires and hot coffee. There were skirmishes and attacks by gunboats February 14th and the soldiers suffered another cold night. On February 15th Grant arrived and ordered an attack by the whole division at once, making good gains towards the fort. At night, all was again still. On February 16th white flags were displayed by the rebels and the battle was over, but Generals Pillow, Floyd, and Forrest escaped of the Confederate side.

Gun at Fort Donelson aimed at Ravine Ole climbed to attack.

Confederate earthworks at Fort Donelson, with Nathan Kalmoe, great-great grandson of Ole.

Ole's unit fought in this successful battle of Fort Donelson, TN, Feb. 14-15, 1862. It was a difficult challenge fighting on the deeply-ravined terrain and trying to move over and through abatis. The 12th Iowa Infantry was under severe fire, but fortunately the losses were light for them, according to Col. Woods' report in Reed's book: 2 killed, 26 wounded. In Ole's company G, only one was wounded. The Union captured 15,000 prisoners, and all their munitions. Kentucky and Tennessee were almost entirely abandoned by the Confederates immediately thereafter.

The 12th Iowa Infantry were among those who collected and guarded prisoners and were assigned to log barracks. Most of the dead for both sides were buried in the field there. The prisoners were sent north and the Union soldiers enjoyed fireplaces and ovens in the barracks there, which greatly increased their comfort after lying out for days in cold rain and snow without tent nor heat from fires at night. They baked corn bread from captured meal and made hot biscuits in those Dutch ovens. The severe exposure of those days, plus the use of the local water which contained sulfur, produced diarrhea in almost 100% of the men, with some getting severely ill. Some soldiers, including Ole, continued thereafter to have life-long health problems, presumably the result of this extreme exposure, including recurring tendencies towards fevers, chills, arthritis ("rheumatism"), and diarrhea. Although he served each day of this battle and isn't listed as hospitalized at this location during or the days immediately afterwards, his pension records said these symptoms continued on and off throughout his life.

The battle at Fort Donelson was the first real success of the war for the Union. There was much publicity and many people, including governors, came to visit the battlefield and help the wounded. A resolution was passed in the Iowa legislature to honor the soldiers. This was also the battle at which Gen. Grant became known as "Unconditional Surrender Grant," as he negotiated the terms of surrender. It was a play on the initials of his first and middle names.

Many commendations were given for the soldiers' valiance. In a letter by Governor Samuel Kirkwood of Iowa, he wrote, "The Iowa troops made themselves and our state a glorious name. The 2nd regiment had the best chance for the honors at Donelson, but the 7th, 12th, and 14th did nobly..." Kirkwood continued by repeating a compliment from Dr. Hughes, state Surgeon General of Iowa, saying, "...the 12th Iowa is a splendid regiment and fought gallantly at Donelson."

Reorganization

At that time the army was reorganized and Grant's command was then called "Military District of the Tennessee." On Feb. 21, 1862 The 2nd, 7th, 12th, and 14th Infantries of Iowa were brigaded together and then called the First Brigade with Col. Tuttle of the 2nd Iowa Infantry commanding. This first brigade was part of the second division led by Brig. Gen. C.F. Smith, which was part of the Army of the Tennessee, Grant commanding. These four regiments – along with the 8th Iowa – later became known as the "Hornets' Nest Brigade" after the Battle of Shiloh/Pittsburg Landing. A couple of miles from Pittsburg Landing was a small church called Shiloh, for which the battle is sometimes called.

Pittsburg Landing/Shiloh- The "Hornets' Nest"

After some soldiers had collected the clothing and equipment left at Fort Henry, the materials were redistributed. The troops now had much more to carry and transport again. On March 7, Smith's division marched to Metal Landing on the Tennessee River, 12 miles. It was one of the hardest marches of the war, remembered Reed, because each man carried a knapsack, overcoat, blanket, and complete arms and equipment. This was so unpleasant that thereafter the men discarded the knapsacks and just wore their blankets rolled up in a thin, long roll and placed them over their shoulder like a sash. They then spent 7 days on steamers heading south up the river with huge amounts of guns, equipment, horses, mules, and wagons. The 12th Iowa traveled on the steamer, the *John Warner*. The animals and equipment were placed on the lower decks, with the men squeezed onto the upper deck, so crowded that they didn't have room to cook for themselves. Coffee was only obtained by using hot water from the steamers' boilers. They landed at Pittsburg Landing, TN, on March 19 and created a camp about a mile away while waiting for other armies to arrive from Corinth, MS, about 19 miles away. The pleasant surroundings and clean water helped them to recover from their ordeal at Fort Donelson. Ole was promoted to corporal March 25, 1862, which meant he led a small squad of about ten men when the unit was at full strength early in the war.

Gen. Albert Sidney Johnston of the Rebels decided to attack at Pittsburg Landing rather than wait for the Union army to grow still larger, anticipating an attack at Corinth, MS. Reed emphasized in his account of the battle of Pittsburg Landing that much false information was distributed after the war regarding this battle, so he was glad to be able to give an accurate account. Another detailed account of this battle is in *Shiloh 1862* by Winston Groom. So even in those days there were complaints of inaccurate media coverage with some authors not careful to check their facts. Of course "eyewitness" accounts often varied, too.

The terrain was a combination of flat land, hills, ravines, and creeks. At first Gen. Smith was commanding at Pittsburg Landing, while Gen. Grant was still north of there. An injury to Smith's leg worsened so much that it necessitated a trip to the hospital in Savannah, which left his division to Brig. Gen. W.H.L. Wallace. Smith's convalescence made Gen. William T. Sherman senior officer at Pittsburg Landing for the time being.

Grant wrote that the strength of his army on April 6, 1862 was 33,000 effective men, plus about 6,000 more, counting non-combatants such as teamsters who drove the wagons, surgeons, hospital attendants, chaplains, musicians who also carried stretchers, etc.

Gen. Johnston's Confederate forces moving north from Corinth numbered about 40,000 effective men. According to Reed, Grant had 61 regiments, 15 batteries (tactical units of artillery), while for the South, Johnston had 76 regiments, 21 batteries.

On April 6, 1862, Reed wrote that the day was bright and humid and the 12th Iowa infantry got up as usual after reveille, had breakfast, and started to prepare for morning inspection. Several took baths in the creek nearby. They had occasionally heard some artillery fire on Friday at a distance, but as yet had not been called into combat. They were given an extra supply of ammunition and crackers on Friday night, and were told to keep these in their haversacks with their cartridge boxes, ready for an attack. Rumors floated in that there was some skirmishing at the front, but by 8 a.m. the amount of artillery being heard made it clear that a full battle was on. A long roll was sounded on the drums at the regimental parade ground, so the soldiers grabbed their guns, lined up and hurried to the front, commanded by Col. J. M. Tuttle, the division of Gen. W. H. L. Wallace. As they proceeded to Corinth Road they saw troops falling back, saying everything was lost, which must have been dismaying to hear. The 12th Iowa Infantry fought along the edge of Duncan Field at the center of the battle. Eventually the intensity of the fire was such that they needed to fall back from this open field to an area of dense thicket and a ravine. This area was soon to be known as the "Hornets' Nest," the place where they fought the rest of the day.

Early in the fight, Stephen's brigade with Cheatham's artillery on the rebel side attacked them for an hour and had to fall back due to the force of the fire from those Union soldiers in the "Hornets' Nest." Shaver's brigade also tried repeatedly to defeat them and failed. There were four attempts that afternoon by the Confederates under Gibson to charge against these Union soldiers, by orders of Gen. Bragg, but the guns were so fierce that each time the rebels had to pull back. The few men still standing in Gibson's brigade finally left the fighting for the day. The Confederates were making better progress in the areas to the right and left of the "Hornets' Nest" that afternoon. Gen. Johnston was personally leading an attack when he was killed, causing a short lull in the battle. The Confederates decided to get more artillery to concentrate on the five regiments at the "Hornets' Nest." As Hurlbut of the Union side decided to withdraw his division so as to not be cut off from the landing, Wallace saw other divisions withdrawing and so decided to fall back also, but he died before seeing his orders executed. Sweeny got the order to withdrawn his brigade, but didn't manage to communicate it to the 8th Iowa, nor the 58th IL. Tuttle relayed the order to 2nd and 7th regiments and led them out. The messenger he sent to the 12th and 14th Iowa Infantries didn't reach them, so they were left to continue to hold the ground they had worked so hard and effectively to defend since morning.

Diorama of Hornets' Nest at Shiloh National Military Park, Tennessee, taken 2012.

Description of the Surrender of the "Hornets' Nest" at which Ole fought. The sign is at Shiloh National Military Park.

Nathan Kalmoe, Ole's great great grandson, in a Civil War uniform at 12th Iowa's monument along Sunken Road at Shiloh National Military Park, near the "Hornets' Nest."

Nathan Kalmoe, Ole's great great grandson, standing beside the sign marking the place where Ole was captured at Shiloh National Military Park, exactly 150 years later, to the day and hour. Taken April 6, 2012.

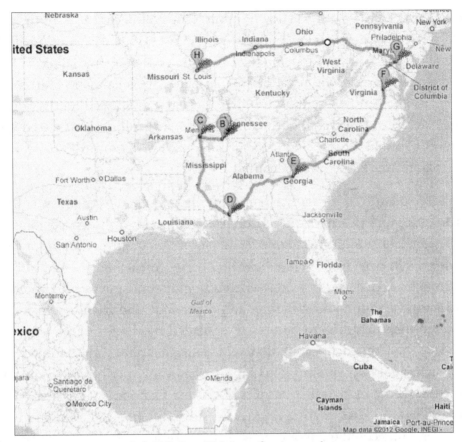

Map made by Nathan Kalmoe of route used to transport
Ole and imprison him in 5 prisoner of war camps.

The soldiers of the "Hornets' Nest" were now in danger of being surrounded. The 12th Iowa Infantry was at the center of the line and had participated in every attack from timber or open field. Only twice did they temporarily move from their spot on all, to make a counter charge to follow retreating rebels through timber, and then retook their places again to continue fighting. They repulsed 12 separate charges that day. The field in front of them was so full of dead soldiers that Reed said one could not take one step without stepping over another dead or injured body, yet not one of Ole's fellow soldiers left their duty, unless taken out wounded. Cartridges had been freshly supplied over and over all day.

When Col. Woods finally gave the order for the 12th and 14th Iowa Infantries to turn around and march away, many had been so engaged in battle that they didn't realize until too late that they were quickly becoming surrounded. Woods placed himself in the front of his men and hoped to go quickly down through the hollow and back to the main road. Nevertheless, these soldiers, while being fired upon on both sides, continued to heavily fire on the rebels before them and watched the line of the enemy fall. For yet another hour the whole rebel army, who had caused Sherman, McClellan, and Hurtburt to withdraw, was fighting against these 2,500 soldiers—what was left of Prentiss's division and two regiments of Tuttle's brigade, both Confederate and Union reports Reed stated. The union soldiers continued to fight until it became useless to continue any longer. Some named this place "Hell's Hollow" thereafter.

To get a clearer picture of what that late morning and the afternoon was like for the 12th Iowa Infantry and others, I quote from Reed's book which quoted Johnston's son, William Preston Johnston, in his Confederate father's biography, *The Life of Gen. Sidney Albert Johnston*. On page 620: "Here behind a dense thicket on the crest of a hill was posted a strong force of as hardy troops as ever fought, almost perfectly protected by the conformation of the ground, and by logs and other rude and hastily prepared defenses. To assail it, an open field had to be passed, enfiladed by the fire of its batteries. It was nick-named by the Confederates, by that very mild metaphor, 'The Hornets' Nest.' No figure of speech would be too strong to express the deadly peril of an assault upon this natural fortress, whose inaccessible barriers blazed for six hours with sheets of flame and whose infernal gates poured forth a murderous storm of shot and shell and musket-fire which no living thing could quell or even withstand. Brigade after brigade was led against it. But valor was of no avail. Hindman's brilliant brigades which had swept everything before them from the field, were shivered into fragments in the shock of the assault, and paralyzed for the remainder of the day. A. P. Stewart's regiment made fruitless assaults, but only to retire mangled and disheartened from the field..."

Woods, in his report for the *First Reunion of the Hornets' Nest Brigade*, stated that an aid-de-camp rode up and directed him to face the rear and fall back, stating that Eddington would receive orders as to the position he should occupy. Those orders never reach him and probably could not. The 2nd and 7th had gone to the rear and made it to higher ground, but it became obvious these others were surrounded. Wood wrote that they were so closely surrounded that some of the musket balls from the guns of the rebels intended for Union soldiers struck their own Rebel soldiers on the other side. Nevertheless, the 12th and 14th Iowa Infantry continued to fire on the enemy that was blocking their passage to the landing. Some of the enemy fell back, and the Union soldiers attempted to quickly get through. The enemy continued to move towards them, coming from behind and blasting them continuously. The enemy in front was shooting at them at short range.

Col. Woods, who had been twice wounded, got off his horse and turned command over to the senior captain, Eddington.

Eddington continued with his own report in Reed's book, stating that Woods was near the tents of the 3rd Iowa when he was wounded. They continued to encounter a large number of rebel soldiers, Gen. Polk's division. Their column halted. Eddington went to look for Woods, seeing how dangerous the situation was, to find out why they halted. He couldn't find him and didn't know where he was, so since he was the next senior officer, he ordered "right dress" which was obeyed immediately. He ordered the commanders to confer for a moment and they determined ammunition was almost gone. A rebel rode up with a white flag, demanding they surrender. Eddington asked his rank and the rebel said he was a lieutenant of Gen. Polk. Eddington ordered him to leave saying he didn't want to talk with an officer lower in rank than his own. The rebel left and fighting continued. Soon another rebel officer, a captain this time, rode up with a white flag and demanded surrender, saying he could not stop the fire of his men. Eddington said he had thought of surrendering, but his men were fighting men, so he should not send any more officers with white flags. What Eddington was hoping for at that point was just enough time to make it to the river where there was much water and that others could come to their rescue. But no one did.

Ole, a Prisoner of War

Ammunition gone, they had to surrender the men as prisoners of war at about 5:30 p.m., which concluded the fighting for that day. Tuttle, with the 2nd and 7th Iowa, after reaching the landing, had heard continued heavy fighting and tried to send soldiers to assist the "Hornets' Nest" troops, but before reaching them the guns went silent and so realized they had surrendered. Since Prentiss was the most senior officer there at the time, having worked so closely with the 2nd Iowa, it was decided to designate all these troops as Prentiss's division at the time of surrender.

Reed quoted many commanders' reports on both the Union and Confederate sides in his book. He said some believe the fighting of the Iowa soldiers at the "Hornets' Nest" kept the Confederates so occupied that it enabled the rest of the Union forces to make it safely back to the landing and may in effect have saved Grant's army. Reed wrote, "...the final summing up of the evidence will convince any unprejudiced searcher for the truth that the the valor of the troops at the "Hornet's Nest'" saved the day at Shiloh. And who shall say what the result of the great content would have been had Shiloh been lost on Sunday and Beauregard's army left free to attack Buell on the next day? Is there not a very strong probability that such a reverse would have so strengthened the 'Peace at any price' party, then just coming to the front, that the armies would have been recalled and the Union dissolved? All honor, then, to those who that day withstood the onsets of the whole rebel army, and gave their lives, or suffered wounds, and the horrors of the prison pens, that the Army of the Tennessee might not be destroyed, and to those who by saving the army from defeat at Shiloh April 6, 1862, saved the Union" (p. 61).

Reed quoted Gen. Trabue of the Confederate side who in his report wrote that Brig. Gen. Withers was given the "honor" of capturing Prentiss' division and assigned Col Shorter to be in charge of the prisoners as they were marched to Corinth, MS, about 22 miles. The prisoners did not know how long their imprisonment might be, or even if they would live to fight again. Many did die in prison, and many more, like Ole, were so sick they might have died. His imprisonment lasted seven months and he was moved to several locations before being exchanged.

Reed said that after the surrender, the Union prisoners were marched 5 miles away that same night. After prisoners of war were removed, the Union gunboats shelled the battle area to clear them of Confederate troops. It is heart wrenching to think of the thousands upon thousands of men lying wounded and dying, parched, all night at Shiloh in the rain, crying out for help and in pain. It was an impossible task to tend to so many after the exhausting battle of the day. As Reed quoted Grant from his memoirs, "it would have been possible to have walked across the clearing in any direction, stepping on bodies without a foot touching the ground." Grant spent the night partially sheltered under a tree at camp with his men rather than taking shelter in a tent. The tents had been taken down earlier in the fear that the battle would move to this camp along the river at Pittsburg Landing. So the wounded, sick, and exhausted soldiers all spent this night out in the rain.

It was impossible to ever make a complete, accurate account of the dead, and many bodies couldn't be identified after lying out exposed up to 48 hours. 2,361 were buried as unknown at Shiloh Cemetery. Many were listed as missing in action, and not later identified. Regarding the 12th Iowa Infantry for this battle, Reed's chart shows 479 engaged, 17 killed, 419 missing, 43 wounded and left on the field, 33 wounded and missing, 10 died of wounds in hospital, 9 died of wounds in prison, 65 died of disease in prison, and 4 were missing, never heard from, supposed to have been killed.

The prisoners dressed each others' wounds in a cornfield, after a five mile march, using jackknives for surgical implements. The *Decorah Posten* obituary of Ole Rocksvold said at Shiloh he accidentally got a ramrod through the hand while loading his gun that day.

The prisoners then had to lie down that night on the wet corn field, with rain pouring down on them, without any supper, believing, as the captors tried to convince them, that the entire Union army was beaten. This was untrue but used as propaganda to dishearten these prisoners. According to Quartermaster J.B. Dorr, quoted in Reed's book, the prisoners lay down small firs to lay upon on the wet fields that night and endured a terrible rainstorm all night.

The second day of battle at Shiloh, April 7, resulted in a sound defeat for the Confederate army who then retreated to Corinth, but of course the rebels would not have explained that to the prisoners. Perhaps, though, they may have been able to learn or guess, seeing the condition of the rebel soldiers and their demeanor in Corinth, but perhaps not. This day also provided time for those still lying on the battlefield to be tended by their comrades.

I wish we had a letter from Ole describing this battle and his time of imprisonment, but none has been found. We don't know why the particular letters written during the Civil War were saved starting in 1863 until he was mustered out. Were there other letters written that were lost? Since we don't have a first hand account from Ole of the battle of Shiloh/Pittsburg Landing, you may be interested in reading a couple of other soldiers' accounts in *Civil War Eyewitness Reports*, but it takes a strong stomach to read.

Nevertheless we are extremely fortunate that fourteen letters written by Ole during the Civil War were preserved to give us a fuller picture of the person he was and his perspective as a soldier, in addition to many letters written thereafter. According to James McPherson, 90% of Northern soldiers were literate and 80% of the south, but other books I have read have estimated total literacy for soldiers much lower, even as low as 50-60%. So some soldiers were not capable of writing letters unless they dictated them to someone else to write. Of course the level of ability judged as "literate" may vary. In the case of Ole, he must have been educated in Norway before he came at age 21 since we have his writing in letters and other documents near that time. It isn't known how much English he knew when he arrived, but he became so fluent so as to be asked to write the history of Glenwood Township for a book on the history of Winneshiek County in his later life.

The Horror of War

I would like to pause and comment at this point, that I find it very painful to write about this battle of Pittsburg Landing/Shiloh and think of the suffering and grief of all involved.

Some people tend to glamorize war, highlighting the bravery, self-sacrifice, strength, and mental and physical endurance of those involved. Those aspects are certainly very important to acknowledge. I feel the strongest lesson learned from this battle's accounts is how horrible and wasteful war is. I believe it is important to avoid unnecessary wars, exhaust all other options before getting into a war, working hard to prevent them in the future whenever possible. That is one way we can honor the sacrifices of these soldiers.

Reed's chart states that their total for prisoners taken from the Union side for April 6, 1862 at Pittsburgh Landing/Shiloh was 2,885, with 959 Confederate prisoners taken. Deaths for the Union side: 1,754, Confederate 1,728, wounded Union 8,408, Confederate 8,012, for a total of casualties for the Union 13,047, Confederate 10,699, with a final total of 23,746 who were killed, wounded, or became a prisoner that day. This was a loss of about 30 % of the Union fighting force. Think of the many husbands, fathers, sons, brothers, and friends who were lost! You will learn later that there were also females disguised among the soldiers as well, who were also lost.

Prisoners Marched to Corinth, MS

Continuing from that first day of capture, Quartermaster J. B. Dorr's report, quoted in Reed's book, stated that the morning of April 7, the prisoners received a one-third ration of moldy crackers and bacon to eat. They then had to stand for two hours, awaiting orders.

Cavalry then came riding up to say the Union army was in pursuit, so the captured Union soldiers were immediately marched the 19 miles towards Corinth, MS, via Monterey. Along the way the prisoners saw many wounded, as well as Confederate regiments hurrying forward. The road was in terrible shape, running through several swamps. Since many were sick and wounded, they made slow progress and didn't arrive in Corinth until about 4 p.m. It was drizzling part of the time as they marched. When they were close to town they could see the earth banks the rebels had constructed and three pieces of artillery. 400 more prisoners joined them. The prisoners waited in Corinth until night through a heavy rain storm until they were at last put into train cars. At ten p.m. officers and a few others were allowed to stay on the porch of the train depot for the night. The next morning, April 8, they traveled by train to Memphis, arriving about 6 p.m. The morning of April 9 they received their rations and got a meal in a hotel. Dorr stated that many people there were in support of the Union and gave prisoners provisions, cigars, and tobacco. On April 10 they reached Granada by noon and Jackson, MS, in the afternoon, with large crowds awaiting their arrival at all stations. They saw Gov. Pettis, Executive of the State of Mississippi. On April 12, they left Meridian at noon and reached Mobile, AL, about 9 p.m. At Mobile Dorr met John Forsythe, a colonel of a regiment and editor of the *Register*. The prisoners were moved from the train cars to a steamer, the *James Battle*, and stayed at the dock until noon the next day.

Col. Forsythe asked Dorr on April 13 if there was anything he could do to make Dorr more comfortable. Dorr declined. At noon they started their trip to Montgomery. Two other boats left carrying a group of prisoners to Tuscaloosa, AL. Dorr stated that all officers above lieutenant rank were going to Talladega. Before noon on April 15 they reached Selma and said good bye to the senior officers who left by boat for Talladega. Dorr went ashore and bought a few things, saying he received a "petty insult" from a lady. They left about noon for Montgomery, arriving about 10-11 p.m. and remained on the boat all night.

On April 16 the prisoners left the boat about 9 a.m. A large crowd came to watch as they were marched to a cotton shed, which was the prison. It was about 330 feet long by 180 feet. On the sides were sheds, roofed with slabs, iron and tin, about 18 feet high. There were double doors at one end of the building, one door at the other, with a railroad track running next to the structure. Occasionally citizens would stop by to see the prisoners. At night they lay on the ground since the sheds had no floors.

The prisoners spent April 17 trying to make their accommodations as comfortable as possible The weather was warm, so they didn't have to suffer due to the lack of blankets or warm clothing. Sinks were in one corner of the prison and with 600 hundred captives in this yard, hygiene was definitely an issue.

Coping as Prisoners

On April 18, they were allowed, while guarded to go into Montgomery, a city of about 10,000 people, and buy a few things with the little money they had. Dorr stated that when captured all he had was "one pair of boots, one pair of socks, one pair of pants, one pair of drawers, two shirts, one overshirt, one cap, one blanket, a jackknife and 75 cents." He said some of the prisoners had borrowed money from him for items they needed, but couldn't afford to pay him back right then. On April 19, they were given a small amount of hay and a plank so they could make a platform to sleep on. They heard that an attack was made on Fort Pillow and that Halleck had arrived in Pittsburg.

Dorr wrote April 21 that there was nothing to entertain them while prisoners so they created ways to amuse themselves to pass the time. They read, walked, sang, played ball, and pitched quoits. Their rations were less than half a regular soldier's rations, and very poor quality. They included: moldy crackers, a little rice and beans, bread, corn bread made from corn and ground cobs without salt, stinking beef, a little sugar, and no coffee. They survived by buying more food from poor whites in the area.

In *Campaigns and Battles of the Twelfth Regiment Iowa Veteran Volunteer Infantry*, page 105, Reed cited Dorr's April 24th report entry about prisoner life, that the Union soldiers were ingenious and figured out a way to "relieve the rebels of their spare change." They found sweet briar roots and clay, using those substances to make pipes and sell them. On May 2, Lieutenant Bliss was shot by a guard. Bliss was buying milk and a woman was making change for him. The guard ordered him to leave. Bliss said the woman was making change and he would come very quickly, but the guard shot him instantly. May 3 was the burial, but only a few officers were allowed to attend it. On May 5 they heard they would be exchanged and be free by next week, but it turned out to be a false rumor. Dorr wrote on May 10 that they heard more unreliable rumors about how the war was going, and that Joe Coe of Company E died. On May 11 they kept hearing rumors, but didn't know what to believe. On May 12 they realized they might not be released soon after all.

They read in the local paper on May 17 that Corinth was being vacated by the rebels as Union troops approached. They also heard rumors that Mobile, AL, was captured by the Union. On May 21, some of the officers and privates heard they were to be exchanged soon and they started making descriptive rolls about the soldiers/officers - such as name, height, hair and eye color, age, profession. On May 22 it seemed the parole would just involve privates. Other prisoners from Tuscaloosa arrived. A few were paroled, but many were sent back again. On May 24, soldiers started to write letters to send home in anticipation of being paroled. They heard about 40 prisoners from the Tuscaloosa group escaped while they tried to send them back to prison. On May 25 it sounded like at this point the officers and privates were to be separated, with privates transported by train to Macon, GA. By May 28 Dorr was freed and his diary report ends, but Ole remained a prisoner.

Health Effects from Prison Life

Among Ole's military pension papers, there are documents, some of which he filled out by hand, that describe the trouble with his health during imprisonment and the rest of his life. Soldiers filled out such forms when applying for their pensions. Soldiers John Johnson, Hans Hansen, and Anton Anderson all substantiated that Ole had trouble digesting the sour corn bread and other poor quality and rancid food the prisoners were given. As a result, Ole suffered greatly from starvation, diarrhea, chills, and fever, to the point that these soldiers wondering if he was going to survive. Many others suffered this way during imprisonment as well, and some did die in captivity. Ole wrote in the pension forms that he had trouble the rest of his life with arthritis, intermittent fevers, pain, and gastro-intestinal difficulties, likely due to the extreme exposures and starvation while a prisoner and during his three years of service.

Memphis, TN, Mobile, AL, Cahaba, AL, Macon, GA, and Aiken's Landing, VA as Prisoner

Ole was moved as a prisoner from Shiloh/Pittsburg Landing, TN, to Corinth, MS, Memphis, TN, Mobile, AL, Cahaba Prison near Selma/Montgomery, AL, and Macon, GA, at Camp Oglethorpe. An incorrect listing of Andersonville Prison appeared in the *Eggebraaten-Kjos Family History* book. At Macon he stayed the longest, five months. Finally, he was sent to Libby Prison, Richmond, VA, where he and his fellow soldiers were exchanged on James River above Fort Monroe at Aiken's Landing/Gardens, VA, Nov. 10 or 12, 1862 (documents vary on the date). He was a prisoner 7 months, but he survived.

The newly-released prisoners were then sent to Annapolis, Md., and from there to St. Louis where the regiment was reorganized due to the many who had died or resigned. Reed wrote that Col. Woods was then in command of the 12th Iowa Infantry . Captain Townsley was in charge of company G, Ole's company, at this point. It appears that Ole had the chance to go back home during this time of reorganization at St. Louis, based on a later comment in a letter dated Dec. 27, 1863 in which Ole mentioned he had not seen Anne, his girlfriend and future wife for "almost one year" at the time of the letter writing.

Back at Benton Barracks and First Letter

Bev Anderson Swenson, Ole's great granddaughter, found a total of 14 letters written during the Civil War by Ole. During Ole's time in St. Louis at Benton Barracks again, we have the earliest known letter, dated Jan. 5, 1863. Any prior letters he may have written were either not saved or somehow got lost or destroyed. This Jan. 5, 1863 letter was written to Hans P. Ruen, the husband of Ingeborg Strandbakken, who was the sister of Ole's future wife, Anne. Hans and Ingeborg lived on a farm near the Rocksvolds. The letter is not in good shape and some writing is illegible. The first two pages in the envelope clearly fit the date, but the third and fourth pages, based on content, do not fit the date, referring instead to 1863 at Vicksburg.

Ole's First letter

Translation

[Translator: Benton Barracks was in St. Louis, Missouri]

Benton Barracks, January 5th, 1863

Good friend Hans P. Ruen and family,

So as not to disregard my obligation and pledge, I am sending you a few lines that will be of little interest to you, since there is really little worth telling about. We are back in Benton Barracks and do not know for how long. It is common knowledge that the Union Brigade, which was formed immediately following the Battle of Shiloh *[Translator: also known as the Battle of Pittsburgh Landing]*, will be demobilized and the Iowa troops sent to Davenport, Iowa, for reorganization. *[Translator: several words not legible, on a crease]* . . . regiments, and if this is the case, then it will be our destination as well, something we all welcome, inasmuch we do not wish to remain here.

Anything I might have to tell you regarding the recent . . .

[end of page]

[second page]

. . . carnage has no doubt been reported in the daily papers in the past few days.

As I mentioned earlier, because I really have nothing suitable to include in this letter, I must resort to telling you things of little importance, so as not to leave most of this little piece of paper white *[Translator: empty]*.

I'll first tell of a spectacle that occurred last night, driving a harlot from the camp. A bunch of drunks were inside *[Translator: a building]* when *[Translator: blotted out, but probably is something like "the door"]* was kicked open. She appeared and was immediately dragged out and driven away while stones rained down on her. She *[Translator: very difficult to decipher the handwriting here, but he seems to be describing all the cursing and screaming she was doing]*, while those pursuing her were laughing and yelling, and all her pleading didn't help her. They chased her away from here until she was no longer _____[?]. They said that she was _____ *[Translator: Cannot decipher the handwriting of the last 7-8 words, nor could my Norwegian wife make any sense out of them whatsoever. One of the words looks like it could be "Been"/"legs", and another looks like "peena"/"attractive"/"beautiful".]*

Things are quiet here in the camp, and there are not many troops either. The 37th Iowa Regiment, commonly called the Silver Gray or Gray Beard *[Translator: Both designations written in English]* (men between the ages of 45 and 80) left here today for town to serve as *[Translator: Difficult to decipher the entire word, I see Gerald Giving has written "provisioners", which is no doubt correct]*, since they were regarded as unsuitable for any other kind of service.

[end of page]

[third page] THIS THIRD PAGE CLEARLY DOES NOT BELONG TO THIS LETTER

. . . *[Translator: The last sentence at the bottom of p. 2 appears to end there. The first words at the top of p. 3 are the continuation of a sentence that is NOT the sentence at the bottom of p. 2. What begins at the top of p. 3 is Ole's description of the Battle of Stones River in Middle Tennessee between General Rosencrantz of the Union Army and Confederate General Bragg, one of the bloodiest and most crucial battles of the war.]* . . . at the fortress[?] between General Rosencrantz and Hardee and Bragg. The battle had not ended on New Year's Eve, but the enemy had to withdraw *[Translator: It was actually January 3rd, according to Wikipedia.]* A huge number of troops were killed on both sides. It is said that half of the troops of the Wisconsin Regiment were killed, among them a Lieutenant Colonel and a Captain. Also six Captains were wounded. Most unpleasant news. Most of General Rosencrantz's ammunitions and baggage train was captured.

Nonetheless, the Battle of Vicksburg, Mississippi has already begun. General Sherman opened fire on the enemy batteries on the back side of the city. He had a significantly-sized army, and on the first day, things quickly *[Translator: Word/words blotted out.]* He took three of their large batteries, ammunition and weapons, as well as over 100 prisoners *[Translator: Could be 700]*. Our flotilla is entering on the river side, but so far without much effect. Huge numbers of troops are being sent there daily now as reinforcements, and a huge . . .

[end of page]

THE ACTUAL THIRD PAGE OF THIS LETTER IS MISSING

[fourth page]

Anders Egge asked me to greet you. He is lying in the hospital in town and is no better that when we last saw him. *[Translator: This page has blotches of ink everywhere, and much of it is illegible. He continues to write about the condition of Anders Egge, which does not appear to be very good. It is virtually impossible to make sense out of the following sentences, can make out several words here and there, nothing more]*

Your ever devoted

Ole P. Rocksvold

Please excuse both my writing style and my handwriting. My hand is shaking too much to be able to write any better now.

O. P. R.

Translation by Jim Skurdall
Fjellveien 27 / 1470 Lørenskog NORWAY
Cell phone from the U.S. 01147 90 11 23 29
E-Mail: jim@skurdalltranslation.com
Web: http://skurdalltranslation.webnode.com/en/

Ole's Second letter

On Jan. 19, 1863, Ole wrote from Rollo, MO, to Anne Gilbertson/Gilman (Anne Guld-brandsdatter Strandbakken), his future wife. It is the earliest-dated letter we have found addressed to her. The translation follows:

Translation

Rolla, Mo. January 19, 1863

To my well-regarded lass, Anne Gilman, (Editor's note: Anne went by multiple last names, not unusual for Norwegian immigrants)

Having now once more moved to another encampment since last writing to you, I am sending you a few lines so that you do not lose track of us altogether. We left St. Louis in a direction different from what I described in the letter. Instead of Davenport, Iowa, we headed for Rolla, Missouri, 116 miles from St. Louis. A dispatch reached General Curtis on the 10th of this month informing him that the enemy had taken Springfield, Missouri, together with two other towns, and all private as well as government property they could not take with them was destroyed. These rumors soon had us on our feet and moving toward the foe. We have now been in Rolla for a week, and there is hope that we soon shall …

[second page]

… return again to St. Louis, as the most recent report says that the enemy has been driven out of the state and into Arkansas, having had 7,000 troops captured, together with a number of killed and wounded. So here we have nothing to fear.

I can tell you a little about our camp life here, and conditions are about the hardest we have had so far. Our camp is around a half mile from town, on a hill so it can be quite windy. We only have small tents sleeping five men each, with no heating, so that when we awaken in the morning our blankets are covered with an inch of frost, and, as you might imagine, it is no fun lying there or getting up in the morning. So we talk about past times when we were lying in the arms of our sweethearts and how we are now so far away from our beloveds. It is the last thing we talk about in the evening and the first as soon as we awaken each morning. But communication …

[third page]

… with you happens only when dreaming, and I believe there is not a night it does not happen, and in the morning everyone has his story to tell. I have often told my tentmates about my dreams of you at night and I am not in the least bashful in admitting my fondness for you and my expectation of reciprocated feelings. Since my last departure, I have not heard anything from Iowa and expect to find several letters here, and, likewise, I expect to hear from you before long.

Dear Anne, write to me soon, if you have not done so already, for under the present circumstances nothing is more precious to me than hearing from you.

[continued on the next page]

I have nothing more to write about now and in closing wish to let you know that I have been in the best of health so far and hope to hear the same from you.

Cordial greetings from your ever devoted

O. P. Rocksvold

Address your letters to:

Co. G, 12th Iowa Vol
Camp Benton, St. Louis, Mo.

Translation by Jim Skurdall

Ole's Third Letter

On Feb. 15, 1863, Ole wrote from Benton Barracks to his "unforgettable Anne" again. It is so touching to read how he describe how he could never forget her. The translated text follows:

Translation

Benton Barracks, St. Louis, Mo.

Feb 15, 1863

Unforgettable special friend, Miss Anne:

Your most welcome letter dated the 8th of this month arrived today and was read with greatest pleasure. Slowly but surely your first letter arrived, and it was likewise the first letter I have ever received from a young lady.

I cannot properly express nor thank you for your encouraging and honest words articulated in the letter. You also say that you are happy to see from my letter that I have not forgotten you. Oh no, dear Anne, I would be more likely to forget my own existence than forget you. I wrote to you a few days ago, and, not knowing if you had returned home, the letter was sent to Lansing as was the one preceding it. You must send for it so that it does not end up in the hands of another, otherwise "var det de same" *[Translator: not sure what he means here, perhaps that the content of the two letters was about the same, "otherwise they were the same"]*, and I ask you, dear Anne, to pardon the content …

[second page]

… of said letter, if you receive it. I was perhaps a little too insistent, wondering if I would hear from you again, and for this reason I asked if you had forgotten me. But I retract this question after having received this little letter, which satisfies my curiosity in every respect.

I do not have much news to report that you would find of interest. The only somewhat comical thing that has happened in the past several days was when a number of paroled prisoners came into camp, including 13 Indians belonging to our army, who were captured near Little Rock, Arkansas. Their names were as strange as their brutish appearance.

Regarding the prisoners just mentioned, I must cast a glance back to the position we achieved a year ago with the capture of Fort Donelson. It was a day of rejoicing, for we had defeated the enemy and had superior strength. After having beheld our prisoners as well as newspaper reports *[I assume it is what he means by "Prisse"]*, we were all happy, spirited, and proud of our accomplishments. And we believed that this ungodly war would have been over by now and each of us would have returned home.

[third page]

The hope of going to Davenport, Iowa, mentioned in one of my first letters, is dead and gone. Our officers, and Governor Kirkwood as well, have been diligent in trying to achieve this, but without success. With courage and hope we accept the call of duty in this new year and hope that God will be with us and everything will turn out for the best. *[Translator: the handwriting of the next passage is very faded and on a crease in the paper. Not enough is legible to make sense of what he wrote, at least for now.]* … and that affords renewed strength, and strengthens hope for a happy outcome.

You wrote that you have had a photograph taken and are thinking of sending it. Please do it soon, dear Anne, while we are here, for I do not know when we might receive orders to move on. Send me a copy of you to look at while I think of the original. I shall enclose in this letter a pamphlet with the title "Southern States in Secession", and it was around the same time that I was there. If it passes our censor, then you can see the benevolent conduct of the secessionist states. *[Translator: this is my interpretation of what Ole writes here, and I believe there is irony attached to the word "velvillighed/benevolence".]* Such must be punished, and I wish to do my part in achieving this specific end. There is nothing new to report regarding the war.

[fourth page]

Continue to use the same address as before, until I change it, and if we should move on from here, the mail will be forwarded.

In closing, I greet you from Anders A. Egge. He has been discharged from the hospital and is in fairly good health. 2,000 sick and wounded soldiers are expected here in the next few days. *[he wrote "(from Below)"]*

Everyone in our company is in good health and doing exceptionally well, and I have never felt better than I do now. Greetings from Sergeant A. E. Andersen (who is sitting beside me and writing to a girl in Wisconsin) — May the Lord be with you and with us all is the candid and heartfelt wish of your forever [unto death] devoted friend

O. P. Rocksvold

Translation by Jim Skurdall

Ole's Fourth Letter

On March 14, 1863, Ole again wrote to Anne and said he hadn't heard from her in a month. It must have been so frustrating to have long periods of time go by with mail not getting through. On the third page he make a mention of how hard the first year of service was, during which we unfortunately have no representative letter. Here is the translated text:

Translation

Camp Benton, St. Louis, MO.
March 14, 1863

My Unforgettable and Deeply Beloved Friend
Miss Anne

Feeling so inclined to address you in this manner, I likewise ask you to excuse the boldness of my greeting. It has now been a month since I last heard from you. Your letter dated the 8th of February is the first and last correspondence I have received from you at this time, and I hope that you will soon honor me with another. I have only written one other letter to you since receiving yours, as I have been awaiting a reply, but in view of the present circumstances, I have decided to send these lines. We are now "Under Marching Order" [written in English] and expected to be ready for departure on one hour's notice with four days' rations whenever the order is received, whether night or day. Nonetheless, it remains uncertain just when we actually shall leave. Nor do we know exactly where we are going, apart from that it will be to the south, …

[second page]

… presumably to Vicksburg or Cape Girardeau, with all Iowa troops included.

Dear Anne, let us keep our correspondence regular and not allow it to fade away. Write to me soon, if you have not done so already, and send at the same time the photograph you promised. It would be so very welcome until I once again can see you in person, which is not likely until I have completed my service and have been discharged from the Army. As we now move further south, it is uncertain when we shall return, and the only joy we can have is the thought of what awaits us when we meet again and can live together in complete peace. And receiving your letters of encouragement plays no small part in sustaining my own courage and helping time to pass more quickly. This Law of Conscription is no doubt terrible news for many of your neighbors who loathe and fear going to war, and if it is their lot to be called to serve, nothing will exempt them, and if the Army is to be increased by 600,000 men, then I expect to see some acquaintances from up north joining our ranks.

[third page]

I apologize for speaking of such things that concern you so little, but which are directly related to my own circumstances.

I have been in excellent health the entire time since arriving here, and the same can be said for the soldiers here in general. All are in good spirits and hope that in the future we shall not be subjected to such trials as we endured the first year. There is nothing newsworthy to report.

The next time I write to you, it presumably will be from a different location, and if our departure happens soon, I shall write to you as soon as we have reached a new encampment. In the meantime, you can continue to write to Camp Benton, as the letters will be forwarded to our regiment. So use this address until I inform you myself that it has changed.

The weather is exceptionally good, and today is the warmest I have felt since I was in Macon, Georgia.

In closing, I wish to let you know that you are the object of my thoughts each day and are in my dreams each night, and you can never be forgotten or banished from my memory as long as I live.

[fourth page]

I hope that you, dear Anne, do not forget how very fond I am of you and that I live as much for you as for myself. I believe my destiny can only be fulfilled in sharing life's joys with you, as no other young woman has captured my heart as you have, my Beloved. And when I think of being free again and together with you, feelings of dissatisfaction vanish, though such feelings do not often affect my mood. In no way do I regret being in the Army, and I hope, with God's help, to return home as a veteran, unscathed, and be integrated in the company of surviving friends, and together with you in particular. My most fervent wish is to hear that you and yours, as well as as my friends and relatives, are all alive and well. May we remember one another in our prayers.

Most cordial greetings to you all, and rest assured that you will never be forgotten by your forever faithful Beloved.

Address your letters in this manner:

> O. P. Rocksvold
> Co G 12th Regt, Iowa Vol
> Camp Benton, St. Louis Mo

Translation by Jim Skurdall

This letter is in the original Norwegian to see a sample of his handwriting.

alle havde en Idee her hvem det var, og derfor sikrede
mig, at det nyttede ikke at negte dem at jeg dem,
for de mente de vare mange nok til at tage mig med
Magt. Og jeg jaa do dem, at enhver jom havde Portræt
af nogen Pige, vilde jaa jeg med, ved at møde op med
deres og jaa kan du troe at de kom frem. John
Sanden kom frem med Kari Bramhagen, og Versle
Hjerterud, Hans Shager med Hellene Løvbråthe,
Theodor Slew havde en Sort Halling jente at rise
frem, og atter andre noget Lignende, men alle
maatte give inds, paa Qualiteten, og være enig i at
jeg havde det Baste i bland dem alle, jom og jaa var
let at bedømme. Igaar var jeg i Byen og jiut jom jeg
til Overteer igjen, imodtog jeg dit Brev, Dit friedi
jom ene du skulde have valgt den 8d i Maaneden til
at skrive i, jaa jom dit første var af 8de Februar, og
dette af 8d dennes, Brevet var jint ligo til Cairo, da
Postmesteren i Byen ikke vidste andet end vi vare gaaede
Sydover, og jaaledes tog dit flere Dage end jedvanlig for
Brevene at naae. Vi ere nu her paa stedet, og
den Reise jeg talte om i forrige Brev tilbagekaltt.

og hvorlenge det bliver tilro før Marching Order igjen
vides ikke. For en kort tid siden havde jeg Brev fra
Conrad, og Thilla hilser mig iblandt andet, at de havde
haft et Besøg anlig forhen, af en Dame ved navn —
Anne, Mobrs Kaanaz men siger de det er ikke nöd-
vendigt at sige mere om det, forde tror ikke jeg kjender
hende alligevel, eller kan hjælte hvem det var.

Kjere Anne da du troede, at höre fra mig den gang
du nedlagde dit sidste Brev paa Posthuset, saa maa jeg
beklage at du nok blev skuffet i dine Forventninger,
da jeg til den tid ikke havde Skrevet mere end et Brev
siden jeg fik det förste. Tillige seer jeg af dit Brev
at Sygdomstilfælder ere ganske Hyppige i deres Naborlag
og ligeledes at du selv heller ikke var aldeles Frisk, Dog Haaber
næste gang jeg höver fra dig, at intet mangler, saa at
de övrige Velbekjente kunde snart faa sin Helbred til
bage. Sundhetstilstanden her, er for nærværende tilfreds-
stillende, i vort Compagny ere for det meste alle
friske ingen af dem som du kjender er syge, jeg har
hele tiden siden jeg kom tilbage haft ah urokkerhet
god Helse, og har den frem deles.

Ved Liv af den Brændende Kjærlighedsforstaaelse som

Vagtes imellem Jens Skøger og Hellene Liøbraaten

i Julen. Enstadig Brevvexling har været holdt

op[k]e imellem dem siden han Reiste igjen, samt deres

Portraits ere Vexlet, og fine Walentines har han

sendt til hende.   Vell mit Lys ennestun iellerd

ogtillige er det efter Tatto, og tid til at reve tilsenge

og jeg maa afbryde denne korte Skrivelse, og m[ed]

det Ønske at Tiden ikke var fjernt Borte, at vi

atter kunde Samles, og leve i Roe, og Krig Menneske

Slagteri maatte faae ennde og enhver gaa til sit kjere

Hjem. Sluttelig maa jeg fortelle at dine Brev,

giver mig baadde Kraft og Mod, og ikke minste tra,

sag har til at Betvivle din Oprigtighed. Hvis

jeg atter skal komme i Slag, saa følger din af faa

med denne gang, hver forvisset om at du Alltid

er i Tanker af din til Døden forbundne ven og

Hengivne Elsker. — —   Ole P Rockvold

    Jeg haaber du skriver snart, og Adresser som

før hen,

Ole's Fifth Letter

On Mar. 20, 1863, Ole wrote to Anne saying it had only been a few days since he wrote and thanked her for the picture which he received March 18 and the letter March 19. Ole said he felt blood rushing through his veins when he saw her picture and he was proud to show it to his comrades. The text follows:

Translation

Benton Barracks, St. Louis
March 20, 1863

Most Highly Esteemed and Beloved Anne,

Once more I reach for my pen to write a few lines to you, though it has not been many days since I sent you a rather meager letter.

I am not able by this means to express my gratitude for the admirable[1] manner in which you have kept your promise, both writing to me and sending me your photograph. I received the latter on the 18th of this month, and the following day I received your encouraging and, in every respect, most satisfactory letter.

You can imagine, dear Anne, how happy I was to receive your photograph, and the blood was coursing all through my veins as I opened it and regarded you, looking so natural, as if I had been standing in front of you. And, as you can also imagine, it was not long after the mail carrier had delivered it that I was surrounded by curious lads, for they …

[second page]

… all suspected from whom I had received the letter. And therefore they assured me that it would do no good to deny them the right to see the photograph, for outnumbering me as they did, they would overpower me. I said to them that any of them who had photographs of their sweethearts would get to see mine if they showed up with theirs. And they came forward, John Sanden with his photo of Kari Branhagen, and Versle Hjerterud; Jens Skager with a photo of Hellene Løvbrøttet; Theodor Steen had one to show of a dark Hallingdal girl; and a number of others with similar photos. But all of them had to concede that in terms of quality, I had the best one. This, they agreed, had been easy to determine.

Yesterday I was in town, and no sooner had I returned to my quarters than I received your letter. It appears that you intentionally wrote on the 8th of the month, as your first letter was written on the 8th of February, and this one on the 8th of this month. The letter was sent to Cairo, as the postmaster in town knew only that we had gone south, and thus it took longer than usual for the

---

[1] I cannot, nor can Anne-Guri, decipher the adjective used here, looks like "Poinglige," which brings to mind no Norwegian word that would fit in this context. I assume my choice of the word "admirable" comes close to what Ole meant to express.

letter to reach us. We are still at the same place, and the journey I spoke of in the last letter was cancelled …

[third page]

… and how long it will be before we receive marching orders, I do not know.

Not long ago I received a letter from Evenrud, and Thilla sent greetings and said, among other things, that recently they had the visit of a fine lady by the name of — Anne — but said it was not necessary to say more about it, as they doubted I knew her anyway, nor could guess who it was. *[Right after the name "Anne" Ole wrote in parentheses "Mobro Kaana", which is a more rustic way of writing "wife of a maternal uncle". I don't know why he wrote that. My interpretation of this passage otherwise is that the visitor, the "fine lady", was Ole's sweetheart, Anne, and he is being ironic here].*

Dear Anne, believing that you would hear from me, you posted your last letter, and I must apologize for having disappointed you in your expectations. At that time I had not written more than one letter after receiving your first. Moreover, I see from your letter that there are frequent cases of illness among your neighbors, and that you yourself have not been feeling so well. I hope that you will be lacking in nothing the next time I hear from you, and all my good acquaintances will have been restored to full health. As for matters of health here, things are satisfactory, and for the most part everyone in our company is in good health. No one whom you know is ill. Ever since my return I have enjoyed excellent health and continue to do so.

[fourth page]

Do you know of the passionate romantic relationship that began last Christmas between Jens Skager and Hellene Løvbraaten? They have maintained a continuous correspondence since he left, exchanging photographs, and beautiful Valentines.

Well, my candle has nearly burned out, and tattoo has sounded, and it is time to be in bed, so I must end this short letter with the wish that it will not be long until we can be together in peace, and that war and human slaughter will soon be at an end, and each of us can return home.

In closing, I must tell you that your letters give me both strength and courage, and I have not the least cause to doubt your sincerity. If once more I must go into battle, you will be with me this time as well. Know for certain that you are always in the thoughts of your [unto death] devoted Beloved

Ole P. Rocksvold

I hope you will write soon. The same address as before.

Translation by Jim Skurdall

Ole's Sixth Letter and the Trip South

On April 4, 1863, Ole said they were leaving at 10 p.m. for Dixie, hopefully to Vicksburg. He said he was healthy and could handle anything that comes with the other brave boys and share their destiny. It is amusing these days to read that he would give $10 to be able to see her when the value of money has so changed now! Here is the text:

Translation

Camp Benton, St. Louis, MO.
April 8th, 1863

Dear Anne,

I am sending you a few lines before leaving Benton Barracks. Tomorrow at 10 p.m. we shall depart here and travel further south. I am happy to report that I am in the best of health and can take part with the other brave lads and share their destiny wherever and whatever it may be, hoping at the same time that it promises us good fortune and victory.

A difficult test surely awaits us. It is possible that we shall come in closer quarters [Ole wrote "Closer Quarters", meaning to the enemy] than we have been, but not necessarily, no not at all. There cannot be an engagement without some who bite the dust, and especially at a place like Vicksburg, which at present is the enemy's Gibraltar. It is said to be impregnable, but I hope it is not the case. My dear Anne, I continue to hope ...

[second page]

... that the bullets will, with God's help, pass me by now as they have in the past, and that you, my dear, will remember me in your prayers.

I would have given 10 dollars to have been in your company on a recent visit to town. Last Monday evening we were there for a concert. Forty-two women represented the different states and territories in the Union, together with those that have seceded from the union. The Devil came and persuaded Jeff Davis to found his kingdom, saying he would help him if he could have his soul, and a pact was made, and the Devil took him in the end, and his kingdom was returned to Uncle Sam.

I wrote to Norway yesterday, and at the end of the letter I could not resist adding a sentence concerning you. Dear Anne, I said that I had found what I had been searching for for so many years, as though I were certain, but in an ...

[third page]

... additional sentence I told them that we had known each other for a number of years and understood each other well. I also said that you, and you alone, were the one who had captured my heart, and I said that I hoped I had won yours in return, and gave them your full name.

Dear Anne, you must be so kind as to forgive me my boldness in using your name without your knowledge. Anne, write to me often and do not forget.

Now we shall head south and one or another circumstance can quickly arise so that letters cannot be forwarded. So let us therefore make use of this occasion while it lasts.

I have beheld your photograph, Anne, more than once, and I will keep it close by until I return.

[continued next page]

That is all for now, and though we may be parted, we shall be together again. Never forget this. This is my hope, and receive these lines with the assurance that this hope is well kept in the heart of your faithful friend,

Ole P. Rocksvold

Use the same address as before.
Translation by Jim Skurdall

Ole's Seventh Letter and the Battles and Siege of Vicksburg

On April 9, 1863, the reorganized troops traveled south on the steamer, *Planet,* from St. Louis, MO, towards Vicksburg, arriving at Duckport, LA, on April 14. When Ole's unit set up camp, it was in a corn field with the level of the ground below the level of the river. The soldiers dug a canal to help with transportation from the river to Walnut Bayou and then to the river below Vicksburg. The canal project was an effort to reroute the Mississippi River so that Vicksburg could be bypassed and ignored without a fight! The canal ultimately failed and was abandoned. On April 16 they heard that 7 Union gun boats with supplies were sent down river past the batteries of Vicksburg to see if they could get through. Only one was sunk, so it showed they now had a way to get supplies south of Vicksburg. With this knowledge, Grant decided to change their location and marched the army below Vicksburg.

On April 22, some of the army was sent to join McClernand, some went up the Yazoo River to attract attention away from the actions below the city. The 15th corp constructed a wagon road along the banks of the canal to Walnut Bayou.

On April 26, 1863, Ole wrote from Duckport, Louisiana, about 1500 miles from Decorah, and said the physical distance between them was much further now that he was near Vicksburg, MS. Difficult trials lay ahead, as tomorrow 25,000 men would cross over to the Mississippi side of the river to try to stop railroad connections between Vicksburg and Jackson, MS. A very large number of enemy troops were trying to prevent this mission from being achieved. A frightening and trying time. The text follows:

Translation

Duckport, Louisiana, April 26, 1863

My well-regarded and unforgettable Anne!

Before leaving this camp, I shall keep the pledge I made to you in my last letter from St. Louis, namely, to inform you of that which has befallen me since then. The distance between us now is much greater than I wish it to be, and soon it will be even greater, as we shall depart from here tomorrow. I am already 1,500 miles from you and my home, and only 12 miles from Vicksburg. Dear Anne, you may rest assured that the thought of you will never be lost to my memory as long as I live, and no matter how great the distance between us. The cheerful hope remains in my heart that we shall meet again and that together, in moderation and in devotion to one another, we shall enjoy whatever earthly goods we are given for as long as God permits us to live on this Earth.

Dear Anne! You must understand that difficult trials lie before us. Tomorrow 3 divisions comprising around 25,000 men will cross over to the Mississippi side [of the Mississippi River] and try to stop railroad communications between Vicksburg and Jackson. A confrontation is inevitable, as the enemy . . .

[end of page]

[second page]

. . . has an extremely large number of men assembled there to prevent us from accomplishing our mission. During this expedition we shall have to camp without tents, as each company is allowed only one tent, and that is to be used for the sick and wounded. We shall certainly find ourselves in disagreeable situations, as we did during our journey here from Illinois, for example, having to sleep on top of coffins for lack of any other space. Since our arrival here we have been sleeping on the wet ground, but under tents, which, from now on, we shall sorely miss while sleeping in Mississippi swamps.

But everything must come to an end, and this, too, will end. We have not lost our courage. Several foolhardy raids have been undertaken since arriving here. On the night of the 17th-18th, eight cannon boats and four transport boats passed the blockade at Vicksburg. Only one of the transport boats was sunk by cannonfire. However, the night of the 23rd-24th, six other transport boats set out, and two of them were sunk by fire from the fortress, while four made it by unscathed. There were only a few killed in the entire encounter. The weather is already too warm here for any kind of hardships to which we are exposed. It is [cannot decipher], all that is expected of us.

[end of page]

[third page]

[Cannot decipher] has been that during the first days our regiment was to be consolidated into a battalion, and half of our commissioned officers discharged, and, likewise, our non-commissioned officers not needed in the five companies of the battalion are also to be discharged. Some will have the opportunity of soon being reunited with their dear friends, and if luck is on my side, I myself may count among those so fortunate. It is not that I am so weary of serving that I wish to come home. But where you are, there, too, I wish to be. I had thought I would receive a letter from you before leaving here, but that is not the case now, as we leave tomorrow, and we have not received any mail since arriving here. If only it would come. It is also possible that after leaving here we shall not have the opportunity of sending letters. And that has been the criticism, that we were supposed to receive mail as long as we were down here I do not have time to write more, as I must post the letter momentarily and it is almost impossible to finish because I must hold . . .

[end of page]

[fourth page]

. . . the paper on my knee while I write [illegible here, but I believe he wrote something like] so I hope you can read what I have written. As I said, I do not believe I shall have the opportunity to write to you again until after I have taken part in the impending bloody battle of Vicksburg, during which many will bite the dust. [Words missing or illegible here] I place my trust in the hope that God will [cannot decipher] unscathed from this terrible storm. I march into battle without fear, and hope at the same time that you will not forget me in your prayers. I am in good health and lacking nothing. And I hope to hear the same from you, dear Anne. And, in closing, I can tell you how happy it makes me to have your picture, which is always in a breast pocket and follows me [handwriting almost illegible here, everywhere into battle?] It is possible that before this letter reaches you we already will have engaged in a skirmish.

Farewell dear Anne, and do not forget your friend, devoted to you unto death.

Ole P. Rocksvold
Co G, 12th Reg, Iowa Vol
Via Cairo, Ill. Army of the Southwest

Translation by Jim Skurdall

Overview sign at Fort Donelson National Military Park, TN.

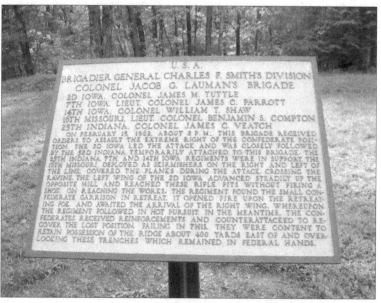

Description of fighting on Feb. 15, 1862 at Fort Donelson, TN
at the National Military Park.

View by the river at Fort Donelson National Military Park, Tennessee, taken 2012. The men with whom Ole fought on Feb. 14-15, 1862, had to struggle up steep, wooded ravines to the left of this picture to engage the Rebels. They also unfortunately suffered all night outdoors in cold and snow without blankets or coats.

Battle of Pittsburg Landing/Shiloh Description at the Shiloh National Military Park, Tennessee, taken 2012.

This sign describes the battle on April 6-7, 1862, in which Ole Rocksvold fought at the so-called "Hornets' Nest" for many hours before ultimately being captured. He was held prisoner for seven months.

Sunken Road, with Nathan Kalmoe, great great grandson of Ole,
at Shiloh National Military Park, TN.

Gen. Prentiss surrendered here 5:30 p.m., April 6, 1862, which included Ole and soldiers from 12th Iowa. The sign is at Shiloh National Military Park, TN.

Shiloh National Military Park sign regarding the capture of Ole and the 12th Iowa April 6, 1862.

Nathan Kalmoe at Iowa's monument at Shiloh National Military Park, Tennessee, 2012. Nathan is the son of Dave Kalmoe and Sharon Bowen, grandson of Florence Ohnstad and Ed Smith, great grandson of Hilda Rocksvold and Ed Ohnstad, great great grandson of Ole and Anne Rockvold.

Nathan Kalmoe and Sharon Bowen at the 12th Iowa monument at Shiloh National Military Park.

Katie Will and Nathan Kalmoe at 12th Iowa Monument
at Shiloh National Military Park.

Engraved quote of Abraham Lincoln on Iowa's monument
at the Shiloh National Military Park, Tennessee.

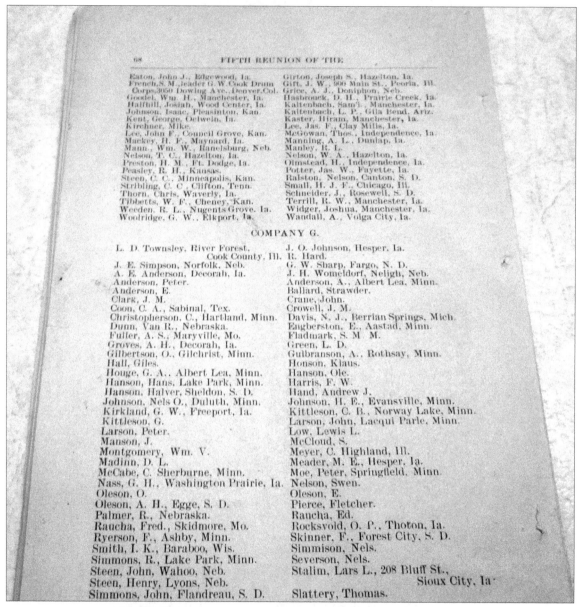

Eaton, John J., Edgewood, Ia.
French, S. M., leader G. W. Cook Drum
  Corps, 3050 Dowing Ave., Denver, Col.
Goodel, Wm. H., Manchester, Ia.
Halfhill, Josiah, Wood Center, Ia.
Johnson, Isaac, Pleasinton, Kan.
Kent, George, Oelwein, Ia.
Kirchner, Mike.
Lee, John F., Council Grove, Kan.
Mackey, H. F., Maynard, Ia.
Mann., Wm. W., Ranelsburg, Neb.
Nelson, T. C., Hazelton, Ia.
Preston, H. M., Ft. Dodge, Ia.
Peasley, R. H., Kansas.
Steen, C. C., Minneapolis, Kan.
Stribling, C. C., Clifton, Tenn.
Thorn, Chris, Waverly, Ia.
Tibbetts, W. F., Cheney, Kan.
Weeden, R. L., Nugents Grove, Ia.
Woolridge, G. W., Elkport, Ia.

Girton, Joseph S., Hazelton, Ia.
Gift, J. W., 900 Main St., Peoria, Ill.
Grice, A. J., Doniphon, Neb.
Hasbrouck, D. H., Prairie Creek, Ia.
Kaltenbach, Sam'l, Manchester, Ia.
Kaltenbach, L. P., Gila Bend, Ariz.
Kaster, Hiram, Manchester, Ia.
Lee, Jas. F., Clay Mills, Ia.
McGowan, Thos., Independence, Ia.
Manning, A. L., Dunlap, Ia.
Manley, R. L.
Nelson, W. A., Hazelton, Ia.
Olmstead, H., Independence, Ia.
Potter, Jas. W., Fayette, Ia.
Ralston, Nelson, Canton, S. D.
Small, H. J. F., Chicago, Ill.
Schneider, J., Rosewell, S. D.
Terrill, R. W., Manchester, Ia.
Widger, Joshua, Manchester, Ia.
Wandall, A., Volga City, Ia.

COMPANY G.

L. D. Townsley, River Forest,
           Cook County, Ill.
J. E. Simpson, Norfolk, Neb.
A. E. Anderson, Decorah, Ia.
Anderson, Peter.
Anderson, E.
Clark, J. M.
Coon, C. A., Sabinal, Tex.
Christopherson, C., Hartland, Minn.
Dunn, Van R., Nebraska.
Fuller, A. S., Maryville, Mo.
Groves, A. H., Decorah, Ia.
Gilbertson, O., Gilchrist, Minn.
Hall, Giles.
Houge, G. A., Albert Lea, Minn.
Hanson, Hans, Lake Park, Minn.
Hanson, Halver, Sheldon, S. D.
Johnson, Nels O., Duluth, Minn.
Kirkland, G. W., Freeport, Ia.
Kittleson, G.
Larson, Peter.
Manson, J.
Montgomery, Wm. V.
Madinn, D. L.
McCabe, C. Sherburne, Minn.
Nass, G. H., Washington Prairie, Ia.
Oleson, O.
Oleson, A. H., Egge, S. D.
Palmer, R., Nebraska.
Raucha, Fred., Skidmore, Mo.
Ryerson, F., Ashby, Minn.
Smith, I. K., Baraboo, Wis.
Simmons, R., Lake Park, Minn.
Steen, John, Wahoo, Neb.
Steen, Henry, Lyons, Neb.
Simmons, John, Flandreau, S. D.

J. O. Johnson, Hesper, Ia.
R. Hard.
G. W. Sharp, Fargo, N. D.
J. H. Womeldorf, Neligh, Neb.
Anderson, A., Albert Lea, Minn.
Ballard, Strawder.
Crane, John.
Crowell, J. M.
Davis, N. J., Berrian Springs, Mich.
Engberston, E., Aastad, Minn.
Fladmark, S. M. M.
Green, L. D.
Gulbranson, A., Rothsay, Minn.
Honson, Klaus.
Hanson, Ole.
Harris, F. W.
Hand, Andrew J.
Johnson, H. E., Evansville, Minn.
Kittleson, C. B., Norway Lake, Minn.
Larson, John, Lacqui Parle, Minn.
Low, Lewis L.
McCloud, S.
Meyer, C. Highland, Ill.
Meader, M. E., Hesper, Ia.
Moe, Peter, Springfield, Minn.
Nelson, Swen.
Oleson, E.
Pierce, Fletcher.
Raucha, Ed.
Rocksvold, O. P., Thoton, Ia.
Skinner, F., Forest City, S. D.
Simmison, Nels.
Severson, Nels.
Stalim, Lars L., 208 Bluff St.,
             Sioux City, Ia.
Slattery, Thomas.

12th Iowa's Fifth Reunion program book-page listing those from Company G.

War Department,

ADJUTANT GENERAL'S OFFICE.

#655,045.

Washington, *Jany 15*, 188 9.

Respectfully returned to the Commissioner of Pensions.

Ole P. Rocksvold , a Private of Company G ,

12th Regiment Iowa Inft Volunteers, was enrolled on the

18th day of October , 1861 , at Decorah, for 3 yrs.

and is reported: On roll from enrollment to Dec. 31, 61, present.

So borne to Feb. 28, 62. March and April, 62, absent

missing in action at Pittsburg, Tenn., April 6, 62.

(Regt. was in action at that date and place.) So borne

to Feb. 28, 63. March and Apr., 63, present, and so to

Feb. 29, 64. March and April, 64, absent on det. ser.

May and June, 64, absent sick in Convalescent Camp

Memphis. July and Aug., 64, present. So borne to

Oct. 31, 64. He was mustered-out at Nashville,

Tenn., Nov. 30/64, with a detachment of Co.

Regimental Hospital records show him admitted with

Diar. Chron. June 13, 64. Disposition not stated

6-15-1889 War dept. Ole Rocksvold sickness record

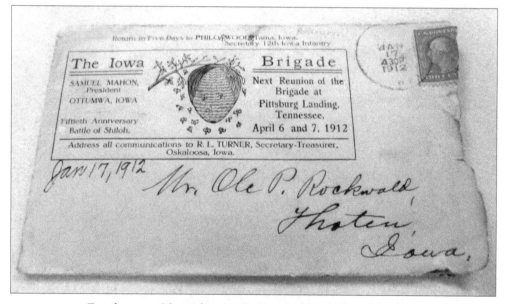

12th Iowa's Fifth Reunion song sheet, close up of top of page 2

Envelope to Ole with an invitation to the 50th anniversary
of The Shiloh Battle in Tennessee in which he was captured.

~ Chapter 4 ~

Vicksburg through the
end of Ole's Service

The nine battles that comprised the Vicksburg Campaign spanned several months, with a siege ultimately forcing the rebels to surrender the city on July 4, 1863. Winston Groom in *Vicksburg 1863* described the battles as thrilling and heart-rending. His book is fascinating, giving more detail on creative strategies of Union attempts to win, complications in fighting in swampy terrain, risk-taking, interpersonal conflicts, and mistakes and bungling that occurred on both sides. While no one decisive battle won the day for the North, the rebels ultimately surrendered because of the North's siege of Vicksburg. In *Team of Rivals* by Doris Kearns Goodwin, on page 528, Lincoln is quoted in a letter to a friend written May 26, 1863, "Whether Gen. Grant shall or shall not consummate the capture of Vicksburg, his campaign from the beginning of this month up to the twenty second day of it, is one of the most brilliant in the world."

The Union army made many failed attempts to capture Vicksburg over the preceding many months, but the battles of the final Vicksburg Campaign itself were almost entirely Union victories. The fall of Vicksburg essentially opened the entire length of the Mississippi River to military and commerce shipping, and it physically split the Confederacy in two by cutting off Louisiana, Texas, and Arkansas. Groom quoted Grant, "The fate of the Confederacy was sealed at Vicksburg." Many lives would have been saved if the Confederacy had acknowledged that fact earlier, but unfortunately the war continued for two more years.

During the Vicksburg Campaign, the command structure included Woods in charge of the 3rd brigade, which was under Gen. Tuttle in charge of the 3rd division, which was in turn under the command of Gen. Sherman of the 15th corps.

Grant led the 13th and 17th corps in battle at Port Gibson May 1 and achieved a firm hold on the east side of the river. Tuttle's division – in which Ole served – left Duckport on May 2 with only what they could carry to go to Richmond. They continued to march for days to Hard Times Landing, across from Grand Gulf, arriving May 7. Fortunately the weather and roads were good. Along the way, they found the owners of the houses had gone, with their slaves taking care of the property until their return. They then got on a steamer, the *Chessman*, to cross the river to Grand Gulf. The steamer was covered with holes from being shot at by the rebel batteries at Vicksburg. The men were given 5 days' rations of crackers and coffee for their haversacks. The soldiers were told that meat would have to be obtained in the country, and they should be careful with their rations because they didn't know when they could get more. On May 8 they started to march to join the rest of the army to the rear of Vicksburg.

While awaiting other troops' arrival, they rested at Rocky Springs on May 10. They found the countryside had been stripped of any food and their crackers were getting exhausted. Some had to steal food of the mules or eat parched corn. During the night cattle were driven in and animals were assigned to companies to kill and eat. They individually broiled the meat at the end of the ramrod, a metal rod used to load the bullet down the barrel of their muzzle-loading rifles. Some also fried meat in a half-canteen. Since it was unknown when there would next be time to cook meat, it was usually cooked completely in the evening, and the leftovers stored for the next two meals. They had to do this for 10 days, because no more crackers or other rations had arrived yet, other than a little corn meal. You can imagine that storing meat in the haversack all day resulted in it not being in very good condition for eating at night!

According to Reed's narrative, on May 11 they moved towards Edward Station, between Jackson and Vicksburg. The armies facing each other now were about equal size, about 50,000 each. They tented at Auburn that night, and at Fourteen-Mile Creek May 12. Since the Confederates were gathering near Jackson, Grant wanted to send several groups there along with the 15th corps, of which Ole was a part, to disperse the Rebels So Sherman led the Union soldiers to Mississippi Springs and then towards Jackson. They reached Raymond the evening of May 13 and fought upon arrival, driving the Rebels through Mississippi Springs. It rained that evening and they bivouaced (stayed in tents) that night east of town. At 3 a.m. reveille sounded, the men quickly ate the beef cooked the night before, and started for Jackson as soon as it was dawn. Because of the rain, they sometimes had to wade knee-deep in water as they made their way, finding the enemy entrenched about one and a half miles from Jackson. McPherson's troops were making their way to their left and they occasional caught sight of them driving the Rebels before them. The 12th Iowa was the first regiment to reach Jackson, the capitol of Mississippi. When they arrived, they found the abandoned camp of the enemy, with food cooked, waiting to be eaten, so the soldiers helped themselves. The Union troops were now in control of the city and spread out to protect themselves from attack. They made fires to dry out their clothing, sought rations, and set up tents. Many bales of cotton were found so the soldiers decided to use them to cushion their beds for the first time since entering the service. Reed said bits of cotton fiber were all over their uniforms the next morning.

On May 15, McPherson's troops were ordered to Vicksburg and Sherman's corps told to hold Jackson and await further orders. The third brigade of Tuttle's division (Ole's) went out four miles and were told to destroy the track for the Memphis Railroad from there to Jackson. To destroy this mode of transportation to prevent its use by the rebels, they would lift up a section the length of the regiment and put the wrenched up rails and ties in piles. They then lit the piles on fire which enabled them to twist the ends of the rails so they couldn't be used again. Company C captured 9 geese which the men enjoyed eating that evening. They captured 20 prisoners, and were ordered to destroy the Confederate's storehouses of their supplies, an arsenal, and an iron foundry used for manufacturing supplies. They also burned public buildings. According to Reed and also Gen. Sherman's memoirs, some of the Union soldiers who had been taken prisoner at Shiloh remembered being taken through Jackson while prisoners back then. Some of these soldiers went over to the hotel called the "Confederate House" to eat, but were refused when they tried to order supper. The owner said it was because they were trying to pay with greenbacks (not the Confederate currency.) Since these soldiers were thus insulted, some of them decided to burn the hotel down. Since Ole was one of those captured at Shiloh, we don't know whether he was among those who tried to eat at the hotel or helped burn the building. There is no mention of this event in his letters.

At 1 p.m. Gen. Sherman was notified there was a battle at Champion Hill and he was to bring his 15th corps there as soon as possible. Reed described Sherman as a very promptly responsive person and within thirty minutes they were on their way to Clinton, ten miles marching without a break. They came upon a train with some food supplies and ammunition. The soldiers received two pieces of hard tack each, which was very welcome as they were hungry after the long march. Even though it was only hard tack, it was very welcome at that point since this was the first issuing of food supplies since Rocky Springs. After time to make a cup of coffee, they continued to Bolton, ten miles further. This march was very difficult due to terrible roads, darkness, broken bridges, and artillery blocking the road at places. Whenever there was a pause, men dropped to the ground, asleep. They had to carefully check to make sure everyone restarted when the march continued, or someone could have easily been left behind, so exhausted were they. Reed claimed that some soldiers slept while marching and would accidentally walk right into the person in front of them!

They arrived at 2 a.m. on May 17 at Bolton to hear the battle of Champion Hill was over and already won by the 13th and 17th corps. Those Rebels left for Black River. Sherman allowed the Union troops to rest until dawn. Then they were ordered to catch up with the Confederates, so they moved in the direction of Bridgeport. Near Bolton they marched past the plantation of Jefferson Davis, the president of the Confederacy, now in severe disrepair. The slaves remaining there asked that the soldiers not take the remaining few head of cattle. At dusk they reached Bridgeport on Big Black River, having marched 22 miles that day, suffering through heat with little water available. They laid a pontoon bridge and crossed the river at dawn, and marched until they were near Vicksburg, close to Haines' Bluff. The cavalry went to Haine's Bluff to scatter the enemy there and the infantry continued to just north of Vicksburg, which prevented Confederates from leaving Vicksburg from the north. The 13th and 17th corps moved in towards Vicksburg from the east, having just fought the battle of Big Black. Ole's group, Tuttle's 3rd brigade, was held in reserve at this point and set up tents for the night.

The morning of May 19 their brigade was ordered to do reconnaissance work near Chickasaw Bayou. Reconnaissance work entails assessing the enemy's location, strength, etc. Rebel soldiers abandoned their guns and they captured 10 prisoners there. The third brigade communicated with the gunboats on the Yazoo River which let them know Grant was in position in the rear of Vicksburg. They were ordered to be ready to attack the fortifications at Vicksburg at 2:00 p.m. Their division, Ole's, was to be held in reserve for this particular attack, with the exception of company C, which brought ammunition to the front line. One of company C was killed. The attack failed, but the Union soldiers built entrenchments and put their batteries within easy range of the enemy for firing.

On the morning of May 20 the regiment moved the regiment forward to these entrenchments, and set up tents on the side of a hill. A trench was made for a battery at their front.

On May 21 communications were opened and rations were received after waiting 18 days for a supply. That must have been a huge relief!

Ole's unit was in reserve for the assault the morning of May 22, but participated in the battle that afternoon with the second and third brigades. The 12th Iowa Infantry was at the head of the brigade attacking along Graveyard Road near the Stockade Redan, a large hill of fortifications of the rebels. They couldn't proceed further due to other troops blocking the advance, so they covered the retreat of those troops that also couldn't get through the Redan.

Having learned Sherman's troops were unsuccessful in scaling the Redan, Grant decided to start siege operations. The 12th Iowa Infantry bivouacked there for the night. They leveled the side of the hill to make places to sleep and also built shades of cane. These troops also helped provide cover for sharp shooters, pickets, and those working in trenches. Rebel mortars from the gunboats as well as guns from land kept a barrage of fire landing within the trenches since they were so close to the Redan, and several were killed. They had to be very careful to keep their heads down or get shot by the enemies' sharpshooters. Their source of water at this time was a spring at the left of their front between the enemy and Union lines. Whenever someone went to retrieve water in the daylight, he ran the risk of being shot by the enemy sharpshooters. Water was sold at 25 cents per canteen in camp. Several were shot doing picket duty. When my son,

Trenches built for protection while Ole was fighting at Vicksburg, 1863. Nathan Kalmoe, Ole's great great grandson, is standing in one to show depth.

Nathan Kalmoe, his wife, Katie Will, and I visited the Vicksburg area in June of 2015, we discovered that Ole was coincidentally fighting that day within a few dozen yards of

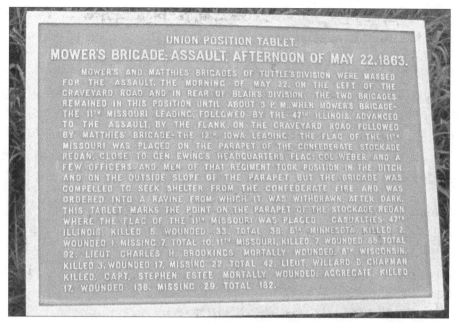

Sign mentioning action in which the 12th Iowa was involved May 22, 1863, during one of the many battles at Vicksburg, MS. Picture taken June, 2015.

another of my great grandfathers, Charles Brown (Karl Brun) on my Dad's maternal side for the 8th Wisconsin Infantry!

Iowa Gov. Kirkwood, Adjutant Gen. Baker, and other officials from Iowa visited the 12th Iowa's camp on June 2. Reed wrote that Gen. Baker wanted to have a good story to tell when he got back so he crawled along the trenches to a picket post, borrowed a Springfield rifle, pointed it toward Vicksburg and fired. There was the usual quick response of gunfire and a bullet struck a tree about 10 feet above Baker's head. Kirkwood immediately dropped the gun and went flat in the ditch, saying "I tell you, boys, that was close, wasn't it?" He then quickly crawled back out. Kirkwood often told the story when he got back to Iowa.

Ole's Eighth Letter

On June 10, 1863, Ole wrote from their rear location at Vicksburg. He had not heard from Anne for a long time and hoped to soon. It must have been difficult when there was a long stretch without a letter. One never knew if it was because no letter had been sent, the recipient lost interest, was ill or dead, the letter got lost, or if there was a delay in delivery. In this following letter Ole relayed a fascinating dream, plus described talking with the enemy at night while doing guard duty. Here is the text:

Translation

Camp of the 3rd Brigade in Rear
of Vicksburg, Miss., June 10th, 1863

Unforgettable and Most Beloved
Anne Gilbertsen!

Dear Anne!

While I have time and the occasion, I wish to write a few new lines to you. I have been waiting to hear from you first, but so far in vain. I hope, dear Anne, that you now have already received a letter I wrote in pencil and enclosed in a letter to Anthon, as I did not know whether you were at home or in Lansing, and I had not had time to reply to your most welcome letter dated April 7th and received on the 2nd of May, as we departed Duckport, Louisiana.

Dear Anne, I know you probably don't think much of my writing to you as part of a letter to another, but I thought that if you should have left for Lansing again, then this would get a letter to you more quickly than if I had sent it to

…

[second page]

… your address. This letter I am writing now I am sending to you, as I assume you are still at home, remembering you said that should you decide to travel somewhere, you would inform me of this, and I have as yet not heard anything.

As mentioned, if you have received the aforementioned letter and can make sense of it, then you see from it that recently we have had to endure rigorous hardships and long marches in the hot weather, have been exposed to danger, and as long as we remain encamped here, we are in greater danger than ever before.

Nothing noteworthy has happened since the last time I wrote, and we occupy approximately the same position, and this for a good reason, if we are to slowly take Vicksburg. For there are enormous fortifications to overcome, and that will cost too much blood to try to storm them. Many unsuccessful attempts were made in the beginning, which cost too many lives and limbs. The intention now is to starve them out, and it is believed that it has been almost accomplished. I heard that General Sherman, after having stood regarding the fortress, said today that the Rebels would not …

[third page]

… be there 6 days from today. It has been a huge job for us erecting fortifications for our own security, together with containing the Rebels, as we have now surrounded them, and their only salvation would be if they were able to break out. One night last week during picket guard duty we stood only 15 rods from their fort and only half that distance from their pickets, and we conversed with them for over 2 hours, peaceably exchanging rather many questions and answers.

As I write this, the cannons are thundering, as usual, and the sharp crack of rifle fire is heard from all sides, with bullets whizzing through the bushes and tree tops, severing leaves and branches that fall on us, and from time to time they bore into and wound one or another of us.

Dear Anne! Last night I dreamed that you were here. At first, I thought we were in the midst of battle, and there among us was a young girl, standing where the bullets were thickest, and it seemed as though a bomb exploded next to her, tearing out her entrails. Soon a grave had been dug for her, and then you came, …

[fourth page]

… it seemed to me, and you took a blanket and went down into the grave, spread it out, took her in your arms and lay her in the grave, and then took a white blanket and spread it over her, after which the grave was filled in. I awoke immediately and found myself 1,500 miles from you, unable to speak a word with you, except by way of my pen.

It would be frightening for you *[he wrote "dem"/them but must have meant to write "dig"/you]* to hear and see what goes on here, but for us the aforementioned thundering of the cannons is now as pleasant to listen to as the sound of cowbells at home. We often sit outside our tents until late in the evening and are entertained by the sight of glowing bombs in the air that are lobbed over toward the town from *[on a crease and barely legible, cannot decipher the name]* in the Mississippi. The bombs have to cover a distance of 3 to 4 miles before striking their target, and we can see them the entire time, together with some 100 cannons along the line, which plow with their glowing shells through the forest, where the enemy is encamped. And we learn from some of the deserters that they wreak havoc among the Rebels.

[Alas, there must be pages missing from this letter]

Translation by: Jim Skurdall

Ole's Ninth Letter

The next day, June 11, 1863, Ole wrote to Anne of exceedingly hard rain which made it very unpleasant since they were without tents and had been camping on a steep slope in which they had dug in for some shelter at Vicksburg. We aren't sure why this letter says he didn't have a tent, but Reed's account said they had tents at Vicksburg. Perhaps some did and some didn't. With the Union's 500-600 hundred cannons blasting towards Vicksburg, at times continuously, imagine the noise and anxiety it would arouse! He said he was in good health and had never been absent from his post when duty called. He said he is the only one in his company (G) that could say this. The text follows:

Translation

June 11, 1863

Dear Anne,

An exceedingly heavy and hard rain yesterday interfered with my letter writing, so I must complete it today. As you can well imagine, a rain like that is more than a little unpleasant for us, as we have not brought tents along and we are camped on a steep slope, which we have dug out to some extent to make it a bit more comfortable. But everything is always changing, and so our camp [the next line is written on a crease and I can only decipher the words "Camp" and "over 3 weeks"]…and how long we must wait is not known. Vicksburg must fall into our hands before we withdraw. We have a line of about 10 miles encircling the city, with 500-600 cannons aimed at it. Just imagine when they all open fire simultaneously! And a grand bombardment that has lasted 18 hours without cessation is soon expected to be intensified.

[end of page]

[second page]

[Please note: a large square, cleanly cut, was cut out of the paper at the top of the page. This did not affect the text on the first page. But it does affect the first four lines on the reverse side, that is to say, on this side of the page. So I cannot translate the first four lines, only individual words: 1st line: "Of which I have…" 2nd line: "…an idea of our…" 3rd line: "…of wretchedness…" 4th line: "…in it. Oh how…" Then I continue the translation of this letter with the fifth line on this side of the page.] Author Bowen's note: Perhaps a censor removed the cut-out piece of paper.

Anne, if only this would soon end and every one of us could leave for home, each to his wonderful loved ones and unforgettable sweetheart, and families, and friends, or, in short, return to all that is loveliest and dearest on this Earth, all that we must give up for the sake of war. I can assure you, dear Anne, that it is this that is such an arduous challenge for me, and much worse than the anxieties of wartime, they do not pain in any way as much as the other. And the thought of the great distance between you and me is the greatest source of my grief and bitterness. But my hope is that when God allows us to see each other again and be reunited, what lies in the past will be forgotten, and our joyfulness will be so much greater.

Oh dear Anne, if only you knew how happy I am when I receive letters from you, I am certain that you would write to me as often as circumstances permit you to do so, as your own dear letters convey.

[end of page]

[third page]

I shall write more often than I have done thus far, as soon as I know for certain your address, and I see that there have been delays of one kind or another. *[The next line is illegible because of a crease in the paper.]*

I must now think about ending this, otherwise you will become bored by reading what I have written, I have written too much already, and more than I intended to write when I began.

In closing, I can inform you that I am to date in good health, and as long as I have been in the Army, I have always been at my post when duty calls, and have not been absent a single time. And I am the only one in our company who can say this. All the others have been ill at one time or another. I hope to hear from you before long, and I shall reply immediately, whether or not I have something interesting to report.

Dear Anne, I wish only for God to bestow on you His blessing, that you may lack nothing. And with that I send you my most cordial greetings and convey my respect to you and your dear relations. And know that you are ever in the thoughts of your Beloved.

Ole P. Rocksvold

Translated by:
Jim Skurdall

Gen. Joseph Johnson was working to bring relief to the besieged city on the Confederate side. The night of June 11, the 12th Iowa Infantry was ordered a few miles north, away from the Vicksburg lines, to resist Johnson's forces at Haines' Bluff. They had to stand all night with their weapons along the Graveyard Road. When it became light they put up their tents, noticing it was the exact same place they tented May 18! The soldiers were told they had to be ready at any moment's notice to march. During this time they were furnishing "fatigue details." Ole's great great grandson, Nathan Kalmoe, explained that "fatigue details" refers to hard labor, and could include digging canals, trenches, etc. Under orders from Gen. Sherman to guard the rear, on June 22 they marched to Bear Creek near Black River. Half of the regiment was on duty constantly as pickets or patrol, guarding the roads from the Black River bridge to Brownsville Road. It was hard work, but better than working in the trenches. On July 2, the tents and equipment left at Duckport two months earlier were brought up to them and set up in a nice grove of trees for a pleasant camping location. Perhaps these were bigger and better tents than the ones they were using during their time in the Vicksburg trenches. Bunks were created in the tents, using stakes, rails, and canebrakes. This was a big improvement from sleeping on the damp ground. They only enjoyed this camping arrangement for two days because on July 4 they heard the wonderful news that the Confederates had finally surrendered Vicksburg. 40,000 Rebel prisoners were captured, according to Reed. The surrender opened up the Mississippi River from the source in Minnesota to the Gulf of Mexico, a huge accomplishment. Grant had made 8 unsuccessful attempts to capture Vicksburg, and the 9th attempt finally worked with the siege. What amazing determination after so many unsuccessful attempts!

At first Grant was going to require unconditional surrender, but then decided he didn't want to have to feed and house so many prisoners, and decided to parole them, with the understanding they wouldn't go back to fighting. He learned later many did go back to fighting instead of going home. Thereafter, for the rest of the war, Grant refused to do paroling since it wasn't effective.

Upon hearing the news of the surrender at Vicksburg, according to Goodwin in *Team of Rivals*, Lincoln wrote to Grant, "I write this now as a grateful acknowledgement for the almost inestimable service you have done the country." The very costly victory at Gettysburg, having occurred on July 1-3, 1863, brought joy and hopes that the war would soon be over, but unfortunately the Civil War went on two more years. Estimates vary about casualties (deaths, injuries, captured and missing) at Vicksburg and Gettysburg, with some estimated Vicksburg's casualties between 6,000-10,000 on the Union side, 3000-9,000 on the Confederate side. For Gettysburg, estimates were about a total of 40,000-50,000 either killed or wounded or missing, with deaths on the Union side estimated about 3,100 and Confederates, about 3,900. Lincoln sent out a celebratory press release which went by telegraph around the country, and fireworks were sent up. Lincoln's joy was somewhat diminished when he learned Meade allowed Lee's army to escape after Gettysburg, left to fight again. Fighting in the Civil War resulted in a much higher death rate than all other wars in which the U.S. has participated, about 1 in 4, according to the official website of the U.S. Army at www.army.mil. About two-thirds of the deaths were due to disease.

Upon hearing the news of the surrender of Vicksburg, the 9th, 12th, 13th, and 15th corps (Ole's) thought they would have the privilege of marching into Vicksburg to behold the surrender and celebrate this 4th of July, but Sherman and Grant were not willing to rest on their laurels. So these corps didn't get that opportunity, but instead got immediate orders to march towards Jackson again and attack Johnson at Black River. So they left their camp and baggage with the sick and others unable to march and were on the move again. The soldiers had to build a bridge over the Black River, then marched 5 miles, driving the Rebels before them. They stopped at a place on higher ground, stacked their guns and lay down to rest until dawn.

Many commendations are mentioned in official reports regarding their work on this Vicksburg campaign. Gen. Halleck wrote, as quoted on p. 136 of Reed's book, "When we consider the character of the country in which this army operated, the formidable obstacles to be overcome, the number of the enemy's forces, and the strength of his works, we cannot fail to admire the courage and endurance of the troops and the skill and daring of their commander. No more brilliant exploit can be found in military history." Grant listed among the Union accomplishments at Vicksburg: 37,000 prisoners captured including 15 general officers, at least 10,000 killed or wounded, many who can never be counted, arms and munitions for 60,000 men, public property, railroads, locomotives, cars, steamboats, and cotton. Much was also destroyed by the Rebels to prevent the Union from capturing those things.

Humor in Time of War

Reed told an amusing story at this point. The men were awakened early the next morning by a braying mule that was tied to the rail fence near the gun stacks. The mule pulled the rail out of the fence and swung it to the ground, causing a row of guns to crash down. Some soldier cried "cavalry" and every person jumped to their feet, grabbing their guns. The Orderly Sergeant jumped up and started giving orders until he twirled around and figured out what had happened and went right back to sleep. So everyone went back to sleep, but not until some of the 8th and 12th Iowa Infantry, in the confusion, had managed to grab some of the new rubber blankets that the recently-arrived new soldiers of 35th had been supplied. Since most of the 8th and 12th hadn't been supplied rubber blankets, they thought it would be good for the 35th to "share." The 35th complained afterwards that perhaps the "Mule Raid" was a ruse to get their rubber blankets. Whenever one of the 35th would go up to someone in the 8th or 12th to ask, "Where did you get that rubber?" the person would reply, 'Draw'd it to be sure."

Jackson and Black River- Skirmishes, Destroying Train Tracks, and Guard Duty

On July 7 they camped in a cornfield near Bolton and it rained so hard that the field was covered with water. The only place they could find to sleep was for each person to lie on a rail of the fence. The ninth corps of eastern regiments passed by July 8 and were very weighed down with all their heavy knapsacks in the unaccustomed heat, so the Iowans advised them to get rid their good uniforms and packs to lighten their loads, as they themselves had learned to do early in their military careers. Marching to Bolton was very hot and there was a shortage of water. The area was dependent on water holes and cisterns which unfortunately had been almost totally exhausted by Johnson's retreating army. In addition, Johnson had made most waterholes unusable by shooting mules and broken down horses and having their carcasses deteriorate in those holes. This predicament forced the Union troops to send a person on a long mule ride out from the area to fill half the canteens at an uncontaminated water hole, come back, and then take the other canteens and go back to fill them and return. On July 9 they skirmished all day with the enemy, reaching the entrenchments by Jackson by midnight.

Reed in his book told of an experience of the 12th Iowa Infantry when a big gun sent a "screaching (sic) shot" that landed in the kettle being used to cook dinner. It caused the men to run and destroyed the pot and the dinner. Another similar and dramatic incident occurred later when some men near Vicksburg had thought some shells were burned out, set them on end, made a fire between them, and put a kettle of beans on top. While they waited for the pot to heat, suddenly one of the shells got red hot and sent the kettle of beans a hundred feet in the air! So they got no beans that night.

Another interesting story Reed told is from July 11 when the quartermaster George Morisey, was sent out to collect forage with 20 men from the brigade. At a plantation, they loaded a wagon with corn and started to return to camp. They saw cavalry approaching dressed in blue, so they thought they were Union troops, but it turned out they were Confederates and got surrounded before they realized. The rebel held a gun to the Union soldiers heads and demanded they surrender. One of the 12th Iowa Infantry managed to slip away, N. H. Spears of Company C. While the Rebels were cutting the mules loose from the wagons, Spears sat on a fence as if to rest. When they ordered him to get off while shooting towards him, he fell backwards off the fence, rolled into the corn, and made it back to camp to tell of the incident. The next morning the regiment went out to guard the train of wagons as soldiers foraged and reconnoitered (surveyed the area of troop information). They found the wagons, but no sign of the Confederates or the other prisoners.

On July 15, Gen. Tuttle reported ill and Col. Woods took over leading the 3rd division and did so until October. The brigade commander during that time was Col. Geddes of 8th Iowa Infantry. After dark that day, the 3rd division moved in to relieve Osterhaus' division of the 13th corps. On the 16th the regiment skirmished and pushed forward until there was active fighting. At dawn on July 17 they discovered the fortifications were abandoned and they took control of the city of Jackson. They moved to a building called the "Deaf and Dumb Asylum" and made camp there, looking forward to several days of rest. So they spent more time than usual in setting up shelter tents this time. However, this longer rest was not to be since the next day the 8th and 12th Iowa Infantry and the 72nd Ohio and 114th Illinois were ordered by Gen. Steele to form a select temporary brigade commanded by Col. Geddes to leave Jackson, equipped with 3 days' rations. They were to break up any camps of the enemy near Jackson, MS. They camped about 3 miles out of Jackson and found a large Confederate hospital there. They also found some of their captured men there, and those who were able to be moved were sent to Jackson. The Union troops left supplies for the hospital and then left the rest of the convalescing soldiers as they found them.

On July 19 they continued marching until they came upon the enemy near Brandon, where one shot from a battery passed over their heads and killed an orderly who was mounted. The Union soldiers then moved into the cornfields where the corn stood over their heights, and moved forward in a battle line. It was very hot and many men were collapsing. Nevertheless, the rest of the troops continued moving forward while artillery fire kept shooting at them and stopped when they got into musket range. The enemy decided to stop shooting and moved back through town. A big thunderstorm then refreshed them in the intense heat of the day. They set up camp in the middle of town and got lots of attention since it was the first time people of this town had seen Union troops. A lady was looking at their equipment with curiosity and remarked she would like to hear the artillery shot. Just then a squad of Rebel cavalry appeared at a distance so the commander had a reason to shoot the artillery, which served to satisfy her curiosity. It also served to shatter the glass in a window and sent people screaming into the house.

Bear Creek Camp

The next day the troops marched to Jackson and destroyed the railroad along the way. They stayed there until July 23 when the city was evacuated. The Union troops then returned to the west side of Black River, where they had been previously. The 12th Iowa Infantry was delighted to move into their camp near Bear Creek and finally get some rest after the stressful and exhausting work of that summer.

Commendations were received for their efforts in Jackson and Brandon. Reed quoted Gen. Mathias on p. 136, regarding Jackson, " I take pleasure in commending Lieutenant Colonel Eddington of the 12th Iowa, Major Palmer of the 8th Iowa, and Major O'Conner of the 35th Iowa, for the prompt and energetic manner with which they placed their skirmishers into the rifle pits before Jackson and were the first officers from our corps who entered the city. The cheerfulness with which the officers and men of that noble brigade endured fatigue and marched under so many privations, and the eagerness with which they faced the enemy, cannot but command the highest praise from us." Reed quoted Col. Woods of 12th Iowa on p. 137 who listed their many accomplishments, and wrote about July 15 when they "met a warm reception from the enemy, and had several wounded – one mortally... Lieutenant Colonel Edington (sic), commanding the 12th Iowa, was prompt and efficient in the performance of his duties, showing he was worthy to command...Lieutenant Reed was always on hand when required....the officers and men performed their duties in a commendable manner."

Continuing Reed's quotes of commendations, Col Geddes of the 8th Iowa wrote about the expedition to Brandon, Miss. with 8th and 12 Iowa, 72nd Ohio, 114th Illinois, and Captain Waterhouse's battery, as quoted by Reed on p. 137-8, "...Forming the 12th Iowa under Lt. Col. Eddington on the right, the 8th Iowa under Major Stubbs on the left, the others in support, I ordered the brigade moved forward for half a mile under severe and continuous fire. Previous to the advance I ordered Capt. Waterhouse to take position in the road, but the distance was so great that their fire could barely reach the point where the enemy's battery was placed, while their rifled guns threw shot and shell into my position with great accuracy. The deep dykes running across the fields made the advance of artillery with the line impossible, consequently they continued their fire from first position, which had the effect of dividing their fire as the infantry advanced. The advance was made through as open field in admirable order, not a man wavered, each regiment marching in line of battle with as much precision as if on review, and the coolness and efficiency displayed by regimental commanders on the occasion renders them much credit."

Reed quoted Lt. Col. Eddington on p. 138-9, regarding July 19, "Continued the march, 12th Iowa in advance, Company B as skirmishers. About five miles from Brandon, artillery fired upon us from the front. The regiment formed in lines of battle on right of road and advanced slowly over very difficult ground, the field being intersected with ditches 8 or 10 feet deep, with briars and bushes on either side. Coming to open field the other regiments halted and the 12th advanced, to a wood where the rebel battery has been planted and passed through a dense thicket going through a rebel camp and capturing an ambulance and some prisoners. After going through the woods, entered, and took possession of Brandon."

At this time while at Bear Creek camp, several took furloughs, and some went home for 30 days. I do not have information whether Ole did get leave at that time. His muster rolls say he was "present" in July, Aug., and Sept., 1863. Did they mark people on leave as "present" for attendance even if on an approved absence? Since Ole said he was the healthiest in his unit, did they mostly give leaves to those who were worn out physically or mentally in order to recover? Reed did write that they gave furoughs "liberally." Except for some scouting and picket duties the troops were able to mostly rest in camp until Oct. 15. During this time Lieutenant Col. Eddington resigned, Major Stibbs became lieutenant colonel and was succeeded as major by Capt. Van Duzee.

An interesting letter written by a soldier to his mother is quoted in Reed's book on p. 133. The soldier, no name cited, describes the tents as arranged into rows with "streets" by brigades, with the 8th, 12th, and 35th Iowa Infantries forming the 3rd brigade of the 3rd division of the 15th Corps, Army of the Tennessee.

The soldier described how the tents were raised 2 feet above ground. The bunks, on forked stakes, were made of canebrake. He had a writing desk and books. He told how wonderful it was to sleep in this camp after spending from May 2 at Duckport until July 27 at Vicksburg almost always sleeping on the ground. During these many, arduous weeks they had also been warned that at any moment they could be roused by the bugle call to get up for action. They had to sleep in their clothes and often not even removing their belts, which made them extra warm and less comfortable. He described the mess tables at camp set with stakes in the ground and a fly (tarp) over the tables to protect soldiers from rain. This letter-writing soldier told his mother that he saw a black ("cullud") boy making supper of codfish, potatoes, biscuits with honey, hard bread, butter, peach sauce, pickles, concentrated milk, and coffee. The soldiers kept the camp very clean, sweeping the streets daily, hauling away the dirt.

Ole's 10th Letter

An undated, partial letter to Anne appears to have been written between July 23- Oct. 15, 1863, while Ole was at this Bear Creek camp. Using descriptions in the letter, locations mentioned, reports Reed gave in his book about where they were and when, and other Civil War records, Nathan Kalmoe, Ole's great great grandson, was able to deduce the possible time span for this letter. Based on the "incredibly warm weather" reference and that Ole's October 11th letter said he hadn't written since August, this undated letter is most likely to have been written in late July or in August.

Translation

[Translator: First page missing, perhaps others. From the content we know that it was written after 22 July 1863, while in camp on the Black River in Mississippi.]

We spent the night in town, and the next morning we burned and destroyed property, and the Beal Road Depot with several hundred bales of cotton inside was burned as well. The railroad tracks were torn up for several miles, and when we had accomplished that, we returned to Jackson, which we treated in the same manner. On the 22nd of July we travelled from Jackson to this place, where we have remained until now. We have marched at least 350 miles this summer, and during the siege of Vicksburg, we had no time to rest. So we have had to endure difficult trials this summer, and many have fallen victim to this demanding routine. I have, thank goodness, remained healthy the entire time and, so far, have not missed a single day.

We are now camped near the Black River in Mississippi, and it is possible that we shall be here for some time, as this army has now accomplished what it was expected to do.

Some of our troops have gone home on furlough, and Anders Egge and another, Dringman Olsen, have left for home from our company, since they have not been home since they enlisted, some of them. They must report back in 30 days, and then two others can leave …

[second page]

… and I have thought about trying my best to be granted leave at the next opportunity and see them again before the time I must serve has elapsed.

Oh, dear Anne, if only I could see you and speak with you face to face, then I would be satisfied with everything else. You are, as before, always in my thoughts, and everything seems so much brighter with the assurance that I have a friend whom I would never trade for worldly happiness of any kind. And I must mention, as I have done many times earlier, that I always carry your photograph, which has been through many skirmishes that would have been unpleasant for the original picture *[meaning Anne, I assume]*, without being damaged. *[Translator: the paper has turned dark here, making deciphering of the handwriting very difficult — my best interpretation of what he wrote in this sentence.]*

In closing, I can tell you that I am in good health and doing well, and I earnestly hope to hear the same from you. Otherwise, I have no other news.

The weather is incredibly warm.

Please give my greetings to your dear relations, and I include you most warmly,

Yours O. P. Rocksvold

Translation by:
Jim Skurdall

After much effort by Reed (several trips to ask at division and corps headquarters and a trip to the chief commissary in Vicksburg), the soldiers who were prisoners of war at Shiloh were finally given "commutation" of rations for the time they were prisoners. Apparently at that time it was the practice to pay soldiers for the rations they were due, but didn't eat, while prisoners, so this would have involved Ole.

While at camp near Bear Creek they started a regimental bakery and built ovens. A baker was given equipment and better supplies so they could make soft bread instead of the hardtack or dense flap jacks they were so used to. This fresh bread was so appreciated that subsequently all the camps that Sherman commanded followed this practice. On Sept. 16 they moved the camp to the Harris plantation, but finding this location too exposed, they returned to Bear Creek. About Sept. 27 the other divisions of 15th corps was sent to Chattanooga. This meant the 3rd division was solely in charge of the line along Black River. They worked little with the 15th corps after that. A few weeks later they were sent to Chattanooga. While they were in transit, Sherman picked up one division of the 16th corps to bring to Chattanooga. Since that division had been guarding the railroad from Memphis to Florence, now the soldiers with whom Ole worked took over that task. Later this third division worked with the 16th army corps.

Voting During War and Breaking Camp

On Tuesday, Oct. 13, election day in Iowa, the Iowa soldiers were allowed to participate. The 12th Iowa Infantry cast 236 votes for governor, with Stone, the Republican candidate, receiving 213 votes and Tuttle, the Democratic candidate and their commander, 23! In the 8th Iowa Stone received 252 votes and Tuttle 11, and in the 35th Iowa Stone got 211,

Tuttle 124. Stone was a veteran of Shiloh and captured as a prisoner of war there. Soldiers generally preferred Republican candidates at that time and Iowa was a Republican state.

On Oct. 15 they were ordered to break up the summer camp, and their division, plus one brigade of the 17th corps marched towards Canton where a rebel force was gathering. These 12,000 soldiers went to Brownsville, Arkansas, 23 miles in one day, not finding any enemy. The next day they continued their march towards Canton. They ran into rebel cavalry and skirmished all day, only able to make 6 miles' distance. On Saturday there were many more rebels with infantry and cavalry to fight. They spent the whole day battling. At night they were assaulted by pelting rain as they slept on the ground the rebels had just given up. On Sunday they traveled south and east and camped at Baker's Creek (Champion Hill). Rebels followed at their heels during the march Monday from Baker's Creek to Black River, with quite a lot of fighting. The 12th Iowa infantry had a very arduous day guarding the train and helping wagons over ruts in the road.

On Oct. 19 they arrived at the Black River bridge and started to create a camp the next day at Clear Creek, nine miles from Vicksburg. On Oct. 21 the tents were brought out and they named the camp, Camp Hebron. They tried to make things as comfortable as possible, with many even building fireplaces in their tents. They hoped they could make this their winter camp, but it was not to be. However, the Vicksburg campaign had finally come to an end.

Ole's 11th Letter

On Oct. 29, 1863, Ole wrote to Anne with a Vicksburg return address. He had been wondering where she was, and hadn't written since August to her because of that. He had learned some information from Hans Ruen. Apparently she had been traveling and Ole wasn't sure where to send his letters, first to Freeport, just outside Decorah, then to Lansing, IA. He also mentioned a rumor of his death. Regarding his recent illness, there are no notes in his pension records. There is one note on Oct. 21, 1862, of an intermittent fever, but I am wondering if it was a mistake and they meant to write 1863 since his previous letters indicated he had not been sick before this (of course not counting the seven-month period he was prisoner.) There is a notation in the pension records that from Aug. 21 to Oct. 5, 1863 he had problems with diarrhea. It seems Ole tended to understate his health problems to Anne- possibly to prevent her from worrying. The text is here:

Translation

In Camp, 8 Miles from Vicksburg, Mississippi
October 29th, 1863

Well-regarded and unforgettable lass
Anne Gilbertsen

A few words from a soldier you know in the Army of the Mississippi.

In a letter from Hans Ruen, which I received yesterday, I learned something again of your whereabouts, and this has moved me to write a few lines to you once again. For the first two months I did not know where to send a letter that it might reach you, and thus I have not written since once in August. And I believe that I addressed the letter that time to Lansing [Iowa]. I sent all the previous letters, I believe, to Freeport [just outside of Decorah]. And H. Ruen says that he received a letter and "sent dig" [not clear whether he means that Ruen replied to her or that he received a letter from Ole and forwarded it to Anne].

Dear Anne, you can imagine how difficult it is for me. Just think that I have not heard from you since the last letter the 2nd of May. I have at times believed that you have not wanted to write to me anymore, but . . .

[end of page]

[second page]

. . . knowing now that you went to Minnesota this summer, it is possible that you have not received many of the letters I have sent you, and thus you have an excuse for not having written. This time I am sending these lines in a letter to Hans Ruen, and I know he will forward them to you.

Dear Anne, you have no idea how often I have wondered why you have not replied to my letters. If you had been ill and unable to write, I would have learned of this in letters from others. I trust you too much to torment myself with the thought that you have become engaged to another, which more then one girl in Iowa has done after her beloved left for the Army.

But there is something else that could be the reason. Hans Ruen informed me in a letter that a rumor has been circulating that I am dead. And I am almost certain that you would have heard such fabrications, since they cannot . . .

[end of page]

[third page]

. . . come from anyone other than envious and slandering admirers, who have neither a conscience nor respect for themselves or others. And once again, as before, I beseech you not to place your trust in such demagogues. I remain steadfast in my desire to secure my discharge at the end of the war and live many happy years in a union with you, dear Anne! And in truthfulness and love share earthly pleasures and cares till death do us part.

News from here is of little importance. Some days ago we returned from an expedition into Mississippi in the direction of Canton. We were away for only a week. There was no battle to speak of, as the Confederates always retreated in the face of our advances, and we did not have enough forces to pursue them all the way to Canton, where they have their headquarters. We withdrew after driving them 20 miles and taking a cavalry regiment prisoner. A lot of cotton and houses were burned and there was pillaging and looting.

[end of page]

[fourth page]

I have been promised a furlough home as soon as two members of the company, namely, Theodor Steen and Hans Hansen, have returned, but rumor has it that furlough can only be taken in the [cannot decipher], and if that is the case, I shall be disappointed in my hope of being able to come home [cannot decipher] less than one year.

I wait for a letter from you every single time the mail arrives, and should you not have a letter on the way to me, please torment me no longer and write to me as soon as you have my letter in hand and send me your address.

I have almost filled the page and must close for now in the hope that my lines will find you in good health, and the same I can report regarding my present condition. [Some words here difficult to decipher as they lie on a crease in the paper — he seems to be writing of a recent illness] . . . and was in the field hospital for the first time. I was there for only 6 days before returning to my company, and I have been healthy ever since. The doctor called my illness [int_ mate?] fever.

The weather has already turned cold, and we have had some frost at night. John and Henry Steen are both ill and in the field hospital, but they seem to be improving now.

In closing, I send you most cordial greetings, and rest assured that you will never be forgotten.

In devoted and everlasting friendship

O. P. Rocksvold

Translation by:
Jim Skurdall

Chewalla, TN, then Back to Black River Area

On Nov. 6, Reed reported, their hopes of staying at Camp Hebron were dashed. Their division were ordered to break up this pleasant camp and join the 15th corps on the way to Chattanooga, TN. The next morning they marched to Vicksburg and got on the steamer, *Thomas E. Tutt*, to Memphis. It was the first time the 12th Iowa Infantry was on a boat that wasn't crowded since it only had one regiment on it this time. (A regiment consists of about 1,000-2,000 soldiers.) They arrived the morning of Nov. 12, and then took the train to Chattanooga. They had some time to enjoy walking around town and then go into camp for the night. Unfortunately, during the night there was fighting between some soldiers foraging for food and a guerilla band. The soldiers were woken by a long drum roll and they were up in line by 3:00 a.m., waiting for dawn to see if they might be needed. No further mention is given of this, so perhaps they didn't need to take action after all.

They waited until Nov. 18 for their train to arrive, but when the officers learned cars weren't available at this time, they received a new order to march to La Grange, 50 miles. A division of the 16th corps had been guarding the stretch of railroad from Memphis to Corinth. Gen. Sherman was trying hard to relieve the army besieged at Chattanooga. Because of the delay in getting train cars to move the troops, Gen. Sherman took the 16th corps from guard duty and left the 3rd division to relieve the 16th for guard duty of the railroad.

Sometimes seemingly small occurrences can have huge ramifications on one's life. In this case the delay in the train's arrival had momentous consequences for Ole and the troops' lives. If they had gone to Chattanooga, they likely would have fought in additional major battles there, and been involved with Gen. Sherman in the capture of Atlanta, the famous March to the Sea, and in action in South Carolina and North Carolina. They would have experienced much more violence and would have had less chance of surviving the war. Even so, Ole did end up fighting and being wounded in the western theatre of the war. But what a huge difference it made because of a delayed train!

A division headquarters was created at La Grange, TN, 270 miles west of Chattanooga, and 50 miles northwest of Corinth, MS. A brigade headquarters was established at Pocahontas, about 25 miles east of La Grange. The 12th Iowa Infantry was assigned to defend the post at Chewalla, TN, eleven miles northwest of Corinth. On Nov. 23 they went by train to their new location, with the horses and equipment within the train cars and the men on top of the cars. They found the 3rd Michigan Cavalry had built log barracks and a stockade, however there was no depot or other buildings at this place where several rail-road bridges stood. They moved into the barracks and Lt. Col. Stibbs became the commander of the post at Chewalla. The most important of the several bridges they guarded was four and a half miles west of the station, which necessitated taking 3-4 days of rations with them when guarding there. The soldiers would return and rotate a different company,a bout 100-200 people, to guard there at a time. They needed that many troops because of frequent attacks by guerrillas and people trying to burn the bridge.

Reed described a large force attacking at Pocahontas Dec. 3 and 4 that made breaks in the railroad. They fought the Rebels on and off for two days. The attacks disrupted their supply lines and communications for a few days.

Ole's Twelveth Letter

At this point, Ole wrote to Anne on Dec. 27, 1863, from Chewalla, TN. He told how much he missed her and still had not received a letter since May 2. He continued to worry that she may believe the rumors that he is dead. Ole was also deliberating about whether to re-enlist. The text is here:

Translation

Chawalla, Tennessee
December 27th, 1863

Unforgettable and Highly Esteemed
Anne Gilbertson

It has been almost one year since I, for the second time, bade you a fond farewell, and, with heavy heart, turned to leave and follow the call of duty to the country where I intend to live and die. To date I have been fortunate in my mission, and I hope this will remain the case until I have completed my service, which is not so far off.

Dear Anne, as you can imagine, this Christmas has not meant a break for me, or held as much pleasure as it did last year, especially in your company. It seldom escapes my memory, and I have endeavored rather vigorously to find an opportunity to come home and visit my many good friends, and none a better friend than you — but thus far I have had no success, and among the others *[the next 2-3 words are impossible to decipher]*. This is partly the reason I have not written more often, but, for the most part, it has been because I did not know where you …

[second page]

… have been the past weeks, and, as a consequence, did not know your address. But a couple of times I have availed myself of the opportunity, as I intend to do this time, of enclosing these lines in a letter to Anthon, and charge him with delivering them to you in person.

Consider, dear Anne, that I have not received a letter from you since the 2nd of May last spring, and if you knew how, each time the mail has arrived, I have looked for a letter from you and have been, up to now, disappointed, you would, I believe, send me a few lines. Please tell me the reason. Do you believe that I am dead, as rumor once had it up there, or have you forgotten me entirely? I hope that neither is true, and, to the contrary, that you will come out and let me receive some words of consolation from you, and give me once again your address, so that I will know where to send my letters to you, and then I would wish to write to you every week. Please tell me if you wish for me to send my letters to you in care of the same name/address as before.

I would imagine that you already know that we have come north from Vicksburg, Mississippi, and now are here in Tennessee, …

[third page]

… between Memphis and Corinth, only 9 miles from the latter place. We have been here for one month.

A large part of our regiment has now re-enlisted for three more years as of New Year's, and are mustered in as veterans. This has awakened my own thoughts regarding what I should do. In the end, I decided that I will opt to be discharged when I have served out my first term. My wish is to enlist for the rest of my life in the service that Nature has created. Remember that. However, I wish to find out just how much time I have remaining, if most of the regiment leaves us, for we only have months, while the others have years. It could be a tedious time for me, but I hope that you will become more diligent in writing to me than you have been, and I'll hardly notice the passage of time.

I must not forget to tell you that a ball was held here over Christmas. The celebration of Christmas does not last long down here. *[Not so easy to know what he means to say in the next sentence, but it seems to be about the very short celebration of Christmas where he is, in contrast to what he is used to as a Norwegian.]* The women in the South are not used to dancing from what I can conclude from their experiment *[he must mean the Christmas ball]*, and many did not even come, citing their lack of skill in dancing as the reason.

[fourth page]

I would like very much to know how you spent Christmas, and I continue to hope that it was a happy and fun time for you, as is always my wish for you.

And I hope as well that you are in good health, and wish this for you most of all, for without good health there can be no pleasure and enjoyment.

In closing, I can report that my health is as good as it has ever been and needs to be, and never before has our regiment had so few cases of illness as has been our situation since arriving in Chawalla.

As nothing of interest has happened recently, there is really nothing new to report. There are a large number of Rebs just a few miles from us, but that is nothing new.

And, once more in closing, I send you wishes for a Happy New Year. I hope that we shall meet in this coming year and shall not be compelled to separate because of my military obligation. I hope that these lines will find you in the best of health as before, and that you will not forget to inform me of the same.

With the greatest respect for you, I sign this letter as your ever sincere friend and beloved

Ole P. Rocksvold
(Address) Co. G, 12th Iowa Infantry
3rd Brigade 3rd Division
15 A C
Memphis, Tenn.

Translation by:
Jim Skurdall

Capt. James Zediker is quoted in Reed's book about a scouting expedition, "Skirmish at Goose Creek, Miss." regarding Company G (Ole's) and Company I. Zeddiker stated there was a report on Dec. 28 of a Rebel lieutenant sighted on furlough near Chewalla, TN. These two companies, G and I, crossed the Tuscumbia River and marched southward into Mississippi, with about 20 on horseback, looking for him. They kept marching on the muddy ground in the dark, searching houses for him and occasionally capturing a "suspicious character." They heard music towards morning. They surrounded the buildings at 5:00 a.m., Dec. 29, while people were dancing. When the Confederates noticed the Union soldiers approach, they tried to escape through the doors and windows, and there were several minutes of gunfire outside the buildings. Loud screams from women were heard inside the buildings. The Rebels finally surrendered and among the 14 captured were a captain and a lieutenant. Company G and I also confiscated horses and arms. Together with the few "suspicious characters" they had previously picked up, the total count for prisoners was 19. One Rebel was killed, five wounded, but there were no losses on the Union side. They were highly commended for their accomplishments.

Reed mentioned that inducements were given at this time for people to re-enlist for 3 more years and if two-thirds of a regiment re-enlisted, they could remain together as an organization. The required number was reached and on Jan. 5 they were mustered in again. Ole finally decided not to re-enlist. He gave no specific reasons why he decided against re-enlisting. Could one of the factors been that he had not gotten regular letters from Anne for a seven-month period and wanted to return to find out what was going on with her? Did he feel it necessary to rekindle their relationship in person? Or did he feel he had served three years and that was enough of a sacrifice for his country?

On Jan. 25, 1864, the Union soldiers were ordered to abandon their posts at the railroad. At one a.m. Jan. 26 they finished packing up, set the barracks on fire, loaded the baggage on the freight train and traveled to Memphis, arriving after dark. Some remained on the train and others moved to other freight cars in the yards to sleep. On Jan. 27 they were supposed to board the Steamer *Delaware* to join Gen. Sherman in Vicksburg. They didn't have enough boats so the whole brigade had to wait until Feb. 1 to travel down the river. While they were waiting, the paymaster distributed two months' pay to each member, which was very welcome. They arrived in Vicksburg Feb. 3, marched to Black River bridge the next day, and on Feb. 4 did guard work for communications and were in reserve for combat while Sherman marched to Meridian and returned. They stayed in camp for a month, practicing their drills twice daily, which was beneficial to new recruits and veterans alike. There had been little time for drilling in the past several months. While stationed at this camp, the 33rd MO, who were recently assigned to their brigade, went to Jackson and returned with a pontoon bridge, prisoners, and wounded. There is a notation in Ole's pension medical records that he was sick Feb. 9 and 10 with diarrhea.

Ole's Thirteenth Letter

On Feb. 22, 1864, Ole wrote to Anne from the camp on the Big Black River, MS. There was much crossed out immediately after her greeting, "Most Beloved Lass," and much crossed out above the date of this letter. We don't know if it was Ole who crossed these lines out, or a censor, or someone else. The text is here:

Translation

Camp of the 1st Division, 16th Army Corps
on *[in English]* Big Black, Miss, February 22nd, 1964

Most Beloved Lass, *[Translator: much that is crossed out here]*

Please permit me once more, dear Anne, to send you a few lines and repeat that of which I have often assured you, namely, that the feeling I have always had for you remains the same and will never leave my heart. You continue to withhold your voice from me, and this has often been a source of concern for me, and at times I have thought that it is of little use for me to continue this correspondence, as long as it remains one-sided. But in keeping with the proverb —from the abundance of one's heart, the mouth speaks —and whenever I have, one way or another, found out where you are, I have sent you a few lines, and several times I have enclosed a few words to you in letters to Hans Ruen, and the last time in a letter to Anton, but I do not know whether or not you have received that because in his last letter to me he wrote that he still had it at home and had not had an opportunity to deliver it to you.

[end of page]

[second page]

Nonetheless, I now have found out where you are and can send my letters to you directly. I have not written so much of late because I have not known where you were. I heard once that you had gone to Minnesota, and then I lost your trail, and only picked it up again recently. Most of those who write to me assume that I receive letters from you, and thus they do not mention you in their letters.

We have come back down to Tennessee again, and it has been almost a month since we left Chawalla, Tennessee. The veterans who have re-enlisted for three years do not always get what they expected. They surely thought they would be on furlough to Iowa instead of down here. Our division came a few days too late to Vicksburg, so that the expedition we should have been a part of had already departed with another division in our place. And so we remain here. No one has heard anything from this expedition, but we expect to hear something any day now.

We have just come in from a review . . .

[end of page]

[third page]

. . . which was held here today in honor of Washington's birthday and included a 34-gun salute.

I have nothing new to report, since every future move is kept so secret that no one is told anything until right before we are to advance. While we are in enemy territory, nothing of importance can be told, for otherwise the enemy would know it as well within a few days.

Dear Anne, I am so happy to have heard not so long ago that you are in good health. And I hope this is still the case. I can also inform you that I am healthy and lacking nothing in my present existence as a soldier, apart from not hearing enough from you. And I hope that you, like so many patriotic women in these times, will sit down and pen some encouraging words to be read by the soldiers to whom they have closest contact, showing sympathy for the destinies of these soldiers, which can strengthen courage for many who are prone to feelings of resignation —which is nothing new among soldiers.

[end of page]

[fourth page]

I hope you will not forget, dear Anne!, that in not such a long time the greater part of the regiment that re-enlisted will be coming home on furlough to enjoy themselves among their friends and next of kin before returning in earnest to the combat areas for another three years, if they are needed that long. And I shall neither ask for the opportunity, nor expect to be able to see home and all my dear ones left behind until autumn, when my term of service is over and I can return and see them all again. And my hope and prayer is that the war will be over and everyone will be able to return to their loved ones. I know it will be difficult to leave behind all my brothers in combat here *[Translator: what follows is on a crease and difficult to decipher, I think he may be wondering if he should return to his comrades]* But I also have a commitment to myself and those I have left behind, and so my place here must be filled by another.

When I wrote above that I hope you will not forget, what I meant by that is when I remain here while the others return home, I hope you will write because we who remain here will then be among new soldiers we do not know.

Now I must end this letter, with words meant to convince you that you are, as always, the only one who dwells in my heart. And I hope and pray that the Lord will keep you and us both in his protection and grant us that of which we are deserving. And I greet you as your true beloved, devoted to you unto death.

O. P. Rocksvold

Address:

Company G, 12th Iowa Infantry Volunteers
3rd Brigade, 1st Division
16th Army Corp Vicksburg
Mississippi

Translation by:
Jim Skurdall

Red River Campaign, Wounded at Pleasant Hill

Sherman's troops returned from Meridian on March 4. Together, they all marched to Vicksburg and camped on Walnut Hills, near their position during the siege. On March

6, there was much excitement as received an order saying three-fourths of the 8th Iowa, 12th Iowa, and 11th MO had re-enlisted so they were granted 30 days leave after turning over their equipment. Those who didn't re-enlist were temporarily assigned to other regiments (which would include Ole.) Col. Woods was now in charge of his regiment and transferred the non-veterans to 35th Iowa.

The veterans going on leave departed March 7 by Steamer *Minnehaha* to Memphis, where they arrive March 12. These soldiers had a terrible time traveling on this steamer. It was falling apart, and kept getting stuck on sand bars along the way. They finally had to abandon it and get a different boat, the *Island City*. The owner of the steamer *Minnehaha* tried to blame the 12th Iowa Infantry for the wreck and billed them for it, but the 12th Iowa Infantry never paid the bill since it wasn't their fault. They were treated to a banquet in their honor in St. Louis on their way home on leave to Iowa. When they got home to Davenport and made it to their respective towns, there were many public receptions and banquets, and many young men in the towns decided to enlist to join them.

There is a notation in the pension records that on March 18-20 Ole was unable to report for duty due to inflamed lungs.

While the re-enlisted men were on furlough, Ole fought with the 35th Iowa Infantry in the series of battles known as the Red River expedition/campaign in northwestern Louisiana. This campaign, primarily the plan of Gen. Halleck, was unsuccessful due to poor planning, communication, and execution. Reed stated that Gen. Banks was ultimately saved by the 35th Iowa Infantry, sent by Gen. Sherman and led by Gen. A. J. Smith. Ole wrote this about this campaign in the biographical portion of his chapter on Glenwood Township, previously cited:

"In 1864 we were sent (6,000) men up the Red River under General Smith to assist General Banks on his raid to Shreveport, LA. We captured Alexandria, taking some three or four cannons there, and twenty-two miles above we captured Henderson's Hill, took four cannons there and two regiments of rebels, one cavalry, the other infantry; then further up we captured a fort and garrison with ten cannons, the name of the fort I have forgotten. At a place called Pleasant Hill where General Banks had been defeated we met the rebels April 9, 1864, and drove them back, covering his retreat to the Mississippi river, a distance of over one hundred miles, having a rebel fence around us of about 18,000 men, which we had to fight every day for two weeks."

It is interesting Ole does not mention in this Glenwood township history chapter that at Pleasant Hill, LA, he was shot in the thigh April 9, and according to medical records, was treated April 10-15, and released back to duty. But he does mention the wound in his letter to Anne, which will be quoted in its entirety in translation in this chapter. Reed condensed a report by Col. Hill, commander of the 35th Iowa brigade, about the Red River campaign which I will describe next.

Col. Hill stated that the brigade of 35th Iowa to which Ole was temporarily attached, the 33rd Missouri, and detachments of 8th and 12th Iowa captured Fort De Russy March 14 with Gen. Mower in command. They marched to Alexandria, LA, arriving March 17, left Alexandria March 21, and marched 22 miles to Bayou Rapides. The Confederates were entrenched there. The Union forces crossed the bayou and marched through swamps and heavy forests for eight miles, then captured 8 picket posts without a shot. They surprised the Rebels in camp at Henderson Hill at midnight, taking 222 prisoners, horses, 4 pieces of artillery, and other equipment. On March 23, the brigade returned to Alexandria. On April 9, 1864, the brigade fought at Pleasant Hill and lost heavily. Col. Hill's report listed three men wounded from 12th Iowa Infantry, but omitted Ole accidentally: Robert Weeden, company F, Hans Hanson and George Kittelson, in company G who fought with Ole. This is where Ole was shot in the thigh (Ole wrote "thigh", but some government documents recorded hip and one said ankle, mistakenly). Col. Hill also listed participation in the following battles: Mansura, LA, May 16, Yellow Bayou, May 17, Bayou De Glaize, May 18, and Old River Lake/Lake Chicot, AR, June 6. The report of Adjutant General wrote that one man of 12th Iowa Infantry was killed at Lake Chicot, but doesn't give the name.

Ole's Fourteenth Letter and last during the War

A letter dated April 18, 1864, written by Ole to Anne from Grand Ecore, LA, (near Nachitoches, east of Pleasant Hill and southeast of Mansfield) explained that there have been many changes and much moving around since he last wrote. This is the last letter that was found written during the Civil War years. The text is here:

Translation

Grand Ecore, Louisiana, April 18th, 1864
My dear, unforgettable friend,

Miss Anne Gilbertson!

I cannot feel satisfied without once again sending you a few lines to inform you that I am alive and still in the best of health. Since last writing to you (some time ago now), we have once more changed location, and many other changes have occurred.

Last month, when the majority of our regiment, or, more precisely, the veterans, returned home, we who are now the veterans had to transfer to the 35th Iowa, and, at the same time, embark on a trip down the Mississippi River and up the Red River with an expedition that was sent from Vicksburg at the same time and has already been here one month. Everything went well to begin with, before joining the army of General Banks. We captured 2 forts and 18 cannons and took 600 prisoners, without losing more than 50 men (dead and wounded). But this all changed as soon as we joined the aforementioned expedition.

[second page]

You have no doubt heard long ago of the bloody battle, the shameful event, that took place at Pleasant Hill on the 8th and 9th of this month. We were given the opportunity to try our hand there on the last day of the battle. We had to go in with all the force at our disposal in order to rescue the Banks army from complete destruction, as they on this day of the battle were retreating pell-mell from the right wing to the left flank along the entire line, with the Rebels close behind. We had formed our line, fully aware that we were the last alternative for saving ourselves and the others. We could not do anything until we had gotten those terrified New York and New England combatants out of our way and behind us, which gave the Rebels time to advance within a few feet of us. But we unleashed a volley at them and, at the same time, let go with a war cry that would have awoken the dead! And our entire line advanced toward them. Our shrieking alone had scared them, and General Kirby Smith, who was leading the Rebel charge, ordered his men to retreat and get away as best they could …

[third page]

… and they ran for God sake *[Translator: looks like he wrote "… and the Run fore God sick."]*. They were in three lines, but soon were scattered in small flocks. They reached a "Kame Brack"[?](canebrake), where they stopped and began firing at us. We happened to be on a bank[?], so that they were able to reach us, although in confused array, and we lost 60 men killed or wounded in our regiment. Two fellows in our company who were behind me were wounded. Hans Hansen Aarnes was shot through the thigh, and George Kittilsen from Calmar was mortally wounded. I got away with some buckshot in my thigh, and it made me so much more alert and was not a serious injury.

We continued for some time, got in close to them and fired off some exceptionally accurate rounds. With my own rifle I avenged the injuries inflicted on my own fellow combatants.

We took many prisoners, and those [Rebels] who were able to escape threw down their rifles and ran. Darkness was approaching, otherwise we would have captured many more. Now it was impossible for us to pursue them any further, and we didn't expect to receive support from our entrapped fellow combatants whom we had rescued, for the previous day they had lost 21 cannons and 170 wagons and several thousand men killed, wounded, or captured.

[fourth page]

We took all our wounded out during the night, while the same night the army of General Banks retreated as fast as their legs could carry them, leaving all their dead and most of the wounded lying on the battlefield. The enemy's retreat was just as hasty, and they left behind much of what they previously had taken from Banks's army.

Early the next morning we received the order to retreat, and no one remained on the battlefield save for those unfortunate souls who lay wounded, pleading in vain that someone might help them out of their dire straits. As soon as the enemy discerned that we had retreated, they quickly returned to take possession of the battlefield and everything [and everyone] left behind by both armies. Our transport boats had headed up the river from Grand Ecore to Shreveport. The enemy now took after them with the intention of either capturing or destroying them. They were blockaded for 3 days and could not move in any direction, so we were without rations. A couple of infantry brigades were finally sent to drive the enemy away, and the boats returned here again.

We have now been ordered back to Vicksburg to join the Army of the Potomac, but General Banks does not want to let us go. We have been under marching orders the past 4 days, but do not know what that means when we finally are set loose, whether to Shreveport or back to Vicksburg. Anders Eggebraaten was in the battle and survived unscathed, but he is now ill, and I fear he may not get back on his feet.

I have no more to write for now, and [from what I have written] you have some idea of how we have fared, while the veterans — perhaps you already have seen some of them — now have the pleasure of meeting loved ones who are almost always on our minds.

In closing I can tell you that I am alive and in good health and I hope to hear the same from you.

Rest assured that you are never forgotten.

Your [unto death] devoted friend

Ole P. Rocksvold

My address is:
Company K, 35th Iowa Infantry
3rd Brigade, 1st Division, 16th Army Corps
Vicksburg, Miss.

Translation by:
Jim Skurdall

It must have been difficult to cope when observing actions that Ole and others considered cowardly and shameful on the part of some soldiers. Sometimes these actions may have caused the Union troops not to achieve their immediate objective, but worse still were deeds that endangered comrades. Another of the many, very difficult aspects of war.

Reorganization and Tupelo

The Union soldiers under A.J. Smith's went back to Memphis June 10 and the 12th Iowa Infantry was reassigned back to the 3rd brigade, 1st division, 16th corps. Col. Woods was commanding the third brigade consisting of 12th and 35th Iowa, 33rd MO, and 7th MN. These regiments had been brought together on June 11 and had served in the same brigade continuously until autumn when the other three non-veteran regiments mustered out.

On April 25, the furloughs expired for those men, some of Ole's comrades, who had re-enlisted. They boarded a train at Davenport, IA, April 28, went to Cairo, IL, then traveled by steamer April 30 to Memphis, reporting for duty there as they arrived May 2. These soldiers received their guns and equipment and were ordered to camp near Memphis. On May 16 Companies A, B, C, D, F, and H, under Lt. Col. Stibbs, guarded the post at White River, Arkansas. The other four companies, including G (Ole's), under Major Van Duzee, remained on duty at Memphis. Reed joked that those at White River had little to do but fight mosquitoes at this very swampy place. After four weeks four companies returned to Memphis leaving only Companies A and F at White River.

In the war pension medical records, Ole is listed as having an intermittent fever May 6-17, 1864, and was returned to duty after that.

On June 11 all the troops near Memphis were brought to witness a public execution. At Fort Pickering, three men from 2nd New Jersey Cavalry had been court martialed, and were marched around the square for all to see. The soldiers were then blind-folded, seated on their coffins, and shot. The Union soldiers were then ordered to march past the corpses. Reed wrote it served as a "warning against future offenses."

On June 13, Ole is listed in the medical records as having diarrhea, and June 15, diarrhea and edema of the feet.

In early June a Confederate force was organizing near Tupelo, MS, planning to disrupt Sherman's communications and the ability to use the railroad in the middle of Tennessee. Under Sherman's orders Gen. Washburn sent a force to defeat/detain the Confederates. Three brigades of Caucasian troops and Grierson's cavalry were led by Col. McMillan. Gen. Sturgis led two regiments of African American troops and three batteries of artillery. Sturgis's men, as they left Memphis, were attacked by Gen. Nathan Forrest's cavalry and defeated as they marched down a narrow road, flanked by swamps. The artillery were captured and the men retreated to Memphis. To replace those troops, Gen. A.J. Smith was ordered by Gen. Sherman to send in the first (Ole's) and third divisions. Coincidentally, my great grandfather on my Dad's maternal side, Charlie Brown (Karl Brun), was also serving in the first division as part of 8th Wisconsin Infantry at this time, but in the second brigade under Col. Wilkins. Since this work involved thousands of soldiers, it is unlikely that Ole and Charlie ever met. On June 18, the first and third divisions of the 16th corps left Memphis by rail, and found the track torn up and a bridge damaged at Colliersville, and so repaired them. Eight companies from 12th Iowa Infantry accomplished these repairs, while the other two, A and F, had duty on the White River. A road was finished to La Grange by June 24 so supplies and people to expedite transportation. Union cavalry were assisting the African American regiments as they made their way back to Memphis.

Some of the African American troops were in shockingly poor condition when they encountered them near La Grange, TN. The African-Americans had hidden in the woods to avoid capture by Nathan Forrest's men and explained how badly some had been treated by those confederates, but no details were given in Reed's account. The Union soldiers were no doubt aware of a previous battle on April 12, 1864, at Fort Pillow, TN, that included the alleged massacre of hundreds of Black troops who were in the process of surrendering, only to be murdered by the Rebels under Gen. Forrest, although Forrest claimed he didn't personally order the murders. According to www.wikipedia.com, the

Joint Committee on Conduct of War determined shortly afterward that the Rebels shot most of the garrison after they had surrendered, and thus considered the actions a war crime. Black civilians were also killed. There are many differing accounts of what happened and after a Congregational inquiry, Gen. Sherman wrote he was convinced that Forrest didn't personally take part in nor ordered the massacre. Many Confederates were angry that the Union had accepted Blacks as soldiers, some of whom were their former slaves. Significantly, Gen. Forrest became the first Grand Wizard of the Ku Klux Klan after the war, but later separated from them.

At midnight on July 4th all Union troops throughout the country celebrated with firing 100 guns in salute. The next morning the troops marched about 101 miles southeast to Pontotoc, MS, where they arrived July 11. This seven day, dusty march was in extreme heat, with many suffering from heatstroke. Some of the new regiments found it impossible to keep up and were "allowed to fall out of ranks" (allowed to not keep rigid formation) and move as best as they could during the cooler part of the day. According to Reed, "The 12th (Iowa) made a record of greatest endurance, by bringing more men to camp each night and in better order than any of the other regiments."

The Union troops skirmished and marched in battle line all day, but were kept from advancing by the Rebels. On July 12 most of them rested there in Pontotoc, but the cavalry continued to Okolona. Early on July 13, the rest of the force marched south towards Okolona. The cavalry continued in this direction, but the infantry suddenly turned toward Tupelo. Then the cavalry was told to turn and follow behind the infantry. When Gen. Forrest of the Confederates learned that Smith was now going east towards Tupelo, he told Buford's division to attack whenever possible. The 12th Iowa Infantry was told to guard the train and marched along its side. There was fighting towards the rear, but they continued marching until reaching Coonewar Creek at midafternoon. Then the Rebels tried to capture the train, approaching through a thicket. The Rebels captured two train guards from Company D, but the two soldiers were able to warn the others by firing their guns. Lt. Col. Stibbs had his Union regiment lie down in a ravine out of sight and when the Rebels came by, Stibbs ordered them to be fired upon, routing the Confederates. Although 12th Iowa Infantry was able to stop them, they weren't able to finish up and collect the Rebel equipment they had captured. At that moment they received an urgent request to help a battery in danger of being captured. So the 12th Iowa Infantry left to help and arrived just it time to save the battery. One of the regiment was killed, 12 wounded and one missing.

There were big losses on the Confederate side, so hot was the firing upon them, wrote Col. Bell, mentioned in Reed's book. This battle is sometimes known as the "Battle of Coonewar Creek." The Union troops then continued their march in the center of the wagon train. As they passed over a piece of corduroy road with swamp on each side, a Confederate battery sent a single shot out at them across the road. (A corduroy road is one with logs placed side by side.) The battery was not in range for them to reach it using their Springfield muskets.. Reed wrote that it would have been deadly to stop the train, and it was impossible to move quickly. All they could do was move forward steadily to prevent a stampede of the train. He hoped they would make their way around the swamp and influence the Rebels to move their battery back. The Union soldiers continued to encounter shots as they marched forward, reaching Tupelo about 8 p.m., having lost one from Company D who was killed instantly. They took over the train depot and an earthworks that the confederates had put up earlier. The 12th Iowa camped two miles west of town that night.

On Thurs., July 14, they were called into battle lines at 3 a.m., which became known as the Battle of Tupelo. Skirmishing started as soon as it was light and the cavalry moved in to support them. They pulled down a rail fence and piled the rails for protection. By 7:00 a.m., the fighting was very heavy against Confederate Lt. Gen. Forrest's four divisions. Forrest started on the north side of Pontotoc Road where the 12th Iowa soldiers were. Reed wrote on p. 155-6 in his book that they watched the double lines of gray uniformed rebels marching towards them and held their fire until they were within firing range, "with a coolness and accuracy which was only excelled by the rapidity with which they discharged and reloaded their muskets. Not a man wavered or fell back; those killed or severely wounded lay where they fell, unheeded by comrades. Those less severely wounded, who were able to get to the rear unaided, left guns and cartridges with comrades; made their way as best they could to the hospital; many of them returning to their place as soon as their wounds were dressed." Many of the Rebels had to find shelter or retreat. By now the Union troops ammunition was becoming exhausted and many muskets were "foul," no longer serviceable. The 7th MN was ordered to relieve the 12th Iowa Infantry while they went to the rear to replenish cartridge boxes and clean guns.

After that, the 12th Iowa Infantry returned to the front in time to face a charge by Chalmers' troops. The Union soldiers were then ordered to charge, with the 12th Iowa Infantry in the front. They drove the enemy back, as far as Harrisburg Landing in Tupelo. The fighting ended for the day, at which time the soldiers treated their wounded and buried the dead.

This engagement isn't mentioned much in battle accounts, but Reed believed that it should be. They were only about 300 Union soldiers who fought off 3 brigades (several thousand soldiers), having killed or wounded 600 Rebels. Confederate reports of the fighting expressed how hard and effectively the Union troops (in this location, the 12th Iowa) fought. On p. 157 Reed quoted Col. Mabry, a Confederate brigade commander in his report, "...the fire of the enemy was so heavy and well directed that many were killed and wounded." Col. Bell, another Confederate brigade commander, wrote that they were under "a most galling fire....The place was truly a hot one, the loss of the brigade in officers and men was immense." Mabry wrote his casualties were 371, Bell 400. Buford's lost 996, and Chalmers' was not given. The losses for the 12th Iowa Infantry on July 14 were one officer and six men killed, 39 wounded. The dead were buried close to where they fell and the name of each person was carved into a tree near the large grave. On p. 157 Reed continued by quoting a poem, but doesn't identify its author:

"Lying so silently, through night and through day;

Moulding, and mingling their dust with the clay.

They left home and kindred, at the call of the chief,

And like reapers went into the harvest of death!

They shirked not stern duty, while shrapnel and shell

Crashed through their blue ranks like missiles of Hell!"

Reed described the unusual circumstances of the death of Lt. Burdick, their quartermaster. He had ridden to resupply cartridges to the front. He stepped behind a tree, more than a foot in diameter. Normally this would have been a safer place to be, but as misfortune would have it, a shot three inches in diameter and five inches long went through the tree, through Burdick, and his horse. The acting adjutant nearby quickly went to him, but Burdick had died instantly. The adjutant swiftly collected his haversack which contained important papers, his sword, and the shot that killed him. Later the adjutant sent the shot home with the personal possessions to Burdick's wife in Decorah, IA. After the war she came to see the site where he was buried, saw how they had carefully identified each man's name carved into the tree, and decided to leave him with his comrades rather than move his body home.

The 12th Iowa Infantry then prepared to return to Memphis, but with several too wounded to move, some soldiers were ordered to stay behind to care for the injured in the hospital. Those selected were some from company B and I. This took tremendous courage to watch their comrades march away, since they had heard of the atrocities Forrest's men had committed on others who were captured at Fort Pillow and Guntown, and by staying behind were at great risk of being captured. These men didn't complain. In fact they told the adjutant that they wanted to volunteer and to rescind the original order so it can be written that they volunteered to care for these nine men, four of whom subsequently died. It was safer for them, however, to keep the written order so they had it in writing to show that they were staying back to care for the wounded and dying. Fortunately those written orders resulted in them being treated as nurses by the Confederates and prevented them from becoming prisoners of war. After their care for the men ended, these brave soldiers received medals of honor for this hazardous duty, and joined the Union forces in the Vicksburg area.

Since Gen. Smith had completed his mission to break up the enemy camp at Tupelo and prevent the reestablishment of railroad communications between Mobile and Chattanooga, the 12th Iowa Infantry, along with other units from Missouri, Minnesota, and Iowa, now moved towards Memphis July 15, with the third brigade as the rear guard. Along the way there was skirmishing. Col. Woods ordered a charge by the whole brigade and the rebels were defeated. Col. Woods decided to about face his brigade and march quickly to Old Town Creek. The Rebels then started to pursue them and the 1st and 2nd brigades joined in with the 3rd to rout the Confederates again, causing heavy casualties again. No further attempt at stopping the Union forces on their way to Memphis was made again. Gen. Forrest was severely wounded in this last attempt. In the 12th Iowa Infantry one was killed and three wounded. The remaining Rebels escaped to the woods and later Gen. Sherman criticized Smith for allowing Forrest to escape to do more damage in the future.

It is clear that Reed was proud of the 12th Iowa Infantry, mentioning in his book each of three days, July 13-15, in which it was in front line of attack. Reed said the 12th "gallantly withstood every charge that it received" and obtained special commendation by Gen. Smith and the whole army. On p. 161 Reed quoted Ingersoll in a book called, *Iowa and the Rebellion* in which is written, "No small force repelled a large force more bravely, completely and successfully during the war." Many other accolades are written from official reports on p. 162-166 in Reed's book.

Long Marches to Several States

On July 16, Smith's army continued the march, arriving at La Grange, TN, on July 21. On July 22 they rode the train into Memphis where they were able to return to their camp. They spent time cleaning and repairing equipment, and had not gotten fully rested before getting orders to march again on July 30. On Sunday, July 31, they got on the train again and landed at Davis Mills, near La Grange, then marched to Coldwater River the next day. Marching to Holly Springs, MS on on Aug. 2, they formed the advance guard. They spread out as provost guards around the town, which means they had policing duties. Reed wrote that this city used to be known as "The Garden City of Mississippi," but the severe effects of war had caused a great decline. This location had been where Gen. Grant established his supply depot in 1862 on his first trip to Vicksburg, with Col. Murphy left in charge of guarding the supplies. The Rebel Gen. Van Dorn quickly captured the area and 1500 men, setting the warehouses and depots on fire. The explosions of the ammunition had left much of the town destroyed.

As the Union soldiers arrived on Aug. 2, 1864, the townspeople did not insult them, as often happened when they came into southern towns. The residents asked for special guards for their houses, explaining that some of the Union troops were their former slaves and they were afraid of what they might do to them in retribution. The women of the town often invited the Union guards in to eat or have tea. The soldiers discovered several men there who were pointed out as Rebel soldiers and arrested them. They had fought in Forrest's command, and one was wounded at Tupelo. The regiment stayed until Aug. 9 when it was ordered to rejoin the brigade that was fighting at the Tallahatchie River. They arrived there Aug. 10 and learned the 7th MN and 35th Iowa had secured the crossing after difficult fighting. Companies A and F rejoined them from White River, AR. They learned that while at White River, the Union soldiers had fought hard and been victorious at repelling the Rebels who attacked them early in the morning June 22 at their partially constructed stockade. It was very hot and they had removed their uniforms while working hard on the construction. They only had time to grab their cartridge boxes and started fighting in their shirt sleeves. They received accolades for their accomplishment, 55 men winning over 400. The soldiers were glad to have their companies back together again.

On Aug. 13 the brigade had a successful skirmish at Hurricane Creek, and stayed there until they had completed construction on a bridge Aug. 21. The Union troops then proceeded to Oxford, MS, where a small group of rebels was driven off. Forrest decided to lead his rebel forces to Memphis, thinking it may not be well protected. 8th Iowa Infantry did a good job of driving them out, however Forrest did capture some soldiers there.

Gen. Smith was ordered to return to Memphis, and thereafter bring two divisions to Gen. Sherman near Atlanta. After such severe fighting in the heat of Mississippi and not seeing much to show for it, the men looked forward to joining the main army near Atlanta.

Sherman had been doing great battles, but had also had great losses. However, losses in individual regiments tended to be fewer. There apparently had been much disagreement about placement and movement of men among the leadership (Sherman, Rosencrans, Washburn, Sturgis, etc.) and there were times when these 16th division troops were going back and forth to Memphis. The soldiers wondered why they were getting these orders. Sherman wrote to Grant April 10, as quoted by Reed on p. 171, that Sherman was anxious to get Smith's men to join McPherson to have 9 divisions of "thirty thousand of the best men in America." As the Union troops crossed the Tallahatchie River Aug. 24, the enemy attacked the Union rear guard, but were defeated, which resulted in 9 rebels killed, 5 mortally wounded, and 11 prisoners.

The Union soldiers camped at Waterford Aug. 25, and then marched into Holly Springs. A delegation of town folks asked for the 12th Iowa Infantry to be provost guards again. Apparently Gen. Smith was known for colorful language and Reed quoted his response to the committee's request on p. 172 by saying, " The 12th Iowa is one of my best fighting regiments. I think it is a doubtful compliment for you _____, _____rebels to want it to guard your ____,_____town, and is an imposition on the regiment to ask them to do it; but if those boys are willing to stand guard they may." So the Twelfth moved forward before the rest of the men and things stayed quiet in town. As the troops left the next day, the 12th Iowa Infantry was the rear guard in the evacuation. In some instances the townsfolk helped the Union men. In one instance, a soldier was accidentally left behind as the troops left town. The citizens hid him as the rebels came into town after the Union troops left. Later after dark the citizens helped get him safely to the camp at Davis Creek.

On Aug. 29 the 12th Iowa Infantry was in LaGrange yet again and under Col. Henderson formed a garrison of one hundred men to guard while the others went back to the camp near Memphis. They thought they would shortly pack and go to Atlanta, but orders were suddenly changed. Confederate generals Price, Marmaduke, and Shelby had combined forces in Arkansas and threatened Little Rock where Union Gen. Steele was in command. So the first division was ordered to help Steel and the third division (Ole's) went by boats down the river on the steamer, *Mattie*, Sept. 2, under the command of Gen. Mower. On Sept. 4, they arrived at White River, and the next day reached St. Charles. They stayed until Sept. 8, then went by boat to Devall's Bluffs, AR. On Sept. 10 the Union troops started marching towards Brownsville, traveling across the prairie 18 miles in one afternoon with only the water in their canteens. They camped in a grove of trees by a slough so they finally had an additional water source. They made it to Brownsville Sept. 11 and learned the Confederates had not entered Little Rock, but went north, possibly intending to invade Missouri.

Reed wrote that someone got the "brilliant idea" of sending infantry, along with some cavalry, to chase these rebels, under Price, and decided Mower's men would be a good choice since they had so much experience marching! I imagine Ole and the others were very frustrated to again get more extensive marching orders going in the opposite direction from the plan to rejoin Sherman near Atlanta! They gathered ammunition and ten days' rations at Brownsville, teams and wagons and drivers. But the teams and wagons would only go as far as the Red River, unload, and then return to Gen. Steele. Gen. Mower ordered one man from each company to collect beef cattle for food and search for a horse to do this. They left Sept. 17, having obtained supplies, and marched north, going through Austin Sept. 18, where the 9th Iowa was camped. The soldiers enjoyed getting to see those comrades again.

Reed related a story about one of the men from company B, Hugh McCabe, who decided this would be a good place to obtain a horse for his mission to find cattle and "borrowed" one and didn't know whose it was. Later it turned out the captain responsible for the horse was McCabe's old neighbor in Iowa. Reed said they enjoyed chuckling about this later after the war was over. The neighbor said his horse was "stolen by the 12th Iowa Jay-hawkers."

On Sept. 19 they crossed the swift-moving little Red River, four feet deep, with the bottom rocky. Some removed their clothes and carried them overhead as they walked across. Once in a while someone would fall and be carried down the river, with the men shouting after him. They marched the next day following the trail of Gen. Shelby's Confederates over very rough roads and along swampy streams. They crossed the White River by walking across it on Sept. 22 and reached the Black River that evening, discovering the bridge was burned, the water too deep to walk across, and the area very swampy. There was no good place to camp, so they just stopped where they stood and spent the night along the corduroy road, trying to cook their own supper and sleep the best they could on the rough road. The "pioneer corps" of the 12th Iowa Infantry was sent forward to make a bridge. At the village of Elgin they found a saw mill got some planks. By Sept. 23 they had a 320 ft. long bridge ready for the army to safely cross. They camped at Miller's church, the same place where Shelby's men had camped three days earlier.

The troops marched up the east bank of Black River about 20 miles per day, going through Pocahontas, AR, and Poplar Bluff, MO, arriving at Greenville, MO, Oct. 2. They found out Confederate Gen. Price's forces were at Ironton, 40 miles north. Price had fought Union troops there, and was now traveling northwest. The Union troops arrived in Cape Girardeau, MO, Oct. 5, having marched 336 miles in 19 days, fording 7 rivers, and building a bridge 320 ft. long. It is hard to imagine both how strong and how exhausted these soldiers must have been! According to Reed, these soldiers had waded through and hauled equipment and artillery over "some of the worst swamps in the country." Sometimes the rear guard had to work all night to get the artillery, equipment and supplies into camp to catch up with the soldiers. For example, on Sept. 30, the 12th Iowa Infantry was the rear guard and had to drag the wagon train out of mud holes all day as they marched from Poplar Bluff to Chipman's Ford. It was very dark and they had to light torches and candles to see the road, arriving just in time for morning reveille at camp Oct. 1. Six of the 19 days it had rained constantly. The roads were sometimes so rough, the stones cut into their shoes. They did all of this on only 10 days' rations. Incredible endurance!

The day they arrived at Cape Girardeau, Oct. 5, five officers and 102 of the 250 men were walking barefoot over the rocks on the rough roads since their shoes had fallen apart! Some had tied coffee sacks to their feet to try to protect them somewhat. It reminded Reed of how, during the Revolutionary War, the army at Valley Forge left blood from their bare feet in the snow. People in the town were alarmed when they arrived, looking as dirty and ragged as they did, thinking they were part of a guerrilla force to attack them. As Reed put it on p. 179, "I presume a dirtier, raggeder set never marched into any town than Mower's men when they reached Cape Girardeau." Their accomplishment was all the more remarkable since they marched faster and better than the horses and mules. Almost all of the animals were no longer fit to use, and half the mules were left behind on the road. Imagine how relieved these soldiers were to arrive at some civilization and be able to communicate with the world! Since they had crossed the state line into Missouri, they now were under Gen. Rosencrans' command.

The soldiers were only given one day to rest in Cape Girardeau while awaiting boats to St. Louis. Price's Confederates were threatening that city. They marched to the steamboat landing Oct. 7, at 2 a.m., with company B, E, and G (Ole's) boarding the steamer *Argonaut*, the rest on the steamer *Armenia*. The upper deck held men, the lower levels of the boats were filled with artillery and cavalry. When the troops arrived, they spent two days getting supplies, and re-outfitting themselves.

On Oct. 10th the Union troops traveled up the Missouri River on boats to Jefferson City towards which Price was marching with his Confederate troops. The 12th Iowa Infantry was on a boat called *Empire* that was too big to manage in waters that shallow, and as a result, the boat was stuck on sandbars for most of eight days. On four occasions, all the soldiers had to get off and use hawsers (heavy ropes) to pull the boat off sandbars while standing on shore. The night of Oct. 13, while they were yet again trying to pull the boat off a sandbar, it got stuck in a position from which they could not move it, nor could they get back on the boat. So they had to spend the night on shore without food, shelter, blankets. To make matters even worse, in the morning there was white frost on the ground and on them. After all these delays, they arrived in Jefferson City Oct. 18 to learn that Gen. Price had turned west before arriving in the city. Part of the Union Cavalry was in front of the Gen. Price's men, with the rest of the Union division pursuing them.

Gen. Sherman protested in a letter to Gen. Grant in strong language that he wanted these two divisions of the 16th corps with him, not near Jefferson City, MO. Reed quoted Sherman on p. 180, "I think it will be found that the movements of Price and Shelby are mere diversions. They cannot hope to enter Missouri except as raiders, and General Rosencrans should be ashamed to ask my troops for such a purpose." Since for now Sherman wasn't granted his request, he at least got permission to take Gen. Mower from them and bring him to near Atlanta. It was hard for Mower and the men to part. He had worked with them for 2 years and had done a great job of leading them and inspiring them to the point that they believed "they could not be beaten." He had earned the rank of Major General leading them. Mower left St. Charles, MO, Oct. 11, and Col J.J. Woods took his position leading the division, with Col. Hill of 35th Iowa, becoming the brigade commander.

Next the 12th Iowa Infantry traveled to La Mine River by train. They found the bridge destroyed so they got out of the train and marched west to Sedalia Oct. 19, meeting up with the rest of the division. They then marched through Lexington, Independence, Blue River, and Kansas City, hearing some skirmishing along the way, but never needing to fight. Price's Rebel soldiers were on horseback and were able to get new horses from the countryside along the way whenever more were needed. Occasionally Price's men would engage the Union cavalry a bit, then leave them alone and move on, ahead of the Union infantry chasing them.

They crossed Blue River Oct. 23, and the fighting in the front got serious, as the infantry marched rapidly all day and into the night to catch up with the Confederate troops, until they had marched 37 miles within 24 hours and reached the river, but Price was already gone. After that some of the cavalry were able to catch up with Price as he had turned south, and they fought at a final engagement near Lone Tree. They captured Gen. Marmaduke and 1,000 men. Price's men had so scattered that by Oct. 26 the infantry, at Harrisonville, MO, gave up trying to pursue them. They stayed there for 3 days to get some rest after marching 176 miles in 8 days!

In Col. Woods' report, cited by Reed, Wood said it was very hard to march so far, especially knowing that there was a railroad all across the state, but it apparently was necessary to use it for transporting prisoners, broken down mules, cavalry horses and riders, artillery, etc. instead of transporting these soldiers! Reed quoted Woods on p. 182, displaying a definite tone of sarcasm, "These must be spared but 'Smith's guerillas' had been diverted to this district, were borrowed in fact, and must expect to march, and they did, through snow and mud; rain and shine; resting only one day in sixteen, reaching St. Louis November 16."

A couple of notes Reed mentioned about specific dates in this march include one from Nov. 3. Col. Woods wrote that the men's clothes were soaked through, marching all day while snow fell. Since there was no wood nor rails with which to make a fire, some officers went into the city and found old sheds and stores where the men could be housed. With that knowledge, the officers got permission to bring the soldiers into the city. Most of the officers stayed in a hotel.

On Nov. 5 at California, MO, (ironic name considering the weather), they camped where there was snow 10 inches deep, but were able to melt it with big fires so they would have a drier place to put down blankets. Reed wrote they slept comfortably until they woke in the morning with a new 4-inch layer of snow on top of them!

At Sedalia, Gen. J. McArthur, succeeded Gen. Mower. Woods went back to leading the third brigade.

A Moment of Humor to Lighten the Stress

On Nov. 8, election day, they left Jefferson City with plans to cross the wide, slushy, waist-deep Osage River. The men followed orders, but Reed cited comments prior to getting into the water, such as, "I will never go through there! Might as well be shot for disobeying orders as die in that river," and similar expressions. Despite so many hardships, Reed wrote they didn't lose their sense of fun. One thing the soldiers found comical was watching a cannoneer sitting on the muzzle of his gun, then suddenly being immersed by being tipped backwards into the water. The soldiers particularly enjoyed seeing some of the officers fall in. Another chuckle was had when an officer with a horse offered to give a fellow officer the chance to ride with him crossing the river. It went well until they got to the middle of the stream when the horse decided it didn't want to put up with two riders, lay down, and rolled both officers into the icy water. The chance to laugh probably felt very good after all the soldiers had been through.

Voting Day

Since it was election day, Nov. 8, 1864, and after they crossed the Osage River, the Iowa troops were allowed to vote for President. Those who had horses to ride got to be the judges. With the voting complete, the soldiers continued on, while the judges stayed back to count the ballots and record the returns. The result in the 12th Iowa Infantry: 190 for Lincoln, 20 for McClellan. Total cast- 210.

After arriving in the dark during a severe rainstorm, the troops camped that night at Westphalia, MO. They couldn't see where they were going so they just stopped where they stood. Each person lay down with his blanket until the rain stopped, when they could finally making fires.

Back to Benton Barracks

The Union soldiers marched into Benton Barracks Nov. 15 where at last warm and more hospitable accommodations were available. They enjoyed sitting around the coal heaters as they had 3 years earlier with the opportunity to reminisce about all they had been through together. In 15 days they had marched from Harrisville to St. Louis, 303 miles with only one rest day. Three days of snow storms were included.

Totals of Marches

Reed's summary of the campaign from Memphis in two and a half months: travel by steamboat, 772 miles, by train, 50 miles, marched 950 miles. This was in addition to the two Mississippi River campaigns, serving together in five states- TN, MS, AR, MO, and Kansas. The troops had only 10 rest days in five months. Other commanders were arguing about who could have them next, they were such accomplished, resilient, hardworking soldiers. I wonder if, after the war, Ole had little interest in going for walks after so much marching!

Mustering Out

While at St. Louis, Reed explained, they received orders for Gen. Smith to bring his 16th corps to help stop Confederate Gen. Hood in Tennessee. However, Col. Wood would not be coming. He had served somewhat beyond his three-year term and mustered out. Some other officers did the same at that time. Smith waited until transportation was available to reach Nashville with his troops. On Nov. 24, Thanksgiving Day, 1864, with Lt. Col. Stibbs leading them, the troops left Benton Barracks, marched into town, and boarded the steamer, *Silver Cloud*. An organization, the Christian Commission, sent apples, other fruits and jellies for the soldiers to enjoy onboard to add to their fare of hardtack. As usual, a delay caused them not to leave until Nov. 26. They traveled down the Mississippi, then up the Ohio River to Smithland, KY, arriving Nov. 28. They joined with other troops that had stayed in Memphis. They loaded them and their equipment onboard, and went up the Cumberland River, arriving in the morning of Dec. 1 in Nashville. These troops rushed to the front line to fight three miles from the city.

However, pension records show that on Nov. 30, 1864, Ole was mustered out at Nashville, Tennessee. So how did he get to Nashville Nov. 30 when the boat on which the 12th Iowa Infantry was riding didn't arrive in Nashville until Dec. 1, according to Reed? Perhaps Ole was on the boat, but got his papers signed the night before arriving, officially saying he had completed his military service. Or did he travel by some other means to muster out from that city? And why didn't he just muster out from St. Louis since there were only two weeks to go of his service? We may never learn the answer to these questions. Nevertheless, after three years he could finally go home!

As I have now completed describing the three years of Ole's military service during the Civil War , here are some additional statistics and reflections on the Civil War and the 12th Iowa Infantry.

Some Facts about the Civil War

There were more casualties in the Civil War than any other war in which Americans fought.

The Civil War records at Vesterheim Museum in Decorah, IA, incorrectly states he was wounded in the ankle at Pleasant Hill, LA. It was actually his thigh, according to his pension records and a letter written by him after the battle.

Statistics on the 12th Iowa Volunteer Regiment are as follows:

Total Strength- originally 926 soldiers. Gained 55 recruits, for a total of 981.

The regiment lost 5 officers and 114 enlisted men killed in action or died from wounds. To disease, it lost 4 officers and 205 enlisted men, for a total of 328 fatalities, almost one third lost. It is hard to conceive of so much suffering and grief for the families and friends of the lost.

For another soldier's view of some of the same battles that Ole was in, see six letters in Abernethy's *Private Elisha Stockwell, Jr., Sees the Civil War.*

Reunions of Iowa Comrades

Ole must have had the desire to keep in touch with his comrades after the war. Nathan Kalmoe, Ole's great great grandson, discovered the reunion records online. In *Reunion of the Twelfth Iowa Veteran Volunteer Infantry,* Ole is listed as attending the 2nd, 3rd, 4th, 5th, 7th, and 8th reunions.

As the soldiers would reminisce about their years of service at reunions, I imagine John Steen, Ole's friend and comrade, would likely have talked about what happened to himself and his brothers with what follows here:

The Steen Family

The Steens of Glenwood Township, emigres in 1853 to Winneshiek County, IA, held the record for the family who sent the most sons to serve in the Civil War (six). The seventh son attempted to join, but was sent home. Four of these sons became prisoners of war, but fortunately all six made it home. All were promoted to corporal or sergeant and all served in major battles. Charlie enlisted in Minnesota's 1st Infantry. Theodore, John, and Henry enlisted in Iowa's 12th, the same unit as Ole Rocksvold. Martin enlisted in 38th Iowa, and Otto was in Wisconsin's 15th.

At Gettysburg Gen. Hancock ordered the 1st MN Infantry in a suicidal charge to hold off the oncoming rebels to buy time until reinforcements could arrive from 200 yards away. Hancock yelled, "We need five minutes. Get me five minutes!" Minnesota's 1st leaped over the wall from which they were protected, fighting with their bayonets, knives, and using rifles as clubs, since there was no time to reload. Only 47 out of 262 survived this charge unscathed, the rest were killed, captured, or wounded. Charlie Steen was wounded in his left thigh, lost his leg, but survived to come home.

Theodore, John, and Henry Steen fought at Shiloh, were captured with Ole, and held prisoner for almost 7 months, and went on to serve in several battles after release. Martin, who enlisted at 16, fought at Vicksburg, Mobile, and other battles. He was wounded at Fort Blakely, Alabama. Otto was captured in the Battle of New Hope Church, Georgia, and spent 9 months in Andersonville Prison. When the war ended, he was released and was extremely undernourished. He did recover and lived to be 84. Ole kept up contact with John Steen after the war. We have a copy of a letter John wrote to Ole after the war, dated April 13, 1906, complimenting him on what a good soldier and leader he was and urging him to come to a reunion of the Iowa veterans. A translation of this letter is included in an appendix in this book.

Women Disguised as Male Soldiers

A surprise awaited me when I was reading the remembrances and speeches listed in the reunion records. Col Stibbs, at the second reunion, stated that he learned after the war that a female, whom he identified in a speech as "Helene Violet B." served 3 years with the 12th Iowa Infantry, disguised as a man. Col. Stibbs said she was present at the reunion, but was dressed as a female and hoped that no one would try to discover who this soldier was to respect her privacy. Since many people attended reunions, including family members and friends, it was feasible for her to come and remain undetected as a former soldier, which apparently was her wish.

I have read before that other women wanted to serve and disguised themselves as well, but this was the first I had heard of anyone in the 12th Iowa Infantry doing so. Another woman who served during the Civil War was Frances L Clalin, who is seen in two pictures on p. 11 in *The Common Soldier of the Civil War*, one with her dressed in women's clothing, and the second with her in her uniform in the 4th Missouri Heavy Artillery and 13th Missouri Cavalry.

In another book, *They Fought Like Demons: Women Soldiers in the Civil War*, it mentioned there are hundreds of documented cases of women serving as soldiers in the Civil War. There may well have been thousands more since many were not documented and never revealed who they were, during or after the war.

It was fascinating to learn of many reasons why so many women served, what they accomplished, and what their lives were like during and after the war. Some women served for love of country and for many of the same reasons cited by men earlier in this book. Others served to be near loved ones, such as a husband, brother, or father who was serving. Some women joined for adventure or to escape harsh or abusive conditions. Still others served to experience a fuller life with more rights, since women at that time were greatly limited as to what they were allowed to do. For example, women at the time were limited as to which jobs they could hold, their pay was lower than men's, and they often weren't allowed to own property.

Like men, besides getting wounded in mind or body, some women paid the ultimate sacrifice. Sometimes when burying dead bodies, soldiers learned only then that a fellow comrade was actually a woman.

Black River area where Ole camped and skirmished, 1863, near Jackson, MS.

Siege description at Vicksburg National Military Park, Mississippi, in which Ole participated, along with other skirmishes and guard duty in the Jackson area.

Plaque recognizing the 12th Iowa's contribution on
May 22, 1863, at Vicksburg National Military Park, MS.

Overview of May 22, 1863 at Vicksburg.

Graveyard at Vicksburg National Military Park.

Monument to Iowa's soldiers at Vicksburg National Military Park, MS.

Nathan Kalmoe and his wife, Katie Will, at the Jackson Courthouse. MS.
Ole helped to guard this town.

Black Soldiers Enter the War. Sign at Vicksburg National Military Park.

John C. Calhoun originated the idea that the southern states should call a convention "to put forth in a solemn manner the causes of our grievances in an address to the other states."

Chief Justice William Sharkey

"Our position is thoroughly identified with the institution of slavery — the greatest material interest of the world."

1861 Secession Convention

Although some people today still claim that retaining slavery in the U.S. was not a main reason for the South seceding from the North, there are many states' documents, such as this excerpt from the 1861 Secession Convention, which prove otherwise.

Interior of Jackson Courthouse, MS. Ole helped guard the town of Jackson after it was captured.

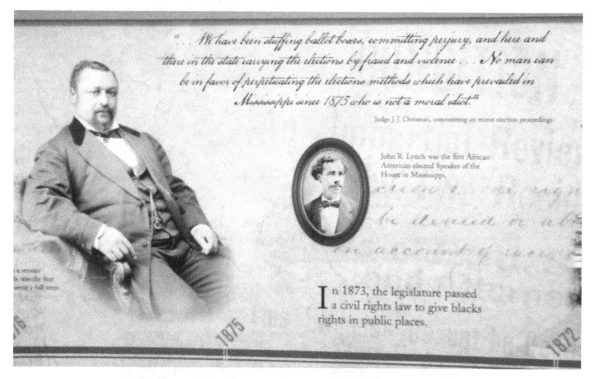

"...We have been stuffing ballot boxes, committing perjury, and here and there in the state carrying the elections by fraud and violence... No man can be in favor of perpetuating the elections methods which have prevailed in Mississippi since 1875 who is not a moral idiot."

Judge J. J. Chrisman, commenting on recent election proceedings

John R. Lynch was the first African American elected Speaker of the House in Mississippi.

In 1873, the legislature passed a civil rights law to give blacks rights in public places.

After the Civil War, there was a period called "Reconstruction" in which laws were written to give former slaves civil rights. Many people in southern states worked to take away rights that were granted to Blacks upon being freed from slavery.

☞ Address: "Chief of the Record and Pension Office,
War Department, Washington, D.C."

Record and Pension Office,

WAR DEPARTMENT,

Washington, NOV 6 1894.

Respectfully returned to the

Com. of Pensions

with the information that in case

of Ole P. Rocksvold

Co G 12 Iowa Inf

(Name also borne

as Rocksvold)

Ort muster rolls

dated Oct 31 & Dec 31st

62 and Feby 28 63

show him

present at

Benton Barracks

Mo.

Mily records

furnish nothing

further as to

[illegible] record.

The medical records show him

treated as follows: as O. P. Rox-

wald, Priv. Co. G 12 Ia. Oct. 21

62. Feb. Intermit: as O. P.

Rocksvold, Priv. Co. B, &c Aug. 21

to Oct. 5. 63 Diarrhoea; as Ole

P. Rocksvold, Priv. Co. G. &c

Feb. 9 to 10. 64 Diarrhoea; as O.

P. Rockwell, Cpl Co — 12 Ia

Mar. 18 to 20. 64 Inflam. Lungs,

retd. to duty: as O. P. Rocksvold

Cpl Co. G. &c wounded near hip

slight (also appears as ankle)

at the battle of Pleasant Hill,

La. April. 9. 64: treated Apl. 10 to

15. 64 Gunshot Wound, returned

to duty: as Priv. Co. K &c. May.

6 to 17. 64 Int. Fev. few, re-

turned to duty; as Ole P.

Rocksvold, &c June. 13. 64 Di-

arrhoea (Chron.); June. 15. 64

Chron. Diarrhoea (Edema,

of feet.)

Nothing additional

found.

BY AUTHORITY OF THE SECRETARY OF WAR:

R. Ainsworth

Colonel, U. S. Army, Chief of Office.

(323a)   Per V,

11-6-1894 Pension Ole Rocksvold one sickness record

～ Chapter 5 ～

Life after the Civil War

Ole Rocksvold mustered out of the service on Nov. 30, 1864 (listed as Dec. 7 in some records) at Nashville, Tennessee, according to pension records. He once again went back to farming in the Glenwood township in Winneshiek County, Iowa, east of Decorah, but the Midwest had been changing while he was gone. Ease of travel and population growth were enhanced through the continued progress of railroad construction in the last dozen years. According to Gesme in *Between Rocks and Hard Places*, in 1854 the railroad reached from Chicago to Rock Island on the Mississippi River and another line went to Madison, WI. It reached Prairie du Chien by 1857, La Crosse, WI in 1858. By 1862, it reached Minnesota, and by 1870, one could travel by train to the Red River Valley (Moorhead, MN, Fargo, ND). So not only was Ole returning to a community changed by war, but also changed by improvements in transportation and communication.

What was it like living in the Glenwood area after the war? Ole stated in his mini biography that the land was very good for farming so it was snatched up by immigrants quickly. The property where Ole and Anne raised their children is at 1233- 258th St., Decorah, IA, about 8 miles east of Decorah. The house currently on the property is not the original house. Ole and Anne's house was behind the current house. A small building on the property, currently used as a garage, was originally a school house and moved there from a little further north near the property. We know Matilda, Ole and Anne's daughter, was a teacher, but aren't sure if she taught in that particular building.

To provide for his family's and the farm's needs, Ole dug a well at "S.W. ¼, N.W. ¼ Section 14," in Winneshiek County, Glenwood Township, according to *Underground Water Resources of Iowa*. It had a depth of 500 feet to the water supply and the supply source was sandstone. By all accounts, Ole and his family were very successful at raising crops and animals. Ole and his family's main crops were oats, corn, barley, and hay. Later he also grew timothy and flax. When I asked the father of the current owner of Ole's property, he said they raise corn, soybeans, hay, dairy cattle, and hogs, not very much different from Ole. The 1886 Glenwood Township map shows that Ole owned parts of sections 14 and 15. His brother Anton's land was just north of his in section 11, later owned by Anton's son, Peter, after Anton was gone. The address for Anton's property is 1268 Coon Creek Road, Decorah, IA.

The farmland around Glenwood was so popular that soon after arrival many immigrants needed to go further west to find good farm land to cultivate. In a 2013 phone interview with E. Palmer Rockswold of Minneapolis, MN, Palmer said his aunt, Anne Elvestuen

Anne Guldbrandsdatter Strandbakken Rocksvold
and Ole P. Rocksvold
Location, likely Decorah, IA, taken either upon their
marriage or early in their marriage, perhaps 1865 - 1870

Rocksvold, was married to Anton, Ole's brother. Aunt Anne told him that Anton and Ole were well-known for making and selling shingles and yokes for oxen in northeast Iowa, in addition to farming. Palmer described both Ole and brother Anton Rocksvold as well-respected leaders of their community with Ole becoming postmaster for 25 years in Toten (Thoten), IA, near Glenwood, and Anton the registrar of deeds. Both were also good writers. Anton did not serve in the war due to health problems and so took care of the farmlands with other family members while Ole was serving in the army.

The wedding of Ole P. Rocksvold (at that time spelled Rockswold) and Anne Guldbrandsdatter Strandbakken took place Feb. 12, 1865, so it was only a matter of months after Ole's return before they married.

Based on what we read in Ole's letters to her, he was completely devoted to Anne and was very anxious to get back to her when he left the service. They were married by Rev. Koren. After the many letters written during the Civil War, we have a gap of time until Aug., 1895 before we have any other preserved letters written by Ole. Presumably they were so busy farming and raising a family that little thought was made to writing and preserving letters. Conversely, it is possible many letters were written between 1865-1895, but just were not saved. Fortunately we have a few letters written by relatives to Ole during the 1870-80's to help fill in the gap of information, as well as many other documents.

What else do we know about Ole's activities once he was back from the war? According to Ernest Anderson's autobiography-family history document, newspaper accounts, and letters, Ole was very community-minded, held many township offices, and was a member of the board of supervisors for two terms. Ole even ran unsuccessfully for state assembly in 1893. In politics, Ernest Anderson described him as a Republican, but not a "standpatter." By that I think he meant Ole was flexible, more moderate, more progressive among the Republican stances of issues at that time, as the word "stand" in Norwegian is similar to our English "stand." However, we also have a ribbon of Ole's which reads, "4th District Delegate Democratic State Convention, Cedar Rapids, IA, Aug., 6th, 1890." So he did change parties over time. The Republican and Democratic party platforms changed dramatically from the 1800's through the 1900's so which party reflected his views the closest on various issues may have changed over time. More about this later.

From several sources of information we learned that Ole had a strong faith in God, and the Psalms were his favorite part of the Bible. He was very active in his church, often volunteering for many committees whenever something needed to be done. He was also elected to many committees and positions in his lifetime, so people must have respected and trusted him.

Glenwood Church Involvement

Glenwood Lutheran Church is located at 1147 Old Stage Road, Decorah, IA 52101. The building that stands there today is not one of any that stood in Ole's time. Since Ole was so very involved in the creation and development of the Glenwood church, it is interesting and pertinent to learn more about its history since it played such a big part in his life. According to *Minutes of the Congregational Proceedings of Little Iowa Norwegian-Evangelical Lutheran Church and the Glenwood Congregation,* the decision to build a sturdier Glenwood church, to replace the initial wooden structure, was made Nov. 24, 1865. The building committee included Ole Ruen, Ole Rocksvold, Hans Blegen, Christina Toyan, and Anders Evenrud. They planned to make a brick church and foundation on the site of the first frame church, built about 1854. The new church was completed in 1873, taking longer than anticipated since the architect was so busy working on new buildings at Luther College and Washington Prairie Church.

Rev. Koren was elected as President of the Norwegian Synod in 1876, so several assistant pastors helped out in the Decorah area until in 1883 a separate pastor, Nils Amlund, was called for Glenwood Church. Glenwood's first parsonage was built at that time with land donated by Ole Ruen. This house burned in March 1927, which caused the loss of congregational records 1864-1927. Copies of records were available in storage at the Washington Prairie church and so fortunately information from the Glenwood church records was still available.

While Ole was a member at Glenwood Lutheran, he volunteered a lot of time there. Besides helping to found the church and build it, he provided much leadership. Ole was on several committees: church furnishings, stewardship, building, school supervisors, parsonage, trustees, fence building, door, heating facilities, cemetery, well deepening, and a committee to seek debaters on the topic of predestination. Ole chaired one pastoral call committee and served on others. Pastoral call committees were responsible for recruiting pastors. Ole was once an auditor of church finances, a delegate to multiple church conventions, and a pastoral assistant. His brother, Anton, was on several committees as well and served as auditor of church finances.

It is interesting to read about various issues this congregation faced, some of which were similar, but others very different from churches in recent times. According to *Minutes of the Congregational Proceedings of Little Iowa Norwegian-Evangelical Lutheran Church and the Glenwood Congregation*, the church more actively intervened in people's personal lives back in Ole's day. If there was a conflict between two parishioners, for example, the congregation sometimes voted to have a representative meet with the disputants to try to make peace. If someone had "sinned," sometimes the "sin" was discussed at a congregational meeting, they voted to condemn the sin, and voted for which person (or committee) to talk with the sinner about it. This person or committee would then give the "sinner" an ultimatum of public repentance with possible atonement for his or her actions, or face expulsion. Sometimes the "sinner" was named in the meeting minutes and sometimes the name was omitted. On a couple of occasions there is a record of having the name in the minutes originally, but later having it expunged.

The congregation voted to do acts of charity for those in need, and also decided when to forgo the collecting of taxes/donations to the church when someone was deemed too poor to keep up the required contributions per person or per family. Since the church was originally the creator of the schools in the area, the minutes tell of decisions about school administration, finances, and also complications regarding church-school curriculum.

The Glenwood Church split in 1887-1888 with a portion of the congregation leaving due to doctrinal differences about predestation. Predestation is a belief that God has selected people before birth to be saved, i.e., go to heaven when they die. This was a very divisive issue back in the late 1800's-early 1900's in the U.S., with some churches breaking up into smaller denominations or creating new congregations because of the conflict. There are various versions of the doctrine of predestation, each with its own contingent of adherents. Some believe that God knew ahead of time who would ultimately believe in Him and then predestined them to be saved. Others believe God caused them to believe, that there was really no choice in the matter, and saved them before they were born. Still others believe there is choice in the matter and the way one lives one's life, in addition to belief in the triune God, Father, Son, and Holy Spirit, are still factors in whether one is saved or not. Some believe the way one lives one's life is a natural reaction to the gift of grace, of being forgiven and saved, and not a requirement in order to be saved.

There were many discussions about: can a person affect whether she or he is saved or not, by belief, by actions, or both? Or is being saved totally a choice of God, preordained, irrespective of what one believes or does? The differences of belief in this doctrine on predestation deeply divided people, with some so strongly believing in their particular view that they felt they could not be good Christians if they tolerated their congregation not adhering to their specific views on this issue. Some sought to have their particular version of beliefs regarding predestation written into their church bylaws. Some members tried to require their pastors to sign documents saying they agreed with a specific view of predestation and would teach only that view to the congregation. There were also discussions about whether a congregation should remain in their synod because of differences about this issue. Some churches voted to get out of the synod.

It sounded from the church minutes that Ole had an "agree to disagree" attitude and advocated that philosophy for helping the church get through this difficult time.

In the case of Glenwood Lutheran, Ole was elected to chair the call committee to find a new pastor during this time of turmoil in the congregation in 1888. The committee developed and got passed a series of statements from which to move forward on this contentious issue regarding predestination:

On 3-26-1888, the call committee elected Ole Rocksvold chair, and O.H. Berg, secretary. Here I paraphrase the 1-6 resolutions that carried on motions unanimously:

1. Discontinue doctrinal dispute and don't participate in it. No agitation, distributing pamphlets, not trying to force opinions on others to get adherents.

2. If necessary for peace, the congregation may choose not to send a delegate to the Synod meeting at this time, but not discontinue attendance permanently.

3. The congregation doesn't want anyone outside the membership to come in bringing discord. The district president may come to visit, but not in connection with the doctrinal dispute.

4. The congregation will call a pastor who has a neutral position, is not taking part in the present doctrinal dispute.

5. Concerning support of higher education, no one in good conscience needs to be feel bound to contribute (note: but perhaps may disagree with positions of those at Luther College).

6. Plan to call Pastor Borge.

After Pastor Borge was called as pastor, some insisted he sign a document stating how he believed on this predestination issue. Borge refused. A group of about 30 left the church regarding the predestination issue between 1887-8. Prior to their departure, Ole spoke at a congregational meeting, trying to get the people to "agree to disagree," but to no avail for some. Since Ole was on the call committee to get Rev. Borge, and there were strong feelings both for and against Borge's selection as leader of their church, it put Ole in an especially difficult position. Ultimately 8 years later, perhaps due to these doctrinal differences, church climate after the split, and/or to a shocking conflict with Pastor Borge in 1896, Ole eventually did leave the Glenwood congregation to go to St. John's Lutheran in Waukon.

In Ole's 4-3-1896 letter to his daughter, Matilda, Ole explained that Pastor Borge, whom Ole helped to call to Glenwood Church, later accused Ole in a letter of being a "liar, thief, and criminal"! This is quite shocking since all sources and documents found so far indicated Ole to be an honest, well-respected leader in the community. There is no record of such an accusation in the church minutes mentioning Ole nor any anonymous person that might have been referring to him. While writing to Matilda, Ole wrote he was enclosing that Borge letter, but unfortunately we don't have a copy of Borge's letter, so perhaps it was lost or destroyed. Ole wrote that he first thought he would confront this pastor before the congregation to deny Borge's claims and said he could even have made those same accusations about Borge. Ole later decided against those options, and left the congregation.

Ole must have been very angry and hurt to be so accused, since he had worked so hard to help found the Glenwood Church, provided much leadership on many committees, and volunteered for so many tasks throughout the years. What could have caused Borge to so accuse Ole? Could Borge have been jealous of Ole's reputation? Was Borge having mental health problems? Had someone else lied to Borge about Ole? Did Borge feel desperate to get more control over the congregation at this stressful time while handling the doctrinal disputes? Unfortunately, unless more documents appear to answer that question, we may never solve the mystery.

After Ole was no longer in the Glenwood congregation, it was dismaying to read many years later the extent to which this congregation did not welcome outsiders- those who were not Norwegian Lutheran. In fact, the congregation actively worked to prevent them from moving into the area. Based on church meeting minutes, there were many who believed they must keep others out due to a fear they might contribute to the delinquency of their children, making sure they stayed in the Lutheran faith at all costs. Unfortunately humankind all too often has been intolerant of others throughout the U.S. and the world, shunning, attacking, imprisoning, and even killing those who are different from themselves. It was hard to read about this intolerant attitude among people who themselves were immigrants in a new country. Unfortunately that attitude is still quite common today in the world.

For those who are interested in more detailed information about Glenwood Church, its decision making, and Ole's participation there, it is included in the appendix on Glenwood Church. I obtained the minutes to congregational meetings from the church's inception until 1934 to provide the information for this section of church history you just read and for the appendix on Glenwood Church.

The Changing Spellings of "Rocksvold"

You may have noticed various spellings of the name Rocksvold already in this book. In Norway, the Rocksvolds were sometimes listed as Roksvoll, Roksvolden or Roxvolden. Ole went by Rockswold most of his life, but switched to Rocksvold sometime around 1895, as evidenced in his letters. So many people in the U.S. misspelled the name since Norwegians pronounced the "w" as a "v" sound, that he apparently decided to give up and spell it the way most people were doing anyway. We have evidence that the misspellings frustrated Ole. In a letter dated Dec. 17, 1894, Ole asked Mr. Robinson- U.S. military pension agent in Des Moines, IA- to correct the military records to "Rockswold." The election results from 1893 when Ole Rocksvold ran unsuccessfully for a seat in the Iowa assembly listed his name as "Rocksvold." So there apparently was a period of time when more than one spelling of Ole's last name was in documents concurrently.

Although Ole's military records have several different spellings for his name, apparently the authorities eventually figured out they were all the same person since his pension records list various spellings when listing dates of illness or other significant dates in his service. Among the spellings of his last name in the pension records were: Rockwald, Rockwold, Rockswold, Rocksvold, and Rockwell, with O. P. or Ole or Ole P. listed for first and middle names. The records were usually consistent in listing him in company G. of 12th Iowa, but one illness record listed him as from company B. It'd certainly be difficult to keep everything straight during a war involving so many people traveling over so much territory, sometimes under very trying and dangerous circumstances.

Here is one last anecdote about the topic of last names. E. Palmer Rockswold, the nephew of Ole's brother Anton's wife, Anne, told me in an interview in 2013 that his father and ancestors didn't originally have the last name of Rockswold, but decided once in the U.S. to choose it. So many people had trouble spelling and pronouncing their original last name of Elvestuen, that they considered changing to a last name of one of their friends. Ultimately they chose "Rockswold," spelled with a "w", not a "v". Palmer didn't mention any subsequent problems with people misspelling "Rockswold," in contrast with Ole's experience.

Ole's Siblings

What happened with Ole's siblings after emigration? With the help of Ernest Anderson's autobiography, letters between relatives, and some census data, we have some information.

Helene and Family

Fortunately we have several letters to give us insight into Helene's family. Helene was the only sibling who didn't emigrate with the family in 1853 and as far as we know, never visited the U.S. For reasons unknown Helene moved in as a small child with her mother's sister, Marie Rensvoldbrug, and her husband Haaken. Perhaps it was due to poverty or to the parents having their hands full caring for the twins, Ole and Anne Mathea, and younger brother, Anton. Helene got married in 1848 to Lars Johansen Dahl, a teacher in Vestre Toten, and had had two of her four children by 1853, the year the rest of her birth family emigrated. She and Lars decided to stay in Norway at the family farm and raise their children there.

Helene and Lars Dahl had three children, Helene Marie, Julius who was an engineer for the water works in Christiania (later called Oslo), and Karl, a teacher in Ost Toten, who died of heart trouble in 1915. Here is some information gleaned from letters by family members in Helene's line.

It sounded like the winter was bleak in Vestre Toten, Norway in 1878, because a letter dated March 18, 1878, was written by Helene's daughter, Helene Marie to Ole and Anne describing deep snow lasting until the beginning of June is some places, grain freezing in the fall, and farmers forced to buy almost everything they needed to live. Without much to sell, people's debts were mounting. She thanked Ole for the wonderful and expensive gifts and was troubled by not receiving letters for so long, wondering if her letters weren't getting through due to a change in the way the addresses needed to be written. She mentioned Kjersti's sister, Marthe Hagesveen, was bedridden now with illness in her limbs. She said Peter and Karl, her siblings, wanted to send pictures of themselves since there was no way for Ole and Anne to see them otherwise. Helene Marie said if she was still living this summer, she planned to take pictures because currently she had no pictures of her husband and herself. She was only 29 at the time, but no mention is given of what health problem could possibly cause her to die so young. As it turned out, Helene Marie ultimately lived to age 71. In several letters Helene Marie and other relatives have commented on Ole's generosity, giving them many gifts, the *Decorah Posten*, or sending money.

Coping with serious family health problems was the theme of a later letter from Helene Marie, 4-23-1884. In it she thanked Matilda so much for her letter that had brought tears to her mother's eyes. Kjersti's sister, Marthe, had now died at age 92, and had been an invalid for ten years and 10 days. It is interesting she listed the length of time down to the number of days, perhaps because it had been such an ordeal? She wrote that Marthe had always been patient, never complaining, and believed it was God's will so she trusted it served His purpose that she was an invalid. Marthe was cared for by her daughter, Mathea, in her home all that time. She said her father, Lars, came down with typhoid fever and people avoided their road to stay away from this disease. Helene Marie nevertheless came and helped her parents, usually daily. Her mother, Helene, had to give him medicine drops every hour and a half day and night and she did that by herself for two months, nursing him back to health. It took a big toll on her mother, Helene. Her health went downhill, her hair turned gray and she generally aged a lot. They were hoping to build a new house at Roksvold farm since the old one has seen better days.

Hilda Øistad Garaas and Henrik Garaas, date unknown, but likely around 1906-7, close to the date they married. Location somewhere in Norway, likely near Hamar. Hilda is the daughter of Helene Marie Roksvold Dahl and Bernt Øistad, granddaughter of Helene Roksvold and Lars Dahl and grandniece of Ole and Anne Rocksvold. Helene was Ole's sister who didn't immigrate to the U.S. with the rest of the family, but stayed to farm with her husband in Norway.

Helene Marie also told of heart-breaking news that her daughter, Hilda, was a deaf mute, but there was a special school in Hamar to help her. Hilda was learning to speak, but it was hard for Helene Marie to leave her daughter "defenseless" there among strangers. As Helene Marie cried when Hilda left on her ride to that school, Hilda used sign language to ask why she was crying. Hilda stayed there in Hamar with an elderly mother whose daughter taught at the institute for the deaf. It was very expensive and Helene Marie missed Hilda terribly, but believed it was best for her future. They sometimes wished they were in America, but several things had prevented them from moving. She said half of her hair had turned gray from worry.

Lars Dahl let his mother-in-law, Kjersti Kjos Rocksvold, know in a March 6, 1886 letter, that Lar's son Peter Julius graduated first in his class at a public technical school in which students from all over Norway attended. He said Peter was working at a machine shop in Kristiania and Karl graduated first in his class at the teacher's college, called "seminary" at the time, and was teaching in East Toten the past 5 years. The position of precentor (leader of worship) in East Toten was open and the pastor was encouraging him to apply. Lars said his daughter, Helene Marie, had married Bernt Øistad, and was living in Kristiania with their three children. The oldest was Laura Matilda, age 15, who lived with Lars and would be confirmed that year. Lars said there had been many renovations, designed by Peter, to the Roksvold farm and the farmhouse is taller now.

Helene Dahl wrote to her mother, Kjersti Kjos Rocksvold on March 8, 1886, saying she was excited to get a letter from her and experienced the warmest of feelings and gratitude. She lamented that it has been 33 years since she last saw her mother when the family emigrated to the U.S. She said it is strange to think of her mother as now elderly and she herself was now 57. Kjersti had written that her husband Peder, Helene's father, had died. Helene wished her mother a smooth passage herself when her time came to die and thought of the joy of being with God and the hope they would all be united one day in heaven. Strangely, Helene wrote that this was " the first letter I have written to you and it may well be the last," perhaps referring to Kjersti being elderly and perhaps dying soon.

Why would this be the first letter Helene would write to her over 33 years or was it an proofreading error? It is hard to believe she hadn't written previous letters to her Mom, especially with the fervent expressions of love for her and thanking her for everything she has done since she was a child. Helene mentioned her husband still taught 39 weeks per year and she did housework, spinning, sewing, and weaving. They were both in good health.

Helene said the house renovation was almost complete, continuing in the 3-8-1886 letter. The house was still one story high but taller, so probably a higher ceiling/roof was created. They were painting the house inside and out. There was a large living room on the south end with 5 large adjacent windows and a large kitchen on the north end. In the middle there was a small room on the east side and opposite it is a large entryway. It was a very expensive project. They had a poor harvest, most of the grain crop froze, and the potatoes were badly damaged. Helene enjoyed getting the picture of Ole, and said he had changed so much she could hardly recognize him.

Helene Marie Roksvold Dahl Øistad, told Matilda that Helene Marie's daughter Hilda was exceptionally gifted and had learned to speak aloud and read and wasn't using sign language as many deaf-mute children have done, in a letter dated 3-26-1893. Helene said that Helene Marie's husband, Bernt Øistad, moved to the U.S. seven years ago and she had not heard anything from him for 5 years! Their daughter, Laura, moved to the U.S. in 1891, but no mention was made if her husband has visited Laura. How difficult it must have been for Helene Marie to be raising her 3 children after her husband abandoned them! And what could have been the reason?

Helene Marie broke the news to Ole in a letter dated 11-3-1903 (perhaps 1902 since the number is hard to read) that their crops were ruined due to frost. She was glad to get the letters from Ole stating he got home safely after his trip to Norway and was so honored to have him visit. She said Hilda kept saying she can "never, never forget her most cheerful, kind and pleasant uncle." A letter dated 3-14-1910, written by Helene Marie to Ole, thanked him for the "magnificent long letter" last month and commented on how lovely and steady his handwriting is at his age (78). She said it was exceptional what he was still able to do on the farm in Dakota, that they usually had great harvests, but was sorry to hear that some of Ole's crops got ruined by a hailstorm and his son's crops were all lost. She stated what great courage it takes to endure such losses. She loved reading the *Decorah Posten* newspaper editions that Ole kept sending. It sounds

Laura Øistad and Anton Roseth.
Likely taken in Minnesota, possibly in the area of Boyd. Laura was the daughter of Helene Marie Dahl and Bernt Øistad, and granddaughter of Helene Roksvold and Lar Dahl. She was the grandniece of Ole Rocksvold.

like Helene Marie felt very close to Ole despite having most of their contact be through written correspondence.

Helene Marie was delighted to get two letters from Ole recently, and was sorry to hear that Ole's eyesight was weakening, in a letter of 3-21-1915. She had heard from him that he was now living with son Norman and his wife, after having a conflict with Willie and his wife. Helene Marie thought it was "shameful" and mean how Ole was treated. (This situation will be discussed in more detail later.) Ole had sold his farms in Dakota and Iowa and was now living with Norman. He had asked in his letter if he had been unreasonable regarding the situation he had apparently described and she stated absolutely not. She was happy that daughter Laura and Anton were were doing so well in Boyd, MN, and wished she could see them, but didn't want to travel alone overseas. She said if Ole would come back again, she would travel with him back to the U.S. for a visit. Her brother Karl was dead at 58, after heart trouble, a stroke, arteriosclerosis, and mental "instability," but stated he was not mentally ill. There was a huge number of people at the funeral and a "sea of flowers." Hilda and Henrik had paid off their mortgage for their house. The war raged (presumably referring to WWI) with no end in sight. They could still buy wheat flour from America and considering themselves lucky to be able to still do so.

Helene Marie's brother, Peter Dahl, wrote a 12 page letter to Ole 11-4-1921, thanking him for his letter and acknowledged the handwriting isn't quite the same as decades ago when he wrote. He recalled that the same hand had held a firearm in "an historic struggle for freedom and humanity," which left powerful impressions on him and many others, although most of those have already died. Peter thanked Ole for the wonderful gift of *Decorah Posten* issues which brought reports of family life and Norwegian American activities which Peter appreciated so much. He was glad to hear Ole was in such good health, that his eye sight was a bit improved and that he could travel to a specialist this fall to see if anything more could be done to help him see better.

Times were hard in America and Norway, and goods were very expensive in Norway, and Peter gave examples. Peter believed the reason for the high costs were ruthless, unscrupulous speculators in the business community and cunning labor union leaders who arranged high salaries for themselves. Peter thought the labor leaders brought about higher wages for the workers through negotiations, but also gave themselves much higher salaries. The prices would go higher, the wages subsequently went higher and it was a vicious cycle. They sometimes had trouble finding buyers for their products because the prices were raised so high. Tens of thousands were unemployed then. The last two strikes, railroad and general strikes, did not succeed. This, all according to Peter.

A third factor in the economic woes of Norway was that the Norwegian currency's value had fallen. Peter said the U.S. had brought the Old World to its knees. England, Sweden, Denmark, and Norwegian currencies had lost a third of their value. He felt there were greedy middle men who raised the prices of imported goods. He said there were unscrupulous business people who had imported luxury goods at an unprecedented scale to earn lots of money in a short amount of time. Big shipowners lost many steamships to German torpedoes in the war and had ordered new ships at exorbitant prices, in the hundreds of millions. Peter stated the Bank of Norway had allowed speculation and lent out enormous amounts of unsecured money not backed by gold reserves.

Peter wrote he was sorry to weary his uncle Ole with this depressing discussion, but wanted to provide an overview of the situation. He said personally he and his wife worked in the city for 40 years, and 42 years, respectively, and had tried to save up a little for old age. Because of these financial problems - events in the world and corruption, they only had a quarter of what they originally had saved. They had no living children, with the only one born dying shortly after birth. With their financial state, they would have hardly been able to afford children anyway, despite being very frugal. Unfortunately his wife had been in fragile health, but still tried to take care of the household. Only the wealthy seemed to find domestic help. Peter himself had a weak left foot since childhood, but said he did not complain.

90th birthday greetings were extended by Peter to Ole in a 3-5-1922 letter. Peter spoke of 9 milestones in Ole's life, but didn't mention if Ole had listed them in a previous letter or if Peter just thought of the nine himself. Peter mentioned the third milestone being Ole's service in the Civil War in which for "24 performances" he played a role. Perhaps he was referring to 24 battles, but it is unclear. Peter listed milestone 7 as the trip back to Norway, "as agile as a youngster...even with unblemished teeth." Another possibility for the 9 milestones might be the 9 decades of his life, since the letter was written for Ole's 90th birthday. Peter said he has only known Ole from a distance, and now at advanced age is still "an independent spirit" and a 'self-made man,' a real veteran and a man of honor par excellence." Peter sent a greeting from his wife and called himself "your humble and most grateful nephew," as he inquired about Ole's health and eyesight.

After Ole had died in 1922, Peter wrote to Matilda 2-3-1924, describing the last couple of years of writing to Ole, her father. Before that, Peter's sister had written to Ole for many years. After she died in 1920, Peter started writing to Ole upon his 89th birthday in 1921. At that point, Ole was blind and had to dictate letters. Peter was so sad to read in the *Decorah Posten* of the death of Norman (Anton Norman, Ole's son), and then some weeks later, the death of Ole and his memorable funeral. He complimented Matilda on her grammar in Norwegian as "impeccable" and called her writing style "exemplary". Peter was writing to giving Matilda answers to questions about family history, perhaps in request by her son, Ernest, as he wrote his autobiography-family history assignment for college that year. Peter described for them what he knew of the ancestors.

Anne Mathea and Family

Moving on to Ole's other siblings, his twin sister, Anne Mathea, married Hans Evenrud from Brandbu, Hadeland, Norway, at Glenwood Township in Iowa in 1856. They had twin girls who died in infancy, Karoline and Theoline, next gave birth to Matilda (Tilla), Pauline, and Henry. Tilla, Pauline, and Henry all married and had children. Pauline married Paul Mickelson and had 8 children: Anna, Alma, Herbert, Leon, Ray, Mabel, Tilla, and Esther. They settled in the area around Polk County, in MN. Henry married Matilda Nilselokken and had 4 children: Harold, Muriel, Ruby, Esther. As far I can tell, they remained in IA at that time. Matilda (Tilla) married Anton Kirkeby, and had 7 children: Ida, Henry, Hans, Carl, Bernard, Alfred, George. I don't know if they all stayed in IA, but George ended up dying in Union Co., Oregon.

Paul and Pauline Evenrud Mickelson family.
From left, in back: Alma, Mabel, Herbert, Roy, Anna, Leon
From left, in front: Esther, Paul, Pauline, Tilla.
Pauline was the daughter of Anne Mathea Rocksvold Evenrud
and Hans Evenrud, and the niece of Ole Rocksvold.

Anton and Family

Ole's brother, Anton Peder, married Anne Amundsen Elvestuen and they lived on the first farm his parents bought when they arrived in America. They had four children, Peter, Clara, Emma, and Albert who all married and had families, plus helped raise Hillman Christian Kirkeby. Anton was confirmed in one of Rev. Koren's first classes, but never attended more school after arriving in the U.S. at age 14 except for one month. According to Ernest Anderson's autobiography, Anton nevertheless became one of the best writers in Winneshiek County and held the position of County recorder in 1883-4. Anton held every office in the township and volunteered at church. In addition, Anton was talented at drawing people's portraits in a few strokes. Anton tended to have health problems throughout his life and died from asthma age 47.

Anton Pederson Rocksvold with his wife, Anne Amundsen Elvestuen, likely taken around 1870's, marriage was in 1873, Decorah, IA. Anton was the younger brother of Ole Rocksvold. They were the parents of Peter, Clara, Emma, and Albert.

Anne Strandbakken's Siblings

I have no letters, and only one contact, a Sivesind relative, among the descendants of Anne's siblings: Maria, Ingeborg, Hans, Elena, Anders, Hans O., and Berthe. Maria married Hans Sandbeck, Ingeborg married Hans Ruen, and Elena married Guldbrand Gorgen. Hans died at 18 years old. Anders married Berthe Sivesind and Berthe married Joseph Babcock. There is additional information about each of them and their descendants in the *Kjøs-Eggebraaten* book.

Ole and Anne's Family Life

After Ole and Anne's wedding, Feb. 12, 1865, according to Ernest Anderson and documents in Ole's pension records written in Ole's own hand, they had 10 children: George Paulus (1865-1890) who died at age 24 (details to follow); Matilda (1867-1951) (spouse

The Ole and Anne Rocksvold Family, taken approximately 1890-1894.
In back from left: Theodor Olaf, Manda, Matilda
Middle Row from left: Carl, Emma, Ole, Anne, Hilda
Front row from left: Peter William "Willie," Anton Norman "Norman"
George had died in 1890. Theodor Victor had died 1871.

Anders O. Anderson); Carl Oscar (1868-1945); Theodore Victor (1870-71) who died of croup in infancy; Emma Theodora, (1872-1912) (spouse Oscar Amunrud); Manda Augusta (1874-1967); Theodore Olaf (1876-1894) who died of pneumonia at age 18; Hilda Oleana (1878-1964) (spouse Edward Ohnstad); Anthon Norman (1880-1922), called Norman (spouse Tilda Foss); and Peter Wilhelm (1882-1957), called Willie (spouse Helen Bengsten). Anne's mother, Marthe, died in 1871 of heart failure and dropsy.

A deed dated April 9, 1877, was signed by Ole and Anne Rockswold for land in Winneshiek County. So they apparently decided to buy 260 more acres for $2,000. There are maps in the appendices to show locations of farmlands at various years.

George Rocksvold, son of Ole and Anne Rocksvold
Decorah, IA, likely taken 1885-1890

George Rocksvold had a tragic farm accident at age 12 in 1877. According to Ernest Anderson's autobiography, George crushed his left leg between cogs of a threshing machine. He stood on an icy surface on a windy day while driving the horses, and fell. His leg was amputated six inches below the knee. Accidents with these type of machines were common at that time. Over the years improved guards were developed to prevent hands and legs from getting caught. George got an artificial limb and remained very active. He was able to walk so quickly and well that strangers didn't realize he had an artificial limb. Tragedy struck George again at 24. He got "brain fever," also known as the Grippe or influenza, and died.

Pauline Evenrud, Mathea's daughter, wrote to Matilda Rocksvold 10-3-1878, saying she was so sorry to hear of "Georgy's" accident, and wished she could come to see him, but could not at that time. She asked for a reply as soon as possible to find out how he was adjusting. She added she was very lonely and that her husband and Fred (unknown person) were out until 11 or 12 every night. The only pleasant news she had to tell was of a pleasure trip when her husband "allowed her" to take the horse and buggy for a ride.

So three of the Ole and Anne's ten children had illnesses that took their lives while still young, one as an infant (Theodore Victor), one at 18 (Theodore Olaf), one at 24 (George). Another son, Anton Norman, only lived to 47, barely closing in on middle age. It must have been so difficult in those days that most families couldn't reasonably expect to have all their children grow up and lead full lives. In addition, many women still died in childbirth at that time. I have read that at that time people sometimes even waited a while to name their babies, until they saw whether they were going to survive. Perhaps they were trying to partially steel themselves against possible loss. But as my mother, Florence Ohnstad Smith, described the many losses suffered by her mother, Hilda Rocksvold Ohnstad, grief from multiple losses was sometimes so debilitating that Hilda would go to bed for days and not come out of the room. There is no way to truly shield one's heart from the loss of one's child.

In addition to farming, for twenty-five years Ole was postmaster for Thoten, a part of Glenwood township. As a result, the Rocksvold family had frequent visits from neighbors while they were busy doing their farm chores. In *Kjøs-Eggebraaten Family History*, Lyla Ruen wrote people enjoyed the hospitality when they came to the Rocksvold farm to pick up their mail, as mail delivery to each home wasn't available back at that time. She also wrote that Anne was a very good mother and housekeeper and was "handy with the needle" as she sewed attractive clothing for her children.

Much insight can be gleaned about Ole's life and personality in a series of letters he wrote in the late 1890's to early 1900's. Letters Ole received from relatives and friends, and correspondence sent between relatives, also contain valuable information which add to our understanding of the person he was. Translations of the letters I am summarizing appear in the appendices of this book , if you would like to read the originals in their entirety.

Politics and Ole

On 10-8-1893, Andrew (also known as A.O.) Anderson wrote to his future wife, Matilda Rocksvold, Ole and Anne's daughter. After discussing other topics, A.O. mentioned reading in the *Decorah Posten* that Ole got the nomination for Democratic representative in the Iowa legislature, and asked if Ole went to Chicago as candidates generally did in the fall. Andrew then told Matilda that he had argued with Ole about politics some years ago. Andrew said he was "young and foolish" and carried it too far, and regretted it, especially with someone so much older than himself. He said the next year the arguing was worse, but that was the last of it. He said he had not disputed with Ole since and planned to never do it again as it was not proper at all. Andrew said he thought Ole and "Drake" (unknown person) were down on him on that account.

A.O. wished he hadn't been so "radical," and now when he and Matilda had developed their relationship he had pondered whether to ask her if Ole had ever mentioned the arguing. Andrew wrote that he knew Ole wouldn't care if Andrew didn't side with him because he was "too much of a practical and sensible man for that." Andrew said he had more respect for Ole than for anyone else there, even if they passed "impolite words." He described Ole as better posted (well-informed about current events.) He hoped Ole may not even have thought of the arguing since. Andrew didn't like to have to write about it, but he felt he wanted everything known between Matilda and him and hoped she would understand. Andrew asked her to let him know if she knew anything about these arguments and hoped Ole had forgotten about it. He also hoped he would be able to act in such as way as Ole would be pleased.

The issue of Ole running as a Democrat when he had been Republican for so long, raises a question. Why switch parties? Nathan Kalmoe, Ole's great-great-grandson and a political scientist, pointed out that the issues of prohibition and tariffs may have been factors in his decision. According to Wikipedia, Horace Boies served as governor of Iowa from 1890-94 and was the only Democrat that served as governor from 1855 to 1933. A former Republican, Boies switched to the Democratic party when the Republicans started supporting prohibition of alcohol and high tariffs, which hurt farmers. He was defeated during the hard times in 1893, the same year that Ole ran unsuccessfully for IA assembly as a Democrat. So perhaps that was the reason for Ole's switch of political parties. However we have no documentation about Ole's personal reason(s) for switching parties. It apparently wasn't a good election year for Democrats. In the article "Honored by Iowa Democrats," in the *New York Times*, Sept. 5, 1893, which Nathan located, it explained more about the Boies' party switch and about his opponent, Frank D. Jackson, to whom Boies lost that fall.

Nathan Kalmoe also found a research article, *Ethnocultural Voting Trends in Rural Iowa, 1890-1898*, in which it appears Winneshiek had a history of voting for Republicans, so Ole had less of a chance to win when he decided to switch parties sometime before running in the assembly race. Author Bruce Gunn Kelley, noted a pattern in voting related to cultural background and religion in Iowa at that time. He categorized the religious groups into the "liturgicals" and the "pietists." Liturgicals were those people whose religious beliefs emphasized faith alone for salvation, while Pietists believed they were divinely called to change the world, so that faith and "works" (actions) were essentials in their beliefs. Based on pre-1896 data collected by historian Paul Kleppner, the liturgicals tended to vote Democratic, while the pietists tended to vote Republican at that time. Cultural groups associated with more liturgical beliefs were Irish Catholics, German Catholics, and Bohemian Catholics. Cultural groups associated with more pietistic beliefs were the Dutch Reformed, Norwegian Lutherans and Swedish Lutherans. Those who were more mixed (about 55/45%) voting Democratic over Republican, respectively, were German Lutherans. Those mixed (about 55/45%) voting Republican over Democratic, respectively, were Danish Lutherans. Since Winneshiek County was predominately Scandinavian Lutheran (Norwegian, Swedish, Danish), most were voting Republican at that time.

You will remember in the 20th century there were changes in the platforms of the two parties which caused many people to change the party with which they were affiliated. Kelley explained that times were turbulent throughout the 1890's and the distinctions started to shift in voting patterns. There was much discontent among farmers as deflation caused them to get less for their crops, yet the interest in their debts continued constant. There was a depression in 1893 and much upheaval in the election of 1894, as voters tended to blame the majority Democratic Congress and President Cleveland for the troubles. By the 1896 elections, the Republicans were forming coalitions and were regarded as the moderate party, continuing to grow support nationally and in Iowa.

On Oct. 19, 1893, Matilda wrote to her future husband, Andrew (A.O.), referring to the dispute Andrew had had with Ole. Matilda later married Andrew June 11, 1894, so they must have been "courting" at that the time of the letter or were at least good friends since she showed concern about the dispute. She was teaching away from where Andrew lived. It was postmarked Washington Prairie, IA, near Glenwood, and sent to Inwood, where they ultimately lived together after marriage. Matilda wrote she finally was taking the chance to answer his long letter. She had tried to write earlier, but she kept getting stopped by people who wanted to talk, or wanted her to accompany them to a store or post office, or wanted her as company in their home, etc. Matilda also said Ole Ruen died and Matilda's mother looked poorly at the funeral. (Anne died July 4, 1895, age 55).

Finally on page six of the 10-19-1893 letter, Matilda brings up the dispute, so perhaps she was feeling uncomfortable bringing it up. Matilda wrote that Andrew asked in his letter if she had heard anything regarding the disputes he and Ole had had some time ago. She said she had heard something, but not very much from Ole and that he hadn't even mentioned Andrew's name since that time. She said others mentioned the dispute to her, but she can't remember specifically what was said, just that those two were "against each other." Matilda asked, "Were you really disputing so very much that you think he remembers yet, too? If so, I really do wish it had never taken place." She thought she should have asked Pa about it when she saw him Sunday, but since she didn't know the real cause or if it was his fault or Andrew's, nor the substance of argument, she thought it better not to say anything and keep still. She hoped it was forgotten and that they both would "feel towards one another as they ought to do."

Matilda said she was longing to have a talk with Andrew and was glad he was coming for Christmas, 9 weeks away. She said she was sorry she hadn't written sooner, but there had been much "disturbance" this week, but didn't allude to what. (Perhaps the funeral?) She hoped she wouldn't miss any more school days (perhaps to weather?) or she might have to teach on a Saturday to make it up. She said she would be starting work at the other school, but not until the first or second Monday in Nov., but didn't say which school. She signed her letter, "With much love, ever your sincere and loving Matilda." The closing for the letter may indicate they were in a close dating relationship by this time.

Here is the text, translated by Jim Skurdall, of the 10-3-1893 *Decorah Posten* article announcing Ole's nomination to run for assembly in IA.

> "*Decorah Posten* 10-3-1893
>
> The Democratic County Convention met at the courthouse on Saturday, the 30th of September, with A. Bernass presiding.
>
> Upon completion of the necessary preparations, nominations were opened for a representative to the legislature. The nominees were O. P. Rocksvold, Dan Shea, M. J. Volland, Dessow and I. Zuckmeyer.
>
> In the first round of voting, Rocksvold received 54 votes, Shea 9, Volland 32, Adams 2, Dessow 6, Zuckmeyer 6.
>
> In the final round, Rocksvold received 75 and Volland 40 votes, after which Mr. Rocksvold was declared to be the party's nominated candidate. "

Another letter written by Matilda to Andrew, 11-3-1893, is relevant in that it mentioned Ole running for Iowa assembly and included a newspaper clipping about it, the text of which will follow shortly. Matilda said she had company and was up late "fooling around" with a group of young relatives such as brother Theodore plus Oscar Amunrud, but wished she could have been writing to Andrew. She said the mail only goes out twice a week, so she wanted to get her letter written and mailed soon. She was to teach in the first school house east of Washington Prairie Post Office, about a mile from there on Waukon Road. She hadn't been in the school building yet, but heard they fixed it up nicely. Matilda found it hard to described how her mother, Anne, was - sometimes quite well, other times poorly. Her Mom said she couldn't sleep well and some nights not at all. Her father had been gone about a week, but Matilda expected him back tomorrow. The girls were working in the cornfield and she was the housekeeper, with much more work than she had time to do. She occasionally tended to her grandma, Kjersti Kjos Roksvold (who died Mar. 9, 1895 at 95 years old, 4 months before Matilda's mother, Anne). Tending to Grandma Kjersti's needs was a lot of work for Matilda as Kjersti's room was upstairs and she almost never left it. Only once that fall did Grandma Kjersti come downstairs to dinner, and then Kjersti thought she was lost. Matilda wrote to not think or feel sorry for all the writing about "you know what." That it is fine and she doesn't think anymore about it. Perhaps this "you know what" was regarding the dispute between Ole and Andrew? There are no more clues about the topic.

Here is the text of the undated enclosed clipping that was sent with the 11-3-1893 letter. There was no citation from which newspaper it came. It has "1893" hand printed on it:

> "O.P. Rocksvold, democratic candidate for representative, was in the city Saturday. All who met him were free to say he was a pleasant and good hearted man. There are very few men in the county who have a more thorough knowledge of public affairs than Mr. Rocksvold. A constant student of political issues, and a thoroughly honest and consciencious (sic) man, which qualifies him for the position the democracy of Winnesheik county have nominated him. He has resided near Thoten in Glenwood township for over forty years; is an old soldier, and Norwegian by birth. A vote for Rocksvold is a vote for honest government."

I was not able to locate in the Luther College archives this paragraph among the political articles in the two local newspapers in the Decorah area that summer or fall of 1893 to identify the date when it was printed. Unfortunately his election bid to be the representative of Winneshiek (as it is spelled today) County in the Iowa legislature was unsuccessful. Ole Rocksvold, 1931 votes, W. H. Klemme, 2636 votes.

On Sept. 22, 1894 Ole, at age 62, applied for a pension for his service in the Civil War. He went through a lot of bureaucratic hassles to get it. Ole had to get several fellow soldiers and family members to write documents to vouch as having served with him or had witnessed his health infirmities during and after the war, such as rheumatism, piles, fever, chills, heart trouble, and a bullet wound in his right thigh. Apparently there had been some instances of fraud so the government was trying to be extra careful before granting pension money. There are many pages of forms over subsequent years, many in poor handwriting by clerks, but apparently Ole's pension eventually got approved and increased over time as his health worsened, requiring more paperwork.

Ole Rocksvold's post- Civil War letters that we have start with the date 12-17-1894 when he wrote to the government to have them correct the spelling of his last name, Rockswold, which had been misspelled repeatedly in military documents. As mentioned earlier, he eventually gave up and just went by "Rocksvold" because by 1895 he was signing letters with the "Rocksvold" spelling. Translations of all of his letters are in the appendices so they can be read in their entirety. Some other letters Ole received from relatives and friends also appear in the appendices. They were selected to give the reader a sense of what life was like living then and there, plus provide more clues into Ole's personality and the relationships Ole had with these people.

Matilda Rocksvold and A.O. (Andrew) Anderson's wedding picture, June 11, 1894, Decorah, IA. Matilda was the daughter of Ole and Anne Rocksvold. They made their farm home at Inwood, IA.

Ole's Family in 1895

What was happening with Ole and Anne's children by 1895 when we have Ole's next letter, dated 3-20 and continued 3-22, 1895? By this date, Matilda, the oldest child, was 28, married to A.O. Anderson, and living on a farm in Inwood, in the northwest corner of Iowa. None of Matilda and A.O.'s three children, Irene, George, nor Ernest, had been born yet.

As for Ole and Anne's son, Carl, 26 years old in 1895, was single, and remained so all of his life. Daughter Emma was soon to be 23, married to Oscar Amunrud, and pregnant with her first child. The couple eventually had 7 children- Alberta, Olive, Edna, F. Norma, Reuben and Roy (twins), and Magdalene. They farmed in Wibaux, in eastern MT, near Beach, ND. Ole and Anne's daughter,

Matilda Rocksvold, fourth from left, with a group of ladies, perhaps
friends or fellow teachers.
Matilda was the daughter of Ole and Anne Rocksvold. Likely taken near
Decorah, IA, in early or mid-1890's.

Matilda Rocksvold and A.O. Anderson wedding at Ole and Anne Rocksvold's house.
June 11, 1894, Glenwood Township, Decorah, IA.

Emma Rocksvold Amunrud, daughter of
Ole and Anne Rocksvold
Picture taken probably 1888-1894
Location unknown, likely Decorah, IA

Hilda Rocksvold, daughter of Ole and Anne
Rocksvold, mother of Florence Ohnstad
Smith, grandmother of author, Sharon Smith
Bowen. Location, unknown, likely Decorah,
IA, taken probably about 1888-90

Manda, was soon to be 21 at the time of the letter in March, 1895, was single, and remained so all her life. She did housework for others, and suffered from mental/cognitive health challenges which were not clearly defined, living for some years in an Iowa "institute." Based on her letter-writing, she was literate. As mentioned earlier, Theodor Olaf died at age 18 , one year prior to this letter. Hilda, my maternal grandma, was 16 in 1895, and didn't marry Edward Ohnstad until she was 32. Anton Norman was 14 at the time of this 1895 letter, and he married at age 27. Peter William (Willie) was 12 then. More will follow later about Hilda, Norman, and Willie.

Ole, almost 63 year old, wrote to Matilda and A. O. to let them know that Ole's mother, Kjersti, had died after much suffering and being an invalid in their home. He wrote he was glad she was at peace with God. Ole mentioned that Pastor Hellestvedt came to the house the day of the funeral and spoke at the church. He mentioned that about half of those in attendance were from Pastor Borge's congregation and were warmly welcomed. So it sounds like sometime between Jan. 7, 1890, the last time Ole's name is mentioned in Glenwood Church minutes, and this letter, 3-20-1895, was when Ole changed his membership from the Glenwood church to St. John's Lutheran Church in Waukon where Pastor Hellestvedt was pastor at the time. I attempted to get a copy of any church meeting minutes at St. John's to see if Ole's name was listed in there, but the people there weren't able to find any that had his name mentioned.

From left: Carl, Anton Norman (Norman), Peter William (Willie)
Rocksvold, sons of Ole and Anne Rocksvold
Picture taken probably between 1910-1915. Decorah, IA

Kjersti's and Anne's Deaths

Interestingly, when Ole's mother, Kjersti, died March 9, 1895, Ole had her buried in the Glenwood Church cemetery in the Rocksvold family plot beside her husband and other family members. He mentioned he didn't have permission to bury her there since he had left the congregation, and had gotten a message to that effect. However, he said he acted as if he didn't know about this rule and no one bothered him about it after that.

Ole mentioned that he traveled with Pastor Hellestvedt and Pastor Jacobsen to the conference of the Decorah district at Springfield Church. He loved the experience so much that he described it as being in "an ocean of God's love." Ole also mentioned in this long letter that his wife, Anne, continued to be very ill with a bad cough, difficulty breathing, was very tired, sore, and tender all over. He said her current condition was about the same as she had been at the time of Theodor's funeral the previous year. She had also developed dropsy (edema), for which Dr. Wilcox had had some success in treating. He added he was sending Matilda and A. O. clover, Scotch barley and oats to plant.

Ole's wife, Anne, died on July 4, 1895, age 55, but we have no letter from that time until 2-14-1896. Her death isn't mentioned in this letter, written 7 months later. According to Ernest Anderson's autobiography, Anne died of a "hemorage (sic) caused by cancer under her left arm." My mother, Florence Ohnstad Smith, had heard Grandma Anne had heart trouble, so perhaps she had both ailments or there could have been a misunderstanding since Florence wasn't born until 1920. Since Ole's mother, Kjersti, had died March 9, 1895, he lost both his mother and his wife within 4 months. It must have been a very painful time to have two major losses so close together. And this in addition to the grief from previous losses: infant son Theodore Victor died in 1871, Ole's father in 1885, son George in 1890, and son Theodore Olaf in March 1894. When Anne died, there were still children at home for Ole to care for as a single parent. The living children at the time of Anne's death were Matilda, 28, Carl, 27, Emma, 23, Manda, 21, Hilda, 16, Anton Norman, 14, and Peter William, 12. My mother, Florence Ohnstad Smith, said her mother Hilda did much of the housework and child care for her younger brothers after her mother died since the older siblings had moved out of the home and already had jobs by that time.

Ole mentioned it had been so long since he had heard from Matilda, he was wondering if they were "dead or alive." Many people had been very sick with terrible coughs, including Ole, but he was finally getting better. Ole said the ladies aid bought an organ for the church for $100 by Mason and Hamlin. The Decorah Lutheran Church had bought one for $1500 for their church from Aase Haugen. Carl, Oscar, Manda, and Ole went to hear a concert on it by Louis Falk, whom Ole described as the best organist in America. Falk was an organist in Chicago and also a professor there. It sounds like Ole was very interested in music since he made a point of describing the organ purchase and the concert.

Ole sent four bags of Salzer Barley to Matilda, which Ole mentioned in his April 3, 1896 letter. Ole wrote that he was very upset by a "love letter" he received from Pastor Borge of the Glenwood church. This story was previously mentioned in the section about the Glenwood church history and Ole's part in it, but in this letter there was more about the circumstances leading up to receiving the letter. Ole wrote that he had gone to Rev. Borge's house to get a baptismal certificate for "Tonny" (probably a childhood nickname for Anton Norman), but didn't find him home. He then asked Borge's wife to prepare a birth certificate for him and Willie at the same time. (Note: This occurred around the age of confirmation for Norman so perhaps that is why they wanted to get those copies.) When Tonny went to pick up the certificates the next day, Borge had him wait while he wrote a long letter to Ole and sent it along with Tonny to bring home to Ole. Ole further mentioned that the date of confirmation would be either the first or second Sunday after Easter. He also described bad snow and stormy weather even though it was April.

Hilda, Matilda's sister, had developed an abscess on her kidney and was in much pain along with another illness, unnamed, as described in Ole's 9-9-1901 letter to Matilda. Dr. Wilcox has made a housecall every other day for 4 weeks. Yesterday Dr. Wilcox and another person, Dr. Jule, had put a needle in the abscess and made a two-inch incision because of the extent of the liquid within. They withdrew about a half gallon of pus! Hilda was doing better, woke up from the anesthetic, her fever was down, and she was "calm and compliant, never uttering a complaint." He also mentioned extreme weather, going months without rain, and then getting rain in torrents. What a challenge to deal with such weather as a farmer!

Ole's Trip to Norway

Ole wanted to return to the land of his birth. In a letter to Matilda, May 16, 1902, Ole mentioned he was planning a trip to Norway with Ole Kjørlien in Decorah. Ole Rocksvold was now 70 and both Oles originally planned to time the trip so it would be exactly 50 years since they emigrated, but decided instead to go "now or never." They departed New York City June 6, on the *Celtic,* the White Star Line's largest ship. (Incidentally, the White Star Line's ship, the *Titanic,* sunk ten years later.) Carl sold out his land to Oscar and was coming home to circumvent the need to find someone to take care of Carl's farm.

On his first leg of the trip to Norway, Ole sent a post card from Washington, D.C, June 4, 1902. He visited Gilbert Haugen, representative from Iowa in the 57th Congress, 4th district, the new library building, and museums, and Washington Monument. At the White House, Ole saw Theodore Roosevelt leaving the building, but didn't get to meet him. They also visited the Departments of the Army, Navy, Agriculture and the Treasury building. They had dinner at the Havigs' house, "one of the finest evenings of his life." (I don't know who the Havigs were.)

Ole sent a letter from the Dahl farm at Vang, Valdres, Norway on July 15,1902. He had been moving around a lot. Ole and he spent a week in Christiania (later called Oslo), with many special attractions, and on Midsummer's Eve or Day (known as "Sankt Hans") they took the train to Eidsvoll. Then they went to Trøkstad in Ulsager (Ellensaker) for an excursion to Gardemoen where 6,000 men were stationed. Next they went to Minne, stayed overnight and then traveled by boat to Gjøvik. Ole said it was magnificent to sail on Lake Mjøsa, but the dry weather made the scenery not as lovely as usual. They stayed overnight at Gjøvik and the next morning hurried to the Rocksvold farm. Relatives and friends were waiting for them since the Decorah Posten had tipped them off that the two Oles were coming! Niece Helene Marie looked older due to the many cares she has had in her life. Helene Marie's daughter, Hilda, wasn't home when the two Oles arrived. She was sewing in Hamar, but wanted to be home when Ole came back again to visit later during his trip. Ole stayed at the Rocksvold farm for a week. He was able to attend the funeral of Mathea Hagesven/Hagenstue, his first cousin, July 3, then July 4 traveled to Hadeland (where his wife's family was from), and on the 8th took a steamer to Røkenvik to Odness in Sondre Land.

Next they went to Valdres, where they were at the time the letter was written, and planned to stay a few more days. Ole said the people there were the most hospitable he knew. Wherever they went, Ole and Ole were given the best accommodations and the hosts went to great lengths to entertain. Ole Rocksvold also had the chance to walk on a glacier. Next they went to Laerdal, Bergen, Hardanger, "Waas" (Voss), then Trondheim. After that they planned a quick trip south to Toke and would stay a while before they returned in late August, but he couldn't give a more detailed itinerary at that time. Ole wrote that he wished he had more time at the Rocksvold farm because there were so many people he didn't have time to see, but said he would do better next time, when he returned during this same trip. He said he felt great to be in these wonderful surroundings and walked further in one day than he usually did for a week in America.

A ten-page letter couldn't contain all that Ole had experienced, when he wrote on Aug. 4, 1902 from Trondheim. He recapped the earlier part of his trip in more detail, then went on to mention travels to western Norway, Vang, Grindeheim, Gudvangen, and Stalheim. He was greatly impressed with the waterfalls and mountains and the fjords there. He went to Bergen, climbed mountains and saw museums there. In Trondheim he found the cathedral spectacular, as well as many historical sites and other places of beauty. The two Oles planned to leave Aug. 6 for Hamar, then go back to Toten for more visiting, and then on to Christiania by Aug. 15. He planned to leave for England Aug. 17, and from there on Aug. 22 would leave for the U.S. He was healthy, but it had been unusually cold so he needed to wear his overcoat most of the time.

Back home again in Iowa, while writing 9-29-1902, Ole told Matilda he could not have hoped for a better time on his trip, everyone was so kind to them. He had gotten home Sept. 6. Unfortunately his coughing problems returned again. He hoped to visit Matilda in person that fall to tell more about the trip. He had visited with Hilda Rocksvold (Øistad), Helene Marie's daughter, and Helene Rocksvold Dahl's granddaughter. Hilda was deaf and Ole described her as "magnificent" and said they had good conversations together. Since we learned earlier that Hilda was taught to speak, not just use sign language, we can surmise that she spoke to Ole rather than had a signer translate. Hilda waited on him "hand and foot" while visiting and said she wanted to come to America. She and her mother accompanied him to Gjøvik as he was leaving and waved handkerchiefs as long as they could see each other as he departed.

Ole said the Norwegian relatives sent their greetings. He was experiencing pain in one side so it was hard to get up from a chair. He mentioned Iver and Kari Berge and Joseph moved to Northwood, ND (west of Grand Forks). The *Kjøs-Eggebraaten* book indicates that Kari was a niece of Anne Elvestuen Rocksvold, Ole's brother Anton's wife.

Health Challenges and Family News

Ole regretted that he had been a poor correspondent when he wrote to Matilda on March 13, 1903. He wanted to come out to visit in the fall or winter, but had had a bad cold and didn't feel well all of the fall, either. They didn't thresh until right before Christmas and had 12 acres of corn to husk after New Year's. Peter didn't finish threshing until after New Year's and had been sawing lumber all over Allamakee County (east of Decorah) with Carl. On March 23 they were to leave for their farm in North Dakota. They were bringing 4 teams of horses and had 300 acres to plow and sow. Carl and Albert (probably Anton's son) planned to be farming that summer and Peter had been thinking about going there to help them set up, but then returned since he had so much to plant and thresh. Emma was going to keep house for them. She had been working at Haugen's in Decorah earning 5 dollars a week, a pretty good wage. Ole received a letter from Hilda Rocksvold in Norway with a picture of her, which he enclosed for Matilda to look at and return, saying he had received a picture last year of Helene Marie, Laura, and Hilda last year.

There is a letter from Ole to Matilda with no date on the first page that we can likely presume was written April 30, as the fourth page is dated May 1, 1903. Based on the contents of the first page it was written after Ole's Norway trip. He discussed friends and acquaintances dying, and said that Alberta, Emma's daughter, came home from school, but was now back for spring term. Emma wrote to Hilda Rocksvold in Norway while visiting Ole and had gotten quite good at writing in Norwegian. He hadn't gotten a letter from Carl since he left for Dakota (Northwood). Albert, Ole's brother Anton's son, was up helping Carl while Peter was gone. Emma came along to keep house there, too. Ole wrote that Carl and Peter's land was 6 times the acreage of the Rocksvold farm in Norway, which Ole's estimated is about 50 acres, including forest, hayfields and cultivated fields. Ole brought back gifts from Norway on his trip, but not enough to meet demand. He had a total of eighteen brooches, but only had 3 left. He planned to mail them to Matilda, Irene, and George. He apologized that he had no present for Ernest and A.O. that he could put in a letter. Ole waited one day to mail this letter to see if Matilda's letter would arrive before mailing it. He had received a long letter from Matilda May 1, and thanked her. He did not get a letter from Carl, but they were very busy plowing 200 acres.

Emma had told Ole she found it hard to be alone from 6:30 in the morning until 7 or 8 in the evening while the men worked out in the fields, Ole explained in a 5-28-1903 letter to Matilda. Emma said she thought she would go visit Northwood, ND, to see people there, including the Berges. Ole mentioned he might be elected as a delegate to the church meeting in Duluth. He had promised Helene Marie that he would visit her daughter, Laura, in Boyd (near Montevideo, MN). He thought he might do that on the way to Duluth. Ole resigned as postmaster after 25 years at Thoten effective July 1. They planned to close the Thoten post office.

"Quite a Bit Left of Him"

On Dec. 21, 1903 Ole wrote to tell Matilda the Norwegian relatives were asking for a photo of him, especially those who weren't able to see him during his 1902 trip there. They said they were surprised to see there was "quite a bit left of him" after being gone so long from Norway, saying that many people, after coming over from the U.S., tended to "dry up so there is nothing left but skin and bones"! He mentioned that Matilda must have heard of the wedding of Emma by now. He said he had received only one letter from Carl, and it was good, both in handwriting and content, so "there was no need for him to be ashamed." (Perhaps Carl found learning to write English a challenge or didn't feel very confident about it.) It sounded like Peter took more risks than Carl about going into debt in the hope of cultivating and growing more crops.

Continuing from 12-21-1903 letter, Ole asked if Hilda (probably his daughter) had written anything to Matilda about "the wedding" and she had said no. For this wedding, Ole mentioned that Peter was putting up a temporary addition to their house, 20 feet by 32 feet, to make room for 60 to eat at a time. So perhaps it was the wedding of a sibling of Peter Rocksvold, son of Anton, Ole's brother. The wedding had 200 guests. Ole also mentioned that Pastor Hellestvedt "became so difficult to work with" that he had to resign and now Pastor Fjelde has been called. Ole also mentioned that Matilda must have heard that Emma had twins recently. Ole said they gave the twins each 3 names which he felt was "extravagant." He joked that at that rate Emma was going to use up all the names!

Matilda learned that Ole's hand had been trembling, he must necessarily use a pencil now, and apologized for his penmanship, Ole, said in a 2-10-1905 letter at age 72. It had been unusually cold and snowy, with many roads impassable. Sometimes the mailman couldn't get through. It had been -35 degrees (below zero) the previous week. Ole mentioned not hearing from his daughter, Manda, nor "any of them" for a long time. Ferdinand Kirkeby said Manda told them she would be home for Christmas, but Ole said they didn't see her. He encouraged Matilda to write to Norway because Helene Marie and the family got so excited when receiving any letters from them. Ole said he had to stay indoors most of the winter, but nevertheless had been to Decorah several times and to church every other week. He said to tell George to write or else Ole wouldn't write to him.

In the same 2-10-1905 letter, Ole also mentioned his twin sister, Mathea Evenrud, was in bed sick with cancer in her internal organs. The doctor was predicting she would die within two months. She had known for 6 months, but didn't tell anyone because she didn't want an operation. Now it was too late and had spread through her bloodstream. He said she was composed, but trembled a little, and said the Lord's will be done. Ole awaited a letter from Helene Marie, but heard in the last one that her daughter, Hilda, was getting married this fall. She had been engaged for ten years to a man (Henrik Garaas) who worked at a repair shop and was a good mechanic. They were both deaf, but spoke, read, and wrote in Norwegian. Ole also mentioned that Karl Sagvold, one of Helen Rocksvold Dahl's children, was now a teacher. Ole also said he hadn't heard from Karl in Mandan, ND and Ole hadn't written for a long time. Ole's felt they had little interest in whether Ole was alive or dead. (Perhaps because Karl hadn't taken time to write or perhaps there were other issues we don't know about.) There were descriptions of crops and weather challenges, but Peter and Albert were doing well. Ole had a bad cough and difficulty breathing, but would respond to George and Irene's letters soon.

Contact with a Civil War Comrade

Ole received a letter from his comrade in the Civil War, John Steen, April 13, 1906, asking if he was going to the dedication of the monument to Iowa at the Civil War battlefield at Shiloh Nov. 23, 1906. The Illinois Railroad was offering half-priced tickets for the veterans to make this trip. John said he moved to Wahoo, Nebraska, almost three years ago. John reminisced about he and Ole being the first two to be selected for guard duty as they arrived at Camp Union Oct. 26, 1961, and were the first to make corporal. The cold and suffering of Fort Donelson was also remembered. John said he visited Rev. Koren in Minneapolis last Nov. and he was still intellectually strong. John sent greetings to Ole's sister, "Mrs. Evenrud," (Anne Mathea) and to the old friends and neighbors. He recalled visiting Mr. and Mrs. Hans Ruen and also Andrew Strandbakken three years ago. He asked if Ole was taking another trip to Norway. John's wife went 3 years ago and stayed 14 months and wanted to go again. John said many were going this year, but he preferred not to go when there was a crowd.

Twin Mathea's Death

On April 19, 1906, Ole wrote to Matilda's family to let them know Mathea died on the 12th. She predicted she would die on Maundy Thursday and she did! Ole also mentioned that Anders Strandbakken, Ole's wife's brother, was now completely blind, went to the hospital in St. Paul for treatment for 2 months, but it didn't help and was back home. He would write more about Mathea later since the postman was coming soon.

Ole said he was mailing corn to Matilda and A.O., mentioned in a letter, 5-4-1907. Other news included Edgar Wangsness dying of typhoid fever and Ole had been sick with the influenza.

Buying Beach, ND, Property

Ole traveled to Golden Valley, ND, near Beach, to look at land and found Section 23 T 141 R 105 and the north half of section 23 available, he wrote to Matilda in June, 1907. He said it was the loveliest he has ever seen so he bought it for $17 per half-section. (A section of land is one square mile or 640 acres.) It was 7 miles north and one mile east of Beach. The value of this land had increased greatly and Ole thought perhaps Carl would have been more successful coming here instead of northeastern ND. There had been no crop failures there so far. Carl was going to come and look at it, and if he liked it might sell the farm where he was currently. Carl sent a picture of Matilda's farm with a snow drift 5 feet high between the house and barn, taken April 27. Carl hadn't been able to begin planting until mid-May and it was still freezing almost every night then. Ole went to St. Paul for the annual meeting in Northfield (probably a church conference). This time he wasn't a delegate, so he just went for one day. Ole was healthy.

On the third of July, 1907, Ole signed a document selling the partial sections of 14 and 15 he had owned in Winneshiek County to G.G. Lundtvedt and Bramine Lundtvedt for $2,000.

Ole wrote to Matilda on Oct. 17, 1907, that it had been so long since he wrote them, he couldn't remember when it was. Ole hired someone to plow the land he bought near Beach last spring and had someone check to make sure the hired man did a good job, and he had. Ole went there with Carl to look it over in July to see if Carl wanted to move there and sell the other property. The crops looked good and they had a lot fewer weeds than in northeastern ND. There were rumors Albert was engaged to a Danish girl and would stay up in northeastern ND, even if Carl would sell everything. Albert lived with a family from which he wanted to buy land at $25 per acre. Carl was looking at land a mile and a half from Ole's near Beach, ND. Ole was the first person from Winneshiek County to travel out to Golden Valley. When Ole told them how good it looked, several from Iowa went out there, looked at the crops and decided to buy land there. Ole said on his Iowa farm the oats have been the worst ever, but barley was quite good. Corn was better than expected. He also was growing potatoes, timothy, and flax.

Ole had arranged an option for land for Carl if he wanted it, but Carl didn't respond for a long time, so the person sold it to someone else. In this 11-19-1907 letter, Ole explained he had received a letter from Carl saying he wanted it after all, but Ole told him it was too late. Most of the land out in Golden Valley had been sold now. Ole had recently returned from his third trip there. Ole traveled by train to St. Paul. Since more people from Glenwood were on their way to Golden Valley from there, also, he traveled with them by car and wagon. Ole looked at more land with a company secretary and decided to buy a quarter section more, with Carl in mind, in case he wanted that land. Carl had sold his land now in the Red River Valley (area near Fargo, ND, Moorhead, MN) and planned to come down that winter. In this letter Ole repeated the rumor that Albert planned to marry a Danish girl. On his way home from Beach, Ole went to Casselton and Northwood, near Fargo, ND, to visit people who had wanted him to visit for a long time, including Gilbert Tangen. He was gone 2 weeks, traveled 1,725 miles by train, and at least an additional 300 miles by automobile near Golden Valley. Ole's hired help threshed while he was gone from his farm, and a good yield in barley, oats, and corn was achieved.

Carl sent Ole a $800 bill of exchange towards the purchase of the land near Beach. In this Dec. 31, 1907 letter, Ole wrote that as he traveled through Mason City he heard that Hilda had been preparing a reception for the "newlyweds" but doesn't say who they are. (Based on the month and year, it must have been Ole's son, Anton Norman and Tilda

Foss.) The reception was Dec. 28, was great fun, and they had over 100 people, with many staying until dawn. Ole got a notice that his pension claim from the government for his service in the Civil War was approved. This was the last letter we have postmarked from Iowa before he moved to his land north of Beach, ND.

Ole's Move to Beach, ND

Now it was moving time for Ole. In a letter written March 31, 1908, Ole told Matilda he had arrived March 20 at the newly-purchased land near Beach, ND. Temporarily son Willie, daughter Hilda, and Ole were living in a house two and a half miles from the land. It was owned by a widow who had moved into Beach. It is 20 square feet with two rooms, plus a shed for two cows and Moxi, a horse. The other 4 horses stayed in a tent. Ole planned to build a barn first, 32 ft. X 18 ft., and then a house 24 ft. X 16 ft. to live in that summer and later use it as a granary. Ole said their half-section here was known as the prettiest and best in the whole valley. He planned to grow oats, so they would be busy building, disking, and breaking the new land. Mr. Noben would help break the land, too. They had plenty of snow that winter to provide good moisture for a bountiful harvest for fall. People who cut the hay from it would be asked to give him some. A huge number of newcomers were arriving this spring, with 5-10 carloads of livestock coming daily from WI, MN, IA, IL, IN, and ND. The Stondal Company had only 5,000 acres left to sell, far from town, hilly, and poor quality. Hilda liked this new location and was looking forward to seeing their farmland. Ole said he was fortunate they had a house to live in, as many were camping outside. They brought a 22 disk drill, walking plow, disk, drag, 2 wagons, and a buggy, 150 fence posts, oak lumber, stove, beds, table and chairs, bedding and food to be independent. Since they were 5 miles from a coal mine, they could pick up loose coal for 1 dollar. After they moved to their own land, they would be only 3 miles from the coal mine.

On March 9, 1909, Ole wrote from Decorah to Matilda. It sounded like he spent the winter there. Ole planned to visit Matilda's family on the 23rd and said he should tell her the surprise that Edna Amunrud was coming along, but he won't say any more. They had a beautiful winter in Decorah. Anton Kirkeby sold everything at an auction. He heard the winters in (western) Dakota were mild and beautiful. He was anxious to get out there again and didn't feel as well here as in Dakota. Hilda, his daughter, wrote she was glad she was not down in Iowa and snowed in. She wrote that the weather there in March was more like May in Iowa. They haven't had snow for a long time.

Ole arrived safely on a trip to Fargo and stayed at Hotel Norden (probably stopping to visit Hilda and others in the area), Ole told Matilda in a 4-1-1909 letter written from Beach. He took the *Flyer* train to Beach and it was packed. The weather was beautiful but had been cold lately.

Someone named Inger Faaren of Red Wing, MN, wrote to Ole June 15, 1909, addressed to "Dear Uncle" responding to a letter from him. She might possibly be a daughter of someone in Ole's sister Mathea Rocksvold Evenrud's line. She said she thought it was a good idea of his to go to Mexico and she hoped he would be able to do a trip there. This is the first mention in any letter of Ole even considering a trip there, but we have no evidence that he ever went. She said she would like to do such a trip herself, but couldn't afford it. She said she was always tired and hoped to live long enough to retire.

Ole wrote from Beach saying he was harvesting oats. The Aug. 24, 1909 letter from Ole to Matilda, added there was a hailstorm July 10 which did some damage so the crop didn't mature evenly, but it was a good harvest nonetheless. The wheat was excellent, no rust, 30 bushels an acre. They had 140 acres of oats, 50 of wheat, 40 acres of flax, lots of potatoes and hay, 7 of barley, but the barley and corn were ruined by the storm. They have had a lot of rain that summer so fields stood under water for long periods of time. There were 30 inches of rain since the middle of May. The rest of the letter was written Aug. 30. A neighbor had helped one day with the harvesting. All in all, it was a good year for wheat and oats. There had been no 100 degree days this summer, 92 was the hottest. They had a grove of a thousand Norway poplars they planted last spring, now 5 feet high. A grain elevator was being constructed in Beach, a flour mill was soon to be built, and a new bank was just started.

In 1910, Ole joined Totenlag, a Norwegian-American alliance formed in that year, to maintain a bond of friendship between people of Toten, Norway, and those who emigrated from Toten to the U.S. The organization continues today in creating friendships and assisting people in their genealogical efforts and I am a member. Sheila Andorfer of the U.S. and Mette Nordengen in Norway helped me with my efforts in research Ole and his ancestors. A picture of the pin Ole wore as a member of the Totenlag is in this book.

Edward Ohnstad, Future Husband of Hilda, Hired

Ole had finished planting 180 acres of wheat, 60 acres of barley and oats, with help. In the May 8, 1910 letter to Matilda, Ole said they had 240 acres altogether and 160 acres of that they plowed that spring, about 7 acres per day. They disked and harrowed twice before planting and then harrowed again and went over everything 6 times, all the plowing done twice and harrowing after planting to make the best growing conditions possible. (Harrowing is using an implement, after plowing, that breaks up the clumps of soil.) They had plenty of rain.

Continuing in his 5-8-1810 letter, Ole wrote that they hired a person for the summer to help them at $35 per month. He was good, hardworking, could run every kind of machine, was good with horses, and so they were very fortunate to have him. (He was describing Edward Ohnstad, Hilda's future husband.) Ole wrote that the hired man's father (Johannes Monsen Ohnstad) lived 15 miles north of Fargo and had a farm of 700 acres. The letter continued May 10. Mrs. Lundtvedt needed an operation in Fergus Falls and Ole accompanied her there until the operation was over, which turned out to be two operations. He stood and watched the operation the whole time. (It is interesting that they allowed that!) They did not get a terrible storm like Iowa had in April, only some cold rain and a little frost. A huge amount of new land was being cultivated this year and the cost per acre was reaching $60, up from in the teens when he bought. They planted 21 fruit trees that spring. They planted 1500 more of the trees they planted last year. They had 11 hogs, 2 cows, 1 heifer, 1 heifer calf, a bull, hen, and a jackrabbit, and, of course, their horses. Hilda had fun with the rabbit. Hilda had a camera and was enjoying taking pictures, but was still learning how to use the camera. In addition to the other horses, they bought a brown mare which Hilda would probably be riding quite a bit.

Ole wrote a postcard in February of 1910, postmarked Decorah, to Ernest, Matilda's son, and said Willie left for Beach and found everything in the best of order (but doesn't say where Willie had been coming from, so perhaps he was visiting Decorah.)

Ole wrote Matilda from Beach on June 13, 1910. (Perhaps Ole went back to Decorah for the winter and they were living near Beach during the months when farming work needed to be done. Our translator, Jim Skurdall, thinks Ole meant to write July 13 instead of June, based on the content). They had visitors from Iowa, Peter and Albert Sivesind, and O'Bryan and Peter from Waukon. Ole accompanied Albert to Fargo June 29 for a short visit with Carl and Albert. Albert had to be at a school board meeting July 1, so Ole stayed only a short time. The visitors said the crops near Beach looked the best, as east of there everything had dried up, but there near Beach it was lush and green. Ole expected an excellent harvest as long as there were no hail storms, etc. He bought hail insurance, the maximum for a section- 200 acres, $8 per acre, $1600 all together.

In Fargo, ND, it looked bad after a big snowstorm in early May. Ole said that folks there had planted under miserable conditions and since then hadn't had any rain. There were cracks in the ground wider than his hand. The wind was more destructive than the drought, though. Carl and Albert had 35 acres of barley which had not sprouted yet. There were weeds everywhere along the Red River near Fargo, getting worse each year. Some on both sides of Grafton had already plowed their wheat and oats under because it looked so bad. It was very unfortunate for Carl and Albert who lost their entire crop of 160 acres the previous year. At least they got enough of a harvest from the quarter section that they lived on to have enough seed and feed for horses.

Continuing in his 6-13-1910 letter, Ole wrote that the farmland near him looked like the best in the country that year so they had lots to be thankful for. A neighbor from Virginia went home to visit this summer and came back saying during the whole 2,600 mile trip he didn't see any crops doing as well as theirs near Beach. While Ole was away for 3 weeks, there were 3 heavy rains and the flax and corn shot up a lot. The next part of the letter was written July 14, and Ole said it had been very warm, and the day of the letter, reached 100 degrees in the shade. In the area of daughter Matilda's farm at Inwood, in northwest IA, they had hot weather and water was scarce. Ole said they didn't have a water shortage since they dug a well 20 feet deep and had 12 feet of water in it, which they could use for horses and cows. The hardest part was getting hay for winter. They rented a quarter section of land for hayfields five miles away. Not much was growing on it, so he was hoping to let it stand longer so it would grow more. They had had good luck with pigs.

Concerns about Carl

A postscript to the June 13, 1910 letter asked Matilda to keep the following information to herself. Albert, Ole's nephew and Anton's son, had written to Ole saying that Carl, Ole's son, had been having "strange notions" again like last winter and Albert didn't know what to do. Ole felt like he should go and see if there was anything he could do to help. But now Carl had been calmer for some time and Albert said he almost regretted writing to Ole. Ole tried in many ways to get Carl to come to Beach with him, but he refused. Carl was thinking people were trying to poison him. A woman nearby regularly baked bread for them, but Carl refused to eat it and so was making his own. Carl said Mother told him they were trying to poison him. (Carl's mother had died in 1895.) Carl said this year of 1910 would be a dry year with no harvest but after that it would be different. The Lord would turn it into paradise, there would be no vermin, and crops would grow without sowing or planting. Carl had said next year there would be no crops, but Ole said we had had the best crops ever. They visited a French man on Sunday and then Carl conversed completely normally with him. So Ole said there wasn't anything else he could do at the time, as long as he was able to continue working. (Little was understood about mental health at the time and few options were available for treatment.) Carl had said he wanted to continue as hired help, and not be the boss. Carl said the Lord knows what is best, but Ole wrote "if only the Lord knew what was wrong with him."

"Best Farmer" in Golden Valley

On Oct. 26, 1910, Ole wrote to Matilda saying the heat was unusually bad this summer, with some days over 100 degrees and some even up to 104! There were also times with little rain, so the harvests at many farms weren't as big that year. However, he said their harvest was even bigger than last year with over 8,000 bushels. He hired someone named Mr. Butterfield to do the threshing. He said they accomplished more than any farmer in Golden Valley that year with 9 horses, and none got injured. When Ole went to town, he was congratulated as the "best farmer" in Golden Valley based on the yield results reported by Mr. Butterfield of the various farms. Prices had fallen. It was hard to find places to store the harvest. Ole reported that they now had a telephone in their house and also received free mail delivery daily. Ole's son, Norman, wrote that Clara (Albert's sister, and Anton's daughter) got a letter from Albert saying their harvest went quite well that year and that Carl was doing better so that he hardly noticed anything wrong with him.

From left to right: Ole Rockvold, possibly Helen Bengtsen, future wife of Willie Rocksvold, Hilda Rocksvold, possibly Emma Rocksvold Amunrud, possibly Magdalene (child of Emma and Oscar), possibly Oscar Amunrud, likely Willie Rocksvold. Location: likely the farm near Beach, ND where Willie, Ole, and Hilda were living together for a time. Date likely between 1911-1912.

Sight Worsening

Ole said it was magnificent that having been in Beach only 2 years they had the best harvest in the valley, and would make at least $6,000 for the crops, with enough left over for horse feed and seed for next year. Ole said he probably could sell the land for $50-60 an acre at this point, but it made no sense to sell. He wanted to wait until he had made enough for the farm to pay for itself and hopefully return to Glenwood $20,000 better than before they left. He said he had trouble reading in the diminished light now, but said he planned to visit Matilda and her husband, A.O., next month. He hoped to travel through Fergus Falls to see Dr. Skerping about his eyes. The doctor had told him if Ole could stay for at least a week he could help Ole a lot.

Ole wrote on Dec., 22, 1910, to his niece, Irene Anderson, Matilda's daughter, and sent a package at the same time. He said he had promised to send Irene, Alberta, and Olive each a watch when they were confirmed, so now they were in the mail. (Alberta and Olive were daughters of Emma Rocksvold and Oscar Amunrud. A picture of these beautiful gold watches are in this book.)

Disastrous Weather for Crops and Willie Becomes Engaged

On July 11, 1911, Ole wrote to Matilda that the weather in the spring was good with the prospect of a good harvest, but then the weather became very hot, the crops dried up, and were "ruined." They would have to mow down most of the crops for hay. The Amunruds were doing better because they had good showers recently but that didn't happen at Ole's farm, except for a slight sprinkle of rain. He thought they would still have enough harvest so they wouldn't lose their courage. Ole said Emma, his daughter, was quite homesick when she first got out to Beach, ND. Willie, Ole's son, left June 29 for Iowa. Ole said, no doubt Willie wanted to get married and had 1,200 miles to travel. His bride was from the southeastern corner of Iowa near Fort Madison. She boarded there in Beach 5 months and went back the beginning of June. She was a good school marm, but Ole said he wasn't sure she would be a good farm wife, but hoped so. Ole hadn't heard from Willie the last two weeks since he left for Iowa. (Willie and Helen didn't actual marry until Jan. 1, 1913.)

Emma's Health Crisis

Ole wrote to Matilda from Fergus Falls, MN, on March 18, 1912, saying he had to change travel plans suddenly because Emma wrote she had to have an operation. He advised her to go to Fergus Falls and would meet her in Fargo to accompany her to Fergus Falls. Hilda and Ed had arrived in Fergus Falls, too, traveling with Emma from Fargo, since Ole didn't make it in time to travel with Emma. Willie also came to visit Hilda and said he also had to have an operation. Dr. Skerping said Emma had a tumor and was worried about cancer, or a problem with the appendix or intestines. (The handwriting was difficult to read for the translator.) Ole was allowed to watch the whole operation, but hadn't had a chance to talk with the doctor yet. He gave Matilda Emma's address at the hospital in Fergus Falls.

From left in front: Finkel Foss, Anton Norman Rocksvold, Peter William Rocksvold
From left in back: Tilda Foss, Manda Rocksvold, Marie Foss
Date unknown, likely early 1900's prior to Norman's marriage to Tilda Foss in 1907. Location - likely Decorah, IA

On April 8, 1912, Ole gave more details about Emma in his letter to Matilda. They left Fergus Falls, MN, for Fargo, ND, April 4. Emma was very tired and arrived by the end of the day near Argusville, where Hilda, Ole's daughter, and husband Ed Ohnstad, lived. The road was bumpy and she did not feel well with so much shaking after the surgery, even though they took a good surrey (a four-wheeled carriage drawn by 1-2 horses). She felt much better after a good night's sleep. Many relatives visited Easter Sunday. Emma would stay there to rest up for a few days before traveling home to Beach. The doctor wasn't sure how much travel she could tolerate after the operation. The doctor didn't risk taking out the appendix as it could have been fatal. Ole said there was a horrible stench when he doctor cut her open. There was such a huge amount of fluids she had been carrying around that the head nurse said it was the foulest thing she had ever seen. The nurses worked day and night to take care of the incision and kept her as comfortable as possible in recovery. Ole paid $50 for the operation. The doctor normally charges $100 for those living near town.

Albert's Accident

Continuing in the same 4-8-1912 letter, Ole wrote that Albert Rocksvold, Anton's son, had a bad accident and burned himself badly. He fell through loose boards in the grain elevator where the gasoline generator's water tank was and fell up to his waist in the boiling water. He is still in the hospital a month later. Willie visited him and "Albert cried like a baby" when it was time to say good-bye. Ole wrote Albert's brother, Peter, immediately and he called up Albert's sister, Clara, and they went to see him right away. The doctor said they could save his life and his legs, but would need skin transplants. People have offered their own skin for the grafting. Ole wrote that the weather had been cold and miserable. Planting had begun and it looked good so far, but they needed more rain. Willie wrote that the water was knee-high between buildings on their farm a few days ago. There had been lots of snow and it had melted in a couple of days. He wasn't sure when Emma would be ready to travel before they left.

L-R front: Edward Ohnstad, Hilda Rocksvold Ohnstad (Ole's daughter)
L-R back: Peter William Rocksvold, Helen Bengtson (future wife of Peter William)
May 20, 1911, Ed and Hilda's wedding day, with attendants

Emma's Death, June 18, 1912

Unfortunately, we don't have a letter preserved right after the time of Emma's death, so we aren't able to read how Ole and his family reacted to this terrible loss. When Emma died, her husband, Oscar Amunrud, was left with 7 children to raise, ranging in age from almost 2 to 17! Ole sent a postcard to Matilda on July 16, 1912, from Beach, and said they were in good health and things were pretty slow. Ole doesn't mention his daughter Emma's death in this very brief postcard.

Oscar Amunrud and his children, 1923, Wibaux, MT. Oscar's wife, Emma
Rockvold Amunrud, died in 1912. "Ming" was a nickname for Magdalene.
Emma was the daughter of Ole and Anne Rocksvold.

More Disastrous Weather

There was a hailstorm and rain for three weeks in August which ruined many of the crops.
Ole and the others had finished harvesting what was left when he wrote to Matilda, Sept.
8, 1912. Ole said they fortunately had crop insurance, but didn't think the damage was
going to be that bad. Willie asked for 10 percent damage and they have received $200
compensation, but it wouldn't cover the entire policy as they had 400 acres insured. Ole
wrote that Matilda should have been there before the hailstorm to see how beautiful the
crops looked. Nonetheless, they still had a "magnificent crop" with what was left. Oscar
Amunrud's family was doing well, which was the first mention of their family after Emma's death three months prior. Helen Bengtsen (future wife of Willie) visited that summer and returned to teach in Mandan the following winter. Ole hadn't heard from Carl,
but worried that he was dejected when he came home to see his crop ruined. (It sounds
like Ole often tried to accentuate the positive when there were crises- such as calling what
was left a "magnificent crop.")

Ole wrote on Nov. 1, 1912, to Matilda saying they finished getting the harvest in just in
time for lots more rain. The threshers could only work half the time because of rain, and
were waiting for things to dry up to continue. The harvest wasn't as bad as they thought,

ending up with 9,800 bushels all together. They would have had 12,000 bushels if the hailstorm hadn't come. They wouldn't be able to fit all the crops in the first granary, so they built an additional one. It had now been snowing for two days and it was two feet deep in some places. In the area there were thousands of acres of crops still standing, covered with snow.

Ole continued that many neighbors hadn't threshed yet, so he was very fortunate to have finished before this snow came. They bought an additional quarter section of land to basically use for more pastureland. There was a good water supply, 30 acres of fenced pasture, 100 acres already broken and 50 acres to use for whatever they wished. Ole bought at $30 per acre, which he said was reasonable at this time. If the snow didn't melt and they didn't get some good weather soon, they wouldn't get anything plowed. So far they had plowed only 10 acres, and Ole didn't know how they could get anything planted

in the spring if current conditions continued. He might buy another horse so they would have three four-horse teams. They currently had 11 horses and a foal. They planned to plant 4,400 acres the coming spring. Prices for crops were low. They would sell the wheat and flax, but would keep the barley until spring. There was a shortage of railway cars and grain elevators were full. Ole remained healthy and hadn't been sick during the time he had been in Beach. He planned to wait another 2-3 weeks before traveling east.

Long Letter from Manda

None of Ole's letters were preserved from 1913. However, there was a letter, Dec. 14, 1913, written in very large cursive writing to Ole by his daughter, Manda, from Mason City, IA. She was wondering if Ole was returning to Iowa for the winter soon and asked if he could stop and visit her at 503 State

Peter William (Willie) Rocksvold and Helen Bengtson

Street. She was rooming with a girl from Cedar Rapids, IA, through Dec. 29, and had enough room for him to stay with them. She wanted to cook for him, paying the owner of the house for the kerosene used for cooking on the gas stove at her rental. Manda was reminiscing of the old days when everything was "cozy " at home, although it was not easy to get all the work done on time. She wanted to come to Beach to see him and the others there, and even help him to have a traveling companion back to Iowa since his eyesight and hearing were so poor now (Ole was now age 81). She said there were lots of dangers and they needed Christ to help them. Manda wrote that Ole sent her a check in the mail three weeks ago. The check was addressed to Mrs. Ask, but she had told Manda that Ole had sent the money through Mrs. Ask, but the money was actually for Manda. Manda thanked her father very much. (Perhaps Ole had concerns about the money getting deposited or distributed correctly. That may have led Ole to sent the check to Mrs. Ask instead of directly to Manda.)

Continuing in the 12-14-1913 letter, Manda said she wrote to cousin Olive Amunrud (who was 17 at the time) who lived near Ole and wondered how things were going. Manda felt so bad for the seven children (then ages 3-18) who had lost their mother, Emma, last year. She also said it would be difficult with so many children needing to go to school and having such a long distance to get there. Manda had written to Ole via his daughter Hilda, but didn't get a response and that letter ended up in the dead letter office, returned to Manda 3 months later. She knew Hilda was moving to a new house, but didn't know the address. She also wondered if Ole was going to stop in Argusville, ND, at Hilda's on the way back to Iowa, and how he was managing, "batching it" (living like bachelors) with Willie's wife away on a trip. Manda hoped Ole hadn't sold the Beach area farm yet for a lower price than he was asking since prices were now starting to go up again.

Conflict With Willie, Back to Decorah

Ole wrote from Decorah to Matilda on April 11, 1914. Ole had been traveling for 2 weeks to visit at Beach. He said he was now was living at a nursing home in Decorah, but it doesn't say when he had moved. (Since he was capable of traveling so much, perhaps his "nursing home" was more of a senior living center, since he apparently didn't need a lot of nursing help.) Willie's wife had now arrived in Beach and since then Ole hadn't felt like the house near Beach was his home anymore. So he decided to sell his portion of the farm. Earlier, Ole had decided to deed half the land and property to Willie for one dollar. Willie had estimated the land was worth $12,000. Since Willie and Helen thought it was a better deal than they expected, Ole was surprised that he was being treated like a "tramp." Ole wrote he had not had a summer like this one since his time as a prisoner of war in the South. (The handwriting was not so clear here, but the translator thinks he wrote something like Ole had "to work hard, it is a struggle.")

Continuing in this 4-11-1914 letter, Ole wrote that he had told Oscar Amunrud the previous spring he would be willing to accept $10,000 for his share of the farm, but nothing was said to Willie about that conversation. After Ole returned to Beach last winter, Ole thought Oscar told Willie about that conversation between Oscar and Ole. Immediately thereafter Ole got a letter from Willie saying he wanted to buy Ole out and he would set the conditions. Not long ago they bought a quarter section of land and still owned $2,900 on it. The conditions were for Willie to have 5 years to pay at 6% interest. The first payment to Ole would be $2,900 on the land and that Oscar would get 480 acres (and then the next writing is unclear, possibly "to remove from his debt".) Or, Ole could buy him out under the same conditions, in which case he wanted cash payment. Willie also said he didn't want to pay anything towards the debt in Iowa. That was the money that was borrowed in the spring to get started originally out in Beach. Ole had originally paid $6,000, $3,000 of which was still owed. He said that was just Ole's affair. Ole wrote to say he understood that Willie didn't want to deal with everything, and that Willie wanted to leave Ole with the debt and leave himself with the farm. After that Ole got an "ugly letter" saying "Your words are good for nothing" and other "vicious things" that Ole wrote that he didn't want to mention in the letter.

Ole explained in the same letter, that he wrote back to Willie, counter-offering with "very reasonable" conditions, which Willie accepted. They had paid $2454 for the quarter section and Ole wanted half back ($1127), and Willie received Ole's share of the farm and personal property for $8,000. So Ole received a total of $9127, and held a mortgage at 6 percent interest for the payments. Ole would allow Willie to wait until Jan. 1, 1916 for the first payment, and complete the payments by 1920. (The next sentence wasn't clear, but said something about Ole never having taken a cent of the farm income after he returned to Iowa until this winter when he got $52.) Then he talked about the harvest in fall, which resulted in $1,000. Ole spent only one night at Willie's for the visit there, and then spent the rest of the nights at Oscar's. (It is sad to read that Ole didn't feel welcome at his Beach farm home anymore and the financial conflict with Willie. It is very unfortunate they didn't have their financial agreements in writing from the start to hopefully have prevented some of this strain in their relationship. Having dual relationships – personal and work – can often get complicated.)

Ole wrote that Oscar Amunrud, widower of Emma, had a house with 6 rooms and had built another building. They were doing well. Five children were going to school and there was an exceptionally good school in Beach. Ole wasn't sure if he was coming to visit

Matilda before summer, but when he did come he could tell more in person that he didn't want to put in writing. He continued that he was healthy and happy at the nursing home and wanted to stay there the rest of his life on earth. Hilda had written to say she had given birth to another daughter (Olive) in Fargo. She was staying with a family a week before returning home. In his travels he realized he might have been able to visit her in Fargo, but it turned out she was gone before Ole arrived.

Syttende Mai in Minneapolis, MN

Ole enjoyed the Minneapolis Syttende Mai festival for a week in 1914 (Norwegian Independence Day May 17) with Ole Kjørlien. They traveled around that area about 200 miles by automobile, he told Matilda in a letter May 25, 1914. This Ole was the same person with whom Ole Rocksvold had traveled back to Norway in 1902. Ole wrote that he then traveled to Boyd, MN, visiting Anton Roseth and his wife Laura, who was the daughter of Helene Marie Dahl Øistad. They asked him to stay at least two weeks, but he had planned to stay a week and said he really couldn't stay longer. However, rain had made the roads in such terrible condition that insisted he stay until the roads were better, and he did. He said the Roseths have a "magnificent house" and Anton owned 3 lumber yards and shares in two others. Ole added he was in the best of health.

Ole felt like he was "cooked" because it was so hot and felt ill because of it in his July 25, 1914 letter to Matilda. Ole said the hay, corn, and barley crops were good, in fact the hay was the best ever, but it was too hot for the oats to do well. Ole got three large loads per acre. Peter (Anton's son) got 14 loads with about 16 acres left to cut. Ole went to the 50th wedding anniversary of C. Evens (unknown to author) with Norman, Ole's son. There were 400 people there. Ole had heard from Jert Selsvold that in ND they had the best prospects ever for their harvests. Ole hadn't heard from any of the ND relatives recently, though. Peter had a well driller come, drilled 420 feet down, and then dropped the bucket and couldn't get it up, so they will try to drill it out. Kalle and Elling Vangen (unknown to author) returned from their Norway trip and said they didn't like it. Elling said he wouldn't go back even if given a free ticket!

Eyesight Worsening

Coping with his diminishing sight and trying to write at dusk on Dec. 18, 1914, Ole wrote Matilda that it was almost impossible for him to write much now, so his letter would be short. (He was now 82.) He said he was actually writing "by feel." Hilda's family was coming to visit tomorrow. Manda called two weeks earlier saying she was in Calmar and would arrive in Decorah that night and wanted to be picked up. Ole said she "had not learned nor forgotten anything" while she was away. (The next line looks unclear, but the translator thinks it was something about wanting to bring her boyfriend home.) Manda had been told that she had to "learn to behave properly" or she should pack her bags and leave. (No further explanation is given as to what specific behaviors were considered inappropriate.) They were in good health. Tilda, Norman's wife, hadn't been well, but had improved and was healthy again.

Ole apologized to Matilda and A.O. in his letter of Feb. 10, 1915, since he hadn't written for so long, but wanted to let them know he was still alive. They had had a beautiful winter until Feb. 1, then had a terrible blizzard all day and night with a foot of snow and impassable roads. They couldn't plow for 3 days, and then it became very cold. He thanked them for the many pictures. He saw a card from Irene, Matilda's daughter, to Tilda that said it was "shameful" they hadn't written and sent a thank you for the gifts, so that was why he was writing then. The letter continued Feb. 12, saying the weather was so dark that he couldn't see to write yesterday. Tilda hadn't been well, and Norman went with her to the doctor in Waukon. She had a heart condition. The rest of them were well. Manda came home for Christmas and was still there.

Two letters from Matilda had come by March 16, 1915, when Ole wrote to say he should have written long ago in response. The first letter arrived Tuesday when they expected her to come for a visit. Norman drove to Decorah in the morning, thinking Matilda would arrive on the 3 p.m. train. He waited until the 6 p.m. train had arrived. Victor Ruen was waiting for her when the midnight train came. (I don't know who Victor is, but with the last name of Ruen, he could have been a distant relative since there are Ruens in the Kjøs-Eggebraaten family history book.) She could have come out with them in the morning. There had been lots of illness in the area, but Ole's home had been spared. They still had many feet of snow in most places. Ole said Willie had written to say they were fine in North Dakota. Helen won a contest for selling *Beach Chronicle* subscriptions and got second prize and a piano worth 450 dollars. She wanted to win the auto, first prize. Willie said he could sell the piano and buy a Ford car, which Willie thought was better than 2 pianos. Ole planned to travel as far as Fargo the coming summer, and perhaps go up to Carl's. Willie wrote that Carl was thinking of selling, if he could. Ole said they were healthy and he had put on about 10 pounds that winter. (It was good to read that the communication and relationship between Willie and Ole had improved after the conflict regarding finances.)

Ole had put off writing while they were busy haying, he wrote to Matilda on July 27, 1915. It rained a lot, so that interfered with getting the haying done. They had little hope for their corn crop because of rain. Olive Amunrud, Oscar and Emma's daughter, wrote that they had bought a farm again and moved in on a half section of land in Montana,

24 miles from Beach (near Wibaux) and about the same distance from Willie. Of that half section, there were 80 acres of good-looking land for wheat, oats, flax, and corn, with a good water supply. A new town (Wibaux, MT) had been started near there with a store, post office, and blacksmith. They bought the land for 12 dollars an acre from a homesick homesteader. Ole wrote that Alberta and Norma Amunrud, Emma and Oscar's daughters, were still in Beach and Norma was going to Norwegian school. They told Ole the crops looked good there. Ole was thinking of traveling at least to Hilda's (Argusville, ND, north of Moorhead, MN). From there it was easy to get to Beach by train, then to Oscar's, which he would really enjoy doing. Ole hadn't heard from Willie since early spring when he sent him a corn planter. Ole had run the hay fork during haying, which is all he was able to manage. Everyone there was in good health.

More Disastrous Weather in ND

Coincidentally, Willie Rocksvold, Ole's son, wrote to his sister, Matilda, July 26, 1915, the day before Ole's letter, saying another hailstorm came and wiped out almost his whole crop, with nothing more than 20 acres left that would amount to anything. It was fortunate he had insurance, but would have to plow the whole crop under. It was raining so much he couldn't even do that yet since the ground was too soft to work a team of horses.

Willie and Helen Bengtsen Rocksvold ended up having two children, Genevieve and Owen, and eventually moved out to California after not finding success with farming in western ND.

Since Matilda and A.O. were considering a trip to visit Hilda, Ole thought he would also like to go. However, on Aug. 8, 1915, Ole wrote Matilda to say it had been flooding from Fargo to Hillsboro with so much rain that it wouldn't be very pleasant there. Ole's main purpose in going there then was to try to convince them to move away from this "mudhole." It was almost impossible to travel house to house. If he went up there, he would have to stay indoors all the time. Hilda had written to say they were looking for him everyday, and her daughter, Esther, whenever she saw a man coming, would say, "There comes Grandpa." He still hadn't decided whether to go, but perhaps would wait until harvest was over. Ole got three letters from Golden Valley, ND, near Beach, and from Montana. One was from Willie with unpleasant news. A hailstorm destroyed his whole crop, the best crop he had ever had. Ole was including that letter to Matilda. Willie told Ole it was tough to watch everything ruined in a few minutes, 400 acres. It was good he had insurance for $26.40 per acre. Ole was supposed to receive from Willie $480 in interest this spring for the mortgage Ole held on the farm, but with the poor harvest last year, Ole said he could wait. It looked like he would end up waiting another year for the money.

In the same letter, Ole thought he remembered writing in the previous letter that Oscar Amunrud sold his farm and lived in town until June when he got a new farm 24 miles from Beach in Montana, 80 acres. Many Norwegians lived there, with church services in Norwegian and a Norwegian school. They invited Ole to visit, which he would like to do. The weather had been terrible all summer, rainy and cold. Many crops had rotted, but they got most of the hay in. They lost the equivalent of 12 loads. Some farmers lost almost all of their crops. During a rainstorm last week they got 3 inches of rain in a half an hour, and another storm the following Sunday. Then it got cold, 50 degrees, but the last 3 days had been warm and dry. It would be difficult to harvest the oats since they were all tangled and lying in all directions. Oscar said they would lose quite a bit of that crop, too, but he continued to be in good health.

Farmers must have very strong nerves and lots of courage to cope with the ever-changing weather conditions and crises that come with that kind of work!

On March 18, 1916, Ole wrote to Matilda saying they arrived home to Decorah after traveling and found everything in order. Norman, Ole's son, and Norman's wife, Tilda, met them. Ole told Matilda they had had beautiful weather while away, but it didn't say who he was traveling with nor where they went, perhaps visiting Matilda with stops on the way? Many were ill in Decorah now, with over 60 cases of scarlet fever and many deaths. The situation with seed corn was worse than thought previously and most couldn't be planted. Norman had bought two bushels at 9 dollars a bushel. Ole had hired a man for 45 dollars a month to help. He said his pens were bad so it was hard to write and the mailman was coming any minute, so he closed the letter. (So it sounds like Ole may have been doing some farming with Norman now in IA.)

Tornado!

Ole wrote on his 84th birthday, March 30, 1916, from Argusville, ND, to Matilda and her husband A.O. at Inwood, IA. He was visiting at the home of his daughter, Hilda, and her husband Edward Ohnstad at the time. He had arrived three weeks earlier, May 10, and it had been raining almost all the time so they were not close to finishing planting. There was a tornado (called "cyclone" at that time) March 25, the worst they had ever seen since people started homesteading there. The wind blew down about 50 buildings and many people's livelihoods were destroyed, but he didn't hear of anyone dying. On Hilda and Ed's farm, it took down the windmill and a couple of smaller buildings. The wind picked up a buggy shed, lifted it over a binder that stood in its way without touching it, and then scattered the pieces over the field. Where Hilda and Ed used to live, a granary and another building were ripped to shreds and hurled against the house, breaking into the wall in many places. Edward's brother, (Carl) Olaus Ohnstad, lived there now, but fortunately had been in the bedroom when the "cyclone" came and was uninjured. While visiting, Ole said he had been taking it easy, as it was too muddy to do much outdoor work anyway.

Ole continued in the same 3-30-1916 letter, saying the Ohnstads and he drove in an automobile to a church dedication in Moorhead, MN, May 14, 1916. (I was unable to find

out which church by searching the internet and contacting Trinity. The dedication they attended may not have been for Trinity, as I learned their first service in Trinity's new brick church was Dec. 25, 1915. Perhaps it is possible the actual dedication day was May 14, seven months from the first service, but unlikely. My Trinity contact wasn't able to determine that with certainty.) Because of the constant rain, they had to stay in town two days. (Incidentally, many family members who lived in the Fargo-Moorhead area ended up choosing to belong to Trinity Lutheran in the future. Among those were Hilda and Ed Ohnstad, and their children, once they moved closer.)

Ole had gone with the Ohnstads to Perley the previous Sunday, he continued in his March 30, 1916 letter. The rain had stopped for 2-3 days so the roads were fine for travel. There were 5 automobiles at the Ohnstad place. Since the weather had at last improved for several days, they could try to finish their planting that week. The Ohnstads were talking about driving to the annual meeting (likely for church) that sum-

Esther, Olive, Vernon, and Ruby Ohnstad, taken about Nov. 1920, likely at Argusville, ND, or Fargo, ND. Ruby was the twin of Rachel. Rachel died at 2 months old, Dec. 31, 1917. Ruby died at age 3, Dec. 11, 1920. These children were the grandchildren of Ole Rocksvold, and the children of Ed and Hilda Rocksvold Ohnstad.

mer in Fargo. If they went, they were hoping to meet Ole there. Ole planned to go home with the delegates from Winneshiek County, IA, and needed to be home by the beginning of July. Ed and Hilda now had a better farm than they did before. Hilda had her hands

Rachel Ohnstad, twin of Ruby, shortly before her death at 6 weeks old, taken about Dec. 1917, likely at Argusville, ND. She was the granddaughter of Ole Rocksvold, daughter of Ed and Hilda Rockvsold Ohnstad.

full with the children (3 close in age: Esther, Olive, and Vernon) and housekeeping. She had a young girl helping with the baby (Vernon), but no additional help. She sent her greetings. Ole had caught a cold and bad cough, but was otherwise fine.

Norman and Florence Ohnstad, grandchildren of Ole and Anne Rocksvold. Likely taken about 1925-6 on the Argusville, ND, farm of their parents, Edward and Hilda Rocksvold Ohnstad.

Ultimately, Hilda and Ed Ohnstad had a total of 7 children: Esther, Olive, Vernon, twins Ruby and Rachel, Florence, and Norman. Rachel died at only two months old, and Ruby died of meningitis at age 3.

Ole was looking for A. O., Matilda's husband, at the large church convention, but didn't find him so assumed he was home, Ole explained in his June 6, 1916 letter to A.O., Matilda's husband, posted from Fargo, ND. The auditorium held 2400, and was almost filled every day. In the afternoon was a vote on four proposals with representatives of the NS and Hauge Synod (a little difficult to decipher the handwriting here for the translator). They unanimously adopted the proposals with over 1000 men. Ole was a delegate and had not seen the pastor or the other delegates that he assumed were there somewhere. He wrote that he was in good health and doing well.

That June 16, 1916 letter was the last of Ole's letters we have found before his death on Aug. 20, 1922, six years later. We have additional letters written to Ole by others during

Ed and Hilda Ohnstad Children, Grandchildren of Ole and Anne Rocksvold:
From left, Esther, Olive, Florence, Vernon, Norman
Likely on their farm near Argusville, ND, about 1925-6

this time which provide insight as to how he was doing, his relationship to the writers, and life at that time. Here are short summaries of a few of those letters, the entirety of which are in the appendices.

Tilda Foss Rocksvold, Norman's wife, wrote to Matilda, Jan. 2, 1918, saying the Ole's eyesight was somewhat better, but on days when it is dark and cloudy it was hard for him to read. Norman had offered to go with him to the doctor to see if anything more can be done for his sight, but Ole said he wanted to wait for now and see how he was after Christmas.

Norman and Tilda ended up having four children: G. Arla, Grace, Alice, and Roy. When Tilda died in 1928, (her husband had already died in 1922), Alice, age 11, and Roy, age 7, went to live with aunt Matilda and A.O. Anderson. The other two children were old enough to be on their own by then.

Another letter giving us insight into his relationships between 1916 and his death in 1922 is from his niece, Hilda Øistad Garaas, in Hamar, Norway, written Feb. 27, 1921. She was the granddaughter of his sister, Helene Roksvold Dahl, and the daughter of Helene Marie Dahl Øistad. She thanked Ole for sending the *Decorah Posten* issues which was very thoughtful of him. She also appreciated the warm-hearted feelings he expressed

Anton Norman and Tilda Foss Rocksvold Family
about 1920, probably in Decorah, IA
From left: Grace, Tilda, Norman, Alice, G. Arla
Norman was the son of Ole and Anne Rocksvold.

Ole, age 84, with Ohnstad grandchildren
From left, Olive, Vernon, and Esther Ohnstad.

about Hilda's mother who died two days short of 9 months ago. Hilda Garaas missed her Mom terribly. She sent her greetings to the "kind gentleman" whose 89th birthday was coming up on the 30th of March. She wrote that her mother told her she (Helene Marie) had the same birthday as Ole. She wished Ole the best from the bottom of her heart. They were in good health and heard often from sister Laura in Minnesota, whose son was confirmed in May, 1920. Hilda also heard often from her mother's brother, Peter Dahl, in Kristiania (Oslo), Norway. Prices had fallen a lot, with food, clothing, firewood, and housing much less expensive. One hectoliter of coke (coal residue for fuel) cost 18 ½ Norwegian crowns last winter and was now 6 crowns. Hilda's husband also sent his greetings.

Ole Rocksvold and his Grandchildren - 1906
Three are children of Matilda (Rocksvold) and Andrew Anderson
Six are children of Emma (Rocksvold) and Oscar Amunrud
Back Row: Olive Amunrud, Irene Anderson, Alberta Amunrud, and Edna Amunrud,
Ernest and George Anderson on end chairs
Reuben and Roy Amunrud are on Ole's lap
Norma Amunrud in front

Wilhelm Rasmussen, Ole's pastor, wrote to Ole from Waukon, IA on Aug. 8, 1922. This may be one of the last letters Ole ever received since Ole died a couple of weeks later, Aug. 20. The letter mentioned hearing from A.O. Anderson, Matilda's husband, and having spoken to Mrs. Norman Rocksvold, Tilda. He said Ole lived in a nursing home and recollected Ole's strong faith which he noted on the occasion of Norman's funeral. (Ole's son, Norman, had died May 12, three months earlier.) Wilhelm included several Bible quotations about faith and dying in the Lord, plus lyrics to a Norwegian hymn, "I Know of a Sleep in Jesus' Name." Wilhelm said the pastor and congregation would sorely miss him when he dies and wanted to thank him for all the help, encouragement, prayers, love, generosity, and being a good Christian example. He wished Ole a blissful and easy journey to his heavenly home. So apparently he believed Ole would not live much longer.

A picture of Ole being read to by a neighbor, Martin Kirkeby. Since Ole greatly missed being able to read as his eyesight worsened, this picture is very meaningful as he sought out people who would read to him.

Coping with Blindness, Surgery

Ole always loved to read and kept up with all the happenings in the world. Even in the last five years of his life when he could not see, he frequently asked all those around him to read to him so he could continue to learn all he could about what was happening in the community, country, and world. In his autobiography-family history, Ernest Anderson described Ole as knowing more about World War I than anyone around, when he was 85 and blind, and would describe those events clearly for listeners with the pictures he had formed in his mind.

Ole mourned the loss his sight and greatly hoped it could at least be partially restored through a new cataract removal surgery available in Madison, SD. According to Ernest Anderson, Ole traveled there with his daughter, Matilda Rocksvold Anderson, in June of 1922. Unfortunately Ole was sick with kidney trouble the same week that he had the surgery, and so never got the chance to enjoy reading again that he was so seeking. It is not mentioned specifically if there was any improvement in sight after the surgery. Whether or not there was improvement, he was apparently too ill to enjoy it. At first, it looked like he would die there in Madison, SD, but he improved enough to go home with Matilda to her farm at Inwood, IA. This illness led to the end of his life shortly thereafter.

Ole Rocksvold died 11:15 a.m., Sun., Aug. 20, 1922. Ernest Anderson wrote that Ole was the last of his Civil War comrades from his community to die. Members of the American Legion honored him, playing the final taps for his funeral, which was held at the Glenwood Church since it was larger than the Pontoppidan Church to which he belonged at the time of his death, according to the *Decorah Posten*, Aug. 25, 1922.

When Ole realized that his last days had come, he told his daughter, Matilda, he was glad to pass on to a well-deserved rest. Ole was 90.

~

Ole P. Rocksvold was a person of intelligence and conviction, deeply committed to his family and community. Difficult challenges confronted him as an immigrant, Civil War soldier, and prisoner of war. He suffered the grief of outliving five of his children and his wife of 30 years, handled the uncertainties of pioneer farming, and ultimately went blind in old age. He nevertheless persevered to become a beloved husband and father of ten, grandfather of 23, successful farmer, and respected community leader. His love of learning and writing was passed down, with several descendants becoming educators, researchers, and authors. His fortitude, dignity, and life of service are an inspiration. It was a honor to preserve his memory by writing this book.

Ole Rocksvold, location unknown, likely Decorah, IA, taken probably 1910-1915, in his late seventies or early eighties.

350   UNDERGROUND WATER RESOURCES OF IOWA.

Wells in Winneshiek County—Continued.

Owner.	Location.	Depth.	Diameter.	Depth to rock.	Depth to water supply.	Source of supply.	Head below curb.	Remarks (logs given in feet).
T. 100 N., R. 7 W. (HIGHLAND).		*Feet.*	*In.*	*Feet.*	*Feet.*		*Feet.*	
Julius Selmes......	3 miles east of Hesper.	177	6	20	147	Sandstone...	147	
T. 100 N., R. 8 W. (HESPER).								
Frank Darington...	4 miles southeast of Hesper.	224	6	20	194	.....do.......	194	
Charles Casterton..	4 miles north of Locust.	107	6	15	69	.....do.......	69	
T. 96 N., R. 9 W. (WASHINGTON).								
....	Fort Atkinson...	100	6	......	80	....	80	
T. 96 N., R. 8 W. (MILITARY).								
Anthony Bore.....	Ossian..........	224	......	......	60	......	......	
.........do...........		735	......	100		......	......	Yellow clay, 35; blue till, 61; yellow clay, 4; limestone; shale; limestone, 300.
Public school.......	.....do...........	134	......	60		......	15	
....	NE. ¼ SE. ¼ sec. 19.	187	......	28		......		
John Collins........	SW. ¼ SW. ¼ sec. 8.	198	......	40	......	Limestone..	80	Water in white limestone underlying shale.
....	NE. ¼ NE. ¼ sec. 3.	220	......	40		......	50	Surface clays, 40; limestone, 25; blue shale with limestone, 124; white limestone, 31.
....	NE. ¼ NW. ¼ sec. 23.	396	......	48	370	Limestone..	330	Yellow clay, 15; blue clay, 33; limestone, 22; shale (Maquoketa) with interbedded limestone layers, 115; white limestone, 211.
T. 96 N., R. 7 W. (BLOOMFIELD).								
....	SE. ¼ NE. ¼ sec. 19.	180	......	32		....		
T. 98 N., R. 8 W. (DECORAH).								
O. P. Rocksvold...	SW. ¼ NW. ¼ sec. 14.	508	6½	20	500	Sandstone...	380	Clay, 20; limestone, 200; St. Peter, 70; magnesia, 90; Cambrian or Oneota, 117; Cambrian sand, 13. Water also at 175.

Ole's Well

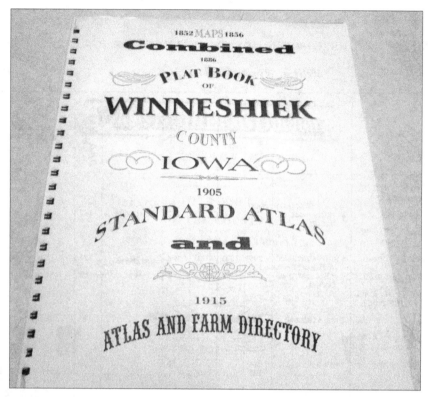

1915 edition of the Winneshiek County Atlas in which
Ole's wrote the chapter of Glenwood County.

Ole Rocksvold data, Winneshiek Co, IA.

On the left, a ribbon from a reception Ole attended for Governor Boies.
He was governor of Iowa 1890-1894. On the right, a ribbon from the fifth
reunion of the 12th Iowa Infantry, Oct. 10-12, 1894, in Sioux City, IA.

OLE P. ROCKSWOLD,
DECORAH IOWA
878617   ACT MAY
R R 6

Commissioner.

U. S. PENSION OFFICE MAR 18 1915

No. 1. Date and place of birth? *Answer.* I was born March 30th 1832 Vestre Toten Norway. Europe

The name of organizations in which you served? *Answer.* I served in Co. G. 12th Iowa Vol. Inf.

No. 2. What was your post office at enlistment? *Answer.* Freeport Winneshiek Co. Iowa

No. 3. State your wife's full name and her maiden name. *Answer.* Mrs. Anne Rockswold nee Miss Anne Gilbertson Strandbakken

No. 4. When, where, and by whom were you married? *Answer.* On the 12th of February 1865 at Glenwood Norw. Evang. Luth. Church, by Rev. U. Koren Decorah Ia.

No. 5. Is there any official or church record of your marriage? Yes

If so, where? *Answer.* With Rev. Paul Koren Decorah Iowa.

No. 6. Were you previously married? If so, state the name of your former wife, the date of the marriage, and the date and place of her death or divorce. If there was more than one previous marriage, let your answer include all former wives. *Answer.* No.

I have not been married more than once

No. 7. If your present wife was married before her marriage to you, state the name of her former husband, the date of such marriage, and the date and place of his death or divorce, and state whether he ever rendered any miltary or naval service, and, if so, give name of the organization in which he served. If she was married more than once before her marriage to you, let your answer include all former husbands. *Answer.* Not been remarried

No. 8. Are you now living with your wife, or has there been a separation? *Answer.* No My wife died July 4th. 1895

No. 9. State the names and dates of birth of all your children, living or dead. *Answer.* George Paulus born Nov. 14th 1865 died Mch. 3rd 1890. Mathilde born Feb 17th 1867 living Carl Oscar born Oct. 9th 1868 living Theodor Victor born Sept. 17th 1870 died Mch 7th 1891 Emma Theodora born Mch. 31st 1872 died June 18th 1912, Manda Augusta born April 1st 1874 living, Theodor Olaf born Feb. 27th 1876 died Mch. 17th 1894. Hulda Oliana born Dec 5th 1879 living Anthon Norman born Aug. 31st 1880 living Peter Vilhelm born Dec. 13th 1882. living

Date March 15th 1915. (*Signature*) Ole P Rockswold

Ole Rocksvold pension record, handwritten description of family

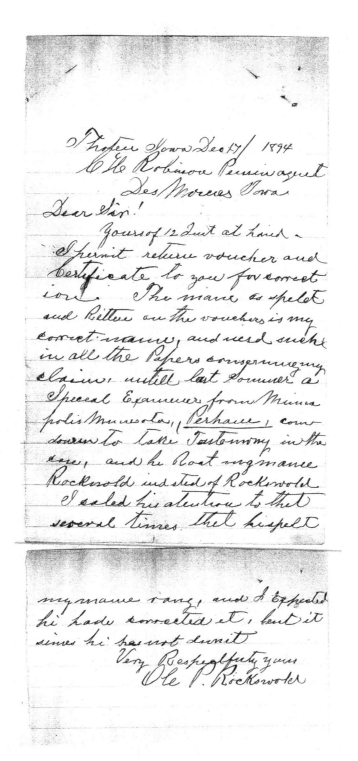

Ole Rocksvold pension record, handwritten letter correcting spelling of last name

Part of Ole's chapter from the Winneshiek County Atlas

CHAPTER XXVIII
GLENWOOD TOWNSHIP

Of several sketches of Glenwood township, none are better than that prepared in 1905 by O. P. Rocksvold, one of the pioneers of the township. It was printed in the "Atlas of Winneshiek County," published that year by Anderson & Goodwin. Mr. Rocksvold says, in part:

"Gjermund Johnson was the first Norwegian settler in township 9B north, range 7 west, which was the way the township was known.

"He located in the southwest quarter of section 31, and built the first dwelling house in the township. N els Throndson and Andrew Gulbrandson Haugen came later the same year, and settled on section 32. These were the only settlers in the southwest part of the township. In 1851 Knut Evenson and others settled in the same neighborhood. In the southeastern corner of the township, Hans O. Eggebraaten and family, Hans Blegen and wife, Ole and Hans Patterson, their three sisters and their old father were the first Norwegian settlers in the east part of the township. .

"Claims were made by Philander Baker, L. Carmichael, John Brant, Jack Brant, George Coney, John Bush, Wm. and John Barthell and others, but they soon sold their claims to Norwegian settlers and disappeared. Samuel Drake came in 1850 to the northwest part of the township, and settled on section 7; his father and brother Nathan came in 1851. Other families settled in the neighborhood but moved away in a short time. In 1851 Timothy Fuller, Russell and Benjamin Goodwater, Wm. Smith and Levi Barnhouse settled in the township, but Russell soon sold out, the others remaining for a number of years.

"In 1852 the Norwegian emigrants began to come direct from Norway, and continued to come until the outbreak of the war, which checked the emigration for some time. A few years later they began to come in large numbers, so that soon every acre of available land in the township was taken up.

"William Smith built a sawmill on Trout river in 1853 and supplied the first settlers with lumber; before that time they had to split logs for the floors, doors and other purposes. Glenwood was well supplied with wood and water, the two main objects for which the settlers were looking. Iowa river running along the north border of the township, Trout river from the south through its center, Coon creek from the southeast, all emptied into the Iowa river at the north part of the township on section 2.

"All of these streams were well stocked with fish, the two last mentioned with speckled trout. Even in the Iowa river a good many trout were caught. Wild game was plentiful, red deer could be seen every day, and I often saw them grazing among the cattle in the summer. Game birds were also numerous, such as prairie chicken, partridges, quail and wild pigeons. The latter were often so numerous in the spring of the year that a flock would almost shade the sun. In 1866 a flock came along and picked up the seed on a ten-acre field that had been sown by hand by the writer of this sketch, so it had to be sown over again.

"Glenwood contained very little prairie land; the most of it was timber with some open patches here and there, consequently was hard to clear for farm purposes. The soil is of the best kind-black loam, underlaid with clay. After fifty years of cultivation it produces the best of crops. The timber varieties are burr oak, white oak, black oak, black walnut, butternut, elm, poplar, and many other varieties.

"I find from the census of 1880 that Glenwood had a population of 1,190. That year the Waukon and Decorah railroad branch was graded, so many of the professional railroad hands were enumerated as citizens of Glenwood, where they did belong at the time being. In 1890 the population was 1,034 and in 1900 just about the same.* Hundreds of good citizens have emigrated to Minnesota and the Dakotas, where land was cheap.

"At the outbreak of the Civil war, Glenwood was not slow to send her sons to the front. Four companies of infantry and one of cavalry were organized in the county, going into the regiments as follows: First company in the Third, second in the Ninth,

---

GLENWOOD TOWNSHIP:-

BY O. P. ROCKSVOLD.

Gjermund Johnson was the first Norwegian settler in township ninety-eight, North range seven, West, which was the way the township was known. He came in company with twelve others, but as they located in the adjoining townships I shall not mention them.

Mr. Johnson located in the southwest quarter of section thirty-one, and built the first dwelling house in the township. Nels Throndson and Andrew Guldbrandson Haugen came later the same year, and settled on section thirty-two. These were the only settlers in the southwest part of the township. In 1851, Knut Evenson and others settled in the same neighborhood. In the southeastern corner of the township, Hans O. Eggebraaten and family, Hans Blegen and wife, Ole and Hans Patterson, their three sisters and their old father were the first Norwegian settlers in the east part of the township.

Claims were made by Philander Baker, L. Carmichael, John Brant, Jack Brant, George Coney, John Bush, Wm. and John Barthell and others; but they soon sold their claims to Norwegian settlers and disappeared. Samuel Drake came in 1850 to the northwest part of the township, and settled on section seven; his father and brother Nathan came in 1851. Nathan is still living on the old homestead. Other families settled in the neighborhood but moved away in a short time. The first Norwegians had formerly stayed in Wisconsin for a year or two, and sent out parties into Iowa to locate. Some went into Clayton county, locating on the Turkey river, others into Allamakee county, settling near Paint Creek, others came to Winneshiek county. In 1851 Timothy Fuller, Russell and Benjamin Goodwater, Wm. Smith and Levi Barnhouse, settled in the township, but Russell soon sold out, the others remaining for a number of years.

In 1852 the Norwegian emigrants began to come direct from Norway, and continued to come until the outbreak of the war, which checked the emigration for some time. A few years later they began to come in large numbers so that soon every acre of available land in the township was taken up. Wm. Smith built a saw mill on Trout River in 1853 and supplied the first settlers with lumber; before that time they had to split logs for the floors, doors and other purposes. Glenwood was well supplied with wood and water; the two main objects for which the settlers were looking. Iowa river running along the north border of the township, Trout river from the south through its center, Coon Creek from the southeast, all emptying into the Iowa river at the north part of the township on section two.

All of these streams were well stocked with fish, the two last mentioned with speckled trout, even in the Iowa river a good many trout were caught. Wild game was plentiful, red deer could be seen every day, and I often saw them grazing among the cattle in the summer. Game birds were also numerous, such as prairie chicken, partridges, quail and wild pigeons. The latter were often so numerous in the spring of the year that a flock would almost shade the sun. In 1866 a flock came along and picked up the seed on a ten acre field that had been sown by hand by the writer of this sketch, so it had to be sown over again.

Glenwood contained very little prairie land, the most of it was timber with some open patches here and there, consequently was hard to clear for farm purposes. The soil is of the best kind, black loam, underlaid with clay. After 50 years of cultivation it produces the best of crops. The timber varieties were burr oak, white oak, black oak, black walnut, butternut, elm, poplar, and many other varieties.

The township was for many years a stopping place for Norwegian emigrants who built their cabins on timber lots of old settlers, where there was plenty of grass,

both for pasture and meadow, so in a few years they raised quite a herd of cattle, and procured oxen and wagons and started west for free homesteads, where many of them are now among the wealthiest farmers in their localities.

I find from the census of 1880 that Glenwood had a population of 1190. That year the Waukon and Decorah railroad branch was graded so many of the professional railroad hands were enumerated as citizens of Glenwood where they did belong at the time being. In 1890 the population was 1034 and in 1900 just about the same. Hundreds of good citizens have emigrated to Minnesota and the Dakotas where land was cheap.

At the outbreak of the Civil War, Glenwood was not slow to send her sons to the front, four companies of infantry and one of cavalry were organized in the county, going into the regiments as follows: First company in the third, second in the ninth, and the third into the twelfth, the fourth into the thirty-eighth and the fifth into the sixth cavalry. All of these companies were more or less soldiers from Glenwood township. A few soldiers also went into the fifteenth Wisconsin as a Scandinavian regiment. It was soon found that all of these boys were of the right kind of material of which to make good soldiers.

A certain family, Thrond Steen and wife of Glenwood, sent six sons to the front, one to the 1st Minnesota, three in the Twelfth Iowa, one in the Thirty-eighth Iowa, and one in the Fifteenth Wisconsin, and the seventh and oldest brother was drafted in 1864, but when it became known that he had six brothers in the army before, they let him go home to take care of his old parents. Glenwood has more than furnished its quota of soldiers; but Decorah got the credit of a good many of them; as they did not think of demanding their enlistment as a credit to Glenwood township so in 1864 when a draft was ordered, four men were drafted in the township.

There are three Norwegian Lutheran churches in the township. The first was built in 1857 and continued until 1870 when the congregation had outgrown it, then a large stone church was built that year by the side of the old one, at a cost of $13,000. A few years later a part of the congregation seceded and built a church for themselves, in 1889. Two years later others joined them; so they removed it to a better location and remodeled it at a cost of $3,000. Another church was built in the southwest part of the township about the same style and cost as the one above mentioned.

There have been two flour mills erected in Glenwood township. One was built in 1868, known as the stone mill on the Trout river, and had adequate water power, for a number of years. Another was built in 1872 by B. B. Sander on the same stream further down; but after a few years the water gave out, so the machinery was sold as scrap iron and the building was converted into a creamery. The stone mill mentioned above was run for several years by steam, but finally was closed as it did not pay expenses.

It may not be out of place to mention the writer as being an old settler, as my name has not been mentioned among the first settlers. I came to Glenwood township direct from Norway in 1853, and have resided here ever since with the exception of three years; when I served in the army. My first occupation was to build houses, clear land and break; was known as an expert shingle maker, making at least 100,000 in one single summer splitting and shaving them by hand. In the fall of 1861 I enlisted in Company G, Twelfth Iowa Infantry, and served three years and two months. I participated in the following battles: Fort Henry, Fort Donelson, Shiloh, where on April 6th, 1862, our regiment was captured at what is known as the Hornet's Nest, and we were kept in prison for six and one-half months.

We were kept at the following places: Memphis, Tenn., Mobile, Ala., Cahaba, Montgomery and Macon, Ga., where we were kept for five months, then sent to Libbey Prison and exchanged on James river above Fort Monroe; were then sent to Annapolis, Md., and from there to St. Louis; when the regiment was reorganized and in the spring of 1863 sent to Vicksburg, and from there to Jackson, Mississippi, where we had a hard time to capture the city, then back to Vicksburg, participating in the siege until July 4th, 1863, when the Fort surrendered, then turned around and went with General Sherman's army and drove the rebels back to Jackson and captured the city again. In 1864 we were sent (6,000 men) up the Red river under General Smith to assist General Banks on his raid to Shreveport, La. We captured Alexandria, taking some three or four cannons there, and twenty-two miles above we captured Henderson's Hill, took four cannons there and two regiments of rebels, one cavalry, the other infantry; then further up we captured a fort and garrison with ten cannons, the name of the fort I have forgotten. At a place called Pleasant Hill where General Banks had been defeated we met the rebels and drove them back, covering his retreat to the Mississippi river, a distance of over one hundred miles, having a rebel force around us of about 18,000 men, which we had to fight every day for two weeks. In the fall of 1864 I was mustered out at Nashville, Tenn., went home, got married the following spring, resumed farming and have been at it ever since. I am now seventy-three years old and feel played out.

Ole Rocksvold's Glenwood chapter with autobiography info

and the third into the Twelfth, the fourth into the Thirty-eighth and the fifth into the Sixth Cavalry. All of these companies were more or less soldiers from Glenwood township. A few soldiers also went into the Fifteenth Wisconsin as a Scandinavian regiment. It was soon found that all of these boys were of the right kind of material of which to make good soldiers.

"A certain family, Thrond Steen and wife of Glenwood, sent six sons to the front, one to the First Minnesota, three in the Twelfth Iowa, one in the Thirty-eighth Iowa, and one in the Fifteenth Wisconsin, and the seventh and oldest brother was drafted in 1864, but when it became known that he had six brothers in the army before, they let him go home to take care of his old parents. Glenwood has more than furnished its quota of soldiers, but Decorah got the credit of a good many of them, as they did not think of demanding their enlistment as a credit to Glenwood township, so in 1864 when a draft was ordered, four men were drafted in the township.

"There are three Norwegian Lutheran churches in the township. The first was built in 1857 and remained until 1870, when. the congregation had outgrown it, then a large stone church was built that year by the side of the old one at a cost of $13,000. A few years later a part of the congregation seceded and built a church for themselves in 1889. Two years later others joined them, so they removed it to a better location and remodeled it at a cost of $3.000.

*Population in 1910, 871.

Another church was built in the southwest part of the township about the same style and cost as the one above mentioned.

"There have been two flour mills erected in Glenwood township. One was built in 1868, known as the stone mill on the Trout river, and had adequate water power for a number of years. Another was built in 1872 by B. B. Sander on the same stream further down, but after a few years the water gave out, so the machinery was sold as scrap iron and the building was converted into a creamery. The stone mill mentioned above was run for several years by steam, but finally was closed, as it did not pay expenses."

∼ Appendix 1 ∼

Glenwood Church: Ole's Involvement

This appendix is for those who are interested in a detailed look at the information contained in the meeting notes in *Minutes of Congregational Proceedings of the Little Iowa Norwegian-Evangelical Lutheran Congregation and the Glenwood Congregation*. You will learn more about the committees on which Ole served, decision making in the congregation, and how the congregation came to be split. Also discussed are issues and information about predestination, relationships with incoming immigrants, the raising of children, secret societies, the "Know Nothing" political party, and the challenge of maintaining one's language and culture in a new country.

The Detailed Church History Based on Church Meeting Minutes

The church was established at a Jan. 12, 1854 meeting at Thrond Lommen's house near Trout Creek, where they divided the those wanting to belong to the Norwegian-Evangelical Lutheran Church into 6 parishes (eventually increased to 8). The source for this information, the book of congregational meeting minutes, was reconstructed after a parsonage fire destroyed the original copy. We are fortunate we have this information at all, thanks to the people at the current Glenwood Church and Pastor Stacey Nalean-Carlson.

First, the bylaws and procedures were created. They recorded in paragraph 3 that all ceremonial acts must conform to the "Norway and Denmark's Church Ritual of 1685" and its Service book, with some modifications as were necessary in this country. They required in paragraph 4 to call only pastors who conformed to the Norwegian Church's requirements and were properly examined and ordained.

The issue of schools is mentioned in paragraph 21 saying school affairs would be conducted by the school council consisting of the congregational council and trustees. The school council would decide school terms, districts, courses of learning, hiring of teachers, and salaries. They also made sure teachers carried out their duties and dismissed teachers if their work was unsatisfactory. So in early settlements of European immigrants in the U.S., schools were often initially created by churches rather than civil government.

Some churches at that time had a distinctive, personal way of intervening in disputes among parishioners. Paragraph 23 of these bylaws for this church states when a member of the congregation has a dispute with or a complaint about another member, he must report it to the pastor and parish assistant. They would try to settle the question. If this didn't work, the disputants were supposed to appear before the congregation. Then the council would do their best to help resolve the matter, citing a directive in the Bible in Matthew, Chapter 18. I wonder how well that idea would go over today.

A short history of the congregation is at: http://www.glenwoodlutheran.org/history, and also in an article summarizing the book, *The Norwegian Immigrant and His Church* by Eugene Fevold, also listed in the bibliography.

At the May 29, 1856 congregational meeting, the parish near Glenwood was divided into two areas, and Ole was made a trustee for area 1, with his name misspelled In the minutes as "Ola P. Ragsvolden." His name was spelled correctly in minutes of subsequent meetings, though, listed as "Ole P. Rocksvold." Church council members were in charge of "churchly concerns." Trustees, having one year terms, were charged with the "secular affairs" of the congregation. There would be a President, Secretary, and Treasurer. The trustees would maintain and preserve all secular arrangements and properties and make assessments for necessary funds. They also had the power to assess and collect money from the congregation for public taxes and duties. Trustees could also assess fees to keep the church running if the minimal contribution required, plus free-will offerings, weren't covering all the expenses. Trustees elected chairmen and secretaries. The future pastor of the congregation, Ulrik Vilhelm Koren, recommended that each communicant pay ten cents to get the church started and to help pay for a $25 fee they needed to send in to the governing body of the Norwegian Evangelical Lutheran Church in America. At the time, Koren was traveling over a large area, serving many places, but was later to become the pastor specifically for Glenwood Lutheran.

On Dec. 1, 1856, they voted to be incorporated. At this same meeting, they wrote that no person could be a trustee unless he is male, over age 21, and a member of this church. It also stated all members of the church may vote.

Rev. Ulrik Vilhelm Koren is Called

On Nov. 29, 1858, they decided to draw up a formal letter of call to Rev. Vilhelm Koren. A letter from Dec. 1, 1856 is mentioned, but for some reason it hadn't been ratified so this 1858 letter is a slightly altered version of the 1856 letter. A salary of 400 dollars annually was to be given and a building for the parsonage needed to be enlarged and repaired. There were some questions about which geographical areas Koren would cover and how to divide the congregations up. They decided each farmer would provide one-fourth cord of wood each year so the pastor wouldn't have to use up the woods by the parsonage. If a farmer couldn't provide the wood, a payment of 50 cents was to be paid to the trustees.

By the Dec., 1860 meeting, the pastor mentioned concerns about the use of God's word in church and home, "conditions regarding the young people," school children, and public offenses during the year, the church's connection with the Synod, and the need to take communion. They also discussed the idea of locating a university in Decorah, and possibly dividing the Little Iowa congregation.

The Origin of Luther College

On March 1, 1861, they decide to divide the Little Iowa congregation and also started to raise university/church academy funds. This school eventually became Luther College in Decorah. A short history of the college is at: https://www.luther.edu/about/history.

These pastors and immigrants in northeast Iowa, southeast MN, and southwest WI were very forward-thinking to so value education to start a college then, even when many of them were not well off and some still lived in sod huts.

Frustrations for the Pastor

On Jan. 9, 1863, Koren gave a report on conditions of the last year, connection of the Synod with other groups and the state. He also mentioned the requirements for church discipline, communion practices, and "grave sins" in the congregation. These "sins" included neglecting God's word, lack of brotherly rebuke, domestic strife, drunkenness, and covetousness of worldly goods. These problems were taking a lot of his time, so Rev. Koren said he didn't have enough time and energy for study.

A Parishioner's Conflict with Rev. Koren

In the Nov., 3, 1863 church minutes, a long-standing disagreement was mentioned. A member had said openly that he hated Pastor Koren. The member had been publically admonished by the pastor and deacon the previous summer repeatedly, and attempts were made to talk with him alone, too, to get him to confess his sin and be reconciled. Eventually the pastor decided that doing "open discipline" in church had been "too hastily undertaken" and wrote to the member for a chance to talk. Koren confessed he had shown a "lack of wisdom and prudence" in the matter which made the problem worse. The member had then confessed his sin and asked to be reconciled. The congregation voted to forgive and reconcile him with the congregation.

School Organization and the Question of Dance

On April 4, 1865, Ole was selected to be one of the 5 supervisors for the school. Among their responsibilities was to collect the fees to cover expenses, including the teacher's salary. They met on this date to say there were complaints of a lack of payment of the school expenses from some families and of small amounts of the teacher's salary. The congregation also discussed the question, "Is dancing sinful or not?" It was decided unanimously that a Christian could not with good conscience dance in "the way this entertainment is usually conducted because it gives occasion for temptation and bad company as well as setting a bad example."

Plans to Build a New Brick Church

On 11-24-1865, the congregational meeting declared a parishioner, by name, was unfit to take communion if he requested to do so because of "neglect of church services, indifference to instruction for his children, unwillingness to come to congregational meetings when he was summoned, etc." At the same meeting, they decide to build a new church of brick, 50 feet X 35 feet, not counting choir area and steeple, on the same property as the current church, with the goal of summer 1868 for completion. Subscriptions would be started to pay for it.

On 12-21-1867, Ole was selected among five people who were to be on the the building committee. Taxation would be used to pay for the stone. Ole's brother Anton, and one other person were elected as trustees.

The Question of Secret Societies

At the 5-28-1868 congregational meeting, they discussed whether it was useful to belong to secret societies. The minutes stated that no member of the congregation did belong to such societies at the time. (My note: At least that they are aware of....!)

Discussions of Slavery, Financial Matters, and a Limestone Church Instead

At the congregational meeting of 12-19-1868, one member of the delegates to the Synod explained the situation regarding the slavery issue, but gave no details about that summary. There was a lengthy discussion. The delegate stated he did not understand the issue before the meeting and had some doubts about the position of the ministers in this matter. During the transactions of the Synod the delegate said the teaching of the pastors was biblical, but the minutes of this meeting do not state what those teachings were. Also at this meeting it was noted that the salary of school master Pedersen was in arrears and a committee of 4 was appointed to resolve this matter, including Ole. It was also decided that the new church wouldn't be made of brick after all, but limestone. Apparently it has not been built yet, even though the plan in 1865 was for it to be done by now.

Two School Districts As They Grew

On 6-14-1869, it was decided the congregation would have two districts for schools, with each school having a different teacher. The new committee of 8 to create these schools included Ole. They would bring their recommendations to the congregation regarding boundary lines, salaries, residence for the new schoolmaster, etc. Andrew Strandbakken, Ole's brother-in-law, was selected as one of three collectors for school salaries.

On 1-12-1870, there was a discussion about certain sins, especially regarding courtship.

More About Secret Societies

At the church meeting on 2-16-1870, after a long discussion, it was decided that secret societies were sinful and Christians should not participate in them for these reasons: there is an absolute promise about the secret society, the misuse of oath, and the association of secret societies with unbelief and atheism. Anton Rocksvold, Ole's brother, was elected to be among three to collect the fall offering. The congregation gave the pastor permission to travel to Norway.

Views on Alcohol Use

On 5-7-1870, a letter was read from the Decorah congregation about the drunkenness of people using Decorah as a market place. It asked that all Christians not be present in places where intoxicating drink is sold. This congregation "agreed heartily" and would try to promote this cause.

On 3-20-1871, there was more discussion of delinquent accounts to pay for the new church, and that collectors had the power to cancel payments for cases of parishioners in need. Anton Rocksvold was among 4 to serve as apportioners for those payments and was also among 6 who were elected to visit young people and guests of the congregation (newcomers).

Temptations for Young People

On 4-8-1872, there was a discussion about temptations of young people regarding several things, including lotteries. They also decided to call an assistant pastor.

What about Delinquent Accounts?

At the church meeting of 1-4-1873, there was a discussion of school issues and a clarification that all confirmed members need to contribute to the cost of the school. If someone didn't, the trustees would summon witnesses to this neglect and make a complaint to the congregation. Unless there was a valid reason for non-payment after admonishment, these people would not have access to communion, sponsorship at christenings, and their children would be denied access to school. A decision about a specific member's open lack of faith and neglect of God's Word was postponed. Ole was selected among 3 for a committee making recommendations regarding where the pastor's parsonage should be-Decorah or Washington Prairie. Glenwood congregation preferred Decorah.

Fencing and Policy on Non-Member Burials

On 6-13-1873, it was decided to fence the church yards of both congregations. A committee of 4, including Ole, was to take care of money, materials, and labor. It was also decided that anyone living within the boundaries of the congregational border for two years without becoming members must bury their dead in the public township cemetery rather than the church cemetery. A committee of 4, including Ole, was to collect the house rent for the pastor.

At the church meeting of 10-23-1873, Ole and 5 others were elected for a committee to get offers for "fitting up the church building." It was decided the reasons for calling Pastor Borge were valid and gave Pastor Koren authority "to look for other help."

On 12-4-1873, Andrew Strandbakken was selected to be among 4 to collect the fall offering.

Intervention in Two Parishioners' Conflict

On 5-12-1874, there was a disagreement between Charles Steen and H. Pasop. Pasop had accused Steen of some wrongdoing. Steen denied the wrongdoing and felt offended. The congregation found no evidence for Pasop's accusations.. It was recommended Steen forgive Pasop if Pasop could not understand his offense, which the congregation felt was not due to ill will. They asked Steen to help Pasop in this matter.

Disputant Leaves

At the church meeting of 11-20-1874, 4 members, including Ole, were elected to take up subscriptions to help with the indebtedness of about $800. They replaced Charles Steen as treasurer, since he had moved to Decorah. Anton Rocksvold replaced Hans Sivesind as auditor. Ole and A. Steen were elected to take care of heating facilities at church. Ole and Ole Ruen were elected to change the doors to the church so they open out. The schoolmaster Berg's salary was set at $25 per month.

Morals and Selling the Old Church Building

On 5-11-1875, They decided to sell the old church. A letter from schoolmaster Pedersen concerning the school situation in the district near Rocksvold School was to be discussed, but only two from that district showed up so they took no action. No details were given about the situation. They discussed the need for supervision of the morals of the children at the "English school." A case of immorality in the congregation was discussed, with a reminder of parental duty to guide their children away from temptation. It was also requested that those who are to fence the church yard get the task done. The church would be sold to the highest bidder, since no offer had yet been made according to the previous plan.

Church Discipline Issues

At the church meeting of 4-7-1876, there was a discussion of neglect of church meetings and church discipline, which is the responsibility of all, not just pastor's assistants. Gossip was a common sin and a hindrance to church discipline. They elected 5 men to be responsible for cases of public offense.

Rev. Koren, New President of the Synod

On 12-1-1876, Koren was called as president of the Synod. Very few were present at the meeting. A motion was made to use the profit from an acreage for the fall offering, which had been done by two parishioners. It was agreed to by 7 people, including Ole.

On 10-4-1877, the account with a specific parishioner will be taken care of for the congregation by Ole Rocksvold and Ole Ruen.

More Discussion on Temptations of Young People

At the church meeting of 2-18-1878, one discussion topic was temptations of young people- against the sixth commandment, dance, etc., and the reluctance of parishioners to talk about these matters.

Membership Questioned

On 12-13-1878, a discussion took place regarding a specific person's request for membership. There was an objection due to "his poor reputations in some respects." A committee of two was elected to inform that person of these objections. Regarding a different person's request for membership, a current member asked for settlement of a dispute with that person before allowing him to be a member. A committee of two were in charge of this settlement. Anton Rocksvold was selected among 4 as trustee.

Temperance Societies

On 3-20-1879, a committee of 3, including Ole, was selected to investigate what needs to be done about the heating apparatus for the church. A discussion occurred about temperance societies. The various views included: they conflict with Christian free will, not all these societies were bad, some felt drunkenness is a civil wrong, but not a sin, some felt if they joined they might encourage weaker brothers. Others felt joining a temperance society wouldn't help weaker brothers because abstinence wouldn't occur because of God's love but instead by coercion. Pastor Koren cited I Cor. Chapters 8 and 9 in the Bible that Christians should plead Christian freedom to choose abstinence, not membership in a society. It was discussed whether being a guest in a saloon is acceptable as a Christian. Based on the conditions of the saloons in this area, it was thought it wouldn't be acceptable, but not necessarily all saloons. They decided to take up an offering for the Negro mission after spring season. Ole asked a question, and the congregation decided the collection of the claim on Christen Svano's house for the sum of the second assessment would fall on him together with interest.

A New Parsonage to Be Built

At the church meeting of 11-10-1880, It was decided to buy 20 acres for the new parsonage, a committee of 5, including Ole, would search for a place. Pastor Quammen was recommended by Pastor Koren and Turmo, citing "declining health," but it didn't say if it was Koren or Turmo who had the health concern.

Questions about Predestination and Assurance of Salvation

On 2-4-1881, Pastor Koren discussed the Church dispute about how far a believer is assured of salvation. This had been discussed at the Conference in Decorah. He warned of the danger of a potential split in the Synod which might cause a delay in the division of the parish until later. Ole was one of 4 elected to be trustees. Andrew Strandbakken was one of 3 elected to be delegates to the general Synod.

Pastor Turmo Leaving

On 11-1-1881, there was a discussion of Pastor Turmo being called to Rock County, WI, which became vacant when Rev. Naeseth was called to Luther College. Pastor Turmo explained his reasons to consider the call. Ole and one other parishioner stated they thought the reasons for him to leave were stronger than the reasons to stay. Pastor Jacobson said he agreed Turmo should take the call. The congregation voted unanimously for Turmo to take the call, if after prayer and examining his conscience, he believed that is what he should do, and that a replacement is found before he goes. Turmo said he had already prayed and examined his conscience, and upon hearing they were approving of it, he would accept the call to Rock County.

Pastor Assistants Elected

At the church meeting on 11-6-1881, 3 assistants to the Pastor were elected, including Ole. Of the six people running, the top three were: Ole, 39 votes, Andrew Evenrud, 29 votes, Hans Bleken, 24, votes.

Sheds for Horses, and the Call of Pastor Borge

On 2-2-1882, Anton Rocksvold, Ole's brother, and 4 others offered to make sheds for horses. He would also take care of the incorporation deed for the congregation. They decided on property for the parsonage costing $2000. They planned to send a call to Pastor M. Borge, Mankato, MN, and if he rejected the call, they would call Pastor O. Norman, Ottertail County, MN, with a salary of $400-500, plus offerings and extras, and gifts in kind.

A Call to Student Hauge

On 8-30-1882, the congregation discussed whether to call student Hauge in Madison as pastor when he completed his examinations. They decided to call him right away. Ole presented lists for pastors' salaries, 1881.

Starting to Audit Accounts

On 11-20-1882, Anton Rocksvold and two others were elected auditors. The congregation decided there should be a proper audit of treasurer's accounts each year.

Insufficient Salary for Schoolmaster

At the church meeting of 12-19-1882, the schoolmaster said he needed more money to support his big family. They decided they could also offer him the precentor (choir director) position to add to his work for the congregation. They were also increasing the attendance area for his school. The congregation decided they felt responsible to "free" the schoolmaster to make a better livelihood, so it sounds like the salaries for teachers were sometimes not adequate to raise a family. A committee of 3, including Anton Rocksvold, were elected to bring a proposal about how to help the schoolmaster achieve the support he needs. They also planned to have Pastor Koren express appreciation to him at the next service. A farewell offering would also be taken. It wasn't clear what the committee would actually do to help him after that. A committee of 5, including Ole, were elected to set up the divisions and terms for the school district. Perhaps a reorganization/reassessment of needs was in order. A committee of 4, including Ole, was responsible for laying out the parsonage site, after consulting with Pastors Amlund and Koren.

"Do Everything Possible Not to Become Involved"

On 3-7-1883, the congregation decided, regarding the predestination controversy, to "do everything possible not to become involved."

The rest of the *Minutes of the Congregational Proceedings* book lists the Glenwood congregational minutes separately, 1883-1933. They were translated by Charlotte Jacobson, Aug. 1982.

Updated Bylaws for Glenwood Church

It lists the bylaws/rules at the beginning, similar to what they did at the beginning of the minutes book. The following were listed as the "symbolical books of the Norwegian Lutheran Church" which give "a clear statement of the teaching of God's Word": Apostolic Creed, Nicene Creed, Athanasian Creed, Luther's Small Catechism, the unchanged Augsburg Confession, and the creed as presented to Emperor Charles V at the Diet of Augsburg, 1530.

> In brief, in order to be an adult member of this church, one must:
>
> a. have been baptized
>
> b. confess adherence to the canonical books of Holy Scripture
>
> c. understand church doctrine at least to the level of a confirmand
>
> d. not indulge in works of the flesh, live in Christian conduct
>
> e. support the congregation and decisions as long as they are not contrary to God's Word
>
> f. not belong to a secret society

The right to speak and vote at congregational meetings were reserved for male, confirmed members at least 21 years old, who contribute to the congregational expenses at least every 6 months, and are "not under church discipline". Exceptions for allowing others to speak at a meeting can be decided by the congregation. Decisions at congregational meetings are made by majority vote, with two exceptions: two-thirds majority is needed to elect a pastor or schoolmaster and also to amend regulations of the congregation.

A pastor or schoolmaster or officer of the congregation can be removed through proper proceedings. Main grounds for removal of a pastor or schoolmaster: stubborn insistence, despite warning, of false teaching; scandalous life; or lack of fidelity in duties of the office. A member can be unanimously excluded according to God's Word, and would lose all rights and partial ownership of church property. It further lists how the board is organized and other rules. The document is dated March 17, 1885, with Anton Rocksvold listed as notary public.

Aug., 1883, Pastor Amlund was elected chair. C. Sivesind was elected to replace Ole as auditor.

Cemetery, Well, Pump, and Windmill Issues

On 6-10-1884, a committee of 3, including Ole, was elected to divide the cemetery into lots and report back. A committee of 3, including Ole, was elected to decide if the well should be dug deeper, and had the authority to go ahead and do the digging, if necessary. The pump needed repair, a cylinder exchanged, and a windmill erected.

A Separate Section for Those Who Committed Suicide

At the church meeting of 10-14-1884, it was decided that a separate section of the cemetery was to be reserved for people who committed suicide. The old rules still stood for non-members regarding burials in the church cemetery.

Handling Delinquent Accounts

On 1-5-1885, the treasurer reported the debts, and there was a discussion about what to do if people didn't pay their subscriptions (bills to cover congregational expenses sent to members). Collectors would visit people who haven't paid and collectors could ask a trustee or pastor assistant to accompany them on this task. Members were encouraged to do what is right and to come to a congregational meeting to say why they weren't paid up.

Fencing, Bill Ringing, and the Meaning of "Free Will"

On 1-12-1886, it was decided that a committee of 3, including Ole, would supervise the work to fence the church yard. They will also build a little house near the church. They decided to pay the custodian a dollar at each funeral that isn't held the same day as a church service. The bell ringer should be paid at such funerals as well. In this case, the custodian was the bell ringer as well. The congregation also gave permission for the ringing of the church bell for a wedding. Those involved in the wedding would pay the ringer. The congregation found a specific member "entirely responsible for paying his free will subscription. If he does not do so, he will be guilty of fraud." (Perhaps a new name was needed for the money donated rather than "Free Will Subscription.")

Caring for the Poor

On 6-1-1886, it was decided that those who needed temporary financial support could receive this from the congregation. Those needing continual support are to be turned over to the county for help.

More on Predestination- Withdrawal from Synod?

At the church meeting of 2-1-1887, due to the strong differing opinions about predestination, a discussion was held to decide whether they could become united as a congregation by withdrawing from the Synod. P.B. Halvorson moved that they withdraw from the Synod. Berg's substitute motion was that since the split wasn't definite, the decision to withdraw should be made later. Vick submitted a written motion regarding withdrawal. After discussion, Ole moved they vote on Vick's motion and if it passed with two-thirds majority, that should be considered the will of the people. Ole's motion passed. They voted, but it didn't reach two-thirds majority. 64-40. Then Ole submitted Berg's substitute motion, it was voted on and passed. So the decision was to wait on deciding whether to withdraw or not.

At the church meeting on 6-16-1887, further discussion occurred regarding whether to withdraw from the Synod. Pastor Amlund wanted Pastor Koren to be a consulting member of the congregation since he was a former pastor. A member said Pastor Koren shouldn't interfere. Several agreed and moved to have him not speak. That motion didn't pass, so Koren was accepted as a consulting member of the meeting. Those who spoke for withdrawing said it was to bring peace and unity if the congregation stood alone. They thought partisanship would eventually die out. Those against withdrawing from the Synod said it wouldn't bring unity, and that the Synod had the right doctrine so they couldn't in good conscience withdraw. They thought the public would believe the reason for the withdrawal was because they opposed some Synod doctrines and that would not be good. The people wanting withdrawal said they didn't want to judge the Synod.

Rev. Koren said he deplored the fact that the congregation was taken up with the idea of separating from the church group to which he belonged, and asked them to not act so hastily. He did not think there were two kinds of faith and if he had the chance to talk in the confessional with each member, most would say they still held their original beliefs, but that misunderstandings were causing the problem. He suggested they hold discussion meetings to learn more about the misunderstandings on this issue. Koren would be willing to come and answer questions. Someone raised a motion to withdraw, but Koren offered a different motion to withdraw specifically stating it wasn't due to the dispute with Synod doctrine. That motion didn't pass. So they decided to address this more in the fall, but in actuality they didn't take it up again until March. In the meantime...

Another Intervention in a Dispute Between Parishioners

On 1-5-1888, there was a complaint of one member, Nik Vik, against another, Ole Nesset. The congregation heard the complaint, but no judgment was made. They told the two to select 5 members to be on a mediation committee, which was done.

On 1-22-1888, a summary was submitted saying the disputants mentioned in the 1-5-1888 meeting minutes had reconciled and said it was due to a misunderstanding. The two thanked the committee for helping them reconcile.

Continued Intense Disagreements on Predestination

At the church meeting of 3-6-1888, Pastor Amlund asked if resigning would help the congregation find unity. Some spoke saying they thought they would achieve unity better with Amlund staying. One asked if Amlund would still serve the congregation if they stayed associated with the Synod. He answered that he could unless there were other reasons to resign. He said he may need to leave soon anyway to go to a warmer climate. The congregation discussed the need to call a new pastor and what to do about the Synod association question. Two motions were presented: One by A.B., which said to prevent a split in the congregation they should put the disputes aside and withdraw from the Synod. Vote, 47 for, 56 against. There was further discussion, with differences of opinion about doctrine. They decided to have a meeting in which the doctrinal differences would be discussed, and theologians would be invited to represent each side of the doctrine of conversion. A committee of 4, including O.E. Nesset, O.H. Berg, Ole Rocksvold, and P.B. Halvorson, two from each side of the dispute, would select the debaters and set the meeting. It doesn't list which side Ole was on. (Note: Since at the 2-1-1887 meeting, P.B. Halvorson moved to withdraw, perhaps Ole also felt that way, since his name is listed immediately before Halvorson's in the committee list, but they may not have listed them in order, two for one view, the next two for the other, but it is a possibility.)

Pastor Amlund Leaving

On 3-20-1888, Pastor Amlund was called to Story County, IA. (which is about in the middle of Iowa, so not really in the warmer climate he said he and his wife were seeking. Perhaps he was actually seeking a less stressful environment.) He described more details about the situation at Story County and said he felt it was his duty to leave because of his wife's health. He repeated that he had said the same at the last meeting – that he couldn't stay here because of her health. A discussion arose about whether to release him from this congregation. On the issue of his wife's health, they agreed. On the issue of the situation in Story, there were different opinions. O. P. Ruen moved that those who accepted Amlund's reasons to leave be permitted to acknowledge that by voting, which they did: 43 for, 2 against. Some didn't vote. Ole moved that the congregation leave it up to Amlund to do according to his conscience and until he leaves he would still be considered in all respects their pastor. Passed unanimously, but two people Nils Vik and Agrim Halversen, wanted the minutes to show they did not vote on Rocksvold's motion. The congregation decided to elect 12 members, "six from each side," to call a new minister:

Ole Rocksvold, Ole Ruen, P.B. Halvorson, Hans Ruen, Tore Bolson, Olaus Skjol (listed on left side), O.H. Berg, Ole Nesset, Agrim Halvorson, Anders Evenrud, Gustav Vestby, Johannes Sivesind (listed on right side of page).

Ole on the Call Committee , Call of Rev. Borge

On 3-26-1888, The call committee elected Ole Rocksvold chair, and O.H. Berg, secretary. Here is a summary of their resolutions that carried unanimously:

1. Discontinue doctrinal dispute and don't participate in it. No agitation, distributing pamphlets, not trying to force opinions on others to get adherents

2. If necessary for peace, the congregation may choose not to send a delegate to the Synod meeting at this time, but not permanently.

3. The congregation doesn't want anyone outside the membership to come in bringing discord. The district president may come to visit, but not in connection with the doctrinal dispute.

4. The congregation will call a pastor who has a neutral position, is not taking part in the present doctrinal dispute

5. Concerning support of higher education, no one in good conscience, needs to be feel bound to contribute (Author's note: perhaps some may disagree with positions on predestination of some of the leaders at Decorah College.)

6. Plan to call Pastor Borge.

Based on the minutes and the above resolutions, it sounded like Ole had an "agree to disagree" or "live and let live" philosophy for getting through this conflict. Apparently some found it hard to have this attitude as you will read as the minutes notes continue. On a motion by Nils Vik, each resolution 1-5 was discussed separately before approval. On resolution 6, C. Toyen objected to calling Pastor Borge because he had been a source of the "Redebjorelse" (Explanation) regarding the dispute. O. Schoel said now that he had heard Borge had done this, he no longer could vote for Borge, but would remain neutral as to voting. Others said this had come up in discussion when they made the committee resolutions, but that Borge had not been a participant in the dispute and was the kind of person they would want to call. Vote to call Borge: 65 for, 12 against. They decided to include the committee's proposal list with the call letter. The congregation also decided to reconsider the earlier decision to hold a discussion meeting as noted in 3-6-1888 meeting minutes. This was unanimously approved. If Borge didn't accept the call, the same committee would look for another candidate. They voted, 57 for and 6 against, to allow Borge to also serve Paint Creek congregation. They also thanked the ladies aid society for buying the organ and carpet.

Twenty-five Members to Withdraw from Congregation

At the church meeting on 9-5-1888, a statement of withdrawal from the congregation, dated Aug. 18. 1888, was presented to Pastor Borge Aug. 20 for the Sept. 5 meeting. On June 16, twenty-five members (Ole's name wasn't listed but the list did include P.B. Halvorson), had sent a request to Pastor Borge for him to renounce the "Missourian doctrine embodied in 'An Explanation' " because they could not accept him as pastor without that assurance." That doctrine said that people are predestined to be saved and go to heaven, that people have no ability whatsoever to affect whether they are saved, and that it was preordained by God who is chosen to be saved. (Author's note: For more information about the dispute, see *Lutherans in North America* and *The Predestination Controversy* in the bibliography for this book.)

The statement noted that despite their "well-founded protest and statement that he has both begun and is continuing to work as pastor in the congregation," Pastor Borge refused to renounce this doctrine. There was a motion at the 9-5-1888 meeting saying Pastor Borge acted "in conformity" with his call to accept the withdrawal statement. It was passed unanimously. Regarding the second part of the withdrawal statement, they stated, "From earlier experiences we see no hope that we can through further proceedings come to a peaceful and blessed conclusion." There was a long debate about this statement after it was read. Several said the previous meetings, including the ones on March 20 and March 26, dispute that conclusion. After further discussion, they decided to cut off debate and not make a judgment about that phrase.

The conflict about predestination and the actions of the parishioners have parallels with today's climate in the U.S. and elsewhere. For example, there was much division during and after the 2016 U.S. presidential election. It has been difficult to get people to talk respectfully and listen regarding their differences of opinion, and work together and compromise for the benefit of all, not just select portions of the country.

On 1-7-1890, a committee of 2, including Ole, was selected to repair the heating apparatus immediately. Ole would sub for Iver Berg as assistant to pastor in Iver's absence.

Church Discipline of a Parishioner

On 12-9-1890, a discussion was held about "church discipline" of a specific man. The meeting notes stated he was guilty of offending the congregation and his wife several years ago by associating with another woman. Pastor Borge discussed the meaning of church discipline and steps to take. Briefly, Rev. Borge said it was a Christian's duty to reprimand a sinful brother in Christ, and if he repented, to forgive him. If he didn't repent, it is the duty of that Christian to consult one or two other brothers to admonish him. If this doesn't help, they should report the situation to the congregation and if he doesn't repent then, they should exclude him. Borge said the reason it had taken so long to meet about this situation was that the man was ashamed to come to the meeting while Pastor Amlund served the congregation. In addition, at the previous meeting, he said he wasn't told the time of the meeting, and so missed it. The man repented and the congregation unanimously forgave him in the confidence he wouldn't sin again. (Could something about this situation also have contributed to the reason the Amlunds left?)

At the church meeting on 5-26-1891, a case of church discipline was listed concerning drunkenness and "loose talk" which was "disposed of in a satisfactory manner."

Buying Insurance for the Parsonage

On 1-12-1892, the church members voted to remove the name of the person described in the 5-26-1891 minutes. Also, they mentioned insurance had been bought for the parsonage.

Burial of People Who Had Left the Congregation

At the church meeting on 4-25-1894, there was a discussion with various opinions of what to do about the people who left the congregation, but had reserved lots in its cemetery for their dead. Some thought it was a legal question. The decision was made to lock the Glenwood cemetery, and none of those who left the congregation may bury their dead in it. Also, only the pastor of the Glenwood Church or a pastor of the Synod may conduct a funeral service at the congregational cemetery. The vote was 17 for, 7 against.

Sunday School in Parishioners' Homes

In the 1-7-1896 minutes, it said the secretary, B.A. Halvorson, had died, so Gustav Johnson was taking his place. They couldn't read the last minutes because they hadn't been entered before B.A.'s death. Sunday school would be continued to be held, as they started a year ago, at different people's homes and at the school houses in the congregation. They felt that this practice of rotating homes for the training is a good influence on both old and young. It was decided Pastor Borge would deliver a lecture in the near future on temperance, "as intemperance in the congregation is an evil which must be met."

A Mystery We May Never Understand

Between the congregational meeting of Jan. 7, 1896, and the Sept. meeting, Ole wrote a letter to his daughter Matilda and son Carl, on 4-3-1896, saying he had received a long letter from Pastor Borge accusing Ole of being a "liar, thief, and criminal," which was mentioned earlier in this book. Ole said he included this Borge letter in with the correspondence to Matilda, but we have not found a copy of it. Ole also said Borge had accused Ole before unsuccessfully and wouldn't be successful this time either, and that these terms would better apply to Borge. Ole wrote he was considering bringing this issue up in front of the congregation, but apparently decided against it because there is no record in the congregational minutes of this ever occurring.

Rev. Borge's accusation raises many questions. For many years Ole had been elected to many committees, volunteered for many responsibilities, and was even on the call committee for getting Pastor Borge to serve Glenwood Church. There were no oblique references to an unnamed person being accused of being a liar, thief, or criminal in any minutes of the meetings, nor of an unnamed person questioning the pastor's behavior. The only mention of controversy regarding Pastor Borge in the minutes in the few years leading up to this letter was when some parishioners questioned the pastor's beliefs on the predestination doctrine, as mentioned earlier. From the minutes it was also learned that the pastor thought intemperance and temptations of young people were issues in the congregation, but those issues are not mentioned in the above accusations in Borge's letter.

Why did Borge accuse Ole of these deeds? Could he have been jealous of Ole's good reputation and accomplishments at the church? Was it a misunderstanding, miscommunication, mistaken identity, or idle false gossip on someone's part that Borge believed? Did Borge suffer from mental illness of some kind?

Perhaps it will remain a mystery unless other documents become available that we don't have now. I noted that after the big crises on doctrine the church went through, Ole's name wasn't listed on committees from then on. Perhaps Ole felt he had done enough volunteering after so many years, perhaps the stress had tired him out, or perhaps he had switched to the St. John's Lutheran in Waukon congregation at this time and so was not available to volunteer at Glenwood Church anymore. He was 64 as of Aug., 1896.

Issues After Ole Left the Congregation

I continue here with some meeting notes and comments about some issues that occurred in this Glenwood congregation after the divisive conflicts about predestation and the split. Even though Ole was no longer there, subsequent events would have affected Ole's relatives and friends. These notes also show the results of decisions the church took earlier and their ramifications.

What follows also includes various church issues that came up, historical context about the Know Nothings political party, and views people had about accepting non-Norwegian immigrants. There are parallels regarding immigrants still today. Also discussed are the challenges immigrants encountered in trying to retain their language and customs as time went on in this increasing diverse land.

On 9-9-1896, a committee was named to get the church repaired, as lightning had destroyed part of the roof and steeple.

At the church meeting on 9-16-1896, it was decided to make a committee to set up some posts at the church so people can tie up their teams of horses there.

The next few meetings only included things about mundane matters, so I omitted those.

Issues of Dance and Drink

On 4-7-1899, the chairman of the meeting, Pastor Borge, spoke a long time about how it does not make sense to allow young people to dance and drink at their homes. He also said it is demoralizing for young and old. Borge said members of the congregation shouldn't allow young people to buy horses and buggies right after confirmation since it became easier to go to undesirable places of entertainment when they have their own transportation. Some young people might spend all the money they earn and never be able to better themselves.

A Vote for a New School, and Help for a Couple

On 1-5-1900, the congregation voted to build a new school. It was decided that people outside the congregation who wanted to bury someone in the Glenwood cemetery should pay $5.00, if they can afford it. Some contributions for a fund for Gustav Pederson and his wife to go to the "Old People's Home" were listed. This is the first time the term "old people's home" was mentioned so perhaps that type of senior housing had recently started to be an option then. Gustav thanked everyone in a letter. He was selling his property and planning to move and apparently the couple needed more money than what was expected to be received in the sale.

On 1-8-1901, the minutes said more money was earmarked to help Gustav Pederson and his wife, and the old people's home was listed as in Stoughton, WI. "Anders Eggen's case was presented and after some discussion the congregation granted him forgiveness." Nothing further is explained. It is interesting to see a trend in the minutes of listing a person's name who has apparently done something wrong, but not telling what the wrong was. Perhaps they had now decided to avoid publically shaming people in detailed permanent records. Also, at this meeting there was a motion about Paint Creek Congregation stricken from the minutes, again without telling what the motion was.

Death by Alcohol

At the church meeting on 2-13-1901, in connection with a recent death due to drinking, several people said members of the congregation should quit going to the saloon and stop giving alcohol to others. Because the congregation considered this issue so important, they noted there would be a special meeting set for 2-27-1901 to discuss the topic further. They also planned a meeting to discuss making a barn for the parsonage.

On 2-27-1901, Pastor Borge gave a long speech about the sin of tempting someone by giving them alcohol, noting the case of Helmer Engrav and the sad death of Knut Thompson, a direct result of drinking. The congregation decided to forgive Helmer for this sin. It was moved and emphasized that it is wrong to go to saloons and wrong to use pocket flasks as this can lead to drunkenness and the previously-mentioned problems. The minutes said there was a "rising vote. 20 votes for." No one is listed as voting against.

Valuing forgiveness from a spiritual standpoint seemed to be important to this congregation and perhaps served social and emotional purposes as well.

On 4-25-1902, Pastor Borge asked for and got permission to visit Norway. Pastor Scarvie at Paint Creek would substitute.

On 8-24-1902, the congregation voted to build a platform in the church for the choir.

At the church meeting on 10-21-1903, the minutes said the Woldum brothers got in trouble for selling "drinkables which were supposed to be patent medicine, but had been used by some as intoxicants, the sale of which has been prohibited." The minutes named this act as "deplorable" and said those who knew about it should have done something to stop it. Martin Woldum confessed that act and spoke, saying he and his brothers didn't know they were breaking the law.

Not Ready for Confirmation

On 1-6-1904, the congregation discussed documents about "Ole Anderson Berge's Case." Ole Berge had left the congregation because his son wasn't confirmed last summer. Pastor Borge said he couldn't confirm him because of a lack of knowledge required of a confirmand. Ole Berge was given a notice to appear at this meeting, but didn't show up. Witnesses spoke and the congregation judged him as unChristian until he asked for forgiveness, quoting Jesus's words in Matthew 18: 15-17. They voted unanimously to put the documents into the minutes and that Pastor Borge should inform the Pontoppidan congregation about the resolution.

Borge Leaves, Rev. Scarvie Arrives

On 7-23-1905, Pastor Borge was called to be treasurer of the Synod and wanted to be released as pastor. They voted to call Pastor Scarvie.

On 8-28-1905, Pastor Scarvie accepted the call to be their pastor.

Details about Service

At the church meeting on 1-2-1906, the congregation voted to omit singing a hymn during the offering, but to just have the organist play. They decided to recite the Creed aloud at the service, for a trial period of 2 months. (It appears the congregation back then made many small decisions that today would be left to the pastor, organist, or choir director to decide.)

On 3-4-1906, Pastor Scarvie received a call to the newly organized Canoe Ridge congregation. The congregation agreed to let him add this responsibility, leading a service there every third Sunday.

New Catechism

On 8-28-1906, there was a discussion whether to use the new Explanation of the catechism, published by the Synod or continue to use the old Pontoppidan version. They approved the use of both.

What to Allow

On 1-8-1907, Professor Preus sent a letter, requesting Pastor Scarvie travel to other congregations to solicit for "S.C. Dormitory." The congregation voted to deny this request. A letter had arrived requesting violinist Skovgaard be allowed to play a concert at the church. This request was also denied. There was an election of officers, with "Rocksvold" listed as trustee, but no first name was given. By this date Ole had not served on committees for several years, so it very likely wasn't Ole. Since Anton, Ole's brother, died in 1886, it couldn't be him either, but it could have been a son of Anton or Ole or some other Rocksvold relative.

On 2-26-1907, a discussion ensued whether to increase the size of the schoolmaster Solheim's house. They voted 16 for, 2 against, 17 abstained, so Pastor Scarvie said they needed everyone's vote. Then the subsequent vote was 25 for, 8 against.

Caring for Parishioner After Fire

On 5-1-1907, they voted to collect money for Gustav Moen who lost almost everything in his house fire.

Ole's Move to ND

On 12-31-1907, the last letter we have that was written by Ole was postmarked from Decorah. The next letter we have, 3-31-1908, was postmarked from Beach, ND, so sometime between those two dates he must have moved to the farm in Beach, where he bought land to live with his son, Willie, also known as Peter William or Peder Wilhelm, and Ole's daughter, Hilda. So we know Ole was out of the area and living in ND for the next few years.

Which Texts Allowed?

On 1-7-1908, Pastor Scarvie asked about a series of texts, and the congregation voted to use the old ones. They also decided the pastor could decide on his own whether to stand before the altar or not at the time of the offering, and authorized Pastor to provide a new ministerial book and communion book. They also decided to borrow money for the debt on the schoolmaster's house. The organist was supposed to find someone to pump the organ.

Since these were the last meeting minutes before Ole's move to Beach, ND, I will discontinue noting many significant and interesting events in the congregation that could potentially have been affecting Ole since he no longer lived in the area.

I will, however, briefly mention a couple of larger issues that occurred in subsequent years which could have affected some of the relatives who remained in the area.

Four Sermons in English per Year

On 1-5-1909 the Glenwood congregation decided to start having four sermons a year in English for those who didn't understand Norwegian.

That date gives us an idea of when the switch away from services in Norwegian started to occur. Peter Rocksvold is listed as being involved in some committees quite regularly at this time, presumably Anton's son Peter, since Ole's son Peter William ("Willie") would have been in Beach, ND by then.

Synod Predestination Position Approved

On 10-12-1913 the congregation voted by overwhelming majority to accept the general proposal on the predestination issue document by the Synod June 11-18, 1913, in Minneapolis. Basically it said that God knows what the future brings for each person, but people also have a choice in their beliefs, potentially affecting whether they are saved. The document also said for Christians not to take away people's "comfort about their beliefs regarding being saved, so as to not harm each other by arguments on doctrine."

Preventing Other Nationalities From Settling There

On 7-19-1914, the congregation met to discuss "what could be done to keep people of other nationalities from settling in the community."

I was discouraged to read this, but the issue needs to be understood in the context of the times.

Most groups of immigrants who came to the U.S. tended to settle near each other, build churches for their communities with services in their own language far into the 1900's, and followed similar customs. According to Joyce Bryant in *Immigration in the United States*, there were so many immigrants coming in by the late 1800's that a political party called the "Know Nothings" tried to thwart the influx and actively tried to prevent the new immigrants from affecting the American populace. The Know Nothings believed the new immigrants would be a negative influence, and so the members of this party tried to create a hostile environment for newcomers.

Some immigrant families and their children tried to blend in as quickly as possible by changing their last names to sound more "American" and telling their children to speak English rather than their native language in the home. My mother and her siblings were told by their parents, for example, to only speak English once they started school, thinking it would assist them in becoming more successful, and fit in better. While the children did ultimately become successful in school and work, this decision unfortunately also led to the children gradually losing the ability to speak Norwegian.

Other immigrants tried to keep quite separate from the rest of the populace, in an effort to increase the chances of their traditions and beliefs being passed to the future generations. Some immigrant groups did this to a more extreme degree, such as the Amish or Hutterites, who even today limit their contact and participation with the rest of the population. Some immigrants decided a blending of the old traditions and new practices were needed to be successful in U.S., however they defined success.

Of course, there are parallels yet today. There are people in the U.S. and in other countries, too, who actively try to prevent or severely restrict immigration into their countries for certain groups of people and for a variety of reasons. Some include fear, desire to keep separate from other cultures and religions, limit population, concern about economic issues, and others.

Committee to Monitor the Selling of Land, and the Issue of Dance

At that same 7-19-1914 congregational meeting, they did a trial vote to form a committee to report back to the congregation whenever they heard of anyone thinking of selling their land. They voted 14 for, 2 against, with many abstaining. The committee would try to find buyers of whom they would approve, i.e., Norwegian Lutherans. After more discussion, they decided to drop the matter for the time being. They planned to meet later with Pontoppidan congregation because their church had also expressed interest in being part of the decision. At the same meeting they noted that it did very little good to speak against dancing, but Pastor Scarvie would nevertheless continue to speak out against it. This was further evidence of the struggle regarding how much to adapt customs and rules to others of the population.

Committee to Seek Norwegian Lutheran Buyers for Land

On 11-29-1914, the church meeting included both Glenwood and Pontoppidan congregations. Pastor Scarvie explained the meeting was to decide what could be done to prevent people of other nationalities from settling in their communities. He said this would make better opportunities for setting up congregational schools. He said he was not opposed to a common school, but felt that there was "too much of common school" and not enough of church school. Pastor Fjelde said he did not think that children could be properly brought up except by the use of God's Word and church school. There was discussion and the congregation moved to elect five men to supervise farm sales. Those who wished to sell would report to this committee. Pastor Scarvie said no one ought to sell his land to an outsider, but instead keep the land for his children and their descendants. He added that people wanted too much money for their land. Pastor Fjelde thought this plan might be too difficult to do. Some thought working with a reliable land agent might help, but others thought it was a bad idea. One parishioner suggested having a "farmer's club" to understand each other better, and Pastor Scarvie agreed that might be worthwhile, but may not accomplish their goals. The vote passed to create the committee, with three from Glenwood (Nils Evenrud, Gustav Johnson, Rudolph Nash), two from Pontoppidan (Olaus Ruen, Johannes Moe). This committee would have the limited authority of seeking a buyer, but if they couldn't find one they should report this to the congregation. This motion was approved unanimously. This decision was to be publicized in the periodicals, "Kirketidende" and "Lutheraneren."

"Not Eager to Settle Among Us"

On 1-30-1917, a meeting was held with Glenwood and Pontoppidan congregations. A parishioner, N. L. Vick, raised the question whether it was worthwhile to have these meetings about real estate and controlling who moved there. It was stated that people of other nationalities were "not eager to settle among us when they knew that we were working against them." Someone suggested that the committee should be authorized to borrow $1,000 in case a farm goes for sale, so they could buy it and hold it "until a suitable buyer appeared." It was mentioned that there was currently a farm in the area owned by an outsider. It was decided to send someone to the owner to find out what price and under what conditions he would be willing for the congregation to buy the farm. Melvin Blegen was elected to do this and report back. Olaus Ruen's and Nils Evenrud's terms on the committee were up. Olaus was reelected and Nils decided he didn't want to have another term, so Hans Levstuen was elected to replace him. They decided to meet again in February.

On 3-28-1917, the congregation met to decide if they wanted to buy the Kruger farm. The person who had been elected to talk to Mr. Kruger was not present at this meeting. The majority of the few present were against making the purchase and they dropped the matter. They decided to keep meeting about once a year regarding these real estate issues regarding people who weren't Lutherans of Norwegian descent.

Governor's Proclamation of English Only During WWI

During the 6-23-1918 congregational meeting, there was a discussion about the Governor's Proclamation that only English be used in church, school, gatherings, and on the telephone during the war. Almost all agreed this was not just and should be ignored. However the pastor explained that all authority comes from God and it was a Christian's duty to obey authority. They voted to follow the law, but asked Pastor Scarvie to write to the governor and ask if Rev. Scarvie could have two services in Norwegian for every one service in English and to be allowed to use some Norwegian in school. Author Karen Hansen, in *Encounter on the Great Plains*, noted that many Norwegians tended to be, among the various immigrant ethnic groups in the U.S., among the most reluctant to drop use of their first language in their daily activities and church services. Nowadays many people recognize the value of keeping one's first language active as well as mastering the language of the country in which one lives.

The 3-28-1917 meeting was the last time I find mention of the committee for preventing people who weren't Norwegian Lutherans from moving into the community. It doesn't say why they dropped the committee or the effort, but perhaps it gradually seemed less important to do. Perhaps the issue got relegated to a lower priority while seeking a new pastor soon thereafter. World War I (1914-18) was also occurring at this time so perhaps priorities changed in people's minds for multiple reasons.

Pastor Scarvie Dies, Many Failed Calls to Be Pastor

Pastor Scarvie became ill, went on a leave of absence, and ultimately died. The congregation had a very hard time finding someone to accept their call as seen in the minutes from 12-3-1918's meeting to 7-14-1919, when Pastor Brevik was announced as accepting the call. They tried calling several people, but were rejected over and over. Could one reason have been their history of so much controversy?

Parishioner Suing Pastor Brevik and Assistants

On the topic of pastors, in the meeting notes of 7-7-1929, there was a "case" concerning a member of the congregation, a trustee explained the situation, but it is not fully described in the minutes.

On 1-7-1930 it was decided that the member in question must withdraw his threat of legal proceedings against Pastor Brevik and his assistants, withdraw his accusation that the pastor was not a Christian and the congregation was not Christian, and must ask for forgiveness. The member must confess his sin against God and the congregation and promise to do better, and promise to cancel all legal proceedings in the case. If he didn't comply, he would lose membership.

Pastor Brevik Resigns and "He Meant It"

On 1-14-1930, Pastor Brevik tendered his resignation. They voted to not accept his resignation, but the pastor said he wanted to be allowed to decide whether he stayed or went. The congregation then said he could decide. Pastor Brevik then said he had resigned and "he meant it." Nevertheless the congregation moved to not accept it, the vote-33 not to accept, none to accept. Brevik, however, stood by his decision to resign. The congregation then elected him to be chair of the call committee to replace himself.

Call Committee Makes a List of 5 to Potentially Call to Replace Brevik

At the church meeting on 1-16-1930, they wrote that since they had so much trouble getting a pastor last time, the call committee should make a list of 5 people, and write the names in the order in which they would try to call them as pastor.

I wonder if there was ever any consideration as to why it was so hard to get a pastor to come there and what could be done differently to be more successful recruiting leadership in the future. No mention of such a discussion is in the minutes, but of course, it may have occurred but wasn't recorded. Being a pastor is very difficult, complicated work, requiring a diverse set of skills and talents. Coming to a congregation that had/is having strong differences of opinion and difficulty making decisions may understandably have discouraged people from wanting to come there at that time.

Number 4, Bredeson, Accepts the Call

On 4-14-1930, the fourth choice of the five options finally decided to accept the call, Pastor Bredeson.

At the church meeting of 4-7-1931, the minutes said they were discussing the decision of how to handle a bill of $550, the fee for Attorney Acres, in the "affair against Pastor Brevik, his assistants, and the board of trustees," by the member whose case was considered on 7-7-1929. The congregation decided to pay the attorney bill.

Rocksvold School

The *Minutes of the Congregational Proceedings* book contains a few more meeting minutes recorded through Jan. 2, 1934, including a couple in which the "Rocksvold School" is mentioned, presumably so named because it was the one next to the Rocksvold farm. We know Matilda, Ole's daughter, became a teacher, and may have taught at that "Rocksvold School." A small building that used to be a school is now on the property where Ole Rocksvold's farm at 1233- 258th St., Decorah, IA, was. The current owner told me it is now used as a garage. The house on the property is not the original house in which Ole and Anne raised their family.

After I inquired about meeting notes beyond 1-2-1934, the people at Glenwood Church only found *The Church Records*, which contains baptisms, confirmations, marriages, and funerals 1927-2002, but no detailed minutes.

Glenwood Lutheran Church is at 1197 Old Stage Road, Decorah, IA 52101-7348.

~ APPENDIX 2 ~

OLE'S POST-CIVIL WAR LETTERS

To: Matilda Rocksvold Anderson, A. O. Anderson, and Family
From: Ole Rocksvold **Date:** Mar. 20, 1895

Translation

Thoten, Iowa, March 20th, 1895

Mr. & Mrs. Anderson,

Your last long letter has gone unanswered for far too long. I injured my right shoulder some time ago and was not able to write. And, moreover, mother had to be cared for day and night, and I had to be available. She had to be lifted in and out of bed several times each hour. Yes, thank goodness, she was able to depart in peace. That had been her wish for a long time, to be released from her mortal body and be united with Christ, where all things are much better. Yes, I have the hope that (in spite of her many faults and sins) the Lord has taken . . .

[second page]

. . . her home, where there is no more illness, sorrow, or pain. "For the former things are passed away." *[Translator: I found this online as Revelations 21:4, King James translation]* She died on the 9th at 2:30 in the morning and seemed to have no pain. She passed away, content and serene, and in death she looked 20 years younger. We were able to easily straighten out her leg that was broken, and it was 4 inches longer than the other.

I bought a casket for her in Waukon, every bit as good as the one we had for Theodor, but this one only cost 18 dollars. Pastor Hellestvedt came to the house on the day of the funeral, which was Monday the 11th. He spoke first in the house, and later he gave a long and most excellent sermon in the church (which was almost full to overflowing). Oline Sivesind said she never before had heard such a good funeral sermon. *[Translator: Ole wrote a word that looks like "Ligkrodsken". "Lig" is Dano-Norwegian for "Lik", "body lying in the casket" in this case, but neither my wife nor I can figure out what is meant by the other part of the word that looks like "krodsken". I simply assume he is referring here to the funeral sermon.]*

[third page]

Around half of those in attendance belonged to *[Pastor]* Borge's congregation, and they were warmly welcomed at the end of the sermon. A message had been sent to me in the morning that our pastor did not have permission to inter someone in the cemetery (we buried Mother in our burial plot). I acted as though I hadn't heard about it, and I heard no more about it. I believe the parishioners wish they had a pastor like Hellestvedt instead of their own. *[Translator: I did some searching online and found out that Rev. J. A. Hellestvedt, after having served in the 1870s as the first Norwegian Lutheran pastor in North Dakota and in the 1880s in Monona, Iowa, served from 1895-1903 as the pastor of St. John's Lutheran Church in Waukon, Iowa, only a few miles from Glenwood. At this time, in 1895, Ole seems to have left the Glenwood congregation and was attending services in Waukon. What Ole writes in this passage, and later in this letter, seems to suggest that Ole may have left Glenwood congregation because, for whatever reason, he was not fond of Pastor Borge. And this perhaps helps explain in part Pastor Borge's criticism of Ole that we encountered in another letter.]*

The day after the funeral, the conference of the Decorah district began in Springfield Church. Pastor Hellestvedt came to our home after the funeral, and in the evening he and I traveled to Pastor Jacobsen's, continuing on the next morning together with the latter to the district conference. It began Tuesday morning and lasted until Thursday evening. There were eleven pastors in attendance and delegates from various congregations, . . .

[fourth page]

. . . in addition to members of the host congregation, so the church was full at all times. Sermons were given by Pastors Dreier, Arvesen, and Rundestvedt, all of them excellent. In the course of two days we got no further than halfway in the discussions that were listed as the first item on the conference agenda. This conference was the one of the most enjoyable times of my life. It was like being immersed in an ocean of God's love.

Pastor H[ellestvedt] and I found lodging with Halsten Nilsen, spending two nights there. We ate dinner at the home of Pastor Bakken. We had a ride of 4 miles both Tuesday morning and Thursday evening, but we had our team of horses standing in the barn and rode with him, so the trip posed no inconvenience. *[Translator: Difficult to interpret what Ole writes here. Perhaps he meant to say that he left his own team of horses in the barn at Pastor Jacobsen's and that they continued on from the Jacobsen farm with Pastor Jacobsen's team. And as for "4 mile", meaning 4 "miles", Ole is certainly referring here to American miles, since Springfield and Glenwood are neighboring townships. A Norwegian "mil" is equal to 10 km or 6.2 miles, but they did not travel 25 miles to get to Springfield Church.]* Clara Nilsen, that is to say Mrs. Helgeson, asked me to greet you from her. Helgeson was there too. He had come home from California. He said he had traveled west on the Northern Pacific and returned on the Southern Pacific.

[fifth page]

March 22nd

I interrupted this letter for a couple of days, in order to be able to pass on some important bits of news later.

Baard Halvorsen died on the 15th of this month after having been ill less than a week. He came down with "La grippe" *[Translator: the flu]* and it developed into pneumonia. There was not chance of his recovery. His wife, Julia, may have died in the meantime. She was still alive yesterday, but Dr. Wilkax *[Wilcox?]* told her there was no hope. She got sick right after Baard, and his funeral was postponed a day or two because it looked as though they might be able to hold a funeral for them together. Their two eldest children are also ill, and it is said that the eldest will soon fall prey to the Grim Reaper. The youngest child, a girl, born last January, is, as far as I know, the only one in the family in good health at this time. Julia has the same illness Baard had, and, I assume, the children as well. The funeral was on the 19th. The church was full to overflowing, . . .

[sixth page]

. . . as almost everyone in both congregations attended. Pastor Borge was at home and conducted the service himself. And, disregarding the occasion, his sermon, in my opinion, did not make half the impression on the listeners that Pastor Hellestvedt's made at Mother's funeral.

Oline Sivesind is very ill. She became bedridden very soon after Mother's funeral. On Wednesday the second of this month our congregation held Ladies' Aid at Kari Ruen's, the largest attendance we have had, with a large number coming from Borge's congregation.

Your mother is now about the same as she was last year after Theodor's funeral. She sometimes has trouble sleeping, and she is worn out and weak. A month ago she began to suffer from dropsy *[edema]* again. Welkox *[Wilcox]* was able to rid her of it, however, . . .

[seventh page]

. . . for some time after that her entire body felt sore and tender. *[Translator: there seems to have been a Dr. Wilcox in the area at the time, a highly respected country doctor, so whenever the name appears again, I shall simply write it as "Wilcox".]* Now she seems quite well, apart from a bad cough and difficulty breathing. As you can imagine, she is not very strong. She is easily exhausted simply from eating and has to stop to rest repeatedly. Yet she says she is not ill.

Oscar and Emma will be moving to Waukon the end of this month. There will be a lot of building there this summer. Someone told me recently that 66 houses are already contracted for, so there will be lots of activity. Louise Ruen has rented a 7-room house and they *[Oscar and Emma]* plan to live there with her to begin with. She intends to stay in the house with them. Oscar was at our place this winter. That is about all I have to tell about them now.

[eighth page]

Together with the clover, I am also sending you barley and oats. I can hardly imagine that you have that kind of barley out there, Scotch Barley, and it is about one cent per gross. I think it will produce a higher yield than regular barley. *[Translator: Ole is certainly referring to "yield" when he uses the verb "folde" in this context.]* The oats are also of good quality and high yield. You can sow both the barley and oats on the best land you have and it will sprout better than *[Translator: Ole wrote "Old summer Grøn", must refer to a brand of seed.]* I am sending you enough clover for two years. My idea is that you can sow half of it this spring and the rest next spring, about 10 acres at a time. After that, you'll produce enough seed yourself. I think this should be your goal for now *[Translator: Ole writes "dette vill bli Object for dig"; "should be your goal for now" is what I assume he means.]* Another time I can write more about how best to use it.

Well, this will have to be enough for the time being. I assume that everyone you know here is in good health, apart from those I have mentioned in this letter.

Sending cordial greetings from everyone,
I remain your

Ole P. Rocksvold

Translation by Jim Skurdall

To: Matilda Rocksvold Anderson, A. O. Anderson, and Family
From: Ole Rocksvold ***Date:*** Feb 14, 1896

Translation

Thoten, Iowa, February 14th, 1896

Dear Children!

It has been such a long time since last we heard from you, so we don't know if you are dead or alive. For quite some time I have been expecting a letter from you every mail delivery day. And though I am still waiting, I'll send you a few lines nonetheless, and hope to receive a reply.

I have had such a bad cold since Christmas that I have been coughing day and night, but I believe now I am over the worst of it. A couple of bottles of medicine have helped me feel better. We have had almost an epidemic here, most everyone with the same symptoms, some very ill, others with more mild cases, but it is all kin to that most reprehensible illness known as the flu.

[second page]

This Christmas we purchased an organ for the church, a Mason & Hamlin, a good little organ. The Ladies' Aid paid $100. It cost $145 at the shop [*Translator: "at the shop" written in English.*] Mina Toyen plays it. You have perhaps read in *Decorah Posten* that "Decorah Menighed" [*Translator: it means "Decorah Congregation". Perhaps he means "Decorah Lutheran".*] received a pipe organ costing $1,500 from Aase Haugen. [*Translator: One of the nursing homes in Decorah today is called the Aase Haugen Home.*] We were there for the concert — Carl and Oscar, Manda and I. We'll never hear organ music of that quality again, as the organist was America's best, Louis Falk. He is paid $2,500 a year to play an organ in a church in Chicago, and he is, in addition, professor at the well-known music school there. This fall three churches in Decorah each have acquired a pipe organ at a combined cost of $4,275. "Decorah Menighed" [*Translator: see my earlier note*] has the best organ of them all.

[third page]

We have had good snow for driving with the sleigh from Christmas until now, mid-January, and we have hauled a lot of ice, so the house is now almost filled. Tomorrow we are meeting in the brick schoolhouse and are going to try to start a farmers' creamery. Cream sells now for 11 cents, and for a number of reasons the routes are so broken up(?) that they bypass(?) each other, so collecting the cream gets to be too expensive, and there is too little cream. [*Translator: Difficult to make out everything he is writing here, some of what he writes is anglicized, but I seem to have got the main idea.*]

Last Monday we had a regular blizzard. It blew all day and the snow was so heavy it was almost impossible to see. It snowed a little on Tuesday as well, so we have enough to be able to drive home "Sommer Veen" *[Translator: Don't know what this is supposed to mean — "the same way"(?), or "over the summer roads"(?).]*

We have not sold "Gri" yet *[Translator: maybe he means "grisene", the hogs/pigs.]*, but we'll have to do so soon. It does not look like the prices are going to get any better. The price now is around $3.80 to $3.90. Some time ago they paid 4 dollars.

[fourth page]

Emma received a letter from Hilda, "in to Dags Maele" *[Translator: not sure what this is, perhaps he means that the letter took two days to get to her?]*, and she says *[Translator: looks like he wrote "for later", but it is surely "for tæler", in today's Norwegian "forteller", meaning "writes/says/reports"]* that she visited you not so long ago, but she writes nothing about how you are doing. Hope you are in good health.

If you are planning to sow barley in the spring, then I'll have to send you a new variety called *[looks like]* Selsor Barley. It has large and strong straw and will stand up in *[looks like]* "Begisle" *[Translator: perhaps he means "frozen"]* soil, and it is *[looks like]* "foldrigt" *[Translator: perhaps "rich in" something]*, and it is *[looks like]* "tellig fit for *[Translator: perhaps means "equal in toughness, resilience, etc.]* to oats. You can let me know if you are interested.

I have nothing more to write about, except to tell you that we are all in good health and under the circumstances doing well. Alberthe(?) is growing big and tall *[Translator: not sure if I have deciphered his handwriting correctly, but this seems to be what he has written.]*

Cordial greetings from you

O. P. Rocksvold

Translation by Jim Skurdall

To: Matilda Rocksvold Anderson, A. O. Anderson, and Family
From: Ole Rocksvold ***Date:*** April 3, 1896

Translation

Thoten, Iowa, April 3rd, 1896

A. O. Anderson and family

Dear Children,

The last letter we received from you has remained unanswered until now. I have been longing to hear from you, seeing as things were not going so well the last time you wrote. But I hope now you are all in good health.

Oscar, Emma, Alberta, Carl, and Clara made a trip to Waukon today, as the weather has improved a bit. But the past couple of days we have had real winter weather. Tuesday night we had more rain than we have had for a long time, but it didn't rain here as much as to the west of us. Smith Bridge washed out, and now "leger nede" *[Translator: I assume he means that the bridge is now lying on the river bank somewhere.]*

[end of page]

[second page]

After that we had colder weather than we had all winter. *[Translator: April 3, 1896 was a Friday; I assume the heavy rain was on Tuesday, March 31, and that Wednesday and Thursday was very cold. As he mentioned, it had warmed a bit on Friday.]* The soil is still frozen, so it won't suddenly be time for plowing and planting and other spring farm work.

Last Monday I sent you 4 bags of Salzer barley. *[Translator: Salzer seems to have been a seed company in the 1890s.]* I sent Tonny to fetch it from Karelius Ask, but he wasn't able to get it *[the barley]* cleaned *[Translator: Ole wrote "Cleand"]* because he did not find him at home. You can sow it in the best soil you have, and you can expect an abundant crop "for legger seg ikke ned" *[Translator: I assume he meant to write "for den legger seg ikke ned", which, I believe, means in this context that it won't freeze.]*

Not so long ago I received a "love letter" *[Translator: quotation marks my own.]* from Pastor Borge. I went out there on March 24th to get a baptismal certificate for Tonny, but I didn't find him at home. So I asked his wife to request that he prepare certificates for both Tonny and Willie at the same time.

[end of page]

[third page]

Tonny went in and fetched his the next morning, and he was asked to stop by again and pick up Willie's before returning home. No sooner said than done. When he returned, he had to go up to Borge's office and wait while Borge wrote a long letter to me, in which he enclosed the certificate. You will find a copy of Borge's letter enclosed in this letter to you. I really don't know what I am going to do about this. I said to Berg that the pastor probably took a few more pot shots at me for the fun of it. *[Translator: This is my interpretation of "nok Skude for lit moro en gang til".]*

There are three points *["Points" written in English]* in the letter I am concerned about, namely, that he calls me a <u>liar</u>, a <u>thief</u>, and a <u>criminal</u>. The question is: which of us fits the description. He tried the same thing once before, but could not prove anything, and certainly he will have no more success this time. And then he must reserve for himself the epithets he has used to characterize me. He'll not get off the hook so easily. I think I would prefer . . .

[end of page]

[fourth page]

. . . to summon him before his congregation and have him retract what he said about me and ask for forgiveness. Then I would not pursue the case further.

I wrote to Hilda a while ago and sent the letter to Canton, South Dakota. I don't know if she received it, as she had already left for your place.

There has still been no decision regarding the date of confirmation, but it will be either the first or second Sunday after Easter.

In closing, I must tell you that everyone here is in good health. Alberta was not feeling well a while ago, but now she is fine. Hilda will have to stay with you as long as she likes.

Greetings from us to all of you.

Your
O. P. Rocksvold

Translation by Jim Skurdall

To: Matilda Rocksvold Anderson, A. O. Anderson, and Family
From: Ole Rocksvold ***Date:*** Sept. 9, 1901

Translation

Thoten, Iowa, September 9th, 1901

Mrs. & Mrs. A. O. Anderson,
Dear Children!

I can imagine that you have been waiting to hear more about how Hilda is doing, so I'll send you a few lines.

She wrote to you herself last Friday, but I don't know whether or not she told you everything about her illness. Over the course of the past two to three weeks, an abscess developed above her left kidney. She had a lot of pain, in addition to the other illness. Dr. Willcox has made a house call here every other day over the past four weeks.

Yesterday, Sunday, he decided to try to determine the content of the abscess. He stuck a *[cannot decipher the word describing the needle]* needle all the way through it from the back causing pus to begin running out. He telephoned Dr. Jule in Decorah, saying that he needed him to come and help him, and he arrived very soon thereafter. Poor Hilda, she had a tough day, but she made it through the ordeal in good shape. They made an incision about two inches to the left of the backbone, and the incision was over two inches in length. It was deep enough so that the pus came running out, at least half a . . .

[end of page]

[second page]

. . . gallon. When they had emptied and cleaned it out, they put in two rubber tubes and a linen cloth larger than a handkerchief in the cavity before bandaging it up.

When she awoke from the anesthetic, she felt much better, and she had a peaceful night. The doctor returned today to wash out the wound, and now she is sleeping soundly. Her fever seems to be diminishing, and so we all hope that she has survived the worst. Poor Hilda, she is so calm and compliant, never uttering a complaint.

We had almost no rain whatsoever from the 4th of July until last Saturday night, but we have had almost continuous rain since then. And it looks like it will rain again tonight. We have had to feed the animals for three weeks, as the fields have been so dry that there hasn't been a blade of green grass for a long time.

Now I must close. I shall try to send you a letter as soon as possible and let you know how the year has gone, and much more. From your father

O. P. Rocksvold

Translation by Jim Skurdall

To: Matilda Rocksvold Anderson, A. O. Anderson, and Family
From: Ole Rocksvold **Date:** May 16, 1902

Translation

Thoten, Iowa, May 16, 1902

Dear Children!

I wish to send you a few lines! And it will surprise ["surprise" written in English] you — the content in particular. I have planned a trip to Norway this summer. Several weeks ago I met Ole Kjørlien in Decorah, and he was planning a trip to Norway in the summer, and, for a long time, we had talked about making the trip together. I have always said that we should wait another year, so that it would be 50 years since we left Norway. But it is now or never. We'll leave New York City on June 6th on White Star Line's largest ship, the "Celtic".

Carl sold out to Oscar this spring, and he will be at home at the beginning of the summer, so my absence will be no problem. And since I feel strong enough to undertake the journey, it might as well be now.

We have had a lot of rain the past two weeks. No corn has been planted down here yet, and there is still some plowing left. Has been impossible to plow, as it has been so muddy. The steeper fields have been washed out something awful and must be replanted in part.

[end of page]

[second page]

For the second time now, Klara Berge is back in LaCrosse for an operation. Her health began declining very soon after Ovidia died. She went once to Dr. Will Kax *[Translator: perhaps he means Wilcox]*, but he himself was already too frail to do anything for her. Then she waited another month, but finally she had to be sent to LaCrosse for an operation. She was back home again after three weeks and seemed to be all right. But then she began having the same problems again. She couldn't eat anything, so she had to be sent back again. It has been a week since she left, and she was so weak that they couldn't do anything with her until she regained some strength. She has to be fed intravenously.

The first stay at the hospital cost around 200 dollars, and this stay will not be any less expensive. A subscription has been initiated to help her, enough, I think, to pay for the first operation. Klara Sivesin has raised over 100 dollars herself, and Emma Rocksvold has raised quite a lot. And there are others out making the same effort.

[end of page]

[third page]

Last Monday, May 12th, Olaus Berge married the daughter of Jens Ask. We attended the wedding.

Dr. Will Crex *[Wilcox?]* is played out *[Translator: he wrote "Plaid out".]* He traveled to Hot Springs, Arkansas this spring hoping that it would help his recovery, but it did not help at all. John Williams told me a few days ago that he *[the doctor]* wishes to return to Decorah. He *[the doctor]* is blind and almost deaf, and he has other illnesses as well. He *[John Williams]* told me this spring that the last trip he *[the doctor]* made to see Ovidia Berge took its toll. He had traveled 60 miles in the cold and stormy weather. He was back home at eight o'clock in the evening and left immediately again for the Berge farm. Manda was there, and she had telephoned him. He went there, and that was the last doctoring he ever did.

While I was writing this, the Berges received a telephone call from LaCrosse that they could come and pick up Klara. They cannot do anything for her. In their opinion, she will soon go the way of her sister. Hard news for the old folks.

[end of page]

[fourth page]

Hilda is now in Decorah and has been there for a couple of weeks. She is working for John Telford. She absolutely wanted to move to town. She is as strong as she was before, and perhaps in better health than before she became ill.

Here at home things are reasonably well. We are all in good health and have not been plagued by misfortunes of any kind. This spring I sold hay, oats, wheat, clover, and timothy, all at a good price, although I did not ask the highest price.

There are many other things I should have mentioned, but they *[cannot decipher]* before you have deciphered the rest of this letter.

If you have any greetings you would like me to take along to Norway, you must send them immediately. It would be nice if you could write a good letter to Hilda, who is a deaf-mute and you will receive a letter in return finer than anything you have ever seen. So write a letter directly to her, or send it along with me.

In closing, I wish to especially thank George and Irene for the Christmas gifts I received from them.

Most cordial greetings from your father

O. P. Rocksvold

Translation by Jim Skurdall

To: Matilda Rocksvold Anderson, A. O. Anderson, and Family
From: Ole Rocksvold ***Date:*** June 4, 1902

Translation

(Postcard)

Washington D.C., June 4, 1902

Mr. ____? A. O. Anderson
Inwood, Iowa

Had this card *["card" written in English]* in my pocket, so I sat down in the park "opposite the Caputyle" *[opposite the Capitol]* to write these lines. We were able to choose the route to New York we preferred, either via "Neagara" *[Niagara Falls]* or Washington, and we chose the latter. Arrived here at 1:30 p.m. and went first to the Capitol to find Gilbert Haugen, M. C. *[Assuming that this meant Member of Congress, I found Gilbert N. Haugen, Republican, representing Iowa in the U. S. House of Representatives/57th United States Congress]*, then to the new library building *[perhaps Library of Congress]*, which is the *[a superlative, cannot decipher]* of all the government buildings. Then we visited museums, went to the Washington Monument and then to the White House and saw the President *[Theodore Roosevelt]* leaving *[cannot decipher]*. Then it was on to the Departments of the Army and the Navy and Agriculture, and the Treasury Building. Then we were guests of the Havigs until late in the evening, had dinner, one of the finest evenings in my life.

Sincerely yours,

O. P. R.

Translation by Jim Skurdall

To: Matilda Rocksvold Anderson, A. O. Anderson, and Family
From: Ole Rocksvold ***Date:*** July 15, 1902

Translation

[I shall use footnotes to comment in this letter]

Dahl[1] farm near the church at Hensaasen[2]

Vang, Valdres, the 15th of July, 1902

Dear Children![3]

I have sent you[4] a few lines only once since I left, and I do not remember where it was that I wrote them. I have not stayed long at any one place. I spent a week in Christiania[5] visiting the city's special attractions, and there are so many of them that are worth seeing. On "Sankt Hans"[6] we took the train to Eidsvoll[7]. We got off the train at Trøkstad in Ulsager[8] for an excursion to Gardemoen[9], where 6,000 men are stationed. From there we continued on to Minne[10], where we stayed overnight. Then traveled by boat to Gjøvik.[11]

[end of page]

[second page]

How magnificent to sail on Lake Mjøsa and see the beautiful rural communities on both sides of the lake! But it has been so dry, that the beauty of the landscape is not seen to full advantage. We stayed overnight in Gjøvik and the next morning made haste for the Rocksvold farm. There they were waiting for us, as the Decorah Posten[12] had tipped them off. Sister Hellene looked good.

---

[1] I thought this Dahl name might have a connection with the Dahl name used by Ole's widowed sister, Hellene, in the Norwegian Census of 1900. But more sleuthing revealed that Dal/Dahl was the farm name of Hellene's husband, before they took over at Rocksvold. So the Dahl farm in this letter appears simply to have been one of the places where Ole found lodging during his stay in Valdres.

[2] In 2003 I translated a book of about 100 pages for a woman named Elaine Ask in Chatfield, Minnesota. It was a history of the very same church, Hensaasen (Hensåsen) Church in Vang. Here is a link with a photo, scroll down, the white church. It was dedicated in September 1902, so it was under construction when Ole was there: http://norske-kirkebygg.origo.no/-/bulletin/show/567822_heensaasen-kirke?ref=checkpoint

[3] Perhaps this was sent to Mathilde, who was to share it with her siblings.

[4] He uses the archaic plural "you" form "eder".

[5] Today Oslo, which was the original Viking name. It was changed to Christiania during the long rule of the Danes and not changed back to Oslo until the early 1900s.

[6] Midsummer Eve (June 23) or Midsummer Day (June 24).

[7] Where Norway's Constitution was adopted on May 17, 1814.

[8] Written Ullensaker today.

[9] Formerly a military base; today Oslo's main airport. Ole, as a Civil War veteran, perhaps wanted to see a Norwegian military facility.

[10] Today Minnesund. It is at the south end of the very large Lake Mjøsa.

[11] On the west shore of Lake Mjøsa. I assume they took "Skibladner", the world's oldest paddle steamer still in operation. It was christened in 1856, so I wonder if perhaps Ole took it on the first leg of his journey of emigration to America? Here is a link in English: https://en.wikipedia.org/wiki/Skibladner

[12] You no doubt know *Decorah Posten* newspaper. Here is proof of its international circulation.

Although she is lame, she gets by with a cane. Hellen Maria looks older than she is on account of all the cares she has had in her life. Hilda was not at home. She was sewing in Hamar. She wants to be at home when I *[Translator: Neither I nor my wife can decipher the handwriting of this word, must be something like "visit"]* there again. Was only at home a week this time. Mathea Hagesven, my first cousin, had died just before my arrival, and I attended her funeral on Thursday, July 3. The next day, the 4th, we traveled to Hadeland, and on Monday the 8th . . .

[end of page]

[third page]

. . . we took a steamer from Røkenvik[13] to Odnes in Land.[14] Then we continued up to Valdres, where we still are and where we plan to remain for a few more days. The inhabitants of Valdres are the most hospitable people I know. Wherever we go, we are given the best accomodations, and our hosts go to great lengths to entertain us. While I sit here looking out the window, snow can be seen in the mountains surrounding us, and other places as well. Yesterday I walked on the snow crust of a glacier in the mountains. In a couple of days we shall head north to Lærdal[15] and Bergen, and perhaps to Hardanger and "Waas" *[Translator: Voss]*, before continuing to Trondheim. From there it will be a rapid journey southward to Toke,[16] where we must remain for a time . . .

[end of page]

[fourth page]

. . . before our return voyage to America, which will be in late August, if everything goes according to plan. I cannot give you a more detailed account of our travels. That will have to come later. I didn't have time while I was there to visit many who live near the Rocksvold farm, but I'll do better next time. It feels good to be here in these wonderful surroundings, and I can walk further here in one day than I can in an entire week in America.

Must close now, the mailman is waiting.

Your father,
O. P. Rocksvold

Translation by Jim Skurdall

---

[13] Røykenvik, on the large lake called Randsfjord.

[14] Søndre Land, a municipality at the north end of the very long and narrow lake.

[15] Inner Sognefjord.

[16] Neither my wife nor I can be sure what place name he has written here, but it looks like it could be "Toke". There is a "Tokke" in the interior of Telemark. So this remains a mystery, unless someone has better luck in deciphering Ole's handwriting here.

To: Matilda Rocksvold Anderson, A. O. Anderson, and Family
From: Ole Rocksvold ***Date:*** Aug. 4, 1902

Translation

Trondheim, August 4th, 1902

Dear Children!

I have just returned to the hotel from the cathedral, where I wandered around below and then up through the tower to the very top, and everything one sees in the course of such wanderings I cannot possibly describe. I'll have to go back to the beginning of my trip and give you a synopsis of it, and that will be the extent of it for now. I don't remember where I was the last time I wrote. It has been a very pleasant trip overall, apart from places in Norway where it has been too cold for comfort. The ocean crossing was wonderful, as was the entire journey to get here.

[second page]

Arrived in Gothenburg, Sweden from Hull in England, then traveled by rail to Christiania *[Translator: now Oslo],* where we arrived on the 18th of June at 6 o'clock in the evening. We remained there one week and saw many of the city's landmarks, then took the train on Midsummer Day to Frøgstad in Ulsager *[Translator: Ullensaker].* After spending the night there, we continued on the next day to Gaardermoen, a military base where 6,000 men are stationed. *[Translator: today Oslo's main airport].* Traveled in the evening to Minne *[Translator: at the end of Lake Mjøsa],* where we stayed the night. The next morning we took the steamboat to Gjøvik, and the following morning we took another vessel to Rocksvold. We did not show up unannounced, as I had planned. Gossip in the 'Decorah Posten' had alerted folks there to our imminent arrival. It was strange coming to familiar places again. I recognized the landscape, if not the people. The railway tracks now pass very close to the house, causing a lot of damage …

[third page]

… to the property. After a couple of days of rest, I was out visiting old familiar places, and even though I did not know the present occupants, I received warm welcomes nonetheless. Only spent one week in Toten. Matea Hagesven, my first cousin, had died recently prior to my arrival, and the funeral was a week later. I was an attendant in her wedding 55 years ago, and I was the closest relative she had, apart from her two children. Pastor Winsnæs thought it quite remarkable that I should show up now after having been away for such a long time. The day after the funeral we caught a ride to Augedal in Hadeland from the Lier Station at Sivisund *[Sivisind].* That was the 4th of July, and we celebrated it at Høkorsen in the middle of the ridge between Toten and Hadeland. It rained all …

[fourth page]

… day and was rather wet when we arrived. The next morning we had to go up to the Egge farms, as we had greetings to pass on to them. The following night we stayed with old Ole Tomt. The next day was Sunday, and before continuing, I have to tell you the different places we have been on the Sundays since arriving in Norway. The first was at Out Savior's Church in Christiania; the 2nd in Aas Church in Toten; the 3rd in Næss *[Nes]* Church in Hadeland; the 4th in the new church at Hensaasen in Vang, Valdres *[Translator: see footnote no. 2 of my translation of Ole's letter dated July 15th, 1902]*; the 4th *[Translator: he must mean the 5th]* Sunday at Fillefjældet between Valders and Lærdal. Was on the site where the Thommos Church stood. It is fenced in and a stone *[with an inscription]* tells that it was torn down in 1808. The next was in the cathedral in Bergen, where Pastor Peter Dreier from America preached the sermon.

[fifth page]

The last Sunday, which was yesterday, we were in the cathedral in Trondheim. Now I must begin to speed up a little. Monday morning we took the steamboat from Røkenvik to Ondnes in Land, and the same evening caught a ride to Hatilsveen at Tonsaasen, where we slept that night. The next morning we continued on to Hotel Petersburg, then to Fagersaen[?], and from there to Løken, where we stayed two nights and took a side trip to visit relatives of O. Kjørlien. Traveled then to Hotel Wangsness, and from there up to the rural district where Hensaasen Church is located. There is no road, but one can get through in a wagon. Everything has to be brought in with pack horses, but nonetheless I ate more rømmegrøt there than I've eaten the past 50 years in America. Then we continued on to Hotel Grindeheim …

[sixth page]

… near the main church at the Vang parsonage, where we met Pastor Borge and Pastor Askevold from Decorah. They came from Bergen and were on their way to Christiania. We, on the other hand, went the same evening to visit Gulleran Løften, who had been in America and writes now and then for 'Decorah Posten'. We drank a couple glasses of beer, and then in our honor he ran up the Star-Spangled Banner, which Anundsen and Hamre had sent him from Decorah. We returned to Grindeheim, where we spent the night. Caught a ride the next day to Skogstad, the next hotel, then on to Hotel Framnes near Tjenvandet[?], a lake at an elevation of 6,000 feet above sea level. Traveled on the same evening to Nystuen[?] near Fillefjellet, where we spent the night. Sunday morning we traveled over the north side of the mountain to Lærdalen. Stopped for awhile at Maristuen, a magnificent hotel, then continued down to

Borgund stave church, which we visited before proceeding to Lærdalsøren in the evening.

[seventh page]

We stayed that night at Hotel Linstrøm, leaving the next morning on a steamship bound for Gudvangen. Before arriving there, we took on board more than 200 passengers from a German steamship that was too large to enter the smaller fjord. The group comprised Germans, Englishmen, and mostly Americans, and it took over 100 horses *[and carriages]* to take us up to Stalheim. The view of mountain and fjord from near Gudvangen is one of the most splendid you will ever see. Cliffs drop straight down 4,000 feet and there are equally impressive waterfalls. Kjelfossen waterfall near Ramsøi farm plunges from such a height and has drops of 1,500 feet where the water does not touch the cliff. Ate dinner at Stalheim and traveled on to Vossevangen, and from there the next day to Ulvik in Hardanger, staying two days. From there we traveled by steamship to Bergen, where we remained for almost a week staying at …

[eighth page]

… Matians[?] Hotel, which afforded us most comfortable quarters. We went on excursions almost every day, climbed mountains, and saw much of interest through the binoculars I have. Bergen has many special landmarks and two good museums that are admired by foreign tourists, who say they are the best they have seen. Wednesday evening, July 29th, we left for Trondheim aboard the steamship "Erling Jarl", arriving Friday morning. There we checked into Hotel Dovre. The first thing we did was walk to the cathedral. We got there too early to be able to have a look at the entire interior, but there was a lot to see nevertheless. Sunday morning I went to the worship service there and was able to see more after the service. But yesterday, August 4th *[Translator: Ole has no doubt written this over two days]*, joined a guided tour through the church from top to bottom, and in every room and chapel we listened to the explanations …

[ninth page]

… and descriptions, were shown photos, and received information regarding the cathedral's history and how it will look when it is completed. I won't try to tell about everything we learned. That would exceed my ability. Have taken many excursions, there are so many historical landmarks. It is an exceptional city, and the surrounding area is glorious — large farms, attractive houses, and fertile land. Tomorrow, August 6th, we shall travel on the express train to Hamar, from where we'll soon be back in Toten. We'll not have so much time there, as we must be in Christiania on the 15th and depart from there on the 17th for England. The "Celtic" leaves Liverpool on the 22nd and we already have our tickets for the return trip and must arrive promptly.

[tenth page]

I have been well the entire time and healthier than I have been for a long time. As I have mentioned earlier, I have spent almost a week in each of the three largest cities in Norway, which has given us time to see everything. This letter is much too long, and you will be worn out reading through to the end, and yet it does not begin to describe everything I have experienced on this trip. Norway has had an unusually cold summer, so we have had to wear our overcoats most of the time. I have written several letters home, one of them almost as long as this one. Hoping that this letter will find you all in the best of health and that none of you have met with any misfortune. And so I shall close for now.

Your father

O. P. Rocksvold

Translation by Jim Skurdall

To: Matilda Rocksvold Anderson, A. O. Anderson, and Family
From: Ole Rocksvold **Date:** September 29, 1902

Translation

T____en(?), Iowa, September 29th, 1902

Dear Children,

Much too much time has passed since I last wrote to you, but time passes quickly, and I can't keep up.

I had a pleasant and comfortable trip to Norway and home again. I was in good health the entire time, and those I met there, whether strangers or relatives and acquaintances, were both courteous and kind. I could have wished for nothing more. I arrived here on the sixth of September and found everything in order at home.

I have not felt so well, as I "gik i armen" *[Translator: Do not know what he means by this; perhaps his own expression.]* shortly after arriving home. Have never gotten over the coughing or the bronchitis I have had for some time. I hope it does not return again at full strength.

[end of page]

[second page]

Shall not write any more about the trip in this letter, as I do not have time.

Perhaps I shall come out for a visit sometime this fall. I had to promise old Sørensen that I would come and visit him. We were together on the return voyage over the Atlantic.

Hilda Rocksvold, she who is deaf, is a magnificent lady. We had many conversations and became good friends. I could not have made her happier than to simply let her wait on me hand and foot. If I did so, then she thought I was most agreeable, and she was content. I did have a nice present for her that she appreciated very much, and she said she would have liked to return to America with me. She and her mother accompanied me to Gjøvik, and they stood on the pier and waved with their handkerchiefs as long as I could see them.

[end of page]

[third page]

Today Iver and Kari Berge and Joseph moved to Northwood, North Dakota for good. They sold their farm this summer to Helmer Webjørnsen for 5,000 dollars, and they held an auction last Wednesday, selling all their personal property at good prices. So they left here with about 6,000 dollars. Well done! They were invited to our place yesterday afternoon, where a surprise party had been arranged for them.

Have not done any threshing yet. Carl is with Peter this fall and out by the ocean now. He perhaps won't be coming here for several weeks. We'll have a poor corn crop *[Translator: He writes "Corncrop". In Norwegian, "korn" means "grain", but as he is living in Iowa, he no doubt means "corn".]* Much of it has frozen, and it is wet as it can be.

I have had a pain on one side for a week now, and it has bothered me a lot. Can hardly get up from a chair.

[end of page]

[fourth page]

It is raining again today. The clover is growing and everywhere it is almost "kuehøi" *[Translator: High/tall as a cow?]*. No difference whether it is "indraat" *[Translator: Not sure what he means here, "harvested/cut"?]* or not, it is really thick wherever you look.

Everyone in Norway said to kindly greet you. I have not written to anyone there since arriving home. I wrote to Laura and received a reply. They had not heard from her for a long time and were worried that she had met with some misfortune.

Everything is fine here.

Cordial greetings from your father

O. P. Rocksvold

Translation by Jim Skurdall

To: Matilda Rocksvold Anderson, A. O. Anderson, and Family
From: Ole Rocksvold **Date:** March 13, 1903

Translation

Thoten, Iowa, March 13th, 1903

To Mrs. and Mrs. A. O. Anderson and children:

There is really no excuse that I have not written to you for such a long time. But I dread starting, since I am such a poor correspondent. Nonetheless, I shall try to put down a few lines.

I had thought about traveling out to see you last fall or winter, but nothing came of it. I came down with a bad cold before Christmas, and I was not feeling so well the entire fall. Didn't finish threshing until not long before Christmas, and had 12 acres of corn to husk after New Year's. Peter didn't finish threshing until after New Year's. Since then he has been sawing lumber over in Allamakee County, and Carl has been with him until recently. On the 23rd they are leaving for their farm in North Dakota. They have bought $400 worth of machinery that is being shipped up there ahead of them

[second page]

They are taking 4 teams of horses. Peter has bought two teams, and Carl has bought 3 horses, as he only had one. He bought a horse from Henry Evenrud for 150 dollars, and a team in Decorah for 260 dollars. Peter paid almost 600 dollars for the two teams he bought. So all together, with saddles and other accessories, they paid 1,200 dollars. They are taking along 500 bushels of my Silver Mine oats. They have 300 acres there to plow and sow, so they have their work cut out for them.

Carl and Albert will no doubt "blir om Farmingen" this summer. *[Translator: not sure if he means they will be farming up there. Probably.]* Peter will most likely go up as well to help them get set up, but he will return here in the summer, as he has a lot to plant, and he wants to have his threshing done by fall.

Emma is going up to keep house for them. She just came back from Haugen in Decorah, where she has been since the first of November this past fall. She has earned 5 dollars a week, a pretty good wage.

[third page]

Last Saturday, the 7th of March, we had a pleasant celebration in Waukon. It was the Silver Wedding Anniversary for Pastor Hellestvedt and his wife. The congregation found out about it from relatives in Minnesota and decided immediately to organize a celebration. All the preparations were kept secret, so they did not know anything about it until half past eight Saturday morning. They were supposed to be in the church at half past ten. It took a while before they believed what was happening. Finally John Erie drove up to their home in a fine carriage to take them to the church. When they arrived, two pastors welcomed them wearing their vestments, Pastor Ulsager, who is married to Mrs. Hellestvedt's sister, and Pastor Jostad from Minnesota. When they entered the church, it was filled to overflowing, and among those sitting there were Mrs. Hellestvedt's sisters and their husbands. Pastor Jostad gave a moving speech, and the Waukon Choir had rehearsed for the occasion.

[fourth page]

I was asked to lead them out of the church and up to "Higskole Holem i Becman Block" *[Translator: perhaps to the high school?]*. I went ahead of them, and they didn't know what was happening until they saw the head table, set for 100 guests. And no one needed to be ashamed of the dishes that were served. Over 200 persons came, and had the weather not been so bad, there certainly would have been more. The gifts were not expensive, but very nice: a fruit dish, sterling silver worth 35 dollars, a set of knives and forks of the same kind worth 27 dollars, and there was a large gravy spoon they received from Chicago.

Recently received a letter from Hilda Rocksvold in Norway, in which she enclosed a photograph of herself. I shall send you some of the letters I have received from Norway, and then you can read what they think of me there. I received a photograph of Helen Maria, Laura, and Hilda last summer in Norway, which I am enclosing here. Take good care of it, as I may want it back.

[fifth page]

I still have not written back to Hilda in Norway. I should also have sent you the letter I received from her a week ago so you could see what someone who is deaf and dumb can learn.

I should have written a letter to George, but don't have time now. But he shall receive one. Alberta sent a letter to Irene yesterday. She dictated and wrote without anyone saying anything to her. She quickly reads any book we give her.

I was in Decorah for three days at the district meeting. Returned home yesterday evening. We are all in good health, as is everyone around here.

Greetings to you all, and by all means remember to greet George from me. Your father,

O. P. Rocksvold

Translation by Jim Skurdall

To: Matilda Rocksvold Anderson, A. O. Anderson, and Family
From: Ole Rocksvold **Date:** ca. April 30, 1903

Translation

[Translator: No place or date. The letter was written in 1903, after Ole's trip to Norway in 1902, and from the content of the letter we know it was written after Easter Sunday, which in 1903 was April 12th. Furthermore, it becomes clear from what he writes that the first three pages were written on the last Thursday of April, which was April 30th. The last page was written on May 1, 1903. You speculated that he might be writing to Mathilda, and this seems correct. In the sentence he wrote in English he mentions that he has no presents from Norway for "Earnist" and "Papa", meaning, I assume, Earnest and Andrew.]

Just learned from a telephone conversation with Klara Sissind(?) that Hilda, the youngest sister of Mrs. Hellestvedt, is dead. She participated in the silver wedding anniversary of the pastor and his wife in Waukon on the 7th of March, and immediately thereafter she married, and now she is dead. Yesterday we learned from a phone conversation(?) that Henning Telsvold(?) in Thompson died and that the funeral will be held on Saturday. And Ottilie Præstesæler, wife of Henry Lørlien, may also have died. She has been in labor and the doctors said there is no chance of her surviving. They are now living in Pleasant Township. There has not been much illness this winter, nor is there now. Alberta was at home for several weeks, but the spring term at school began, and she couldn't miss that. She wrote to Irin while she was here, and also a letter to Hilda Rocksvold in Norway, which she enclosed in the letter I sent. She learned to read Norwegian quite well while she was here *[Translator: I assume he is referring to Alberta, while she was at home.]*

[end of page]

[second page]

Have not had a letter from Carl since he left for Dakota. Peter came down two weeks ago, but he had actually left a week earlier and stopped for a week in Northwood. Albert is up there on the farm with Carl while Peter is gone. Emma also went along to keep house. They took along eight large horses, but they lost one of them right away, so now have only seven. They built a good stable for the horses while Peter was there, plus they had to buy hay and wheat seed. The greater part of the land was unplowed, so they'll have plenty to do before they can plant. Pretty sure I'll get a letter from them with the next delivery. The last time I wrote to Norway, I told them that Carl and Peter's land is six times the size of the entire Rocksvold farm in Norway with its forest land, hayfields, and cultivated fields. Last summer I estimated that Rocksvold has a total of about 50 acres.

[end of page]

[third page]

Brought back a few things from Norway last fall, but not enough to meet the demand, so there is not much left. Had a total of eighteen brooches, but this is most of what I have left. Thought I would be coming out last fall or winter and could bring it myself, but now I must enclose it in a letter, or else it will remain lying around the house. I have just three left. One for Mathille, one for Irin, and the best(?) for George. *Am sory I have no present for Earnist and Papa, thet I can put in the letter. [Translator: I have copied this last sentence as Ole wrote it in English.]*

Hans Sanbek is now in the "Galehospitalet" in Independence. *[Translator: A reference to Independence State Hospital, built in 1873 as an asylum for alcoholics, geriactrics, drug addicts, mentally ill, and the criminally insane, https://en.wikipedia.org/wiki/Independence_State_Hospital as you can read in the link.]* I took him down a few days before Easter. He seemed to be quite content. I don't wish to end the letter today, as I may receive a letter from you tomorrow, Friday.

[end of page]

[fourth page]

[Dated May 1st]

Yes, indeed. I received your long letter today. Thank you so much. Did not receive a letter from Carl, however, but they are certainly much too busy to write. They have 200 acres to plow.

In closing now I can tell you that we are all in good health and doing well.

Cordial greetings to you all

Your father
O. P. Rocksvold

Translation by Jim Skurdall

To: Matilda Rocksvold Anderson, A. O. Anderson, and Family
From: Ole Rocksvold ***Date:*** May 28, 1903

Translation

Thoten, Iowa, May 28, 1903

Mr. and Mrs. A.O. Anderson, Inwood, Iowa

Dear Children!

Received your letter dated the 13th of this month and see that you received my last correspondence.

Here it has been raining almost every day or night the past two weeks, and I believe we have had about 20 days of rain this month. So we scarcely have been able to get anything done. Still have 15 acres of corn to plant. Have not been able to do any planting since Thursday, which is a week ago today. It is so wet that we cannot go where we need to plant. There are a few farmers here who have not begun planting at all.

Received a letter from Emma in North Dakota on the 25th. It has been quite dry there this spring, but recently it had rained some right before she wrote. She says that things look very good there now, but it has been cold, and the hay was late. They were not finished with planting yet and were going to plant more barley, and later more flax (next page).

(second page)

I have not received a letter from Carl either. I suppose he doesn't have time to write, nor is he used to doing so. They have decided to lease a quarter section next year, the one between the two quarter sections they farm. There are good buildings on it, so they can live just one mile from their farm. At present they have to go two miles to the outer boundary of the one farm, and they have to take along meals for themselves, as well as something for the horses. Their neighbors are impressed with the work they are doing and with their machinery, which they think is better than anything they have around there. They all would like to acquire the same for themselves as soon as possible. (Translator: The next couple of sentences are written in English: "The 20 Da_ek (?) Drill they have thay (sic) is a Dandy. The Gangplow (?) the same, rend (?) easy and do(es) good Work, allso (sic) the 22 feet wied (sic) Drag." I suppose what he means by "Gangplow" is a plow you walk behind. I've written this as Ole wrote it and used (sic) here and there)

Emma finds it rather tedious sitting home alone from 6:30 in the morning until 7 or 8 in the evening "og heller rigtig frisk" (Translator: What he wrote at the end makes no sense, perhaps he wanted to write in Norwegian something that meant "and she doesn't think it is very healthy either." Speculation only.) She says that when they have finished spring planting and other work she is going to go to Northwood and stay for a couple of weeks, there where the Bergs live. You ought to write to her. Her address is: Acton, Walsh County, North Dakota. If the letter hasn't arrived before she returns home, they will forward it to her.

(third page)

After all the rain we have had recently, we really had a downpour Tuesday night. Tuesday noon it rained harder than I have ever seen, but then it cleared up, so we thought it was over. But that night it began again, and it was the hardest rain we have had all summer. Coon Creek and the Iowa River flooded the bottomland and washed out the cornfields. Our newly sprouted fields look nice and were not damaged by the rain. The hayfields are in excellent shape now and will yield a bountiful crop. Our piglets are not doing well this year. Had 10 sows, two of which had no young, and one died giving birth. All we got from the 7 were 14 young. Have bought a sow with 9 young and must buy one or two more. Have 14 cows to milk and one of them broke a leg last Sunday, so we had to slaughter it.

If I choose to do so, I can travel as a church delegate next month to the annual meeting in Duluth. Several have made it known that they would like me to go. The delegates will be elected on Whitsuntide (Pentecost Sunday) after the worship service.

Last summer I promised Helene Maria Rocksvold that I would visit Laura this summer, and if I do travel to Duluth I shall stop in Boyd.

(fourth page)

You really ought to write to Helene Marie Rocksvold in Norway. She would welcome a letter form you so very much. If you knew her, you would love her. She always sends greetings to you in every letter I receive from her. Her address is: Bøverbro Station, Vestre Thoten, Norway, Europe. I still have not replied to the last letter I received from her. I had just written to Hilda, and thus had nothing new to report.

A week ago I submitted my resignation as postmaster of Thoten, Iowa to the Postmaster General, to take effect the 1st day of July, at which time the Thoten Post Office will be discontinued. I will have served in the position for 25 years. (Translator: What follows was in English: "Mail will then go to Nassett (?), and will be carried to the House (sic) by the Mail carier (sic) Nassett (?) to Corman (?) and have it three times a Weeke (sic). Emma Amunrud's Adress (sic) is Frankville.)

Nothing more to report and this letter is long enough anyway. We are all in good health and doing well, and we hope the same is true for you. Please greet Mr. George from Grand Papa, and tell him he would like very much to see George.

Greetings to you all.

From your father
O. P. Rocksvold

Translation by Jim Skurdall

To: Matilda Rocksvold Anderson, A. O. Anderson, and Family
From: Ole Rocksvold **Date:** December 21, 1903

Translation

Næsset, Iowa, December 21, 1903

A. O. Anderson and family!

Dear Children!

As it has been such a long time since I last heard from you, and you from me, I wish to send you a few lines now together with my photograph.

I received a letter from Norway this past October which contained a request from relatives and friends to send a photograph of myself, inasmuch as there were many of my former friends and acquaintances that I was not able to meet during my short visit. They were surprised to learn that there was still quite a bit of me left after such a long absence from Norway, for they had heard that Norwegians, after a number of years in here in this country, tend to dry up so that there is nothing left but skin and bones.

[second page]

I had a dozen photographs made in the fall and sent six to Norway, and there is a market for those I still have. It shows how I looked when I traveled to Norway last year, and how I still look now. Helene Maria Rocksvold wrote in the last letter (dated the 10th of October) that they had had 5 inches of snow for a week, and most of the hay(?) was still outside, and the potatoes were still in the ground, but she said that they had gotten everything in. It had not been much, but it had been better than the previous year. They promised me a letter from Hilda at Christmas, but I did not write until late November, so I don't expect a letter at Christmas.

I suppose you have heard about Emma's wedding, so I need not write anything about that. Christian Kirkeby had an accident two weeks ago. He fell and broke his right leg at the ankle. There is hope that it will heal.

[third page]

I don't imagine you have received a letter from Carl. I have only received one from him, and he says it is the first letter he has ever written in his life. It was good, both the handwriting and the content, so there was no need for him to be ashamed.

Albert Rocksvold came down again to Emma's wedding, so I was able to hear from him everything about their farming and crops. He said it was unusually dry up there this summer. They only had two brief rain showers from the time they planted until they harvested, so they only cultivated two inches deep. But they had a good harvest nonetheless. They only sowed 30 acres in wheat and got 730 bushels, plus 2,200 bushels barley, and 1,600 bushels oats, all of it of excellent quality. They were [can't decipher] 28 dollars an acre for their land this fall, that was for one quarter section, all of it plowed and ready to plant in the spring, but there are no other buildings there other than a granary.

[fourth page]

This quarter section lies a mile from the quarter section on which they live, and the farm there lies between theirs. They could have bought it this fall for $28.50 per acre, and it has fine buildings on it, a good house, 2 barns, a large granary, everything in good condition, and 200 acres plowed this fall, but the farm is 280 acres, and Carl didn't wish to risk going into so much debt. Peter, however, was keen on doing it. They could have used or rented the quarter section next year. If they had sold, they could have had a good 500 acres ready for next spring. Albert says that he and Carl could easily have planted it in plenty of time in the spring, if they had two more horses and another planter like the one they have with a 20 dask drill. *[Translator: Sometimes it was not so easy to follow what Ole was describing. Obviously, the recipients of the letter knew what he was talking about, so his description is a bit sketchy and not so easy for an outsider to follow.]*

Thorvald Kirkeby is at Carl's now while Albert is down here. He'll stay there through the spring and will be with Peter in the winter at his sawmill(?).

[fifth page]

Well, I guess I'll tell a little about our own harvest this year. Toward the end of the summer it looked like it would be the best harvest ever for the grasses and hay, but no one thought the corn would amount to anything, as it was so late this year, but the corn crop was the best of all. *[Translator: Again, I'm assuming that with "Cornet" he means "corn" and not "grain", even though in Norway "korn" means "grain" and "mais" is the word for "corn" in Norwegian.]* Much of the barley and oats were flattened before they headed out, and a great deal rotted on the ground. Everyone predicted that I would get 60 bushels barley to the acre, and I was of the same opinion, but most of it remained lying in the field, and the same with the oats. Nonetheless, I harvested a good 3,000 bushels of barley, oats, and wheat all together, even though the quality was not so good. So I can't complain. Cut a lot of hay and got it all in the barn. Set aside 15 acres of tomatoes for seed and thought I would get a good 12 bushels to the acre, but one stormy day washed away two-thirds of what I had planted.

[sixth page]

I asked Hilda if she had written to you since the wedding, and she said "no", so I shall write a few words about that. It was quite a large affair for late fall. Peter had finished threshing a few days earlier, and he set up a temporary room on the south side of the house, 20 feet by 32 feet, with rain-tight walls and a good roof, and he installed two heating stoves. They were able to set a table for 60 at a time. They had around 200 guests. The bridal couple received gifts of money and other presents worth almost 200 dollars.

We now have a new pastor. Hellestvedt became so difficult to work with this summer that he had to resign, and we called Pastor Jacob Fjelde from Lac qui Parle County, Minnesota, and he arrived here last November, presided over three worship services and was installed here by Pastor Bei(?) on the second Sunday in Advent. He is a very capable man and still quite young.

[seventh page]

Well, having come this far in my letter, perhaps you have had enough, but although many letters I have sent to Helene Maria Rocksvold have been this long, she says that she never tires of reading them and is always full of praise.

You may have heard that Emma Ammunsrud gave birth to twin boys. Pastor Fjelde christened them on December 10th. I was present, but I do not remember the names. They have three names each. That's somewhat extravagant, in my opinion. If they are born two at a time, they are soon going to use up all the names. They are in good health and are growing rapidly.

Enough for this time. Sending you all greetings from us. Don't forget to greet George from Grandpa, and Irene as well.

Merry Christmas to you all from your father

O. P. Rocksvold

[more on the other side]

[eighth page]

I just received a letter from Norway from Hilda Rocksvold written on

December 8th. It took only 12 days to get here. Everyone was fine when she wrote, and she asked me to greet you.

O. P. R.

Translation by Jim Skurdall

To: Matilda Rocksvold Anderson, A. O. Anderson, and Family
From: Ole Rocksvold **Date:** February 10, 1905

Translation

Decorah, Iowa, February 10, 1905

To Mr. & Mrs. A. O. Anderson:

Dear Children:

Yesterday I received your letter dated the sixth of this month and read that you have not received a letter from Hilda for some time. So I shall try to send you a few lines.

Must use a pencil, as my hand trembles and I would scarcely be able to write with a pen legibly enough for you to be able to decipher it. We have been having an exceptionally bitter winter. The snow is almost three feet deep in the woods where it hasn't drifted, and in the fields and along the roads it has accumulated …

[second page]

… in large drifts making them almost impassable, so there are only a few routes we can take.

Last week the thermometer registered below zero temperatures most of the time. It was 35 below in the morning. The mailman has not been able to get through on a number of occasions.

You asked about Manda. I have not had a letter from any of them for a long time. [Can't decipher] we have heard from them. Thorvald Kirkeby came down again last fall, and, after he was back to full health, he had been working during the summer close to where they live.

[third page]

Likewise, Ferdinand K. was working a few miles from them this summer, and he had just visited them when he returned home. They had quite a good harvest: 2,500 bushels of wheat, 1,600 bushels of oats, and 1,000 bushels of barley. They had the best harvest for miles around. They worked the land better than those who had tractors, and, in addition, last fall they had ditched and drained the land, and that gave them a big advantage in the spring.

The one quarter section of the farm lies a mile and a half from where they live, and a bit higher …

[fourth page]

… so there was no water and they were able to plant earlier.

Peter Rocksvold plans to take a trip up there soon, and he may possibly sell his share of the farm to Albert. Peter is thinking about buying a farm at home. It looks like Christine and Anne are going to get some acres of Albert Sivisind's land, build themselves a house on it, and live there from now on.

We have not had a letter from Manda, nor have I written to her. Ferdinand Kirkeby said she had told him she would be coming home for Christmas, but we didn't see her.

[fifth page]

You mentioned that Irene had not received a reply to her letter to Alberta. The reason for that is probably that an ill-behaved boy, the son of Andreas Kongsrud, took her letters, tore them up, and threw them away. She'll have to try and write again. Alberta says the same thing, that she hasn't received replies to her letters.

As for our harvest last fall, it was quite good. The oats didn't mature as they should have, since they lay in the field from early on, but it turned out well. Good crop of barley, and we harvested wheat with the oats, so I think we'll make it through January *[Translator: must have meant to write February.]* and avoid having to buy extra flour.

[sixth page]

We had one of the best corn harvests we have ever had. There were some soggy acres of course, but in the end it was not at all as bad as it looked earlier. We had only planted 35 acres, but I don't believe we ever harvested more when we had many more acres in cultivation. Have 1,000 bushels left. This fall we had 70 hogs, have 50 now.

Have 12 horses this winter, so stable space is crowded, and there is really nothing more for them to do than eat and drink. I had thought of selling a couple of them, but nothing has come of it.

[seventh page]

Just before Christmas I received a postcard of the Rensvold Railway Station from Hilda Rocksvold in Norway, together with Christmas and New Year's greetings from them all. I have enclosed the card in this letter, so you can see it. Rensvold Station is less than an English mile south of the Rocksvold farm, and on the postcard it looks just as it did when I was there. I had written to Helene Maria just before I received the card, and I have not written since. I guess I ought to do it soon. They are always so delighted to receive a letter from us. You ought to write as well, either to Helene Maria or to Hilda, and they would be so happy, and you would have the pleasure of receiving a letter in reply.

[eighth page]

I guess this letter is long enough now, so I shall close. It is probably no [can't decipher} to read it, but wait for a Stormy Day [he wrote "Stormy Day"], and be patient.

I have stayed indoors this winter, have been to Decorah several times and go to church every other Sunday. Those are my outings. I am in good health and have nothing to complain about. It is the same for the others here.

Be sure to greet Mister George [he wrote "Mister George"] from me and tell him to write to me soon, or else I won't write to him.

And, finally, cordial greetings to you all from

O. P. Rocksvold

Translation by Jim Skurdall

To: Matilda Rocksvold Anderson, A. O. Anderson, and Family
From: Ole Rocksvold ***Date:*** January 20 and 24, 1906

Translation

Decorah, Iowa, Route #6, January 20, 1906

Mr. and Mrs. A. O. Anderson, Inwood
Dear Children and Grandchildren!

It has been such a long time since I wrote to you that I do not remember when the last time was. I have tried several times, but either something prevented me, or else it didn't seem to me like the right time, and so I put it off until later. Last summer, when I was in Minnesota, I promised Andrew that I would write if I didn't plan to visit you on the way home. But neither did I stop by, nor did I write. I wasn't feeling well, as it had been raining every day.

As you can imagine, Laura is doing very well, has everything she desires. They have a big, beautiful house, the finest in town when it was built. But since then, Anton, Laura's husband, has built homes for many others. He is a trained carpenter and master builder. He built the Norwegian church there, as well as the large schoolhouse in town. He quit building a couple of years ago, and now owns 2 lumber yards, one in Boyd, and one in a town called Watson, 16 miles north of there. His businesses are doing well. I was there for almost two weeks, and when I left for home, both of them were almost in tears.

[second page]

They said that they had not had a visit from a relative since they came there, and they felt that I really ought to stay for 3 months after having come so far to see them. But it was getting to be time for haying, so I really had to get home.

We were expecting some of you to come here for Christmas. Ida Kirkeby said that you had spoken of the possibility, and we were often in Decorah and were on the lookout for you.

Recently the snow has drifted so heavily that it is almost impossible to get through. Here on our own fields the snow is about two feet deep, and the drifts two or three times as deep, so we have had a mail delivery only every other day. Today has been beautiful, and about half the snow has melted.

Mathea Evenrud is ill and has to stay in bed. Her days are numbered. She has cancer of the internal organs, and the doctor said she won't live more than two months, and she may go in the next two to three weeks. She says she has known this herself for the past 6 months, but didn't let anyone know because she didn't want to undergo an operation. Now it is too late to do anything, as it has entered her bloodstream. She is very composed, trembles a little, says the Lord's will shall be done. Her trust in Him is both an obligation and a release, and her only hope and consolation is that having suffered through a painful illness she will end her days in God's grace and come home to dwell in the temple of God's people.

[third page]

The last letter I received from Norway, from Helene Maria Rocksvold, was on the 14th of October, and it had taken 11 days on its journey. She said that I should expect a letter from Hilda, her daughter, at Christmas, but I have not received anything yet. The last I heard, Hilda was to be married last fall. She has been engaged to be married for ten years. I was supposed to receive a photograph of both Hilda and her husband. They plan to live in Hamar, where he has a good job at a repair shop there with decent wages by Norwegian standards. He is a good mechanic. They both would like to come to America, but I have not dared say anything to either of them, as he is completely deaf, as is Hilda. But he can speak, read, and write their Norwegian language.

I received a photograph from Norway recently, from the teacher Karl Sagvold and his family. It was taken in their house. He is a brother of Helene Maria. He is a huge fellow, I estimate he weighs about three hundred pounds. He looks like he has added a lot of weight since I saw him, and he was stout, quite fat, at that time. The photo confirms that they live well in their home. I did not have an occasion to visit them at home, so this was my first opportunity to see the house.

I haven't heard from Karl in Mandan, North Dakota, nor have I written to them for a long time. My impression is that they have little interest in whether we are dead or alive.

[fourth page]

January 24 (Jan 20-24), 1906

Peter receives a letter now and then from Albert, so we can keep up on how they are doing. They had a good harvest there this year. But part of it was ruined by too much rain. The wheat was left standing in the rain for several weeks, as it could neither be staked?/stacked? nor threshed. But nonetheless it didn't turn out so bad. They had 160 acres in wheat, 50 acres in flax, and almost 100 acres in barley and oats. The harvest around here last fall was good. We got a huge amount of hay, and all of it into the barn. The oats remained standing, but were thin, as it was poor seed, and the same with the barley. The corn turned out well. For a long time it looked like it would be a meager harvest, but the long autumn gave it time to ripen.

We sold 4 horses in the fall. I got 225 dollars for a mare and a foal, and 125 dollars for another horse. Tony [Tommy?] sold a bronco for 60 dollars. We still have 9.

Tell George and Irene that I'll write to them next time. I received a letter from each of them. My health is fairly good, but I have a bad cough and difficulty breathing. All the others here are healthy, as well as most of our neighbors.

In closing, greetings to you all from

O. P. Rocksvold

Translation by Jim Skurdall

To: Matilda Rocksvold Anderson, A. O. Anderson, and Family
From: Ole Rocksvold **Date:** April 19, 1906

Translation

Decorah RFD No. 6
April 19, 1906

Mr. and Mrs. A. O. Anderson and children,

Shall try to send you a few lines to let you know we are still alive. I should have written to you long ago, but have had a few complications from time to time.

First let me tell you that Mathea Evensrud died on the 12th of this month, which was Maundy Thursday. It was three months to the day that Dr. Stevens first visited her, and at that time he said she wouldn't live more than three months. He was right. Around a week before she died, he told some women friends who had come to visit her that she would die Maundy Thursday, and she said the same thing to Pastor Skarve several days later, but he thought it rather strange that she could be so certain of her prediction. I probably should write more about her death, but that will have to come another time if I am to post this letter this evening.

In my last letter to you I forgot to tell you that Anders Strandbakken is completely blind. He was in St. Paul last fall in the care of Dr. Bøkman and lay in the hospital for almost two months,

[second page]

… but it didn't help, and he returned home shortly before Christmas.

Today we began planting for the first time. It was not possible up until now, but the weather is finally stabilizing.

Well, must close, the mailman is coming. I'll write again soon. We are all in good health and hope the same is true for you.

Your

O. P. Rocksvold

Translation by Jim Skurdall

To: A. O. Anderson **From:** Ole Rocksvold **Date:** May 4, 1907

Translation

Decorah, Iowa, May 4th, 1907

A. O. Anderson!

Today we are shipping seed corn to you. I bought a part of it *["a part of it" written in English]* in Decorah before last Saturday, and I got the yellow corn from McBusker. It is tested and insured. The yellow corn I have is not good, so I didn't want to send you any of it. I have tried the white corn several times, and almost all of it sprouts and grows. So you can plant some of it. I didn't get much more than half of the seed corn I had expected due to mistakes in sorting, so half was lost. Won't get any from Charlie Haalhvedt.

[second page]

So I don't have any more seed corn to spare *["spare" written in English, looks like "spore"]*. But when I get out I'll see if I can find any more that is good and fill up the sack.

There was a large funeral yesterday for Edgar Wangsness. He died Sunday morning on his farm in North Dakota, and his father got there in time to see him still alive. He died of typhoid fever.

I have not felt terribly well this week, have had influenza *[can't decipher several words]* before, but am somewhat better now.

Greet everyone

O. P. Rocksvold

[third page]

The yellow corn in the little bag is not the same kind that is in the large bag. I bought it today and I think it is good corn. [Can't decipher] is enclosed.

O. P. R.

Translation by Jim Skurdall

To: Matilda Rocksvold Anderson, A. O. Anderson, and Family
From: Ole Rocksvold ***Date:*** June 20, 1907

Translation

Decorah, Iowa, June 20, 1907

A. O. Anderson and family, Inwood, Iowa
Dear Children!

As it has been so long since I last wrote to you, I'll try now to send you a few lines.

First I wish to tell you that I took a trip to Dakota. I didn't travel to the northeast part of the state, where Carl lives, but rather to the southwest corner, to a place called Golden Valley, in Billings County, North Dakota. Beach is the last station in Dakota on the main line of the Northern Pacific Railroad, only two miles from the Montana line. This valley and a good deal more land belonged to what was called the Missouri Slope Cattle Company, and they held homestead land as well as railroad land and no one ...

[second page]

... dared approach them up until five years ago, when the settlers came and took homesteads and soon became too strong for the cattle kings, and they had to sell out. A company from Madison, Wisconsin and St. Paul, Minnesota called Stavdal(?) Land and Investment Company purchased 167,000 acres from the Northern Pacific Railroad Co., which owned every odd section for 40 miles on either side of the railway line. All even sections are homestead land, and also make up 167,000 acres, so there was room for a lot of settlers.

It is four years since they began selling land, and now all the homestead land is taken, and the company has sold three-quarters of its land, leaving about 40,000 acres. The land is unusually good land, and attractive. There is ample water, and there is igneous coal almost everywhere.

[third page]

Beach is 626 miles from St. Paul, and 375 miles west of Fargo. I arrived there in the evening of May 22nd, and in the morning we traveled in an automobile south of the town through several townships to the largest coal mine. The coal shafts are 20 feet deep, and the coal is good. A man was there chipping it loose, and you could take as much as you wanted for one dollar. This mine was on homestead land, but no one wanted it.

Almost all the land up to 12 miles from town was taken, and homestead land much further out. The price for the land varied from 12½ to 15 dollars per acre. I saw a flock of cattle that had grazed on the land all winter, and they were all in good condition.

We returned to town at noon, and after lunch we drove north of town. I grumbled a bit that …

[fourth page]

… the best land was taken and you had to travel far from the railway line and take land that no one wanted. Mr. Smith, the agent, said then that he would show me a piece of land they had held back and had not shown to anyone, and I could see what I thought.

We drove 7 miles north of Beach, and one mile east, and came to Section 23, T 141, R 105, and to the north half section of Section 23. It was the loveliest land I've ever seen, with grass taller than any I had seen anywhere else, and immediately I had the impression this wasn't [can't decipher]. A German sitting next to me in the automobile said: "By gosh, that is the finest piece of land I have ever seen." I didn't dare show how impressed I was, because it was clear that he wanted the land for himself. After supper, someone came and took the German out to show him the town, while I stayed there and purchased the land.

[fifth page]

I paid 17 dollars an acre for the half section. I was the first from Winneshiek County to buy out there and got the most beautiful land for a better price than the others. I'm enclosing a map of North Dakota and you can see where I'm located. The yellow squares show land belonging to the company. The [can't decipher] are sold, and the white(?) are homestead land. If you lay out the section map and count 7 sections north and one section east you come to the north half of Section 23, which is my land, 8 miles from Beach, twice as long to town as you have, but have just as good roads. The coal mine is 1½ miles my land. If Carl had come here instead of where he went, his land would now be worth 10,000 dollars. It was just when folks were coming in large numbers. He could have taken a homestead near town and bought additional land very cheap. I talked to one man who came around that time, and he sowed 500 acres of his own land.

[sixth page]

He had a 35 horsepower engine and 10 plows, and a roller that [can't decipher] and pressed it down, so it was ready for sowing flax. He plowed an average of 25 acres per day. It cost 3½ dollars per acre to have the land plowed. Flax on sod yields 20 bushels per acre, and it was sold in Beach for 3 cents more per bushel than it was worth in Minneapolis, as it goes to places on the East Coast where the bushel *[Translator: difficult to make sense of this sentence, which seems to have no real ending.]* I saw 6 steam-powered plows in a small area, and the day I was in Beach there were 26 steam-powered plows for Golden Valley being unloaded from the train. *[Translator: Again, this is my interpretation. Difficult to know exactly what he is writing here.]*

There has never been a crop failure since folks came to Golden Valley. Wheat of many varieties, oats, barley, spelt, clover, timothy, everything grows here and thrives, especially oats and barley. In many places oats, yielded 80 bushels per acre. And the cattlemen who were driven away from there to the hills of Montana bought everything they could for 40 cents a bushel

[seventh page]

I wrote to Carl as soon as I arrived back home, and he wants to go out to Golden Valley in the middle of July and have a look. He hopes he'll be able to sell his land up north.

I received a letter from Carl the first week of this month and he still had 40 acres of barley to sow. He enclosed the same photograph that [was taken?/that I saw?] at your place on April 27th showing a 5-foot snowdrift lying between the house and the barn, and the river seemed to be just as high. They couldn't begin planting until mid-May, and it froze almost every night, so the children(?) were in half the day.

Traveled to St. Paul on Saturday, and on the 11th of June there were many who traveled together to Northfield to the annual meeting. I stopped there for a day on my way home. It was a large gathering, over 1,200 persons, but since I was not a delegate, I was not so interested in the proceedings, and I returned home the next day.

[eighth page]

We had cold weather almost continually up to last week. Since then it has been better. The landscape is greening, the grass is growing nicely, but the corn is not doing well. Don't have much hope for it.

I imagine you will be tired of reading this when you get this far. It is time to close. We are all in good health and doing well. No unpleasantries of any kind. I hope we'll hear the same from you.

Greet Mr. George from me. He has grown so much so he is now a [can't decipher].

Most cordial greetings to all of you.

From your

O. P. Rocksvold

Translation by Jim Skurdall

To: Matilda Rocksvold Anderson, A. O. Anderson, and Family
From: Ole Rocksvold ***Date:*** October 17, 1907

Translation

Decorah, Iowa, October 17th, 1907

Mr. and Mrs. A. O. Anderson
Inwood, Iowa

Dear Children!

It has been such a long time since I last wrote to you that I have forgotten when it was. I am sure I haven't written to you since the last time I was in Dakota. As you know, I was out there and bought a half section of land. This was in the month of May. I had not had it for a full two months before a homesteader who lives on the next section offered me $500 *[Translator: he writes "at tjene paa en quarter af det". I am not sure if the homesteader offered him $500 for the quarter section, or if the homesteader offered Ole $500 more for the quarter than he had paid for it, in terms of what he paid for the entire half section. I think the latter is probably true.]* I regarded it as a good offer and didn't know what I ought to do. I had written to Carl and told him that he ought to sell everything there where he lives …

[second page]

… or else come out first to Golden Valley and have a look at the land there. I told him to suggest a time, and I would meet him in Fargo and go out there again. I eventually received a letter from him suggesting that we meet in Fargo on the 24th of July, and that is what I did. When I bought the land, I could only see what the land looked like, and the dead grass of the past year. I liked the idea of going there now and being able to see how the crops looked, before I decided whether or not I wanted to sell. After seeing everything, I thought, if I have one quarter section, I can just as well have two, and I hired a man to plow 100 acres for me at 3 dollars an acre, 50 cents cheaper per acre than I had paid earlier. And I still have a contract with him that he will plow the rest of the half section for the same price.

[third page]

He was only able to plow 80 acres, as it got so hot that wasn't able to finish the job in compliance with the contract. Mr. Smith, the agent in Beach, inspected the land, and told me that he had done a good job, so I sent him 240 dollars for what he had plowed.

Carl really liked the land and liked seeing the crops that all looked so lush and were so far ahead of the crops up there where Carl lives. And everything so clean, no trace of any weeds. Up where Carl lives the weeds have taken over and become worse with each new year. Doesn't look like one can ever get rid of them. Carl couldn't buy any land, as he had not sold what he has. But now he has the opportunity to sell, and perhaps he has done so.

[fourth page]

It looks like Albert is going to remain up there, if Carl sells everything. There are rumors that he is engaged to be married to a Danish girl and intends to stay there. He is still living with the family he wants to buy land from. Albert wants to buy a quarter section a mile and a half from where they live. The price is 25 dollars per acre for everything.

Carl also looked at a half section of land a mile and a half from mine and closer to town. He likes it a lot. It is both fine-looking land and good soil, as flat as my land, but there is a "Colley" or creek running across it, so that takes away some acres. The price is $18 per acre, and they could have sold it long ago, but have been holding it for us, and I could have bought it for 17 dollars an acre.

[fifth page]

I was the first person from Winneshiek County who traveled all the way out to Golden Valley. Last fall there were many who went to Hettinger County, 25 miles south of Dickinson and about 70 miles east of Beach in Golden Valley. When I returned home after the second trip out there and told folks about the crops I had seen there, and told them that now was the time to go out there before the best land was taken, and that now they could go out and see what was growing there, there were a number of them who left immediately, and almost all of them bought land. And they all came back and told the same thing, that they had never seen crops like that anywhere, and it is true. A couple of them went out there in September after they had begun with the threshing there, and they got jobs working on the threshing machines.

[sixth page]

Oats averaged 75 to 80 bushels an acre, but there was one field that yielded 120 bushels an acre. Wheat was about 45 bushels to the acre, and flax from 15 to 30 bushels an acre. The lowest yields were on land that had not been plowed until June. They said that they simply had to buy land, even though they had not thought about it before. The two bought a section together. The name of the one fellow is Hans Jørgensen, from Springfield Township. He said that if I had not told him in such detail of how things were out there, he would never have traveled there himself. Now he seemed satisfied. The company understood that I had done them a favor, so that is why I was able to buy the half section at a dollar per acre cheaper than the others had paid. I was also offered 5 dollars a day and free railway fare and expenses paid for taking folks out there, but I have not done that yet.

[seventh page]

Carl and Albert had good yields, and they finished the fall planting. They got 2,200 bushels of wheat, 1,000 bushels of rye, and 600 bushels of oats. Wheat sells for a little over a dollar in Grafton, and barley brings about 90 cents.

As for the harvest here on our farm, oats were about the worst they have ever been, barley was pretty good. We have only threshed the timothy and the little bit of flax we had. Sold the timothy for 240 dollars and still have 8 bags. The flax yielded 16 bushels an acre and we didn't get it all as some was flattened. The corn is much better than we expected, some is wet, but most of it is good. The potatoes *[Translator: Hard to make out, looks like "raanede stenet I Joden", I think he means to say here that they "rotted while still in the ground".]* but we have enough for our own use.

[eighth page]

Ole Næs, or Sætra, was in Norway, and I got him to visit Rocksvold and our relatives there. He said they were all doing well and in good health. They have sold the farm and moved to Gjøvik, where they now live. Not long ago I wrote them a letter of 13 pages.

Hilda hasn't come home yet from Mason City, but I think she'll be coming soon.

Received a letter from Irene that I have not answered yet, as I am so poor about writing, so she'll have to excuse the wait.

Expecting the mailman any moment, so shall close for now. We are all in good health.

Cordial greetings to everyone

Your

O. P. Rocksvold

Translation by Jim Skurdall

To: Matilda Rocksvold Anderson, A. O. Anderson, and Family
From: Ole Rocksvold **Date:** November 19, 1907

Translation

Decorah, Iowa, November 19th, 1907

Mr. and Mrs. A. O. Anderson
Inwood, Iowa

Dear children!

After recently returning from my third visit in Beach, North Dakota, I wish to send you a few lines and tell you about the trip. Had an option on a half section of land for Carl with no fixed deadline, but I didn't hear anything from him, whether he had sold everything or not, so I wasn't able to act on the option, and the land was sold for 320 dollars — more than I would have paid. Then I received a letter from Carl telling me to close the deal, but it was too late. Wrote to Carl that I wanted to "Pack my Knapsack and start out [can't decipher]" *[Translator: Words in quotation marks written in English].*

When I arrived in St. Paul, I found a whole bunch of land seekers who were heading west, and three of the company managers were accompanying them, 20 persons altogether. I had a sleeping car both ways, paid for by the company. George Selsvold and John Syslak from here in Glenwood also went along. Selsvold bought 160 acres. Arrived in Beach on Wednesday, the 6th. Thursday morning we set out in 2 large automobiles and 2 wagons.

[second page]

Most of the land in Golden Valley has been sold. Of the 167,000 acres the company had, there are scarcely 7,000 left.

The next day I drove together with company secretary, Toffte, to the north side of town, where I have land, and he said there was a good quarter section left, and none of the other land seekers were asked to come along with us. He said he knew that I had recruited many customers for them, and he said that the half section I had an option on had been sold for one dollar more per acre than I should have been able to purchase it for. In appreciation for my efforts, he wanted to show me this quarter section, which was the best-looking and highest-quality land. He said it had not been shown to anyone, as it would have been snapped up immediately. It has an open lake, there are outcroppings of coal on the edge of a gulley. Six miles in a straight line from town, and the road from my half section to town passes it. Toffte said he could have sold it to a man who has a homestead close by for 20 dollars an acre, but he offered it to me for 16 dollars an acre. At the end of our conversation, I got it for 15 dollars an acre. The best deal I have made. Am sure it could have sold for $10.00 more per acre than I paid. I am sure Carl will be most satisfied with it; it was for him that I bought it.

[third page]

Carl has sold his farm in the Red River Valley, and when he has hauled out all the crops, he plans to sell his horses and equipment and come down this winter. They had a good harvest there this year, even though they planted late: 2,250 bushels of wheat, 1,000 bushels of barley, and something over 600 bushels of oats. Albert plans to remain in the Red River Valley. The rumor is that he is going to marry a Danish girl.

On the way home from Beach this time, I took a side trip from Casselton 20 miles west of Fargo and visited Northwood. They had expected me to visit during my first trip to Beach and were very upset that I did not come. I was there for 4 days, but they thought 4 weeks would have been more to their liking. Visited Gilbert Tangen. They have an attractive school there. They asked me to greet you when I write.

I was away for almost 2 weeks this time and traveled 1,725 miles with the railway. I have now traveled 5,275 miles by train, and no less than 300 miles by automobile out in Golden Valley. And I feel in excellent health after all the traveling.

They were threshing here while I was away. The yield was 525 bushels of barley, 700 bushels of oats, the most we have had, both in terms of quantity and quality. The corn is quite good.

[fourth page]

We have better corn than any of our neighbors and the reason for this is the good seed corn we had. Are almost finished with raking and will have almost as much as last year.

Expecting the mailman any minute, so I must close and send off this letter.

Fond regards to you all

Greetings from your

O. P. Rocksvold

Translation by Jim Skurdall

To: Matilda Rocksvold Anderson, A. O. Anderson, and Family
From: Ole Rocksvold **Date:** December 31, 1907

Translation

Decorah, Iowa, December 31, 1907

A. O. Anderson, Inwood, Iowa

Wish to send you a few lines on this, the last day of the year. We all got home late on Christmas Eve, but safe and sound. Had worship service on Christmas Day and everyone attended. On December 26th I was in Decorah, as Carl had sent me a a bill of exchange for eight hundred dollars as the first payment for the land I bought for him. This was more than we had agreed on for the first payment, as I paid 75 dollars down this fall. So I had to send a draft myself.

When I came to Mason City I heard that Hilda was busy preparing a reception for the newlyweds. It was held on Saturday the 28th.

[second page]

As you can imagine, it was a really big affair, don't really know how many were there, but I think there were over 100 altogether, and everyone seemed to be satisfied, and many stayed almost until dawn. And, of course, there were many beautiful presents *["Presents" written in English.]* The weather was exceptionally beautiful, and no snow on the ground. It began snowing on Sunday and continued until late that night. So we have sleighride conditions again, but it has been blowing, so there are large drifts. It isn't very cold.

Hilda has had a bad cold since the party. I hope it won't last long. Peter is all right again and has been since I came.

Hans Saubek is a bit better, but not yet in good health, so none of them came to the reception.

[third page]

Tilda is healthy and seems to be getting along fine. Tomorrow, New Year's Day, we shall have worship service, as we did on Christmas Day.

I received a notice from the Pension Department that my claim was allowed and a certificate sent to the Des Moines agency for payment, dated from April 1, 1907.

Don't have anything more to write that would be of interest to you, so this will be it for this time.

Wishing everyone all the best for the new year from

O. P. Rocksvold

Translation by Jim Skurdall

To: Matilda Rocksvold Anderson, A. O. Anderson, and Family
From: Ole Rocksvold **Date:** March 31, 1908

Translation

Beach, N. D. March 31, 1908

Mr. A. O. Anderson and Family,
Dear Children and Grandchildren,

Am going to write a few lines to you now to let you know that we arrived in Beach the evening of the 20th, and Willie and George Selsvold arrived on Saturday night the 22nd in their [railway] cars. Elmer Berge, who came in one of our [railway] cars, and Helmer Sivisind, who came in one of George Selsvold's cars, were held up for 24 hours by livestock inspection agents during the transfer in Minneapolis. They said their papers were not in order, so another inspection had to be made. Each had to pay an extra 6 dollars. The horses made it through all right and arrived a day later. Both horses and cattle stood the trip well.

[page two]

The weather was excellent when we arrived here, no sign of frost in the ground. A couple of days later it turned stormy and lasted almost all week. The folks here said that all winter long they had not had storms lasting so long. Last Saturday, Sunday and Monday were beautiful, and many began disking their fields, but another storm today. It is good to get some snow and moisture in the earth. It is well soaked now.

We are living for the time being in a house 2½ miles from our land. It belongs to a widow named Mrs. Greffet. It stood empty all winter, as she now lives in Beach. I knew about the house and wrote about renting it before we came. It is a cozy place to live and is on the way from town to our land.

[page three]

The house is 20 square feet and divided into two rooms. And there is a small structure for 2 cows and Moxi. We have the other 4 horses in a tent, 14 x 18 feet, and they get along fine there. The first thing I am going to build is a barn for the horses and cows. All the building materials are here. I brought long poles for framing and have boards for the walls and roof. It is going to be 32 x 18 feet. The materials we have to buy cost around 100 dollars, but it is first-class lumber. I plan to build a house 24 x 16 feet that we can live in this summer and later use as the granary. And we also have tents that can be used. The half section we have here is regarded by many here as the prettiest and best in the valley, and I believe it is.

[page four]

We are going to be very busy building, disking, breaking new land. I want to plant oats on all of the land, and it is worth it to spend the time preparing the soil well.

I met Mr. Noben the first day I was in town and he said he planned to break my land first. It might turn out to be a big chunk of land. There was a lot of hay cut on my land last year, as there was more there than anywhere else, and when I find out who cut it, they will have to provide me with all the hay I need, and I don't think they will refuse. The old settlers here believe we'll have a bountiful harvest this year, as the soil has absorbed plenty of moisture from all the snow we've had. We also had mostly rain the month of May.

[page five]

There is a huge wave of newcomers moving here this spring. There are about 5 to 10 carloads of their livestock arriving every day, for the most part from Wisconsin, Minnesota, and Iowa, as well as Illinois and Indiana, plus eastern North Dakota. The Stondal Company, which owned 167,000 acres, only has 5,000 acres left. Most of that land is a long way from town, is hilly, and of poor quality.

Hilda likes it here and is looking forward to coming to our farm. She hasn't seen it yet. I think we are more fortunate than most of the other newcomers, as we and our horses and cows are well protected from storms. I think many of the others have to camp outside, both they and their animals, as there are few settlers who can accommodate others besides themselves.

[page six]

As for the equipment we brought along, we have a 22 disk drill, a walking plow, a disk [can't decipher], a 4-section drag, 2 wagons, and a buggy. Also have 150 fence posts and some oak lumber, a stove and beds, tables and chairs, plus other things we need, such as bedding and a good supply of food provisions, everything that can help us be independent. We are now living 5 miles from a coal mine, and went there to pick up loose coal. It costs 1 dollar "a Tun minnd ut" *[a ton when mined?]*, and when we come to our own land we only have 3 miles after that *[Translator: not really sure what he is saying here]*.

Can't think of much else to write this time. Have received so many postcards from Irene, Earnest, and George, and I hope you will excuse me for not having replied to any of them. How is Manda doing? Is she in good health and getting along all right?

Most cordial greetings to all of you from your Father and Grandpa.

O. P. Rocksvold

Billings County, Beach, N. D.

Translation by Jim Skurdall

To: Matilda Rocksvold Anderson, A. O. Anderson, and Family
From: Ole Rocksvold **Date:** April 28, 1908

Translation

Postcard, postmarked 28 April 1908

To Mrs. A. Anderson, Inwood, Ia

Mrs C co Haldet *[Translator: I don't understand what he has written here.]*

I received the lovely card you sent me. Send you greetings in return. Thankful to hear you are in good health apart from an occasional cold. *[Translator: The last sentence was difficult to make out, but I think it is what he meant to write.]* Greetings from us to all of you. We had winter yesterday. It snowed all day.

Translation by Jim Skurdall

To: Irene Anderson ***From:*** Ole Rocksvold ***Date:*** January 13, 1909

Translation

[page 1]

Miss Irene Anderson
Inwood, Iowa
RFD #3

Decorah, Iowa, January 13th, 1909

To Irene Anderson, Inwood, Iowa

Have received many cards from you in Iowa. This card shows the front of the big store in Beach, where they wanted Hilda to work as clerk. I came home on the 5th of this month. Received a letter from Hilda. They have had awfully cold weather since I left. I am healthy and feeling well.

From your Grandpa

[page 2]

Photograph of the store in Beach, North Dakota

Translation by Jim Skurdall

To: Matilda Rocksvold Anderson, A. O. Anderson, and Family
From: Ole Rocksvold ***Date:*** March 20, 1909

Translation

Decorah, Iowa, March 20, 1909

A. O. Anderson and family, Inwood, Iowa

Want to send you a few lines in advance, as I am thinking about coming out there to talk to you. I want to leave Decorah on Tuesday morning, the 23rd and arrive in Inwood the afternoon of the same day. I really shouldn't tell you that Edna Amunrud will be coming with me to surprise you, so I'd best say no more.

Have had a beautiful winter up to now. It wasn't until yesterday that the snow began to melt and create some puddles, but for the most part all the fields are still covered with snow. The road to Decorah is open. I was there yesterday, but had poor road conditions on the way home.

Anton Kirkeby held an auction last Thursday and sold all his horses and other livestock, as well as his farm machinery and other things. The auction went well and he received good prices for almost everything he sold, and he received more for some things than he had expected.

[page two]

I hear the weather out in Dakota is mild and beautiful and has been like that since late January, and I wonder if perhaps they have not already begun with spring planting. I've been longing to get out there again. I don't feel as well here as out there. I feel alright, but nothing like I felt out there last summer.

Hilda wrote that she is glad she is not down here and still snowed in. She says the weather there is more like it is in May than in March. Haven't had snow there for a long time, and the most beautiful weather.

Shall not write a lot here, as I'll be out there soon.

Fond greetings to you all from your

O. P. Rocksvold

Translation by Jim Skurdall

To: Matilda Rocksvold Anderson, A. O. Anderson, and Family
From: Ole Rocksvold **Date:** April 1, 1909

Translation

Beach, April 1, 1909

Arrived safely in Fargo. Train on time. Had my trunk transferred to M. P. Depot. and stayed overnight at Hotel Norden. Departed the next morning aboard #3, the Flyer. The folks in the 12 coaches of the train were packed in like sardines. *[Translator: Next words difficult. He may be saying he was used to it after riding troop trains. Not sure. This card is a mixture of Norwegian and English.]* Ed Curtin from Decorah was on the train, but I didn't see him until we had come to Beach. Have not met Williamsen(?) but hope to come home this afternoon. The weather is beautiful here, but it has been cold for several days. Fond greetings to you all from

O. P. Rocksvold

Translation by Jim Skurdall

To: Matilda Rocksvold Anderson, A. O. Anderson, and Family
From: Ole Rocksvold **Date:** August 24, 1909

Translation

Beach, North Dakota, August 24, 1909

Mr. A. O. Anderson and family, Inwood, Iowa!

Dear Children,

I should have written long ago, but I keep putting it off, and I cannot even remember the last time I wrote to you. Right now we are in the middle of harvesting. We have harvested a little over half of the oats, some of which are still green, and there are patches where everything is flattened. The hailstorm we had on July 10th did some damage and the crop has not matured evenly. And in the densest patches there is some rust. But it is a good crop nonetheless. Good quality. The wheat is excellent. It was hardly affected by the storm. No rust either. It is no. 1 in quality and a large quantity as well, in some cases 30 bushels per acre.

[page two]

We have 140 acres of oats, 50 acres of wheat, and 7 acres of barley, but it was ruined by the storm, so nothing to do about that. There has been so much rain this summer, so large parts of the fields have stood under water for longer periods of time, which has done some damage to the crops. Have had about 30 inches of rain since the middle of May, so can understand that no irrigation is needed here. The ground was so wet in some places that the steam plow couldn't be used. That was the case with us, we couldn't use everything we should have. Have 40 acres of flax, but some of it was planted late, and anyway, this was not a good year for flax, it was too wet. There was a lot of flax planted around here, we had perhaps the smallest crop.

There is a man in Beach, James Smith, who planted 2,000 acres. He has 8 sections of land and plowed almost all of it. His plans are to keep expanding until he has 5,000 acres under cultivation. He has been using two gasoline rigs all summer, day and night, right up until now. Now he has stopped his night operations. He is going to use 8 foot belt binders *[Translator: can't make out the last line]*

[page three]

A man who lives 4 miles west of us does harvesting and plowing at the same time. When he has gone around a field once with an 8 foot binder, then he hooks up 6 sixteen-inch plows behind the engine and the binder inside(?) and does both the cutting and plowing at the same time. Mr. Logan doesn't live far from us. He runs 4 large binders behind his engine.

August 30th

As you can see, I began this letter a long time ago, then put it aside until today. So shall add something now, also as a reply to your letter, which I received on Saturday. All the harvesting needed to be done at the same time, so we had to use all the machinery we had. *[Translator: can't make out every word in the next lines. He tells that two days of heavy wind ruined a bit of the wheat crop, and that was a sorry sight.]* Had a neighbor helping one day and were able to save a lot of it. Have some oats left, but will finish up tomorrow.

[page four]

Taking everything into consideration, it will be a good year. The wheat is excellent and the oats good, although it has some rust from the dense patches and where there was standing water, so the warm weather caused some rust. But it didn't do a lot of damage. Have had no frost yet. So it looks like the late planting of flax will be as good as before. Lots of potatoes too. If the hail hadn't done so much damage to the corn, I think the corn crop would have been just as good here as in Iowa, even though there wasn't a leaf left on a stalk after the storm on the 10th of July. But we have cooking corn [fodder corn?] at least, the stalks are from 6 to 8 feet high. No 100-degree days this summer, 92 has been the warmest, and that is enough for all the crops to grow. There is more grass here, and higher, than we have had for a long time. We were able to "set up" *[Translator: not sure what he means, whether stacking to dry, or putting into the barn]* almost 50 *[looks like "Tun", does he mean "tons"?]* of hay, and did it in 7 days and had to travel 2 miles to the hayfields.

[page five]

Received a letter from Ed Gorgen some time ago. He wanted me to appraise some land that lies 20 miles north of us, land that he has been thinking about buying. Willie and I drove out there yesterday, but we didn't accomplish much. No one is living there, it is in the Badlands, and it was impossible to find section corners. *[Translator: difficult to make out some of this]*. I think I'll tell him not to try to acquire this land, although there are some good parcels. But it is too far to the market, and he would have problems with poor roads. Stendahl Company bought a ranch with 13,000 acres this spring and immediately sold the land to settlers. It is 25 to 30 miles south of Beach. A branch line of the Northern Pacific Railroad is expected to come through there. Most of the land sold for 18 dollars an acre, and it went like hot cakes.

[page six]

We already have a lovely grove, planted a thousand Norway poplars last spring, they were tiny, but many of them now are an inch and a half thick and 5 feet high, and still growing. We are often asked how we manage to get them to grow so fast.

A milling company is building a concrete grain elevator in Beach that is supposed to hold 100,000 B[ushels], and as soon as it is finished, they will begin building a flour mill large enough to mill 600 barrels a day. It is supposed to be completed by June 15, 1910. There is a new bank in town as well. Ed Curtin of Decorah brought several railway carloads of horses, and he helped found the National Bank with $25,000 in start-up capital, and it has been open for several weeks.

I suppose this is enough for now. I still have a lot to do. I shall respond to your letter next time. Fond greetings to George, Earnest, Irene, and Edna.

Greetings from your Pa and Grandpa

O. P. Rocksvold

Translation by Jim Skurdall

To: Ernest Anderson **From:** Ole Rocksvold **Date:** 2-1910

Translation

Postcard 2-1910

Mr. Ernest Anderson

Inwood, Iowa, RFD#3

Have received so many postcards from you, and it has been such a long time since I sent anything, so I decided to send one today. I have a bit of a cold, but otherwise everything is fine here. Willie left for Beach on the 7th of this month and he found everything out there to be in the best of order.

Cordial greetings from your Grandpa

Translation by Jim Skurdall

To: Matilda Rocksvold Anderson ***From:*** Ole Rocksvold ***Date:*** May 8 & 10, 1910

Translation

Beach, North Dakota, May 8, 1910

A. O. Anderson and family

Dear Children,

Should have written to you a long time ago, but nothing has come of it. And I don't want to offer up a bunch of excuses, as they might not be very convincing.

Wanted to tell you that we have done all the planting, finished up yesterday evening. Have sowed 180 acres of wheat, and 60 acres of barley and oats. 240 acres altogether, and 160 acres of that we plowed this spring, averaging a good 7 acres a day.

We have 9 good horses, and the 5 best of them have pulled "gangploven" *[Translator: I assume this must mean a large plow you walk behind.],* and we have used it to do all the plowing. The spring planting and all spring activities have never gone better than they have this spring.

[page two]

We disked twice and harrowed twice before we planted, and harrowed again afterwards, so we went over everything 6 times, and all plowing was also done twice, and harrowing after planting. It is in the best condition possible, and we have had rain a number of times, so the soil has plenty of *[can't decipher].* 20 acres that was broken last year was intended for wheat, and it was disked first, but then we decided to put it into flax, and shall break 40 more acres, so we'll have 60 acres of flax this year. *[Translator: Difficult to make complete sense of what he wrote here. This is how I interpret it.]* So we'll have 300 acres under cultivation this year. The same 5 horses that did the plowing also have to do the breaking, and they manage well. *[Translator: With the word "bræking" I assume he means breaking new unplowed land.]*

We have hired a boy for the summer and pay him 35 dollars a month. He's a good boy and hardworking, can run every kind of machine and has a good way with the horses, so we are fortunate to have found him. His father lives 15 miles north of Fargo and has a farm of 700 acres.

[page three]

May 10

Just as I was beginning to write on Sunday, we had [can't decipher], so I was hampered and could not continue until today. I began breaking new land yesterday and had to be there.

Since returning here this spring, my health has not been as good as in past years. But I am better now than I have been recently. I came up here a little earlier than originally planned.

Mrs. Lundtvedt had to have an operation, and Pastor Fjelde recommended a doctor in Fergus Falls, Minnesota, Dr. Sherping, and since Mr. Lundtvedt couldn't make the trip, I had to accompany her and remain until the operation was over. Was there for 3 days. It was no inconvenience for me, but I had to take a different road than I usually do. She actually had two operations at the same time, had two different incisions, so I imagine she is sore. And it was warm, 84 degrees in the shade. I stood watching the entire time, and saw a man *[can't decipher the rest — I am not completely sure that with "Jeg stod og sog paa hele tiden" he means that he stood watching the operation, but that is what it appears to be.]*

[page four]

Here we did not have a terrible storm like the one that hit Iowa and other places in April. We didn't have any snow, but some cold rain, and afterwards a few nights of frost.

There is a huge amount of new land being cultivated this summer. 74 new gasoline engines arrived this spring. There were 104 steam and gasoline engines in use last summer, and they are being used again this year. Two brothers have purchased 6 new engines and have signed a contract with a land company in Montana to break 10,000 acres, and it all will be done this year. The price of land has skyrocketed here, but I believe it will level out soon. One man was offered 60 dollars an acre for his farm, a half section, but I would by no means want to trade with him. I think we could sell this farm for just as much, and perhaps a little more than our Iowa farm.

[page five]

Willie probably mentioned when he was there that Jert Selsvold had 100 acres of flax lying under the snow this winter. He finished threshing the day I arrived on March 22nd, and he got 1,800 bushels and sold it for $2.07 a bushel. He made about a thousand dollars by letting it lie. The quarter section he bought for 18 dollars an acre he sold now for 35 dollars an acre.

The trees we planted last spring are all doing well. Have only planted 21 fruit trees this spring. But we planted 1,500 more of the trees we planted last year.

Have 11 hogs. We had a large sow, and she gave birth to 11, but she killed one when she lay on it. And we have 2 cows, 1 heifer, 1 heifer calf, a bull, a hen, and a jackrabbit. I mentioned the horses earlier. So that is all our livestock. Hilda has a lot of fun with the rabbit.

[page six]

Hilda now has a camera, and I can imagine you would like some pictures. But she has a bit to learn first.

And one more thing. The team we bought this spring has a brown mare, half white and half red, and a good traveler. I ordered a saddle from Chicago, and when we have completed the spring planting and everything else, she will probably be doing some riding. She was out for a ride on Sunday.

This will be it for now. I hope this finds you all well.

Fond greetings from your

O. P. Rocksvold

Translation by Jim Skurdall

To: Matilda Rocksvold Anderson, A. O. Anderson, and Family
From: Ole Rocksvold ***Date:*** June 13 and July 14, 1910

Translation

Beach, North Dakota, June 13, 1910
[Translator: he meant to write July]

Mrs. Mathilda Anderson!

Dear Daughter!

Your letter of the 8th arrived yesterday, and I see that you would like to hear from me right away, so I won't delay.

Recently we had visitors from Iowa, Peter and Albert Sivisind(?), and O'Bryan from Waukon. O'Bryan and Peter just stayed one night, as they were on their way to Glendive, Montana, and then they plan to return via South Dakota with the Milwaukee Railway. Albert stayed an extra day, and I accompanied him to Fargo, as I had planned a short visit with Carl and Albert. We left here on Wednesday June 29th, as Albert had to be at a school board meeting on July 1st *[Translator: June 29, 1910 was in fact a Wednesday. Ole meant to date this letter July 10, 1910.]* He is treasurer. So that is why I was here for such a short time.

[Page two]

The Iowa visitors really liked being here. The crops here are the best they have seen this year. East of here everything has dried up, but here everything is green and lush. And as long as we do not have any hail storms or other destructive weather, we can expect an excellent harvest. The corn here is just as high as it tends to be in Iowa around this time. The later planting of wheat appears to be the best. It has not matured as much as the earlier wheat, but it is thicker and lusher and will be better overall. While I was away, there was a small hailstorm, but not big enough to do any damage. We have hail insurance on 200 acres, 8 dollars an acre, 1,600 dollars altogether. It is the maximum insurance one can take out for one section.

Things looked bad down toward Fargo. They had a big snowstorm in early May, so they had to plant under miserable conditions, and since then they haven't had any rain. The soil is completely parched and the cracks in it are wider than my hand. The searing wind has been more destructive than the drought.

[Page three]

Carl and Albert have 35 acres of barley that has not sprouted, and probably has not yet. The soil there was more parched than anything I saw. Along the Red River there are weeds everywhere. A terrible sight. Seems to get worse each year. Canadian Thistle is thick, many per square foot, but it isn't the worst there is. There is something they call sour weed. It takes over everything, and where it grows Canadian Thistle doesn't have a chance.

Some of the wheat looked like it might have a chance to produce something if there was an end to the hot wind, and they got some good rain, but it hasn't happened. Many farmers on both sides of Grafton had already plowed their wheat under, and as for the oats, it wasn't any better, actually worse.

[Page four]

This is hard for Carl and Albert, as they lost their entire crop on 160 acres last year, but they got enough from the quarter section they live on that they had seed and feed for the horses and didn't have to spend money on that.

Out here we have a lot to thank the Lord for. Judging by everything I have seen and heard regarding the situation around the country, nowhere are prospects for a good harvest so promising as here. We have a neighbor from Virginia who went home for a visit this summer and arrived back here last Sunday morning. He said that on his entire trip of 2,600 miles he had not seen any crops that could compare with ours. That is saying something, considering that he traveled through 10 states.

It was really remarkable, during the week I was away we had three heavy rains, and the last flax and corn we planted had shot up so much I didn't recognize them. And we have had rain several times since I returned.

[Page five]

July 14th

We have had some warm days, and today it is 100 degrees in the shade. The grain is growing too fast because the weather is so hot. [*Translator: difficult to make complete sense of what he writes in the next sentence, but the essence is that things would be better if it were not so warm.*]

I see from your letter that it has been plenty warm there too, so much so that water is scarce. That is not the case here. We dug a well 20 feet deep and have 12 feet of water in it. It is almost as soft as rainwater, and we use it for the horses and cows. The worst thing here is getting hay for the winter. We have rented a quarter section for hayfields. It is about 5 miles from us. Today I drove there to see if we could begin haying, but there was hardly anything, so we'll have to let it stand until after the harvest in the hope that it can grow some.

[Page six]

We have had good luck with a pig we bought during the winter. We bought two last year, but slaughtered one of them last fall. The sow had eleven piglets, but one died, and the other ten have turned out well. We slaughtered the sow this week, she weighed 335 pounds dressed, and we sold half to the one butcher in Beach for 18½ dollars, and we could get 50 dollars for the 9 pigs we have left. Jert Selsvold got one of them. When Ole Pedersen was leaving, Willie took a photo. It only shows the house and the horses and buggy. I'll send one, but it's really not so good. What you see on the left side is going to become a wheat granary. It is finished, but now we are using it as a summer kitchen. As soon as a photo is taken showing all the buildings, I'll send you one.

I can't remember any more that might be of interest to you, and the letter is longer than I planned to write when I began, so this is enough for now.

We are all in good health and doing well.

Fond greetings to everyone from your

O. P. Rocksvold

[Page seven]

Keep this to yourself!

The reason that I traveled to Carl's was this: Albert wrote that Carl had been having his strange notions again that he had last winter, and he didn't know what it would lead to. When I received his letter, I felt I had to go and see if I could do anything for him. But he had been calm for some time, and Albert said he almost regretted having written to me. I tried in many different ways to get him to come here with me, but he wouldn't hear of it. He believes people are trying to poison him. A woman who lives near them bakes bread for them, but Carl won't eat it and bakes his own bread. Only a few times did he talk such nonsense while I was there. He said that Mother had told him that they wanted to …

[Page eight]

… poison him, and likewise that 1910 would be such a dry year that they wouldn't have a harvest, but that it would be different after that. Next year the Lord would turn the place they lived into a paradise. The Earth would be rid of all vermin, and only [can't decipher] crops would grow and without sowing or planting. He said that next year Golden Valley would not get any crops, but we have had the best crops ever. We had an invitation from a Frenchman on Sunday and there were many people we didn't know. Carl conversed with them almost the entire time, and you could not hear a single word that suggested that there was something wrong with him. So there is nothing to do but leave things as they are, as long as he works, but only as hired help, he doesn't want to be the boss. He says the Lord knows what is best. Well, if only the Lord knew what was wrong with him.

O. P. R.

Translation by Jim Skurdall

To: Matilda Rocksvold Anderson, A. O. Anderson, and Family
From: Ole Rocksvold **Date:** Oct. 26, 1910

Translation

Beach, North Dakota, Oct. 26, 1910

Mr. A. O. Anderson and family, Inwood, Iowa

Dear Children,

It is so long since I last wrote to you that I cannot remember when it was. So I'll send you some lines now.

We are getting along as usual. Everyone is in good health and doing well. All the crops are inside now, and we needed all the room we could find. But, overall, the harvest this year was not as big as last year, as we had many days over 100 degrees, and a few up to 104 degrees. So it took some hardy plants to withstand such heat. And at times there was not much rain, although here where we live we really had no reason to complain. We had many rain showers right around here that did not spread to neighboring areas. So we were really fortunate.

[page two]

We accomplished more this spring than any other farmer in Golden Valley. We had 9 horses, and they had their work cut out for them, but they all managed well without any injuries. I mentioned earlier in this letter that the harvest out here this year was not as bountiful as last year, but that was not the case with our farm. We got 6 bushels more wheat per acre this fall than last year. Then it was 22 bushels per acre, this year 28 bushels of wheat per acre, no. 1 hard. Harvested 4,600 bushels of wheat on around 173 acres; 2,100 bushels of oats on 40 acres, and 550 bushels of barley on 13 acres, plus 550 bushels of flax on 55 acres, so altogether we had over 8,000 bushels, and our threshing bill amounted to 650 dollars. That is about 10 percent of the amount [he wrote "of the amount"] we will get when we sell our crops. Mr. Butterfield, who did the threshing for us, said that we were no. 1 in all of Golden Valley. No other farm had yields as good as ours.

[page three]

And when I came to town after we were finished with threshing, I was congratulated as the best farmer [he wrote "best farmer"] in Golden Valley They said that Mr. Butterfield had reported the production [he wrote "the Production"] of each farm, and the yields in general other places were from one quarter to one half of what we got per acre.

The prices have fallen for both flax and wheat. Wheat is now 88 cents and flax $2.36. Willie drove a load of flax to town, what we had threshed, a truckload, and he got 251 dollars and a few cents for it. Have hauled in about 700 bushels, but have only sold 3 loads. Have hauled in 2,100 bushels of wheat and have sold 1,200 bushels at 95 cents. Oats are not worth selling at 22 cents a bushel. We have stored 400 bushels in an elevator, and that's where it will stay until spring. The price for barley is good, 56 cents a bushel, have sold one load, and there are some farmers who want to buy 100 bushels each. We are going to sow 40 acres in the spring.

[page four]

You can imagine that it was not that easy to find room for the entire harvest, but we managed to put away 7,000 bushels, and then fill a number of large wagons. We haul no less than 80 bushels of wheat per team [he wrote "team"], and [looks like he wrote "125 paa team har kjøbt en truck paa 125 bushle." I have no idea what he is saying here.] We have 1,000 bushels of wheat with a good deal of [he wrote "vollater", and I assume he means "volunteer"] oats mixed in. We hauled in many loads of it and they only (he wrote "dokke", and I assume he means "docked"] us 1½ pounds, but then they were ["docke"= "docked"] 4,000 pounds for a carload in [looks like "Dilut", meaning "Duluth"?], and now they take from 5 to 10 pounds, so we want to [wrote "kline", must mean "clean"] ours, have bought a large fanning mill, and we don't want to give ["sell"?] our oats for ["noting" = "nothing"?]. We have plowed something over 200 acres, for some time we had two walking plows going. We brought one along, and we bought one here this fall. We got something over 100 bushels of potatoes on a half acre, sold 20 bushels in town for 25 dollars, have sold 3 hogs for 35 dollars, have one[?] more to sell, and we want to keep 4. We also slaughtered one, it weighed 112 pounds [wrote "drest", no doubt means "dressed"]. We now have a telephone in the house, and we have received ["fri delevry Mail" = free delivery mail] daily. Plastered the house before we started threshing. [Translator: I can't make out much of the last sentence on this page, something about a "portable granary."]

[fifth page]

Had a letter from Norman some time ago. He wrote that Clara had received a letter from Albert, and he had reported that they had harvested 2,000 bushels of grain this fall, most of it wheat, so they are not so bad off after all [he wrote "after all"]. He had also written that Carl was doing pretty well and that he hardly noticed that there was anything wrong with him. I wrote to them some time ago, but have not received a reply.

Well, don't you think that it is quite magnificent that we, who have not been here longer than two years, harvested more than 8,000 bushels and can sell our crops for at least 6,000 dollars and have enough left over for feed for the horses and seed for the farm next year? I think we could sell the farm for 50 dollars an acre, if we asked for it, but as long as we can make [he wrote "make"] 20 dollars an acre by farming it, it makes no sense to sell it. The fellow who did the threshing for us this fall asked if I would accept 45 dollars an acre and said if I would that he would give me 3,000 dollars down.

[sixth page]

I have thought, and have said it too, that when we have got enough out of the farm to the point that it has paid for itself, and [can't decipher several words], then we would sell. I see now that I could get 60 dollars an acre for the farm, so we could return to Glenwood 20,000 dollars better off than when we left [interesting that for "better off" he writes the same in Norwegian, "bedre af", which is not used in Norwegian. Such examples are common for Norwegian immigrants writing Norwegian after they have been in the USA for a long time. Then he writes what looks like "saa har vi det gaa", and I assume he means "saa har vi det godt", meaning "so we are doing well".]

Well, it is beginning to get dark, and I don't see all that well when it is light either, so it is time for me to close. I'll certainly be coming to Iowa next month, and I am thinking of traveling via Fergus Falls and spending a week there to have Dr. Skerping take care of my eyes. He said this spring that if I could stop there for at least a week that he could help me a lot.

Have not had any snow yet, but it looks like a storm is gathering. So this will be it for now.

Fond greetings to you all

Your

O. P. Rocksvold

Translation by Jim Skurdall

To: Irene Anderson **From:** Ole Rocksvold **Date:** December 22, 1910

Translation

Decorah, Iowa,
December 22, 1910

Miss Irene Anderson
Inwood, Iowa

I want to send you a few lines, and, at the same time, a little package by registered mail.

I made the promise once that when you, Alberta, and Oline were confirmed that each of you would receive a "kloke" from me *[Translator: I don't know whether he is referring here to a pocket watch or wristwatch. I'll just call it a watch. The word could also be used for a clock.]* and so now I am endeavoring to keep my promise.

I bought three watches together, and Alberta and Oline have each received theirs already. Yours I have to send by mail. The three watches are completely alike in how they work, but their casings are not alike. It is not possible to find two casings completely alike.

When you open it, press down the spring in the *[can't decipher]*, and likewise, when you close it, press it down again. Hold the casing at the rim and not in the middle, otherwise you will break the glass and *[can't decipher]* the casing as well. I hope you will like it.

Greet George and Ernest and tell them I'll write them later.

Everything is fine here. Arla is healthy and running around all day.

Shall write more another time. Fond greetings to you all and wishing you a Merry Christmas

from Grandpa

Translation by Jim Skurdall

To: Matilda Rocksvold Anderson, A. O. Anderson, and Family
From: Ole Rocksvold ***Date:*** July 11, 1911

Translation

Beach, North Dakota, July 11, 1911

A. O. Anderson and family
Dear Children,

It has been so long since I last wrote, that I can't remember the date. And I do not have good news to report this time.

From spring to the middle of June, things looked good here, and everyone was looking forward to a bountiful harvest, since we had had a couple of rain showers every week. It was not exceptionally warm either. But the last part of June and the beginning of July, it was blazing hot here and dry, and the crops began to dry up and now are ruined.

[page two)

We have 45 acres in barley, and it looked like it was going to be a magnificent crop. But now we'll mow into hay. The oat crop isn't much better; half of it is dead. But if we got rain right away and it didn't get too warm again, I think we could salvage some of it. The wheat is more tenacious, but half the crop has already dried up. The wheat crop is terribly thin, as only the first sprouts *[Translator: can't make out the rest.]* Last year we got 28 bushels per acre. If we get 8 now, we'll be satisfied, considering how things look.

[page three]

Oscar Ammerud and Emma live 7 miles straight south of us, and they'll no doubt have a pretty good crop. Recently they've had several good rain showers, while up here we only got a sprinkling. They'll do well, as long as the weather doesn't turn too warm again. I believe their wheat will be about 20 bushels per acre. I was happy to see that, for they would have lost their courage if they hadn't got a crop. He has 30 acres in flax, and it is excellent, both good and [can't decipher]. He has improved seeds and they are all pleased. Emma was somewhat homesick in the beginning.

[page four]

We have 350 acres in "grøn" *[Translator: think he means "grain" when he writes "grøn"]* and 15 acres in flax. That was the last ground we broke of the half section we have. We "Rented" 80 acres of land on which there is wheat. He [can't decipher] the seed, and is paying half of [can't decipher], and half of the threshing, and will receive half of the wheat. We have 170 acres wheat and 100 acres oats and rye on our own land, and if things turned out this year as last, we would have to build a couple of additional granaries. But we'll be spared that this year.

We have bought another [hard to decipher, "binder"?], but I think we can get by with one. We'll wind up using the "Mowara" ["mowers"?] quite a bit, since we'll mow[?] the oats into hay. *[Translator: hard to decipher his writing here, and make sense of anglicized Norwegian words.]*

[page five]

Willie left here for Iowa on June 29th, almost two weeks ago. He no doubt wants to get married, and he has a long way to go, about 1,200 miles from here. His bride is living in the southeastern corner of Iowa near Fort Madison. She boarded here for 5 months and went back the beginning of June. She is a good schoolmarm, but not so sure if she'll make a good farm wife. I hope so. Haven't heard a word from him since he left. Look for a letter every day.

So, this is enough for now. We are all in good health and hope the same is true for you.

Fond greetings to you all

O. P. Rocksvold

Translation by Jim Skurdall

To: Matilda Rocksvold Anderson **From:** Ole Rocksvold **Date:** Mar. 18, 1912

Translation

Fergus Falls, Minnesota, March 18, 1912

Mrs. Andrew Anderson

Dear Daughter,

You are no doubt surprised to receive a letter from me out here. I had to change my travel route suddenly. When Emma wrote that she had to have an operation, I wrote her and told her to have it done in Fergus Falls and said I would meet her in Fargo and accompany her from there. More about this later.

As I said, I had to change my plans. I had originally intended to travel to Mason City on Thursday, the 14th, and stay there until Saturday the 16th, and then come to your place. But Tuesday evening I received a letter from Beach that Emma would be leaving Beach that evening, arriving in Fargo the following morning. I didn't know if she was traveling alone or if someone was accompanying her. Had I known, I would have gone directly to Fergus Falls. I traveled as fast as the train could bring me there, but she had already been there for 24 hours when I arrived, and just as I got off the Northern Pacific train, they left …

[page two]

… for Fergus Falls on the Great Northern, and I had to stay there until the next morning. Hilde and Ed had also arrived and gone with them to Fergus Falls. And when I heard that she had all these other folks with her, I wasn't worried about her any longer. Ed and Hilda returned home the same evening. And Willie came to Fargo in the evening and came to the hotel and woke me up, but he was staying in a different hotel since he had [can't decipher] and had to leave at five o'clock the next morning. He went to Hilda's and planned to stay there until today and then return home. He told me that he has to have an operation as well, fairly soon. He had had a premonition of this for some time. Doctor Sherping was not very optimistic when he talked to me. He said she had a tumor. *[Translator: difficult to decipher Ole's handwriting in some places: something about an appendicitis…]* and worried about cancer. Her operation was Saturday morning, and, everything taken into consideration, she is doing fairly well. She is not in pain and has been sleeping, but she has hardly eaten anything for two weeks. *[Translator: very difficult to decipher the handwriting of the last lines: the doctor didn't believe she had cancer, but something about intestines, I think, and about an illness she has had for such a long time.]*

[page three]

I've still not had a chance to ask the doctor what he really believes about her situation. I stood and watched the operation and could see that it was much more difficult than Mrs. Lundtvedt's. The doctor operated Saturday, and has had two before 10 o'clock today. If she [difficult to decipher, perhaps "improves"] this week, I think I may go to Hilda's and stay there for a week. Last fall I promised them that I would visit them when I traveled west again. But of course I'll come back here. It is about 80 miles from here to Hilda's. I have written to Oscar and family every day since coming here, and to [can't decipher] and home, and I'll send you a card every day.
And there are many others to whom I'll be writing.

That is all for today. Please write often to Emma. Her address is:

St. Luke's Hospital, Fergus Falls, Minn.

I am pretty well, and everyone who sees me and hears my age thinks the same.

Fond greetings

O. P. Rocksvold

Translation by Jim Skurdall

To: Matilda Rocksvold Anderson, A. O. Anderson, and Family
From: Ole Rocksvold ***Date:*** April 8, 1912

Translation

Argusville, North Dakota
April 8th, 1912

Mrs. A. O. Anderson and family!

Wish to send you a few lines and let you know how Emma is doing.

We left Fergus Falls on Thursday the 4th to Fargo, where we had to stay until the following day. She was awfully tired when we arrived, and she wasn't much better the next day. We arrived in Argusville at 5 p.m., and Edvart was there to take her home. The road was bumpy part of the way, and when we got there she was not feeling well. All the shaking had been too much for her, even though we were riding in a good surrey. She felt much better after a good night's sleep.

Yesterday, Easter Sunday, there were quite a number of Ed's relatives here to see her, and they all invited her to visit them, all nice people. She will have to stay here for a few days before we can begin the journey home. She has to gather a little more strength, as she has been through quite an ordeal. The doctor himself was not sure how much she could tolerate so soon after the operation.

(second page)

The doctor didn't risk removing her appendix, for if blood [hard to decipher, poisoning?] had set in, it surely would have been fatal. He didn't think it was necessary and didn't believe she would be troubled by it later.

Believe me, it was awful to see all the putrid stuff she has been carrying around all these months. I thought she would have decomposed inside, and there was such a horrid stench when the doctor cut her open, and I don't know how many "yards" [he wrote "yard"] of [can't decipher] had amassed in her, and when he removed it came like a deluge, and the head nurse, who attends all operations, said it was the foulest thing she had ever seen. These "Sisters" did their duty to the utmost. They looked after the incision wound day and night and tried to make everything as comfortable for her as possible. I paid $50 for the operation, but he charges those living near town $100.

(third page)

I don't remember if I mentioned the last time I wrote that Albert Rocksvold in Grafton burned himself awfully badly. He had gone to Draiton[?] with a load of wheat, and in the grain elevator he stepped on some loose boards lying on top of the gasoline generator's water tank and fell into it up to his waist. The water was boiling hot. He is still in the hospital there, and it happened a month ago. Willie visited him and he cried like a baby when they said goodbye. I wrote to Peter immediately, and he called up Clara, who went to see him right away. The doctor there believes he can save both his life and his legs, but he will need skin transplants on the wounds. People there have offered ...

(fourth page)

... their own skin for grafting.

The weather here has been cold and miserable since we arrived, began improving a little Easter Sunday, but is the same now again. The new planting season has begun and things look good, but need more rain soon. Willie wrote from Beach that the water was knee-high between the buildings on our farm a few days ago. Had had a lot of snow, and it melted in a couple of days. Everyone is hoping for a good year out there, and even though there is so much meltwater still, they have begun there too.

I don't know when we'll be leaving here. We have to wait until Emma gains some strength before we set out.

So, I guess that will be enough for now.

Fond greetings to you all

O. P. Rocksvold

Translation by Jim Skurdall

To: Matilda Rocksvold Anderson **From:** Ole Rocksvold **Date:** July 16, 1912

Translation

Postcard

Mrs. A. O. Anderson
Beach, North Dakota
c/o Oscar Ammund

Inwood, 7/16-1912

Dear Matilda,

Thank you so much for your postcard, which I received on Saturday. Want to send one back to you now. Everything is fine here at home, and we are all in good health. How are you? I hope you will be feeling all right in a few days. I see from what you wrote that things are pretty slow sometimes and that [can't figure this out] all the time. We were at a party at Swensons' on Sunday and I had a lot of fun. So, must close for now, with many fond greetings.

Translation by Jim Skurdall

To: Matilda Rocksvold Anderson, A. O. Anderson, and Family
From: Ole Rocksvold ***Date:*** September 8, 1912

Translation

Beach, North Dakota
September 8th, 1912

Mrs. Anderson and family!

It has been a long time since I received your letter, which I have yet to answer. I began writing quite some time ago, but I was interrupted, so I'll begin a new letter. The other was old news. We have finished the harvest for the most part here. We still have some oats at Tuller's[?] which aren't ripe yet. Had a hailstorm three weeks ago that ruined a good part of the crops, beat them down and tangled them so that a lot was left lying on the ground. The wheat was so high that we considered leaving 16 inches in the ground, but we couldn't do that *[Translator: difficult to make out what he is writing here.]* We have some wheat stems measuring 61 inches. The average was four and a half feet. We had insurance but didn't think the damage was as great as it turned out to be. Willie asked for only 10 percent damage, and we received that for all the wheat, 150 acres on our own farm and 12½ percent for the wheat and 15 percent for the oats on Tuller's land. We'll apparently receive 200 dollars compensation, not fully enough to pay for the entire policy, as we had 400 acres insured.

(second page]

You should have been here and seen the crops at harvest time and it would have been the most beautiful sight you have seen, and both I and many others thought that the wheat crop would amount to 40 bushels an acre, but the best of the crop was damaged the most. Nonetheless, we have a magnificent crop in spite of the setback. The barley crop was better than usual but was damaged by heavy rain that accompanied the hailstorm. We had almost two inches of rain in a very short time, so the barley stems were soaked through and through and discolored. Our flax is good and almost ripe, as is everything else here.

The large black mare was at the ranch with 7 other horses of ours *[Translator: difficult to make sense of what he is writing here. The mare was to have a foal at this time. They didn't want to pay 200 dollars for her.]* Hellen Bengson was here on a visit this summer. He was here for two weeks and then returned to Mandan to teach school this winter. Have not heard from Carl since he returned home this summer, but I am worried that he became dejected when he came home and saw that his crop was ruined.

Peterson and Mrs. Ramstad have both had operations and are doing well. Mrs Ramstad was visiting in Minnesota and still has not returned home, but plans to come next Wednesday. That is what Mrs. Hegset told us Friday, when we were at her home for Ladies' Aid. Oscar's family is doing well, the youngest is healthy, as are the others ... Edna, Olive, and the boys went to Badland [the No. Dak. Badlands?] today to get plums.

We are all well and hope the same is true for you.

Greetings from

O. P. Rocksvold

Translation by Jim Skurdall

To: Matilda Rocksvold Anderson, A. O. Anderson, and Family
From: Ole Rocksvold **Date:** November 1, 1912

Translation

Beach, North Dakota
November 1, 1912

Mr. and Mrs. A. O. Anderson and family

Am going to send you a few lines to let you know how things are here.

We finally got the harvest in, and it was just in time. We have had a lot of rain all fall so that the threshers could only work half the time. They had to stop many times and wait for things to dry out a bit, and then it would begin again and soak the shocks once more. *[Translator: Ole's handwriting in the next sentence difficult to decipher, but it appears to read "Ellevterne ville ikke tagend raa hvede, og de kunde ikke holde den hjemme, og fölgen blev at lidt eller intet blev trækst." / "The elevators didn't want to accept raw wheat, and they(?) couldn't keep it at home, with the consequence that little or nothing was threshed."]* They finished up on Wednesday, October 23rd, and they were here for 10 days. In the end we had two weeks of dry weather, everything dry as gunpowder, first time since the harvest, so we got all the crops into the barn.

[second page]

So the harvest didn't turn out so bad after all. We did suffer damage from the hailstorm, but in the end we had 4,800 bushels of wheat, 2,360 bushels of barley, 2,000 bushels of oats, 735 bushels of flax, or 9,800 bushels all together. We would have had 12,000 bushels, had it not been for the storm. *[Translator: can't make out much in the next sentence, something about the wheat east of some place.]* I think about 100 acres would have been affected.(?) *[can't decipher some words]* … over 30 bushels per acre. It isn't possible to find space to store all the crops harvested. We built a granary and an addition to another so that we could have space for something over 8,000 bushels, and the threshers remained so long so we managed to salvage another(?) 1,000 bushels of wheat and 300 bushels of flax. I wrote that the threshers left on Wednesday; no, it was Thursday the 24th, and we had good weather until Sunday the 27th, but then it began raining …

[third page]

… and during the night it turned to snow. It snowed all day Monday and most of Monday night, and in the morning there was a foot of snow on the level and in some places it was two feet deep. Here thousands of acres of crops are standing as shocks in the snow, and you can't see anything anywhere but small buttes of snow. Our neighbors haven't threshed yet. We were incredibly fortunate to have finished in good time.

We have purchased an additional quarter section of land. It is the southeastern quarter section of the section we reside on. It was more than anything else to acquire additional pastureland. There is a good water supply there all summer and 50 acres of fenced-in pasture, plus 100 acres are broken, and 50 acres are summer _____? The National Bank of Beach [can't decipher] from Martin Malmin *[can't decipher]*. I paid 30 dollars per acre for it. That was pretty reasonable.

But if the snow doesn't melt and we don't have good weather for a couple of weeks, then we …

[fourth page]

… won't get anything plowed and I don't know how we are going to plant in the spring. We have only plowed 10 acres. I think we'll have to buy another horse so that we can have 3 four-horse teams. We have 11 horses and a foal now. This coming spring we'll be planting around 4,400 acres.

Prices are low for all farm crops here. 70 cents for the best wheat, 35 cents for barley, 20 cents for oats, and $1.25 for flax. We'll sell the wheat and flax, but we'll keep the barley until spring. There is a shortage of railroad cars, so the elevators are full. 2 of the elevators "Bosted"(?)/burst? last Saturday. The 9 elevators in Beach have a capacity of around half a million bushels, and when they are all full, they can fill up a train, 4½ million kt(?).

There is at the very least a third of the crops still standing as shocks under the snow, and it looks like it might have to stand there until spring, and little or nothing ____? threshed, and still so much left to be cut, and that probably won't happen either.

I probably won't be traveling east for another 2 or 3 weeks. I am still in good health and haven't been ill a single hour while I've been here.

Fond greetings to you all from

O. P. Rocksvold

Translation by Jim Skurdall

To: Matilda Rocksvold Anderson, A. O. Anderson, and Family
From: Ole Rocksvold **Date:** April 11, 1914

Translation

Decorah, Iowa
April 11, 1914

Matilde and family!

Just received your letter today, and thank you so much for writing.

I returned home yesterday from Beach, where I had been on a short visit, a little over two weeks. Since Willie's wife arrived, it has not been home for me, and I decided to sell my share of the property, which I did now. Earlier I had decided to deed half of my land and personal property to him for one dollar. He estimated the land was worth 12,000 dollars *[Translator: hard to make out here, something about 500 more, and that Ole thought both Willie and his wife thought it was all a better deal than they expected]*, so I didn't expect to be treated like a tramp, but that was indeed the case.

I haven't experienced a summer like this one since my time in captivity in the South, and therefore I had to "slide mig løs" *[Translator: not sure what he means here, "slite" today means to "work hard, struggle", but if he is still talking about his unpleasant visit with Willie and Willie's wife, then perhaps he means that he had to "leave, as hard as it was to do so". Really not sure.]* I once said to Oscar Annerud last spring that I was willing to accept 10,000 dollars for my share of the farm, but nothing was said to Willie about that.

(second page)

But after I returned home last winter, I think Oscar told Willie what I had said. Immediately thereafter I received a letter from Willie saying that he wanted to buy me out, and he set the conditions. Not too long before that we had bought a quarter section of land and still owed 2,900 dollars on it. His conditions were that he wanted to have 5 years at 6 percent interest, and the first payment to me was to pay the 2,900 dollars on the land so that he would get 480 acres "slaar af gjeld" *[Translator: not sure about this, but seems to mean "removed from his debt"]*, or I could buy him out under the same conditions, in which case he wanted <u>cash payment</u>, and there was one more thing. We owed around 3,000 dollars here in Iowa, money I had borrowed the spring we went out there. This was, he thought, my business, so there wasn't [wouldn't be] much for me after I had paid the 6,000 dollars, and I wrote to him and said that I understood that he didn't want to deal with everything, since he was willing to leave me with the debt while he got the farm, and I wrote that to him, and right after that I received an ugly letter from him in which he wrote "Your words ar good nothing" [quoted] and other vicious things that I won't mention here. So I wrote back with my conditions, which were very reasonable …

(third page)

… and which he accepted. We had paid 2,454 dollars on the quarter section, and I wanted half of that back, which was 1,127 dollars, and he received my share of both the farm and my personal property for 8,000 dollars, meaning that what I received was 9,127 dollars, which I am holding a mortgage on at 6 percent interest. But I gave him time to pay for the land before he begins making payments to me. First payment to me is on January 1, 1916, and the last in 1920. *[Translator: handwriting here difficult to decipher, is something like "I have never taken as much as one cent from the farm income when I returned home, until this winter when I got 52 dollars, so if I should let it go so long, I wouldn't have … can't decipher. Hard to make sense of this.]* We shipped a carload of barley to Milwaukee in the autumn, 1,400 bushels and received 51½ cents per bushel, and there were still almost 1,000 bushels left when I returned home this winter, which he sold for seed, and there were almost 400 bushels of wheat left to sell, and at least 800 bushels of oats, so all of that came to 1,000 dollars. So I don't think I took too much, when I took the 52 dollars. I was there for 2 weeks now, but I only spent one night with Willie and Helen. Otherwise, I was with Oscar. They had built another building. They have a house with 6 rooms *[Translator: difficult to decipher handwriting and make sense of everything, telling about how things looked at Oscar's and perhaps where he slept at their place.]*

(fourth page)

Things are fine at Oscar's. M__ is fat, and _____? as a cannon. All the others are fine. Five of them go to school on weekdays, and Beach has an exceptionally good school.

I am not sure whether I'll be coming to your place before summer, and then I can tell you some things I prefer not to put in writing. I owe Iver many letters, but you deserve receiving this one now. Arla[?] has learned from her mother to play a note on the organ and sing a verse, and she does it well. Gr__? is a little "cranke" [cranky?] now and then, but otherwise fine.

I am in good health and doing well and happy to be in the nursing home, where I wish to remain for the time I have left here on this earth.

Oh yes, I wanted to tell you that just before I left for Beach I received a letter from Hilda that she was in the hospital in Fargo and had given birth to another daughter. She wrote that she was going to stay with a family for a week before returning home. I had been on the road several days before realizing that I could have met her there. But she had already left when I arrived. I later heard that she had arrived home safely with her little daughter.

So, enough for this time.

Fond greetings to you all from

O. P. Rocksvold

Translation by Jim Skurdall

To: Matilda Rocksvold Anderson, A. O. Anderson, and Family
From: Ole Rocksvold ***Date:*** May 25, 1914

Translation

Boyd, Minnesota
May 25, 1914

To A. O. Anderson and family!

Want to send you a few lines to let you know that I am on the way to your place. I traveled to Minneapolis for the city's Seventeenth of May festival, then stayed a week. I went with Ole Kjorlien from Decorah. He has 2 sons and a daughter who live there, and I stayed with them each of the nights. I won't write anything about the festival now. I can tell you about that when I arrive.

I arrived in Boyd Thursday evening and am planning to leave sometime this week, but they won't listen to talk of leaving. They say I have to stay at least two weeks. But I really can't stay that long. It has rained two or three times and the roads are in terrible condition, so they have not been able to take me around much in their automobile. They say that I have to stay until the roads improve and I can go on a good ride.

[second page]

The week I was in Minneapolis I must have ridden at least 200 miles in automobiles.

I am not going to write a long letter this time. Just want to tell you that I am in the best of health and doing well in every respect.

I can't seem to make up my mind when I should leave here. I'll send you a card and tell you when I'll be arriving in Al__d. I have to travel 28 miles from here back to He__ly Falls, and from there 114 miles to Al__d.

It is very pretty around here now. The land here is just as beautiful as around Inwood, nice houses and prosperous farmers. It is very comfortable here at the home of Anton Roseth and Laura. They have a magnificent house and it is well furnished. He owns 3 lumber yards himself and has shares in 2 others. Laura has gotten very fat, but she is healthy and active.

This will be all I have to say for this time.

Cordial greetings

O. P. Rocksvold

Translation by Jim Skurdall

To: Matilda Rocksvold Anderson, A. O. Anderson, and Family
From: Ole Rocksvold **Date:** July 25, 1914

Translation

Decorah, Iowa
July 25, 1914

Mr. and Mrs. A. O. Anderson,

I shall try to put down a few lines to you, but I don't know if you will be able to read them. I feel like I have been cooked. I don't feel well and [can't decipher]. Could have been finished with the harvest today, had it not rained Thursday night and were it not so hot.

The barley crop turned out well, but the oats weren't as good as they could have been, were it not so hot. The corn is good and has tassled. But the hay harvest was the best. I have never seen the hay grow so well here before. On average we got 3 large loads per acre, and the clover is still growing and in full bloom. We'll fill our barn, and Peter has got 14 loads and has around 16 acres left to cut, and may cut 30 "Tun"/tons? *[don't know]*. The clover is knee-high many places there.

[second page]

You have no doubt read in the Decorah Posten about the golden wedding anniversary of C. Evens. Norman and I were there. It was a magnificent celebration with over 400 guests present, and everyone in a festive mood, and the weather pleasant. That is the longest outing I have been on since returning home.

I have not received any letters from Dakota since coming home, but Jert Selsvold came down here for the funeral of his father and he said everyone we know was doing fine and that never before had prospects been so promising for a good harvest.

Peter has had a well driller at his place and has drilled down 420 feet to get water, and then they dropped the bucket down on 375 feet of rope and can't get it back up, so they are going to try to drill(?) it out. *[hard to decipher that word].*

Things here are normal, no one ill, and all doing well.

[third page]

Albert and Klara Johnsen, and Albert and Emma Ask were here last Sunday. They are planning to return home to Mason City this week. Kalle and Elling Vangen have returned from their trip to Norway. I don't think they got that much out of the trip. Elling apparently said he wouldn't repeat that trip if he were given a free ticket.

I was amazed when I saw what Anderson handed me in the box through the car window when I left Inwood. I have hardly dared to use it as I think it is much too nice. I'll certainly <u>not</u> need another Ball__? knife, since this one is guaranteed to cut 500 times with each of the 12 blades. Thank you so much for the gift.

So that will be all for now. I am not sick, but don't feel so well on account of the heat. Everything is fine here.

Fond greetings to you all.

O. P. Rocksvold

Translation by Jim Skurdall

To: Matilda Rocksvold Anderson, A. O. Anderson, and Family
From: Ole Rocksvold ***Date:*** December 18, 1914

Translation

Decorah, Iowa
December 18, 1914

Matilde and family,

Wish to send you a few words, won't really call it a letter, as it seems to be almost impossible for me to write. I received a long letter from Irene, but have not replied, so you see how things are with me.

The first thing I want to tell you is that Hilda, her husband and their children are coming to visit us tomorrow evening. They arrived in St. Paul this morning, but wish to spend the day there today. They had planned to come earlier this fall, but some misfortune or other prevented them from traveling at the time. They are all in good health

[second page]

It is dusk and so dark I can hardly see what I am writing., so just letting the pen find its way. We have been having some cold days and have about 3 inches of snow.

Around two weeks ago we had a telephone call from Manda after ten o'clock in the evening informing us that she was in Calmar and would be arriving in Decorah later that night, and she wanted us to come and fetch her. She has neither learned nor forgotten anything while she has been away. And now she already had plans to *[looks like "tage Romanten her"/perhaps means she wanted to bring her boyfriend home, hard to know for certain]*, and she was told that either she learn how to behave properly or she could pack her things and leave.

[third page]

Well, I said it wouldn't be much of a letter, and so there won't be much more.

We are all in good health and doing pretty well. Tilda wasn't feeling so well some time ago, but she got over it and is now her old self again, healthy and peppy.

So that will be it for now. Wishing you all a Merry Christmas and Happy New Year.

Fond greetings from us all

O. P. Rocksvold

Translation by Jim Skurdall

To: Matilda Rocksvold Anderson, A. O. Anderson, and Family
From: Ole Rocksvold **Date:** February 10 and 12, 1915

Translation

Decorah, Iowa
February 10, 1915

Mrs. A. O. Anderson and family!

I should have written to you long ago, but always seems to postpone doing so. This won't be such a long letter either, but at least long enough to let you know we are still alive.

Nothing much has happened this winter worth writing about. We had a beautiful winter up to the 1st of February, at which time we had a terrible snowstorm, a regular blizzard lasting all day and night. About a foot of snow fell, making the roads impassable, and we weren't able to plow for 3 days. And it is quite cold on top of it all.

[second page]

We have received many pictures from you for which we thank you. I may not have written today either, had it not been for a card from Irene to Tilda on which she wrote that it was really shameful that we don't write and thank you for the things we receive. So, that is what got me going on this letter.

Christian Kirkeby died a little over a week ago. The funeral was last Saturday. He was bedridden for around two months with abdominal tuberculosis. He wasn't able to eat anything the last couple of weeks, and he was so thin, just skin and bones.

Anne still has the cough she has had for so long, but she [can't decipher] many years.

[third page]

February 12th

I wrote the first two pages on Wednesday evening, which had been a clear day, but the next day was so dark that I couldn't see, so I had to put off writing until today.

The snow has been melting day and night and there isn't much left of the heavy snowfall we received.

Albert Rocksvold and his wife came right before Christian Kirkeby died and they were at the funeral. His wife is a little Catholic woman from Württemberg who looks more like a squaw than anything else.

Tilda hasn't been really well of late. She went to the doctor a week ago, and …

[fourth page]

… Norman accompanied her to Waukon today. She has a heart condition, or a [can't decipher] heart.

The rest of us are all quite well. Manda came home for Christmas and is still here.

Norman sold a mare for $165 and will deliver it to the buyer in Decorah on Monday, and Peter sold 3, 2 mares and a horse to the same man for $560. We have had several letters from Hilda and her family since they left. They arrived home safely.

So, this will be all for now, as I have nothing more to write about. I am doing well, am in good health, and I hope the same can be said for all of you. In closing,

Fond greetings to you all

O. P. Rocksvold

Translation by Jim Skurdall

To: Matilda Rocksvold Anderson, A. O. Anderson, and Family
From: Ole Rocksvold ***Date:*** March 16, 1915

Translation

Decorah, Iowa
March 16, 1915

Matilda and family!

I should have written to you a long time ago, but keep putting it off. I received both of your letters. Received the first one on Tuesday evening, the day we had expected you to come. Norman drove to Decorah in the morning, as we thought you would be arriving on the 3 o'clock train. And he waited until the 6 o'clock train had arrived. And Victor Ruen was waiting when the midnight train came in, and you could have come out here with them in the morning. I received your second letter a couple of days later.

The deceased was the same to the very end as she had been for a longer period of time.

[second page]

She was up that morning and ate breakfast as usual, then sat on the bed to read, but suddenly had so much trouble breathing, so they sent for the doctor, and he came immediately. The medicine he gave her seemed to help her, and she lived until that evening. She had no pain.

It was a nice funeral. Her 5 sons and John Erie were pallbearers. There was a sea of flowers. Many attended the funeral, the church was full, and Pastor Fjelde delivered an excellent sermon.

We had a storm not so long ago, but the weather was nice on that day.

[third page]

Today there is a funeral at *[looks like "Stenkirken", wonder if he means the Glenwood stone church?]*. A daughter of Jens Erie died last week. She had measles, and then a very high fever. There has been a lot of such illness around here, but our home has been spared.

The snow is still lying almost everywhere. We have had a lot of foggy days as well on which the the sun has not managed to burn off the fog. In many places there are still several feet of snow.

I had a letter from Willie not so long ago. They are doing fine. Helen had competed in selling subscriptions to the Beach Chronicle and won second prize, a piano worth 450 dollars. She had wanted so much to win the automobile, but failed.

[fourth page]

Willie says that he can get a Ford car for the piano, and that is better than having 2 pianos.

They have snow everywhere there as well, and they are happy for that.

If no obstacles appear, I intend to travel as far as Fargo this summer, and perhaps up to Carl's. Willie wrote that he had had a letter from Carl saying that he wants to sell out there if he can.

I and everyone here in the house are in good health and lacking nothing. I for my part am healthy and have put on at least 10 pounds this winter.

Fond greetings to you all from your

O. P. Rocksvold

Translation by Jim Skurdall

To: Matilda Rocksvold Anderson, A. O. Anderson, and Family
From: Ole Rocksvold ***Date:*** July 27, 1915

Translation

Decorah, Iowa
July 27, 1915

Matilda and family!

Inwood, Iowa

Dear children and grandchildren:

I should have written to you long ago, but keep putting it off, and now we have been busy with haying for a couple of weeks. It has rained more than half the time, so it has taken a long time to finish up. We have most of the hay in the barn now nonetheless, as we haven't cut so much at one time. Now we just have a few loads lying out in the fields before we are done. It will be a lot of hay. And where we cut first, there is now clover blossoming again. Could have finished today, had it not rained last night.

[second page]

We have little hope for a corn crop this year. Last year we were cooking corn the 1st of August, but this year a good portion of the corn will scarcely be two feet high by August 1st. The cornfields are so soggy, it doesn't make any progress, and the soil is full of [looks like Whith Grute?] that will ruin it. The oats are fine, but some have been flattened, and there is bad rust.

I recently had a letter from Olive Amunrud. They have bought a farm again and moved onto it. It is on a half section of land in Montana, around 24 miles from Beach, and about the same distance from Willie. She says it is good land and nice-looking, 80 acres planted in wheat, oats, flax, and corn. They got 3 good horses, 2 cows, and all kinds of machinery except for a binder.

[third page]

They also have a good garden and good water supply. She writes that they all really like it. They have started a new town just 1½ miles from them. There is a store, a post office, and a blacksmith. The town is called B__n? They bought the entire farm for 12 dollars an acre from a homesick homesteader. Alberta and Norma are still in Beach. Norma is going to Norwegian [summer]school.

They say the crops look good out there. I have considered traveling at least to Hilda's, from where it is easy to get to Beach, and then to Oscar's, and I would really like to do it.

How are things with you? Have you given up on the idea of taking a trip or not? If you are thinking of traveling, you must inform me at once, as I must leave at the beginning of next month.

[fourth page]

I have not heard from Willie since early spring. I sent him a corn planter. Olive says that Willie and Helen had visited on Sunday. They came from Beach. They have an automobile, so it took them about an hour to get there.

No other news to report. Everything is the same. Everyone around here is healthy and doing well.

I am the same, drove the hay fork during haying, and that was all I could manage. Everyone here in the family is in good health, and we hope the same it true for you.

Oh yes, I do have some news. Julia Kirkeby was sent to Independence a couple of weeks ago. *[I think there was a mental institution there then.]*

In closing, fond greetings to you from your

O. P. Rocksvold

Translation by Jim Skurdall

To: Matilda Rocksvold Anderson, A. O. Anderson, and Family
From: Ole Rocksvold ***Date:*** August 8, 1915

Translation

Decorah, Iowa
August 8th, 1915

Matilda and family!

Dear Children and Grandchildren!

Received your letter a few days ago, and I wish to send you some lines before I forget. Am happy to hear that all is well with you, and I can report the same from here. I see from your letter that [*can't decipher, "opget"?*] is thinking of visiting Hilda this summer, and the same goes for me. From what I have heard, it has rained so much in the Red River Valley this summer that there is flooding from Fargo to Hillsboro, and it is no doubt worst around where Hilda lives, so it will not be such a pleasant place to visit.

[page two]

The main reason that I wish to go up there is that I would like to try to persuade them to move away from that mudhole. That's what it has been this summer. It has been virtually impossible to get from house to house, and that is why I am not very keen on going there. I would have to sit inside the entire time, for if I tried going out, I would just get stuck in that quagmire. Received a letter from them a while ago, and they say they are waiting for me to come and look for me every day. Esther, whenever she sees a man coming, says "There comes Grandpa." I can't say for sure whether I'm going or not. In any case, I want to stay home until we have harvested. It may be that I'll leave then.

[page three]

Have recently received 3 letters from Golden Valley, and from Montana. One letter was from Willie, written on the 26th of July, and it contained unpleasant news. A few days earlier a hailstorm had destroyed Willie's entire crop, the best crop he'd ever had on that farm. I'll say no more about this, simply send along the letter. It is tough to watch everything ruined in a few minutes, 400 acres of crops. But good he had insurance for $26.40 [*Translator: per acre, I imagine*]. I was supposed to have $480 in interest this spring from the mortgage I hold on the farm, but with the poor harvest last year I said I could wait, and now it looks like I'll be waiting for another year.

[page four]

I think I mentioned earlier that Oscar Amunrud sold his farm this past spring, lived in town until June, before buying and settling on a farm with a half section of farmland in Montana, 24 miles from Beach. It had 80 acres in crops, wheat, oats, flax, and some corn and potatoes. He also got all the machinery he needs on the farm, besides a binder, and, in addition, 3 good horses and 2 cows, plus a lot of chickens. He paid around 12 dollars an acre for the land plus everything else I just listed. Olive says they really like it there. Many Norwegians there, as well as church service in Norwegian and a Norwegian school. They invited me to come and visit, something I'd like to do.

[page five]

Well, the weather here has been terrible all summer, has rained about half the time, and has been cold as well. Have only seen the sun now and then. A lot of the crops have rotted. We got in most of the hay, didn't cut so much at one time. We lost about the equivalent of 12 loads. Some folks lost most of their hay crop. We had a rainstorm a week ago and got 3 inches of rain in half an hour, and we got almost half as much during a shower the following Sunday evening. After that it was cold for three or four days, just like late autumn. Was 50 degrees. The past 3 days it has been dry and warm, so we have seen …

[page six]

… the corn grow a little more and begin to tassle. Otherwise, it is standing in mush. The soil has never really warmed up.

We began harvesting yesterday, and some stakes are under water, so we have to drive around them. The oats are pretty good, but it will be a slow job cutting them as they are all tangled and lying in all directions. We'll lose quite a bit of the crop.

I shall write to Hilda soon and shall greet her from you.

I don't have anything more to report, at least anything worth mentioning, except that we are all in good health and doing well.

In closing I send fond greetings from

O. P. Rocksvold

Translation by Jim Skurdall

To: Matilda Rocksvold Anderson, A. O. Anderson, and Family
From: Ole Rocksvold **Date:** March 18, 1916

Translation

Decorah, Iowa
March 18, 1916

A. O. Anderson and family!

We arrived home safely yesterday evening. Found everything in order here. Norman met us at the depot in Decorah, and soon we were on our way home. They have had beautiful weather the entire time we have been away. The roads were all dry; the snow has been gone for a long time. Both Tilda and the boys are fine after the trip. As for myself, I have never felt better. Many people are ill now, and in Decorah they have had over 60 cases of scarlet fever, with many deaths.

[second page]

Here the situation with the seed corn is worse than many thought. Most of it can't be planted. Norman has tested a good deal of it, and for the most part it can't be used. He has bought two bushels for 9 dollars a bushel, and it is uncertain how good it will be when planted. I've heard a hired man costs 45 dollars a month, and some are already working at that wage.

My pen is so bad I can hardly scribble down these lines, and the mailman will be arriving any minute, so I must close.

Fondest greetings to you all,

O. P. Rocksvold

Translation by Jim Skurdall

To: Matilda Rocksvold Anderson, A. O. Anderson, and Family
From: Ole Rocksvold **Date:** May 30, 1916

Translation

Argusville, May 30th, 1916

Mr. and Mrs. A. O. Anderson
Inwood, Iowa

I wish to send you a few lines to let you know that I am in Dakota. I have been here for almost 3 weeks, arrived on May 10th. It has been raining most of the time since then, and they are not close to being finished with planting. Many aren't even half done.

A cyclone tore through here on Thursday the 25th, the worst they have had since people began settling here. It blew down at least 50 barns and other buildings. Many people's livelihoods were destroyed, but I have not heard that anyone was killed.

[second page]

Here on the farm, the storm took the windmill and a couple of smaller buildings, strewing bits and pieces across the fields. The wind came first from the west, then returned from the east, taking a buggy shed and carrying it over a binder that stood in its way without touching it, then scattered it across the field.

At the place where Hilda and Ed used to live, a granary and an *[automobile garage? looks like, difficult to decipher handwriting]* were ripped to shreds and hurled against the house so that pieces of planking *[can't decipher next two words]* went through the wall of the house in many places and are lying all over inside. Olaus Ohnstad lives there now, and as it turned out, he was in the bedroom and wasn't injured.

[third page]

For the most part I have been taking it easy at Ed's place, as it has been so muddy.

On Sunday the 14th I was in Moorhead for the dedication of a church. We went by automobile. It rained a little in the morning, but we arrived safely. We wound up having to stay there for two days because of the constant rain.

I received a letter from Edina recently. She wrote that they are all in good health and doing well.

Last Sunday I went to Perley with the Ohnstads. It hadn't rained for 2-3 days and the roads were fine for driving. There are no less than 5 automobiles at the Ohnstad place. The weather has been fine for some days now, so they hope to be finished with planting this week.

[fourth page]

They have been talking about driving to Fargo this summer for the annual meeting. If they do, they hope to meet me there. I plan to go home with the delegates from Winneshiek County. I have to be home by the beginning of July.

Ed and Hilda have a better farm now than where they were before. Hilda has her hands full with the children and housekeeping. They have a young girl to help with the baby, but that is all. Hilda and family send greetings.

I caught a cold the past couple of days and have a bad cough, but otherwise my health is fine.

Most cordial greetings from

O. P. Rocksvold

Translation by Jim Skurdall

To: A. O. Anderson ***From:*** Ole Rocksvold ***Date:*** May 30, 1916

Translation

Fargo, North Dakota
June 16, 1916

A. O. Anderson

Wish to send you a card. I have been looking for you here, but haven't found you, so I assume you are at home. A large convention going on here now. The auditorium has a capacity of 2,400. It is almost filled every day. In the afternoon there was a vote on our four proposals together with representatives of the N S and Hauge Synod *[this is what it looks like, difficult to decipher the handwriting here]* and they were unamimously adoped by those representatives entitled to vote, over 1,000 men. I am a delegate to the convention, and I have not seen either the pastor or the other delegate, both of whom are supposed to be here. I am in good health and doing well.

OPR

Translation by Jim Skurdall

∽ Appendix 3 ∾

Pertinent Letters of
Relatives and Friends

Order of letter writers within this appendix:

Matilda Rocksvold Anderson

A.O. Anderson

Pauline Evenrud Mickelson

Helene Roksvold Dahl

Helene Marie Roksvold Dahl Øistad

Lars Dahl

Laura Øistad Roseth

John Steen

Oscar Fridgenlund

Inger Faaren

Manda Rocksvold

Peter William "Willie" Rocksvold

Tilda Foss Rocksvold

Hilda Roksvold Øistad Garaas

Peter Dahl

William Rasmussen

Matilda Rocksvold Anderson - 10-19-1893 *pages 1-8*

Oct. 19. 1893

My dear Andrew.

Will tonight see if I cannot get to answer your good long letter which was received Thursday last.

Thought last night as I was leaving the school-room that I must hurry home and write my letter, but as I was nearly home Mary Williams came along and was bound I should go with her to the store, and when I got back here we had company and could not very well leave the room.

And this evening I was
thinking of writing
just a short letter
and going over to mail it after
supper, but just as I was a little
ways from the gate up here coming
from school some one called Matilda
I have stop." "I have been trying
to catch up with you all the way,"
and turning around I saw Mrs.
John Williams tagging me. And
she says, Come on, go to the P. O.
with me, and off we went.
She is such a nice woman.
People say that they are worth
nearly $10000. but they are just
as common as any body. and
we could never think they are that
wealthy being in company with them

Mary Wilson, a relative of Charles is
working over at Randal Williams
that is Mary Williams father, and
she had been telling some news
here this summer some time, but
none of them ever mentioned
it to me till this evening, as
I was getting out of the cart. she
picked up a pumpkin, she had so
so many in the cart, that she got
over at Randals, some little bits
of nice, and she was bound I
should take one and save the seeds.
Told her I guessed I didn't have any
use for it and she says: "Tell him
it aint good for the cows but
good for pies." and went on that way.
Those people that were here
last night uncle sisters from

Spring Grove and their husbands were trying to plague me a little but did not succeed very well.

These two men were so full of fun and liked to have some thing to say to every body. One of them said this morning I should have his youngest son and the home farm.

Told him I was very glad to hear it and that I was ever so much obliged, but that he would have to answer for it when I came around to hear what the young man had to say. Too bad it isn't leap year.

Father has commenced canvassing. I do wish now that he would come out alright. Mr. Allen from Castilia sent for him and he went there to day.

Ole Amen died last Sunday morn.
and   was buried Tuesday.
                    45 teams were in
          the procession to church
and ever so many met at the church
Rev. Haus from Decorah conducted
the services. and Chas. Golz was
the undertaker.
     Mother was there but I thought
she looked so poorly that day.
     I was at home last Sunday. Went
home Friday evening and went
to Decorah Sat. and father took
me over here again Sunday evening
          Minnie Troyen came from
Chicago Sat. and came home
with us in the evening. She bought
me a Worlds Fair souvenir. A
pretty silver thimble. Had I gone
to Chicago with her the board would not

have cost me a penny, as she has
relations there and she
wanted me to go with
her but I thought I
couldn't go. Said she would not
have lost it for any thing.

You asked me in your last letter
if I had heard any thing in regard to the disputes you and father
used to have some time ago. Have
of course heard something; but
still not very much of any thing
from father, and have not heard
him even mention your name
since that time though others told
me of it, but I cannot remember
what it was only that you were against
each other. Were you really disputing
so very much, that you think he is
members yet, too? If so, I really do wish

it had never taken place. Thought
I should have asked pa about it
and could have had a good chance
to do so Sunday: not knowing the
real cause of it whether his fault
or yours and the substance of it, though
I had better not say any thing at all
and decided to keep still. Hope though
that it is forgotten and that you
both will feel to words one another as
you ought to do.

Am longing more and more to have
a talk with you, yet I am glad that
you are _not_ coming till Christmas
time, for it will be so nice that you
can be here then. Just think! Only
nine weeks more. I shall be so
happy to see you, (so you surely have
heard before) And how kind of Helen
to want to stay when you both leave
her. Hope you have not been to the P. O.
expecting a letter this week and been
disappointed. If so I am sorry but could
not very well help it this time, as there has
been so much disturbance this week some way

But I do wish I could get this
to the P. O. to-morrow morning that
it might get through by Sat.
at any rate; as I shall be longing
so to hear from you again. Am afraid
though that I cannot get it mailed
till to-morrow evening, as the P. O is
3/4 of a mile north and my school-house
about 2½ mi south of here. Cannot
very well go to the P. O first.

My school will be out a week from
to-morrow that is if I do not lose any
more days. Shall have to teach next
Sat. to make up for last Tues.

Will have one or two wks. vacation
before beginning the other school after
all, as the pres. told me this week that
they had changed their mind and
could not have school begin till the
1st or perhaps 2d Mon. in Nov.

Again dear Andrew — good night
with many ———— and much love,
Ever your niece and loving
Matilda.

Matilda Rocksvold Anderson 1893-11-3 to A.O. pg 1-8

Thoten Ia. Nov 3. 1893

My dear Andrew

Received your letter
Saturday evening, but could not
get to answer it so as to have
it sent Monday.

My brother Theodor came
after me Saturday evening and
Minnie came home with us and
stayed till Monday morning
and Sunday afternoon Oscar
Arneirude and quite a number
more young folks came here
and stayed till nearly midnight and
we were fooling around so that
I couldn't get a chance to write.

Could not help but feel that
I would rather have spent the
evening in writing to you; but

you know I couldn't. Would not
have thought so much about
it had it not been that the
mail goes out only twice a week
and I do not like to wait this
long before answering your letters
if I can help it.

Am to have two wks. vacation
and will there begin my other
school. Am to teach in the first
school house east of Wash. Pr. PO,
about 1 mi. from there, right on
the Waukon road. Seems to
be such a nice school house
though I have never been inside,
but heard they have fixed it up in
such fine shape this summer.

Mother is, well I don't know just
what to say, some days she seems
quite well and other days quite
poorly. Says she can't sleep very
well, not at all some nights

Father has not been at home for a while now. Left a week ago last Tues. and we have not seen him since; but expect him back to-morrow evening.

The girls are in the corn field this week and I am the house keeper. Do not think they will get through this week; but one of them will have to stay in next week, as I have not got time to tend to the house work and there is so much of it here it keeps one on the go all the time. Have to tend to grandma every once in a while and she makes so much work, as her room is up stairs and she never leaves it. She was down stairs and ate her dinner once this fall, but that is the only time I know of for ever so long, and then she thought she had got lost.

Have enjoyed this week ever so
much as it is such a change,
from my usual work.

Andrew, hope you have some one
to help you husking now or I am
afraid you will be getting pretty
well tired of it. Here there is
six or seven of them every day.

Clara Rocksvold came home
night before last and is to stay
next week and then will go up
to Bluffton to teach. Is to have
a 4 mo. school at $30. per mo.
and board with her uncle
Ole Kjörlien.

You must not think or feel
sorry at all for writing about
"you know what". That was surely
alright and don't think any more
about it at all.

I wrote you a letter the other evening, thinking I might have found a chance to have it mailed before this, but didn't and as I was so sleepy when I wrote thought I'd write another to day, as I looked it over. Am afraid though that this will not be much better, as I am waiting for the mail man every minute.

Went to a funeral yesterday and how very sad it seemed. It was a little boy 4½ years old, Willie Williams. Think you know Helmer Williams. He married Thrine Nelsefökken and it was there only child. He was playing on a little pile of rails and must

have fallen backwards and a rail
rolled on to him and choked
him the mark showed on his
face and neck. But how pretty
he looked as he lay in his little
coffin, it made me think of an
angel. Four little boys were the
pall bearers. Carl Kirkeby
Albert Berge, Albert Rocksvold
and my brother Norman, they
couldn't keep the tears back as
they walked into church. And
how I pitied his parents and especially
Thrine she is so weak and it is
so hard for her.

Carl came back from Chicago
last Sat. evening says he would
not have missed it for any
thing.

Have never told you that I
have had my ring fixed, but
of course it is not like what is

was before. still I like it now too.

Well cannot get a chance to write any more to day though I should like to.

Closed with all my love and very best wishes to you

Ever and Ever your own
loving Matilda.

A. O. Anderson, *Matilda's husband, Ole's daughter - 10-8-1893 pages 1-8*

Inwood Ja. Oct 8th 1873

My dear Matilda:

Will this evening
endeavor to make a reply
to your dear and loving letter,
which I received Fri. morning
as I was over after a load
of lumber.

Am so glad to learn that
you are so well and happy.
But my dear M, you must
never let it enter your
mind that you was the cause
of me feeling lonesome as I said.
No indeed! I never heard any
thing from you, or about you
either, but what it has caused
me to feel happy and seemed

make me more attached to you.
and if you only knew how
happy I am every time I receive
one of your precious letters.

You know I thought about
seeing you about that time a while
and then gave up going again and after
hearing A. R. had gone I was sorry
I didn't go too. As I knew
that would have enabled me
to meet you. And that was the
only reason. You know it
sometimes takes a reflex that
way although we change our
plans through our own free will.

But Matilda, how I have
wandered what it was that
had happened, ~~as you said~~,
that made you feel so bad and
as you said you didn't think
it would effect either of us now.
I of course know it was about

us. And although you said "Don't
let it worry you one bit but forget
it till we meet." Still it
comes up to me all the time,
"What could it be?" But to be
sure it does not worry me
a particle, since you ~~said~~ you
~~only felt good~~ about it now.
And I will soon forget it I expect.
I imagine it was only slanderous
talk though, as I can't see what
else it could be.

Maggie ~~came~~ home last eve.
G.J. took her up of course and
then he went home to his
folks and came over here
this afternoon again and now
after supper they left for
Canton again.

In the forenoon we were
to church. This seems to have
been an exceptionally good

day to me, had such a nice
sermon and it did me so
much good. There is nothing
on earth that can give one such
<u>real</u> enjoyment and peace of mind
as the Word of God.

Helen says now that she
want care if I go home Christmas
and M. and I planned to go
together. H. is getting more and
more liberal with me. In the
first place you know she said
she wouldn't stay here at all
if I went away and this morning
she started it herself that I
might go then if I wanted too
Well she has been very good all
the time to me and I know
I have done all I can to make

it pleasant to her. And I know
she likes it better here than at
home in many respects.

I have been "playing off"
carpenter now days term building
a corn crib. Will begin husking
corn later part of this week.
We have a splendid corn crop
Think my corn will go at least
between 60 & 65 Bu. pr. A. and
as I am ready to start so early
expect to husk the biggest part
alone and as I have about 30 A.
to go over will have to stick to it
patiently. Kept on exactly one
month last fall.

Well I knew that your
father got the nomination for
Rep. almost as soon as you did got

the "Poster" Wed. and of course I
turn to the locals the first thing
as that is about all I read of that
paper. Was very much pleased to
see it. Did he go to Chicago?
If not expect he want have
time now this fall as candidates
generally have to be around
this time.

Well Matilda, I am now
going to write about something
I never intended to mention
to you at any rate never to write
about it; but as I am
sure you know something
about it before, and on touching
upon any thing regarding politics
it brought it fresh to my
mind again. You surely heard
of how your father and I
argued on politics some years
ago, and that would of course have

been alright if it had not been carried so far; but I was young and foolish or I never would have disputed with a man so much older than myself in such a manner. If my views were different I should have been more reserved about it. and I know I was sorry about it afterwards as I felt that the only thing it made me was enemies and I made up my mind never to argue that way again and especially not with any one older than myself; but the next year it was worse and not better; but that was the last of it too. I never disputed that way since and hope I never shall. as it is not the proper way at all. And I have often thought

Drake and your father were down on me on that account. And you after it got to be as it is with us have wished more than ever that I hadn't been so radical. and more than once have I felt like asking you if your father never made any mention of it. I know he wouldn't care if I didn't side with him as I know he is too much of a practical and sensible man for that but it was not for our arguing Well I know I had as much respect for him then as for any one there. even if we did pass what I may call impolite words, as I knew he was better posted than the average. It may be he has not even thought about it since, and I wish he hadn't. Probably I should not have written about this; but ofcourse I feel like making every thing known to you, and hope you will understand me right. If you know any thing about this pleas let me know. and if he has not forgotten it yet hope he will soon and in the future I hope I can pleas him, or rather be able to act so that he will be pleased.

Pauline Evenrud Mickelson, *Ole's niece*

Translation

Decorah, 3 October 1878

Good Friend Mathilde,

now try to put down a few lines, but it will be rather pitiful, as I am terrible at writing letters. I can report that I am in in good health, and that is the best I can wish for.

I have heard that Georgy had an unfortunate accident, breaking one of his legs, and that the doctor amputated it. Poor Georgy, I suppose he'll be a cripple for the rest of his life. It is so painful not to be able to come home and get to speak with him, but I cannot …

[second page]

… come yet, as the wife has not yet come home. I have felt so lonesome here for some time, and I have been alone every evening, as the husband and Fred are in town every evening until 11 and 12 o'clock. "Birgte"[?] Sunday we had a hailstorm. Afterwards the hail lay in large piles, and glass panes were broken in some places.

I don't have much news to report to you, since here I am not able to learn about anything new that has happened. One thing I can tell you is that about two weeks ago I went on a pleasure outing when the husband let me take the horse and buggy. We were about 8 miles out in the country and had a wonderful time.

Well, I can imagine you are getting tired of reading this rambling, so I'd best close for now. I'll try to write you a better letter another time.

Fond greetings from your devoted friend

Pauline T. Evenrud
Decorah, Iowa

Send me a reply as soon as you can and tell me how Georgy is doing. Greet your mother from me and everyone at home.

Translation by Jim Skurdall

Translation

Decorah, Iowa, May 21st, 1889

Dear Cousin Mathilda,

About a week has passed since I received your letter, and this evening I wish to try to answer it. To begin with, I can assure you that I am in good health, and I hope that these lines will find all of you in good health as well.

On the 17th of May I was at a dance and had a great time.

[second page]

I was at the theater on the 18th, so I really got around last week. I was also very tired, as I didn't sleep Thursday night and was up until 12 o'clock on Friday. But yesterday afternoon I took a nap. I slept from 3 until 6 o'clock. Then I went down to Uncle Anton's, and there I met your friend Maria Berge. And then a few others showed up, Tina Selswold and George and Mathias Kjelsrud, and Lewis Lövstuen, and we began playing cards and had …

[third page]

… a really good time. As you can imagine, it is not very quiet down there on Sunday when we play cards. And then we went out for a walk, Maria B. and George and Tina and Lewis and I and Mathias. Such nice young folks (was cold). It is so dark now, I can't see what I am writing, will have to light a lamp. I've heard there is going to be a wedding in Iowa, so you'll no doubt have a good time. I wish I would be invited.

[fourth page]

Well, time to end my gibberish for now.

Kind greetings to you from your cousin Pauline.

Excuse poor writing for it is written in haste by

Pauline [all written in English]

Be sure and come to town circus day and don't you forget it. Bring a nice young fellow too, if you can. Good night. [all written in English]

Translation by Jim Skurdall

Helene Roksvold Dahl, *Ole's sister*

Translation

Roksvold, 8 March 1886

Dear Mother!

What a surprise was in store for me on Sunday, February 21st. My husband and I and my daughter's daughter, Laura, had gone to church, and when we returned home, there it was, a letter from you.

Mother dear, how often have I wished to hear from you, and now my wish has been fulfilled. I send you my warmest and fondest words of gratitude for your most welcome letter. When I read it, I was flooded with feelings I cannot describe. My thoughts returned to the years of my childhood and youth, when I had you here, and now we are separated by the long passage of years. Just think — 33 years have now faded into oblivion since I bade you farewell, Mother dear. You were already elderly then, and it seems so strange, now that I have grown so much older myself. I'll soon turn 57, and you, Mother dear, are still living.

I see from your letter that Father has been...

[second page]

... allowed to depart this earthly life. Yes, how good this was, for, as I read in your letter, he longed to return home to him who thrones in Heaven on high, and we know that he was old and full of years [biblical]. And the hope that he is saved consoles the sorrow of those who have lost a beloved friend and family member. Mother dear, find consolation in the knowledge that soon the hour will come when you will return to greet Father in your heavenly home. Think of the joy of going to be with God, and there take your place as our Redeemer's chosen bride.

Mother dear, this is the first letter I have written to you, and it may well be the last. If the latter be true, I want to fervently thank you for everything from the time I was a little child. Likewise, my most fervent wish is that when your hour comes to depart this Earth, your passing will be blessed and joyous. Lord, grant us a joyous journey home, that when we awaken beyond death and the grave, we may be reunited in our heavenly home, where we no longer are oppressed by tears of sadness and longing, ...

[third page]

... and friends and relatives never again will be separated.

As for our day-to-day lives, my husband continues to teach school 39 weeks a year. He is in good health.

My health is, thank God, good as well. My housework keeps me busy at all times. I spend a lot of time at the spinning wheel, and at the sewing machine too sometimes. I also manage to do some weaving, part of which I sell.

We have almost completed the renovation of the farmhouse. It will be painted both inside and out. It is still only one story, but it is higher than the old house. It has a large living room at the south end with five large adjacent windows and a large kitchen on the north side. In the middle section there is a small room on the east side, and opposite it is the large entryway. It will be a very expensive project.

We had a poor harvest in these parts. Most of the grain crop froze, and the potato harvest was badly damaged.

I want to thank my brother for the photograph of him. I was hardly able to recognize him, he has changed so much …

[fourth page]

… since the last photograph we saw of him. I also want to thank Mathilda for the calling card she sent.

Presently, we have a daughter of Helene Marie staying with us. This spring she will begin preparing for confirmation in the fall. She is very tall and will turn 15 on the 1st of April.

Please greet all our relations from my husband and me, and Laura sends fond greetings to her great-grandmother. And Helene Marie sends greetings to her grandmother and thinks it is really special to have a grandmother who is still living. She is waiting for a letter from Mathilda. She received a letter from her two years ago and replied immediately, but has not heard anything since then. She sends her cordial greetings and would so much enjoy receiving a letter.

Thank you once again, Mother dear, so long, farewell, it may be my last farewell, as we do not know the hour when our last minute is counted and death arrives with its tidings: Come and follow me.

Most cordial greetings from

Helene Roksvold

Translation by Jim Skurdall

Helene Marie Roksvold Dahl Øistad, *Ole's niece*

Translation

Rensvold Farm in West Toten
18 March 1878

Dear Grandparents and Relatives!

Slowly but surely a year has passed since I first intended to write to you, my dear kinfolk, and the greeting that I bring you today is my dear grandmother's last farewell, which I send to you on her behalf. Almighty God in His infinite wisdom found it a fitting time for Grandmother to lay down her staff, as she was old and full of days. He called her home on Sunday evening at 5 o'clock on the 18th of March last year.

During the many years I lived together with her she was healthy, apart from the last year, when she began to lose her strength. But she was never confined to her bed. Last winter, however, she took …

[second page]

… to her bed and remained there for 3 weeks. Her illness began with a severe case of gout in her right leg, which eased somewhat a few days later. She was then calmer, although she suffered severe chest pain at times. The brief time she was ill she lost so much weight that by the time she died she was nothing but skin and bones. She did not want a doctor to come. As she said, "None but the Heavenly Physician can heal my illness when the time has come." She yielded to God's will and wished to bid this Earth farewell when her time had come. And I wish to tell you of her last farewell to me. I stood next to her bed and she reached out her hand, took my own trembling hand, and squeezed it …

[third page]

… saying: "Now I have begun my journey in Jesus's name. Farewell, farewell, and thank you ever so much for all the wonderful things we have experienced together. Continue to live your life that we might once again meet again there where there is no misery and sorrow." And then she seemed to lose consciousness, and we all thought that she was near death. But she lived another 4 days, although she had almost no voice at all. Her only desire was solely to pray to her redeemer for the forgiveness of her sins and for mercy in Jesus Christ, and comforted by her faith she departed this life contented and peaceful. Yes, blessed be her memory!

My dear Grandparents, how good it would be to see you again, but it will never come to pass in this life, as I have no plans to travel to America. I would so much like to be there, but I dread traveling. I am sure you have a much better livelihood there than you would have here. We rent a house here on the farm and carry on our business, but it is difficult …

[fourth page]

… doing business in such economically hard times. The last two years have been exceptionally bad. Last year the spring was so cold that there was deep snow some places until the first days of June. And in the fall the grain froze everywhere. Farmers are now forced to buy almost everything they need to live, and there is nothing to sell, little money to earn. Things look bleak. But if only this year turns out well, times can change. It is a terrible time to be in business. Everyone wants to buy on credit, and of course the debts mount, and there is never enough money, especially in times such as these.

So, our dear kinfolk over there, we send our warmest greetings and live as well as we can. And may we live our lives so that we might one day meet again where there is no wailing and lamentation. My dear Grandmother, if you …

[fifth page]

… are still living, I send you these fond greetings. Surely it is the last time I shall greet you in this life. And it is my heartfelt wish that when you are deprived of this mortal life you will journey joyfully and serenely to your Heavenly Home and to life and happiness everlasting. Yes, may the Lord help us and shed His grace on us for Jesus's sake.

[Next she quotes one verse of a hymn. Checking online, I see it was written in 1726 by Lauritz Beich and is entitled "Bedre kan jeg ikke fare"/ roughly "I cannot go to a better place". I can only give a fairly literal rendering of the text of this verse she quotes.]:

What is the world that one should

Desire to live in it.

The times are filled

With every sort of wickedness and infidelity.

In our Heavenly Home there is sacred harmony,

There a place is prepared for me,

Where there is life and joy and delight,

Dwelling in God's presence.

My parents send their greetings. They are in good health and doing …

[sixth page]

… quite well. Father is still teaching and has a fairly good salary, and Mother sends her greetings to dear Grandmother and Grandfather. How often have I seen her weep when she takes the photographs of you into her hands, and this is certainly to be expected, knowing that she will never see you again in this life. And my brothers Peter and Carl greet their elderly grandparents. Peter is going to begin at the technical college. He seems able to do about anything he sets his mind to. He does not wish to teach. Carl is at the teacher's college and intends to become a teacher.

Please greet all my kin and ask Tilla Cornelia to write to me. A letter from her would be most welcome.

My dear kinfolk, please accept these humble lines from me with cordial greetings from my husband and children as well, and, of course from

Yours truly

Helene Marie Rensvoldbrug

To
Ole Roksvold and family

Please be so kind as to send a few lines in response, as we are all waiting to hear from you.

[seventh page]

I must apologize for possibly boring you with this humble letter, but when I had finished it and was about to go home to get your address, Father told me that Andreas Ronaas had said that when he visited you, your address had been changed a little, so we began wondering if you had ever received any of the letters I wrote to you, since we do not or have never received any letters from you. I wrote to you after Andreas Ronaas had visited us and delivered to my brothers and me the wonderful and expensive gifts from you. And of course I sent you a letter expressing our most sincere gratitude for the same. Now it seems reasonable to believe that you did not receive anything, I feel almost certain that this is what happened. Likewise, Father sends his greetings and says that he has written but never received a reply, and the reason for this is surely the same. We prefer to believe that this is the reason why we have waited in vain for letters from you.

[eighth page]

Peter and Karl wish to send their grandparents photographs of themselves and hope they will enjoy them, since they have never seen their grandsons otherwise. This summer, if I'm still living, we plan to have photographs taken and send them to you, as I do not have any of my husband or me. I have three children, two girls and a boy. The eldest is 7, the next 4, and the youngest is one year and two months old.

I am also to send greetings to Grandmother from her sister at Hagesveen and say that she is still alive but has been confined to her bed for four years. She has an illness in her limbs. She has had to be lifted into and out of bed day and night all this long time. She has lain ill, but remains patient in spite of her illness. Her husband, Christian, is still living, but he, too, is bedridden.

So now I shall write a fond farewell in the hope that you will not forget to write to me and to my parents' home.

H. M.

Translation by Jim Skurdall

Translation

Rensvold Farm, West Toten
23 April 1884

Dear [first] Cousins!

What a joyous mood prevailed in our family the other evening when I received your most welcome letter. I must hurry to thank you ever and ever so much, for this kindness of — wanting to write. Those of our relations who are older, dear Cousin, can well imagine the feeling in our hearts when we finally heard from our dear kinfolk from whom we had not heard a word for so very long. Father was at our place when I received this letter for which we have waited so long, and he found so much pleasure in reading through it.

[second page]

It was late in the evening when Father returned home, and I thought to myself it would not be long the next morning before Mother would come to hear this new news for herself. And that is precisely what happened. Especially when I read the parts of the letter about Grandmother and Grandfather, her heart was moved. The love between parents and children is so strong, and it has a remarkable power that remains just as intense in adulthood and old age. Tears ran silently from Mother's eyes, and she felt heartfelt gratitude toward you, dear, kind Mathilda, for sending us this news from all of you over there. On Easter Monday Mother and I were together, and we spoke of you and wondered if the old folks were still living, and then on Tuesday the riddle was

…

[third page]

… solved, when I received the letter. First, I can let Grandmother know that her sister Marthe Hagesveen has been released from her earthly bonds. She passed away on March 26th, that is to say, last month, at 92 years of age. She had been confined to her bed for 10 years and 10 days, and during that long time she was not up and about for a single day. She lay in bed apart from the short periods of time she sat on the edge of the bed supported by pillows. She never seemed impatient in spite of the pain she suffered and the long illness she suffered. She entrusted her life to God's will, and she bore her cross in gratitude, knowing that it served the best purpose in the end. Her daughter, Mathea, took her into her home at Nyhaugen and cared for her all these years, day and night. Father and Mother attended the funeral. Christian Hagesveen died 3 years ago. He, too, was bedridden for a number of years.

Otherwise, I'll tell …

[fourth page]

… you how things are with my parents. Father still teaches school 39 weeks each year. He is an experienced teacher who has pursued his vocation diligently now for 42 years. As of the 21st of February he has entered his 60th year. Last summer he contracted typhoid fever and was very ill, and we believed it would end with his death. But it was not the Lord's will that he should depart this life now. Mother was alone with him for a number of weeks. They were living at the school [a farm] and intended to move down to Roksvold to begin with haying, but this contagious illness forced them to remain up there, removed from everyone. People were so fearful that they made long detours to avoid coming to close, since the road runs directly past the house.

[fifth page]

I didn't think I could be afraid of being with my own dear parents, so I visited them often every day. I had no peace, wondering all the time how they were doing. Brother Karl visited them a few times while Father was ill. Mother had a huge burden during that time. Father had to be given drops and medicine every hour and a half, day and night, and she was alone with him. She wanted to care for him herself, as long as she was able, and, as it turned out, she managed to do so. He was ill for two months, then recovered, and no one else contracted the illness. Mother went downhill a lot during that time, her hair turned grey, and she aged a lot. They have both aged considerably, but are healthy now for the time being. This summer they are going to build a new house at …

[sixth page]

… Roksvold, as the old one has seen better days. Father said, when he read how much rye Uncle [Ole] had harvested on his Rocksvold farm that he hadn't harvested quite that much on <u>his</u> Roksvold farm.

Both of my brothers have for a number of years been living away from home.

Peter is a technician and works for plant owner Ingebridtsen at a machine shop in Kristiania. He is not married. Karl studied at the teacher's college in Hamar for 2 years, and right after graduating he took a teaching job at a school in East Toten. The school district is near Anigstad. He is married to a girl from Fladlien, and they have one son named Lars. He will celebrate his first birthday on June 3rd.

[seventh page]

So that leaves me. We still live here at Rensvoldbruget and have a small business, but it is difficult to make ends meet now when you can find a general store under just about every other juniper bush, so there is not much income. I have 3 children, 2 girls and a boy. The name of the eldest child is Laura Mathilde. She turned 13 on April 1st. Hilda turned 10 on April 15th. Peter turned 7 on January 15th. It is with a heavy heart that I inform you that I live with an immeasurably deep concern for one of my little ones. Fate has dealt a heavy blow to my poor Hilda. She is deaf-mute. The Lord in His wisdom has imposed a heavy burden on us and we know that He uses many means to turn our hearts to …

[eighth page]

… Him. Of course we know this, my dear friends, that everything the Lord does has the same aim. Oh my, it is nonetheless awfully difficult for a caring mother to see and experience that one of her children is so handicapped. But thank goodness she is at the same time blessed to be gifted in the senses she has and she does remarkably well compared with other children similarly handicapped. Norway has progressed to the point that there are now speech schools for deaf-mute children. One such school was established in Hamar, and our little Hilda is a pupil there. 40 deaf-mute children attend the school now, and this summer another 30 will be admitted. There are two such schools in Christiania, one with 34 and the other with 84 pupils. Oh, there are so many poor unfortunate children.

[ninth page]

Our little Hilda came to the school on August 20th last year, and she has improved considerably in her ability to speak. It has been a hard struggle, as you can imagine, being taken away from me and left with strangers, a child with no means of defense (cannot hear and cannot speak), having to take things as they are and not know what these persons will do with her. It is impossible for a mother who is not faced with this to understand the worry that at all times oppresses and plagues a mother who is confronted with this situation. I will never forget the moment that I lifted my poor little Hilda up into the cart and they left with her for the Deaf-Mute Institute. I thought my heart would burst when my child made signs to her grief-stricken mother wondering why she was crying. She did not understand that I was crying for her, my poor innocent child.

[tenth page]

She came home at Christmas, and I tried to find the courage to take her back after Christmas. It was a moment of intense pain, our farewell when I was to leave her. She is better off than other children there because she is staying with an elderly woman who is the mother of the teachers at the institute. There are 4 brothers who teach at the school. It is very expensive for us, as we must pay out of our own pockets. It costs us 400 "kroner" per year, and that is a lot of money to pay for a child, especially over here, where our earnings are so meager. It is hard for us, as we have not received any assistance whatsoever, neither I or my husband. And since Grandmother died, we have to pay rent for the house and buy everything for our day-to-day needs, as we do not farm. I have so ...

[eleventh page]

... often wished that we were in America, but a number of things have prevented us from leaving. Now I must soon bid you farewell for now and ask you to excuse me for my long letter, but I so enjoy writing to my dear relatives, from whom I hardly expected to hear anything. I send you cordial greetings from Mother and Father, they are so happy to have heard how you all are doing. Berthe and Christian Skartsæterhagen send greetings to the older folks among you. Likewise, greetings to them from old Hans Brustuen and his wife. They are living and are quite healthy considering their age. And please be so kind as to greet [maternal] Auntie Mathea and her husband and children from me. Many greetings to Tilla Cornelia from me. I see from the letter that she already has many little ones. I have a photograph of her husband and her.

[twelfth page]

I also send greetings to [maternal] Uncle Anton. I remember like a distant dream how he used to carry me on his back sometimes when I was at Roksvold. I was 4 years old when they left for America. And greetings from me as well to [maternal] Uncle Ole, his wife and children. I see that I have many relatives over there, but I know none of you. My warmest greetings to Grandfather and Grandmother. It is remarkable that they are still living and still quite vigorous. Poor Grandmother, who is a cripple, it pains me to think of how she is, and yet it is good that she can walk.

In closing, thank you ever so much to everyone from all of us, and you my dear [first] cousin, thank you ever so much for writing to me. My dear, kind Mathilda, you would make me ever so happy by sending me a photograph. I so look forward to seeing it. I suppose I shall never be able to see you in person.

So long, my sweet friend, and don't forget me. Your humble friend,

Helene Marie

P. S. [written on the left side of the last page]: In the course of the summer I shall send you a photograph of Hilda and me and perhaps of my other children. I am already [hole in the paper here, but she would be either 35 or 36] years old, and half of my hair has turned grey (from worry).

Translation by Jim Skurdall

Translation

Happy New Year!
Now the new year emerges,
Overshadowing the old,
The Star of Hope stands for us,
Under it we build.
That you may be fortunate in all you build
Is my wish for you from the bottom of my heart.
[This is rhymed verse she quotes here---I've provided a literal unrhymed translation.]

Roksvold, 16 January 1888

Dear [first] Cousin!!

My first greeting to you, dear Mathilda, is my warm and heartfelt thank you for the letter and photograph that I received from you last Easter. It was such a joy for me to to be able to see a photo of you who so often has been in my thoughts since that day when I received the first letter from you. Dear Mathilda, …

[second page]

… the photograph is so beautiful, and I naturally assume that you are equally attractive in person. I read in your letter that you are attending English school [American public school] and wish to study. There can be no doubt that you have the gift and the desire to broaden your knowledge and that you will profit by it, especially in a country such as America. I have no doubt whatsoever that you are one of those who will make excellent progress in this regard.

As you perhaps have heard, my son and I moved here to Roksvold some time ago. We were, as you know, also in Kristiania for awhile. But then an acquaintance arrived with whom we had lived for 5 years at Rensvoldbruget. He was on his way to America again — he had been there already for 6 years, so he was well acquainted with the conditions. We arrived at the idea that my husband could accompany him to America, thinking it would be advantageous …

[third page]

… for us in the long term. For I could not leave at the same time as my husband on account of our little deaf-mute daughter Hilda, who lives in Hamar, where she attends school. It has been my most fervent wish to travel together to America. But we decided that we could by no means leave behind our poor unhappy daughter. Thus I decided to move here for the time being, in the hope that fate and fortune might reunite us there far to the west of here.

My eldest daughter, Laura Mathide, has been living here at Roksvold for a number of years, and she is still here. She was confirmed on the 2nd of October 1886 and will turn 17 on the 1st of April. My son turned 11 yesterday, on the 15th of January. He is the youngest of my children. So I do not have so many children.

My daughter Hilda, who lives in Hamar, will turn 14 on the 15th of April. I have only these three children. My son's name is Peter. Hilda still has 2½ years remaining at her school. It will be quite some time before she can be confirmed. She is exceptionally gifted. She is learning to speak aloud and read aloud like other children at this institute, as the school does not use sign language like other deaf-mute children have learned in the past.

Recently, my husband has been living in Minneapolis. He has earned a lot of money since arriving there. He says that it is very expensive for a single person to …

[fourth page]

… pay for board and room there in America compared with what it costs here in Norway.

I see from your letter, dear Mathilda, that Grandmother was still living when you wrote. Has the Lord in His wisdom found it fitting to let her continue to live? I send her warmest greetings and thank her for the greetings she sent me via [word missing, rubbed out.] Likewise, Mother and Father send her their greetings, and Peter also sends his greetings.

Things are fine here at Roksvold and we are doing quite well. Be so kind as to greet all our relatives there. We see from your letter and read it as well in Decorah Posten that Uncle Anton died. Please greet surviving members of his family from us. [The next couple of lines too weak to decipher.]

Thank you for the photograph, and I apologize for the terribly long letter I sent you some time ago.

Farewell, dear Mathilda, sending my warmest and fondest greetings.

Your Marie

[There is something written on the left side of the last page, but it is illegible.]

Translation by Jim Skurdall

Translation

Roksvold, 26 March 1893

Dear [first] Cousin!!

I wish, on behalf of Father and Mother, and on my behalf as well, to greet you and thank you so much for the most welcome letter from you that arrived on the 16th of last month. It was a delight for us all to hear from our next-of-kin over there, both young and old. And how remarkable to think that our elderly grandmother is still living in spite of her advanced age. We live in the hope that the Lord in His infinite wisdom will see fit to allow her to enjoy yet many days of grace before He calls her from this Earth, and that she will achieve that highest of purposes, that to which we all strive, to be among the blessed who depart this pitiful and wretched Earth at the Lord's appointed …

[second]

… hour, when the Angel of Death arrives with his message: "Now your time is here, come and follow me", and she may go to her heavenly home on high and gather together with all family and friends who have gone before her. Yes, this is our mutual prayer to the Lord for our dear mother, grandmother, and great-grandmother, when her last breath has died away and her lips are silent and [cannot decipher] bursts in death.

Dear Mathilda, please convey to our dearly beloved this, perhaps last, wish and, possibly, our last greeting and words of farewell, in the fervent hope that we shall be reunited with her in our heavenly home, where we no longer will be oppressed by tears of sadness and longing, and friends and relatives never again will be separated. How glorious that we shall be able to be together forever more.

We read in your letter that it has pleased the Lord to take a beloved son and brother from your family and home. The Lord's intentions with us are many, may He also help you find consolation in your loss and grief.

[third page]

We are so happy to read that all is well with Auntie Mathea and her family.

Please be so kind as to greet them all from us, each and every one.

So, do you think you still know the person writing to you here? Whatever the case, it is the same person who wrote to you the last time from here. I'll try to put some coherent words on paper. I'll not try to conceal the truth that I dread writing to you, knowing how far beneath you I am in both practical matters and learning. I hope you will excuse the many errors and read between the lines that which I am trying to express.

Things are well here at Roksvold. Mother is well, and Father continues to teach, and if he lives so long and maintains his health, he will celebrate 50 years as a teacher this coming month of May. How long he will continue after that, even in good health, I do not know.

[fourth page]

I cannot say that I have anything new to report from Toten. The world Uncle Ole and Auntie Mathea remember has faded away. Death and the grave have played their part, and so much has changed otherwise, that I doubt anything I tell will be of interest to them. I remember Ole and Auntie, and Grandmother as well, but only as a vague dream. I was 4 years old when they emigrated.

Dear Mathilda, you say that you wish to send a photograph of your deceased brother. It would be so welcome and would mean so much to us if you did so.

As you can gather from this letter, I live at Roksvold. As I remember, I told you that my husband went to America, and now it has been 7 years since he left. I have not heard anything from him the past 5 years and do not know …

[fifth page]

… whether he is dead or alive. As you may well remember, I have 3 children. The eldest, Laura Mathida (her name), left for America in the autumn of 1891. She traveled to the home of a person she knew, someone who has married there now but once worked in our household for 12 years. She lives in Minnesota in a small town called Boyd. Laura wrote to me in a letter after Christmas that she was beginning to think about taking a pleasure trip to visit the Roksvolds in Iowa. She said it would be a two-day trip from where she lives to your home. Laura will turn 22 the 1st of April. She says she has earned a lot of money in America.

My other daughter, Hilda (she who was deaf-mute, is no longer mute, for she can now speak and read aloud), she lives at Roksvold. She has many talents, can do all manner of handwork (handicrafts), and she is diligent and willing to learn. Everything she …

[sixth page]

is shown she is able to understand and do. She was confirmed on 8 June 1890 in Hamar Church, and she attended school in Hamar for 6½ years. She will turn 19 on the 15th of April.

My son, Peter, was confirmed last autumn, in the month of October. One month after his confirmation he moved to Kristiansand (the southernmost town in Norway), where he began as an apprentice in a store and now has been a clerk for a year and a half. He turned 16 on the 15th of January. He is good in reckoning and writing and is well-liked by his employers.

Mother thinks it would be fun to send you a photo of Roksvold, she says she thinks Uncle Ole will recognize the "ladebygning" *[Translator: I think she means an outbuilding of some kind, whether for storing machines or crops]*, but not the house. I don't suppose poor old Grandmother would know what I was talking about …

[seventh page]

… if I tell her that this is her former home Roksvold in Norway.

I can greet Uncle Ole from a few old acquaintances. Old Hans Brustuen is still living and is 88 years old. Hans Roksvold is 65 years old. Johannes Larsen Morterudengen(?), the cobbler, and his wife are 89 and 88 years old. Nils Røstøen and his wife both died some years ago. The Røstøen farm is no longer owned by any of the old Røstøen family.

I must bid you farewell for now with fond greetings to all our kin, both young and old, from all of us. And to you, Mathilda, warm greetings from me

Sincerely,

Helene Marie

Translation by Jim Skurdall

Translation

Roksvold, the 3rd of November 1903

Dear Uncle,
O. P. Rocksvold!

Thank you ever so much for your most welcome letter of the 3rd of last month.

We are delighted to read that everything went well on your long return journey home! It was also very good to learn that the Americans thought they felt in quite good "condition" after visiting Norway. And thank you so much for taking the time to write to Laura. I received four letters, one after another from you; the reason being that <u>one</u> of the letters …

[second page]

… that Laura had written on June 20th had been lost enroute. For a number of weeks afterwards I have written a letter to you, dear Uncle, and I hope you have received each of them. I see from your address that it is a little different from what I wrote, but I believe each must have arrived nonetheless, since your name is known far and wide there in America.

The harvest here was much as you describe it there in your letter. Everything went down the drain due to frost. The barley was completely ruined. We salvaged the potatoes, but do not have as many as last year. Oats very bad. Crop failures all over the districts around here. You read yourselves about the annual harvests in the newspapers.

[third page]

Hilda is still away. She absolutely wanted to quit working in the store where she is now employed and come home to help me over the winter, but they did not want to let her go. So I shall have to put up with being alone here at Roksvold, together with Mother, as I have been before, with the <u>single</u> exception that we had a girl helping us this summer, as you saw. We have a hired boy, of course, the one who has been here for 5 years. He left last autumn, but returned on October 19th. He's a very hardworking young man. And, otherwise, things are well here. The haybarn looks a lot nicer now than it did when you were here,

…

[fourth page]

… as it underwent some major repairs and now looks much more attractive.

Mother is the same as when you were here, as am I. There was an important railway meeting here at our place on Monday, October 13th, and among those attending was also O. C. Præstesaker. He talked a lot about you with me and said, as has everyone else, that he thought you seemed so unusually youthful and vigorous in every respect, compared with all others of your age. And those are indeed the truest words ever spoken.

We here were all so happy to have you visit, something we never expected to happen. Thank you ever so much for wanting to honor us in this manner. It was much more than I can describe. It was pure and simple an unanticipated pleasure for everyone here in the entire family. Brother Karl and family send greetings. And in every letter she writes to me, Hilda reminds me that when I write to Uncle in America I must relay her most cordial greetings. She …

[fifth page]

… "can <u>never</u> <u>never</u> forget her most cheerful, kind, and pleasant Uncle", something she mentions in every letter to me. Hilda left here right after you (plural) left. Everyone who got to know you (plural) for the short time you were here with us asks me to send you their greetings. O. C. Prestesaker asked me to greet you from them.

We have already had two weeks of winter here on the farm, but now the snow has melted — and we have summer again.

When you write to your daughter Mathilda, please greet her from me and everyone from us. We send our greetings to all our kin over there in Iowa.

[sixth page]

If you should ever wish to write to us again, please tell me if you received my first letter written after your return home.

Mother sends her greetings and thanks you ever so much for your visit. Wishing you well, dear Uncle, and thank you so much that you were here, and wishing you all joy and happiness and wellbeing in these later years of your life. May it be long and happy for all of you.

Fond greetings from
Your relative

Helene Maria Roksvold

Translation by Jim Skurdall

Translation

Gjøvik, 14 March 1910

My dear Uncle!

Thank you ever so much for your most welcome letter of the 28th of last month, which I received today. It is simply magnificent to read your long letters and see your lovely handwriting penned by your steady hand. And you are now getting up in years, but you must still be the same youthful man you were when you visited us.

It was indeed remarkable to read about all the work you continue to do on the farm. It can only be described as simply <u>exceptional</u>. I see that the land on your Dakota farm is so productive and that you had an outstanding harvest this past year in spite of the hailstorm, which ruined some of your crops. It is sad that some of the farmers in America have their crops destroyed in this manner. It was so very sad to read of your son's crop losses, that everything was ruined by …

[second page]

… the terrible hailstorm. It is not at all hard to understand that it takes courage to endure such a loss after all the toil and labor and ingenuity.

Once again I must hasten to thank you ever so much, dear Uncle, that you continue to send us the most welcome issues of "Decorah Posten". We derive so much pleasure from reading them and find so much of interest to us on the highly informative pages of this newspaper. We are delighted each time it arrives. We always find something new regarding both America and our own country.

I can greet you from Hilda, she is in good health and doing well. She has no children. I also recently heard from my son, Peter. He writes that they are all well. They already have had 4 children, 3 boys and a girl, but the little girl died last summer on June 13th, at the age of 7 months. The eldest of the boys will turn 8 on the 28th of this month. I hear often from Laura over there …

[third page]

… in America. She writes often. She says they are doing fine and that Anton has plenty to do in the store. And so things are all right.

Otherwise, all is well with all the relatives over here, with the exception of Karl's mother-in-law. She has been very poorly the past year, suffering from mental confusion. She has been with them at home and not at an institution for such cases, but they have to watch over her almost round the clock. More recently she has been calmer, and now she spends most of her time confined to her bed.

As for us, things are as usual except that Mother is worse than before in all respects. She is confined to her bed now, and that happens more often now. She is becoming more frail and there is little she can do now.

I don't remember if I told you when I wrote last time that Mathea Trovin passed away …

[fourth page]

… this past summer very suddenly, she was only ill a few days. We were invited to the funeral, but could not attend. Actually, we have been invited to a number of funerals in Toten since coming here to Gjøvik, and we have not attended any of them.

If I had been ready to travel to America, I could have had someone take me directly to Laura. Last Saturday a young man returned to America who had come from Laura before Christmas and here to us with Christmas gifts from her. This boy came from Troven, so we knew him well before he left for America, and now, as I said, he is on his way back to America again and is going to spend some time with Laura and Anton. As you can imagine, I would have liked to do it, if only because I would have had someone accompanying me. But the easiest will be, dear Uncle, if you make another trip to visit us, and then I promise that I will return with you, and I don't think I would dread traveling either.

Please be so kind as to greet our kin over there from Mother and me. And especially to you Mother and I send our warmest greetings. Thank you again ever so much for everything! And best wishes on the 30th for happy years to come. May you live for many more.

Once more, most cordial greetings from your

Helene Maria

Translation by Jim Skurdall

Translation

Hamar, 21 March 1915

Dear Uncle, O. P. Rocksvold,

Thank you ever so much for both of your letters which I was so delighted to receive, the first around the middle of June, sent from Boyd, and the last written on the first of this month and received on the 17th. And thank you ever so much also for the welcome issues of the newspaper *Decorah Posten*, which, I see, I shall continue to receive in the future as long as — I am living! —

I read that your eyesight has weakened recently, and that is regrettable. Thank goodness for inventions we have such as eye glasses, which help. I so fervently hope that you will be able to keep your eyesight! Otherwise, I see that you are in good health and have not been ill one day since …

[second page]

… we here at Roksvold had the pleasure of having you here with us. Yes, it is a magnificent memory to have, that you really did visit us in living person. The only complaint I have is that it was too <u>short</u>! I am also happy to read that you are now enjoying yourself at the home of your son, Norman, and your daughter-in-law. It is so nice to know that you are doing so well at your age, enjoying some peace and quiet and congenial relationships, and, of course, that you are receiving the consideration that you deserve and that all decent children show their parents, whether mother or father, in their old age.

I also see that you have had other experiences in North Dakota with your son and daughter-in-law. It is awful to think that there are people who can act so shameless and mean.

[third page]

I see that you were treated in an agreeable manner by her. And out in the world she will have her well-deserved reputation, how she acted toward you, dear Uncle. *[Translator: These first sentences on this page difficult, not really sure what she is saying. This is my interpretation.]* I fully support your decision to move to your other son and daughter-in-law in order to find some peace and quiet. I read also that you have sold your farm in North Dakota at a very low price, and according to what you say, this was *[cannot make out what she writes here]*. And likewise the farm on which you live in Iowa. No, dear Uncle, you are not "<u>unreasonable</u>". You asked me if I thought you were, but my answer is "No, absolutely not!"

I see that you think Anton and Laura have such a good life. Yes, what a joy it is for me to know that they are doing so well. And over all the years they have been so good to me. I have received really quite a large sum of money from them altogether.

I see from what you wrote that you were thinking …

[fourth page]

… of me when you traveled to Boyd, and how much I would have liked to have been sitting by your side on that trip so that I also might have been able to see how they are doing in all aspects of their lives. No one could have wished for that more than I did. I see that you are also thinking about visiting Laura and Anton again this summer. In that case you must come and fetch me here so that I can enjoy the visit with you.

As you know, brother Karl is dead. He developed serious heart problems 3 years ago and never regained full health. His condition continued to worsen and during the last half year there were times when he was <u>mentally unstable</u>. He spent the last 10 weeks of his life in Prestsæter Asylum. He received every kind of medical treatment, but nothing helped. His strength ebbed away and the last weeks he lay virtually in a coma day and night.

[fifth page]

He suffered a stroke at 11 o'clock in the morning on the 2nd of January and died on the afternoon of the same day at half past one. He had been unconscious for *[hard to decipher but I think it is "eighty"]* hours. He was at the asylum for 10 weeks and 2 days. Of course he was by no means mentally ill; he suffered rather from heart disease and arteriosclerosis. It was for this reason his death came so rapidly. His funeral was marked by solemn formality with a sea of flowers from far and near from his exceptionally large number of friends and acquaintances from all over, and from relatives. Such an overwhelming outpouring of sympathy for someone of his <u>status</u>.

I read your best wishes to me on my birthday and thank you so much. Though I wish to reciprocate, this letter will arrive several days …

[sixth page]

… late. And I read that you intend to have a photograph taken of yourself on your birthday, the 30th of March, and that you intend to send a copy to me — thank you so much! I certainly do wish to receive one.

I am still in good health, as are Hilda and Henrik. Henrik asked me to tell you that they have paid off the mortgage on their house, and he says that if they decide to sell, he will ask 10,000 "kroner". Both Henrik and Hilda send you their greetings. The house and lot cost them 6,500 "kroner" as it is now.

Well, I don't have any more to write about, and my letter is half as good as yours. I must say that you are really an exceptional man, able to write such long and informative letters in spite of your age.

[seventh page]

The war continues to rage with no end in sight. We have the marked advantage here in Norway of being able to buy wheat flour from America, and we have had it here in the house all winter, wheat flour from America. We found the brand label inside the bag at the top. It was expensive, but so good. We who can still buy from America can count ourselves among the lucky ones. We may eventually have to buy our flour in Norway, and we must hope that the situation does not get any worse than that.

Well, dear Uncle, I wish you all the best. Please greet first and foremost your son and daughter-in-law there at home from me, and any other relatives, when the occasion permits.

[eighth page]

Most cordial greetings and a sincere thank you from me for the letters and for "*Posten*" [*Decorah Posten* newspaper].

In gratitude

Helene Maria

Translation by Jim Skurdall

Lars Dahl, *husband of Helene Roksvold Dahl*

Translation

Roksvold, 6 March 1886

Dear Mother-In-Law!

On the 21st of last month I received a letter dated the first of the same month, for which I thank you most earnestly, also on behalf of my wife. Regarding the main content of the letter, we knew of this already, as a lad from Prestesæterhagen who worked in our household for several years traveled to America last year and came in contact with you. He wrote home and reported, among other things, that my father-in-law had passed away.

The parting of a loved one is always sad, but one cannot justifiably say that his death in this instance is a sad occasion, since he knew that he would be able to live with his family until he reached an age …

[second page]

… at which he would no longer be able to contribute so much. And, in fact, he lived to an advanced age.

What makes his passing more joyous than sad is, most importantly, in my estimation, the fact that the Lord granted him full possession of his senses to the very end, and, moreover, that he was able to acknowledge and confess his failings to God and ask for the forgiveness of his sins, while appealing to those in his presence to do the same. So you see, this is something that each and every right-thinking, Christian person must take delight in and hope that all these prayers found their way up to a merciful and benevolent God. Blessed be the memory of our departed loved one! I enjoyed many pleasurable days together with him while he was here in Toten in Norway.

Many changes have taken place both here and other places on Earth since the departed and I were together.

[third page]

You no doubt know that it has been some time since all our children moved away. Our eldest son, Peter Julius, was educated at one of the country's public technical schools, from which he graduated with honors. In fact, he graduated no. 1 among all the pupils at the school, who came from all parts of the country. Since leaving school, he has been at a machine shop in Kristiania, where he has done his work to the satisfaction of his employers.

Our youngest son, Karl, was educated at one of the seminaries *[teacher's colleges]*. He, too, graduated no. 1, and soon thereafter he began teaching in East Toten, where he has been for a little over 5 years.

Now the position of precentor in East Toten is vacant, and the pastor encouraged him to apply. According to regulations, the school board was to select three of the applicants, who …

[fourth page]

… are now under consideration for the position. Although there were a number of very well-qualified applicants, Karl is now among the top three candidates. Of course, we cannot expect that he will be offered the position, as he is the youngest. No decision has been reached so far.

Our daughter, Helene Marie, who is married to Bernt Øistad, has since last fall been living in Kristiania. They have three children, and the eldest, a daughter age 15 named Laura Matilde, is living with us and will be confirmed this year.

All the buildings here at Roksvold, with the exception of the outbuildings, have undergone many changes. Most of the work that is to be done on the farmhouse has been done, and the rest will be finished next summer. I think it is going to be very nice, both inside and out. It stands where it has always stood, but it is higher now. It was Peter who drew up the plans for the renovation.

[fifth page, incomplete, only six lines]

We thank you for the photograph enclosed in the letter. We think that Ole has changed so much that we hardly recognize him. Ole's daughter, who penned the letter, writes very well and her language is exactly …

[sixth page, also incomplete, is not a continuation of the preceding lines, there must be something missing in between. It looks like the letter was folded and has been torn along the folds, and perhaps the middle portion is missing, as well as the end portion where Lars would have signed his name.]

… write in every home. Many of the older generation who were your friends and acquaintances have passed away. Among those still living are Hans Brustuen and his wife, Agnete. I have greeted them from you. Kristian and Berte Skartsæterhagen are also still living.

[The rest of the letter is missing]

[Written on the left side of the first page is the following]: "The letter from my wife was written in Kristiania by my daughter, who lives there, and who was told that we had received a letter from you. Her address is: Helene Marie Øistad, Korsgaden 27, Kristiania." *[This note is somewhat puzzling. Does he mean that his wife Helene dictated the letter to their daughter, Helene, while they were visiting in Kristiania/Oslo? I assume it is what it means.]*

Translation by Jim Skurdall

Laura Øistad Roseth, *Ole's niece*

Translation

Boyd, April 26, 1905

Mrs. A. O. Anderson!

Dear cousin!

Thank you ever so much both for the letters and these little photographs that I received so long ago. I must confess that it is really a shame that I never take time to write, and I do not dare ask you to excuse me, for it is nothing but laziness.

[second page]

It would be so much fun to see you sometime. You really must see if you can take a trip [writes "trip"] up here to see me, and then I could maybe come and visit you sometime. It might be possible. I haven't had a letter from your father now for a <u>long</u> <u>long</u> time. It was I who wrote last, so I have been waiting for a long time. I read that you have thought about writing to Mother. It would be so much fun for her, as she so …

[third page]

… much likes to receive letters.

Recently we have been having heavy winds during the day. Nothing turning green yet, it is much too dry. We would so much like some rain.

I really don't have any news, since you don't know anyone here, otherwise I might have been able to tell you a little.

Well, this letter is short, but better than nothing. We are all in good health, as usual. I hope you will not follow my example, but rather will let me hear from you when when you are able to write.

Greetings to everyone from your cousin

Laura

Translation by Jim Skurdall

John Steen, *comrade in the Civil War*

2

da en cuñle fraieft, og lidt træn i
ndsen var gjøldende. Saaledes var vi
ogsaa de 2 første Corporaler som blev ud
-nevnt. Det var jo ikke noget stort, men
min, Ole det var det störte som var at
faa da. Og dette har vært for mig en stor
glæde. Og saa var vi tilsammen for at tide
ved Fort Donaldson. Ja den nat staar for
mig ligesaa lys og kold nu som den i
virkeligheden var paa den tid. Hvor den
natten var ubhagelig!!! Jeg har netop
haft brev ifra Captain Soper, Og han for
-teller at i neste November maanedskal
Iowa Battle monuments on the field of Shiloh
Indvies. Dedicated. Han siger at en dag
eller to efter valgdagen nisr. Governor came
-niies and his Staff together with the monument
Commissiones from ~~Duba Des Moines~~ and sur
-viving members of the various regiments
which took part in the battle of Shiloh and
Vicksburg. It seems that they go first to Pitts
-burg Landing and from there to Vicksburg.
Now then, the dedication of the 12th Iowa mon
-ument at Shiloh is a thing I shall not
miss if it is possible for me to go there,
And I wish a goodly number of dear old
company C. could be present. And I believe

3 that if a united effort is made, many of the boys would become interested. The last time I heard from brother Henry he said that of all places he wanted to visit was the Celebrated battle field of Shiloh and his old home in Glenwood Winneshiek County Iowa. If we could get O.P. Rockwood, John O. Johnson, Gulick Hauge, John Steen, Henry Steen, Harvey E. Johnson, Gilbert Anderson, Hans Hanson, Karl Kittelson and others of the boys to attend I tell you it would be a grand affair. I understand that the Illinois Central R R will give half fare Tickets on their lines which would not be very high from Independence or Dubuque to Vicksburg and return, with stop over privilege at Memphis to run out to Corinth and while we are out there we would just run up to the Winter Quarters at Chewalla, say what a Trip, if there could be a squad of us. Please write me and let me know what you think about it. You know the National Encampment of the G A R will hold forth at Minneapolis this year and it would be a nice thing to go there. But I tell you I would ten Times rather go to Shiloh if I could not go to both places. How long

4

did Hans Hanson stay in Decorah
after I left. You remember we were together
at Aarness the last evening I was there
and it was a very pleasant evening. (we had together) I
have in a measure promised myself a
trip to Decorah this summer, and then
I purposed to spend about 4 days with
you at your home, but now that I want
to go south in November it may somewhat
interfere with my Iowa visit. My wife
has an aged Aunt living in Eldorado Fay
-ette County, whom she visits almost every
year. The old lady is now 90 years of age
and the only one living of her fathers kin. A
visit may be made to the old lady this year
if it is I may go along to kind of look
after the baggage. And then look out for
I am coming. I was up in Minneapolis
last November and had a very pleasant
visit with my dear old pastor Rev Dr
V. Koren. It was a pleasure to be with him
he is so strong ~~intellectualy~~ intellectually
and very interesting. But he with the rest
of us is growing old. Wife and I are all
alone this winter. And it is a little lonesome
to live in a 10 room house with the family all
gone. My oldest son is in Manila in the civil service
and my youngest studying Dentistry. (over)

April 13, 1906

I must close now with best wishes for your health and prosperity. Hoping to hear from you soon with encouragement relation to the southern trip in November. Remember me kindly to your sister Mrs Eviurud and to all your old friends and neighbors. I had the pleasure of calling on Mr + Mrs Hans Riien when in Decorah three years ago. They are both wonderfully well preserved and it was a real pleasure to me to see them and talk with them once more. I remember both of them very well before they were married. And I called on Anders Strandbakken at that time. He looks well. I was so sorry to think that my time there was so short I would like to spend a day or two with those good people. At that time brother Otto and I took dinner with Anders Hörsrud + his good wife Helena Lövbraaten. You know I drove a breaking team for Hans Lövbraaten the whole summer of 1854. I was 13 years old in the fall. Well I see the paper is running short and I must stop. My dear fellow Goodby. Your comrade John Olsen

[Translator: What is written at the top of this page, upside down, is in English.]

Translation

Wahoo, Nebraska, April 13, 1906

My dear fellow soldier, former neighbor, and friend, O. P. Rocksvold,

It is now almost three years since I bade farewell to you and old Hans Hanson in Decorah. Oh, how time flies. Looking back without much deliberation it might seem to have been last year, or two years at most. Yes, "Time passes, the clock is ticking, and eternity awaits." *[Translator: In the Norwegian saying there are three rhymed words, "gaar/slaar/forestaar".]* That was not so nice of you to take a trip when you knew so many of your old friends would be coming to Decorah, but we have long since forgotten this lack of courtesy and only remember you as the handsome, sincere, and courageous Corporal Rocksvold of Company G, Iowa 12th. Do you remember that we were the first two of our company to be selected for guard duty at Camp Union, when we arrived on the 26th of October 1861, . . .

[end of page]
[second page]

. . . and when someone with a smidgen of common sense and some backbone was what they were looking for? And we were the first two with the rank of corporal. It was not such a great accomplishment, but, my dear Ole, it was the highest we could climb. And it made me very happy. And we suffered together at Fort Donaldson [Donelson][1]. Yes, in my mind that night is just as vivid and cold as it was in reality. Talk about unpleasant!!! I just received a letter from Captian Soper, and he wrote that this coming November the Iowa Battle Monument on the field of Shiloh *[Translator: last 8 words written in English]* is to be dedicated.[2] He says that a day or two after election day Governor Cummins and his staff . . .*[Translator: Rest is in English]*

Translation by Jim Skurdall

---

[1] Translator: You may already have read this Wikipedia article about the Iowa 12th Regiment: At Smithland, Kentucky, it [*12th Iowa Volunteer Infantry Regiment*] joined General Ulysses Grant for the movement upon Fort Henry, was present at the capture of the Fort. It then moved to Fort Donelson, where it took part in the fight and assault which resulted in victory.

[2] You may have already read this as well:

Iowa Monument at Shiloh
The Iowa Monument was dedicated on November 23, 1906 led by Governor Albert B. Cummins and many other dignitaries. The inscription on the front of the monument is 'This monument is erected by the state of Iowa in commemoration of the loyalty, patriotism and bravery of her sons who, on this battlefield of Shiloh on the 6th and 7th days of April, A.D., 1862, fought to perpetuate the sacred union of the States.' The monument was designed by F. E. Trieble. It is composed of granite from Barre, Vermont. It is 75 feet high and cost $25,000. Photos taken 9/30/08 and 10/10/10. The old photo shows Gov. Cummins, his staff and their wives. The monument is located near the Visitors Center.

Translation

04/13/1906 John Steen letter - English Transcription by Bev Swenson

[continuation of page 1]

...together with the Monument Commission[er]s [from Dubu DesMoines-crossed out] and surviving members of the various regiments which took part in the battles of Shiloh and Vicksburg. It seems that they go first to Pittsburg Landing and from there to Vicksburg. Now then, the dedication of the 12[th] Iowa Monument at Shiloh is a thing I shall not miss if it is possible for me to go there. And I wish a goodly number of dear old Company G could be present. And I believe... [end of page]

[Page 3]

...That if a united effort is [was-crossed out] made, many of the boys would become interested. The last time I heard from brother Henry he said that of all places he wanted to visit was the celebrated battlefield of Shiloh and his old house in Glenwood Winneshiek County Iowa. If we could get O.P. Rocksvold, John O. Johnson, Gulick(?) Hauge, John Steen, Henry Steen, Harvey E. Johnson, Gilbert Anderson, Hans Hanson, Karl Kittelson and others of the boy[s] to attend I tell you it would be a grand affair. I understand that the Illinois Central RR will give half fare tickets on their lines which would not be very high from Independence or Dubuque to Vicksburg and return, with stop over privilege at Memphis to run out to Corinth and while we are out there we would just run up to the Winter Quarters at Chervalla. My what a trip, if there could be a squad of us. Please write me and let me know what you think about it. You know the National Encampment of the GAR will hold forth at Minneapolis this year and it would be a nice thing to go there. But I tell you I would ten times rather go to Shiloh if I could not go to both places. How long... [end of page]

[Page 4]

...did Hans Hanson stay in Decorah after I left. You remember we were together at Aarness the last evening I was there and it was a very pleasant evening. I have in a measure promised myself a trip to Decorah this summer, and then I purposed to spend about 4 days with you at you house, but now that I must go south in November it may somewhat interfere with my Iowa visit. My wife has an aged Aunt living in Eldorado Fayette County, whom she visits almost every year. The old lady is now 90 years of age and the only one living of her father[']s kin. A visit may be made to the old lady this year if it is I may go along to kind of look after the baggage. And then look out for I am comming[sic]. I was up in Minneapolis last November and had a very pleasant visit with my dear old pastor Rev. Dr. V. Koren. It was a pleasure to be with him he is so strong [intellectually-crossed out] intellectually and very interesting. But he with the rest of us is growing old. Wife and I are all alone this winter. And it is a little lonesome to live in a 10 room house with the family all gone. My oldest son is in Manila in the Civil Services and my youngest studying Dentistry. [end of page]

[Page 5]

I must close now with best wishes for your health and prosperity. Hoping to hear from you soon with encouragement relative to the southern trip in November. Remember me kindly to your sister Mrs. Evinrud and to all other old friends and neighbors. I had the pleasure of calling on Mr. & Mrs. Hans Ruen when in Decorah three years ago. They are both wonderfully well preserved and it was a real pleasure to me to see them and talk with them once more. I remember both of them very well before they were married. And I called on Anders Strandbakken at that time. He looks well – I was so sorry to think that my time [at-crossed out] there was so short I would like to spend a day or two with those good people. At that time brother Otto and I took dinner with Anders Horserud & his good wife Helena Lóvbraaten. You know I drove a breaking train for Hans Lóvbraaten the whole summer of 1854. I was 13 years old in the fall. Well I see the paper is running short and I must stop. My dear fellow Goodby. Your Comrade John Steen. [End of page]

[Upside down at top of page 1]

When do you take an other[sic] trip to Norway [?] You know my wife was there 3 years ago. She was there 14 months and she wants to go again. Many will go this year but I would not care to go in so much of a crowd. I prefer a more quiet time and season.

Oscar Frydenlund

Translation

Aurdal, 17 January 1908

Dear Anderson!

I promised to write to you when I arrived home. Unfortunately, I have not had the opportunity to do so until now.

I had a very disagreeable ocean crossing, as I had the misfortune of landing on a ship filled with virtually no one but southern Europeans, and they are, I think, the crudest people there are. There were 2,890 passengers on board, and among them only 10 Norwegians. We had stormy weather the entire time, so we were not out on the deck more than 2 days.

[second page]

Fortunately, I was not seasick, so I guess I should not complain so much.

The voyage itself was very interesting, and we got to see a lot. We left the ship at Plymouth, England, and from there we went to London, where we stayed one day. Then it was on to Harwich, and from there to Esbjerg and right across Denmark to Fredrikshavn. Then over to Kristiansand, stayed there one day and a night. After that, we stopped at all the little coastal towns between Kristiansand and Kristiania, so we got to see really …

[third page — what is marked as p. 3 is actually p. 4, and p. 4 is really p. 3]

… quite a lot. But it was an awfully long journey. We left Soldier(?) on December 2nd and didn't arrive home until the 23rd.

It was terribly cold at Christmas with lots of snow and good skiing. Now we are having remarkably mild and stable weather with the temperature today at 8 degrees celsius [above zero].

I am doing very well here now and doubt that I'll be traveling again for some time, at least not before the first. We have talked …

[fourth page — what is marked p. 4 is actually p. 3]

… about buying Petersborg Hotel, which is situated right next to our property. If we do this, I shall no doubt take it over, and then I'll be bound to this place and unable to travel again.

Have you heard anything from Lauritz and Anders, whether they have been thinking of coming up there again this summer? I would hope that Lauritz would stay with you over the summer. <u>Jente-Mikkel</u> is no doubt [can't decipher] with many Christmas gifts so that he can begin farming in the spring.

Would be fun to receive a few lines from you and hear how things are going.

[written upside down at the top of p. 3/marked as p. 4]

If any of you wind up traveling to Norway sometime, you must come up to Valders/Valdres.

Cordial greetings to all the Andersons from

Oscar Frydenlund
Aurdal, Valders/Valdres

Translation by Jim Skurdall

Inger Faaren, *unknown relative*

Translation

Red Wing, Minnesota, June 15, 1909

Dear Uncle!

Thank you for the letter from you that I received a long time ago. I hope that you are doing well out West, and I can imagine that you are still very busy, as everything is so late this year.

Here you can see how we are going to celebrate the Fourth of July this year *[referring to the first page of stationery]*.

It sounds like a reasonable idea for you to travel to Mexico for the winter. I could use the same kind of vacation myself, but when you don't have the money, you have to be satisfied sitting at home. I am not what I ought to be. I always feel tired. But I guess I'll have to somehow find a way to work another year …

[second page]

… and then retire, if I'm still alive.

Everything is beautiful here in Red Wing now, but it is still rather cold.

Mr. and Mrs. Allen send you greetings. I see them quite often, and they are always so kind to me.

Otherwise, everything is fine with me.

I hope I'll hear from you again soon, and I hope that this fall I'll see you again here in Red Wing, before you leave for Mexico.

I hope the Lord will safeguard your health for many, many years to come.

Most cordial greetings

Inger Faaren
Red Wing, Minnesota

Translation by Jim Skurdall

Manda Rocksvold, *Ole's daughter*

Translation

Mason City, Iowa
December 14, 1913

Mr. O. P. Rocksvold
Beach, North Dakota

Dear Father,

I wish to write a few more lines this evening.

As I said, the paper I was using when I wrote to you last was so poor that I am not sure you were able to read the letter.

I imagine that this is the time that you are about to …

[second page]

… return to Iowa for the winter, and I was wondering if you could make a stop in Mason City on the way. For this reason I am writing to let you know where I am living so you can find your way here. The address is 503 State Street. A girl from Cedar Rapids and I have two rooms together for this month. We have a bedroom and a parlor with a couch. So you see, we have room for …

[third page]

… you, if you wish to stop here for a few days. I am renting these rooms until December 29th and am paying $15 a month, which makes $7.50 for each of us. We have the use of the bathroom and kitchen, and if we wish to cook, we can use the gas stove and pay for the gas we use. The owners use a kerosene stove themselves.

I was thinking of you [plural] during Thanksgiving and wishing that I was close enough to be able to …

[fourth page]

… prepare a nice dinner for you [plural]. I was not feeling well that day and spent most of it in bed reminiscing about the old days when everything was so nice and cozy at home, even though it wasn't always easy to get everything done on time. And I thought about how I wished I could …

[fifth page]

… afford to come out there for a little visit and then return with you to Iowa. I thought it would be easier for you not to have to travel alone and look after your baggage [she wrote "baggage"] when you see and hear so poorly. I think of you often when you are traveling. There are always so many …

[sixth page]

... dangers, and neither of us can get very far without Christ's help and protection. It is best to trust in his word, and he will seek the best for us.

Around three weeks ago I received a check in the mail and later found out that the money had come from you. Mrs. Ask had written ...

[seventh page]

... her own name on it, but when I didn't cash it, she informed me that the money was from you. How did you happen to send the money to her? Whatever the case, thank you so much.

I wrote to Olive today, but I should have done it long ago, as I owed them a letter. And I have not ...

[eighth page]

... heard from them for several weeks. I don't imagine things are going too well for them. And the poor children. It must be hard for them to have so many going to school, and such a long way to go. But I am happy to hear that Alberta could continue with school.

What did you do when Willie's wife was away? I hope that you found someone to keep house so that ...

[ninth page]

... you didn't have to "batche" [I suppose she means "live as bachelors"]. That would have been much too difficult this time of year. I wonder if she has returned now?

Are you going to stop at Hilda's on your way to Iowa? And when is she thinking of coming down here again? I wonder if she received my card and letter, which I wrote after she moved into her new home?

[tenth page]

I have not heard anything up to now, and I would think she could at least find time to write me a postcard.

I wrote a letter to you in the fall addressed to Argusville, as I thought you might stop there for a few days and that you would get it there. I wrote a card to Hilda and asked her to inquire about it. But they must not have ...

[eleventh page]

... done anything, or requested that it be forwarded to Decorah. It was sent to the Dead Letter Office in Washington, and then returned to me three months after I sent it. I hope this letter reaches you and that all is well with you [plural] and that you will have a safe return to Iowa. And I hope the upcoming

Christmas season will be a joyous time in every respect for us ...

[twelfth page]

... and for all our loved ones.

I hope you have not decided to sell out up there for a price lower than you are asking, just when land prices are rising everywhere.

I guess this will be all for now. With fond greetings,

As ever, your daughter

Manda Rocksvold
503 E. State Street
Mason City, Iowa

Translation by Jim Skurdall

Peter William "Willie" Rocksvold, *Ole's son. 7-26-1915*

Beach N.D. July 26. 1915

Dear folks.

Will write you a few words to let you know how things are out here. another hail storm struck here last friday and wiped out our whole crop there is not as much as twenty acres that will make anything and dont think it will pay the expences of cutting I figure it a total loss on the whole thing 245 acres of wheat the best that ever grew on this farm I expected it would go 30 bush

2

per acre and 60 acres Oats
All headded out and 45 of Barly
24 of Flax corn is all gone
and not much left of the
garden. At the price of wheat
now the lose on the wheat alone
is over $9 000⁰⁰ and $2 6 40⁰⁰ Insuren

Insurance on the whole thing
so this year wont make me
rich will have to buy feed
to # plow the crop under and
now it is raining all the time
so I cant even make hay out
of it the field is so soft
it will be many days til we
can get out with a team.
There is quite a lot of damage
done all over the Valley just

3.

took the crop in streaks all
over the county. the storm
kept on for almost a half
hour and the hail stones just
like Billiard balls the only
total loss around is ours ~~Old~~
Oldman Whitmer Part of
Ed. Willisca and port of Rogers
and partly damaged about 8 or 10
sections more around here
and south of Beach the same
way and one storm down
at Burkey the same day.
George Selsvold is about half
hailed out without any insurance
Oscar Ammerud bought a half section
17 miles north of Wibaux this summer
got 80 acres of crop and 3 horses and

4.

and two cows. and some machinery
paid $12 per acre for the whole cheese

Will have to close for this
time hoping you wont have
any hail down there.
From.
Will

Tilda Foss Rocksvold, *wife of Anton Norman Rocksvold, Ole's son. Pages 1-6*

Decorah Ia Jan 2 – 18
Dear Matilda! —
I'm going to
try and write you a
few lines to day have
been going to do so
for the longest time
but seem like its so
hard to get started to
write I'm owing so
many letters that I
must get at it now I
have just finished
one to Hilda now
had a Xmas card from
her she says they are all

well she says you had been
up there visiting them that
was nice she hurley must
have her hands full now
with the 2 babies dont
see how in the world
she can get along alone
How are you now are you
feeling strong again
after that spell you
had when you was
down here? we are
all well baby is getting
to be quite a girl
now and is real good
Grandpa is feeling good

he says his eyes are better
now then they were
and I notice that to
some days he can see
pretty good ofcorse
when its dark and
cloudy he can see to
read any we have been
saying norman could
go along with him to
see some Dr but he
says he thinks they
will get better as he
thinks they are now
and so he wants to
wait and see later

well xmas is over again
and the new year started
don't time fly fast tho
I've stayed right home
all the time
Anna Kirkeby is gone
to now she died christmas
morning at 5 oclock and
was burried Friday she was
awful sick at last they said
Albert has been down here
since before xmas Hilmen
didnt come down I spose it
was hard for him to get
away. I didnt go to the
funeral as it was just

terribel cold that day grandpa
and Norman went we have
been having som cold weather
lately but not any know to
peak of. How is every body
and every thing up there havent
had any letter from home
for some time thought may
be some body would come
down for xmas I looked for
Irene and George you know
you was saying when you was
here that may be they would
come down and Arthur to
have spoke of it the way Celia
wrote once but no one come

well I must quit with
my writing and go and
take baby as she is crying
excuse poor writing
and I wish you all
a happy new year.
Lovingly Tilda,
write when you find time
would like to hear how
you all are

Hilda Roksvold Øistad Garaas, *grandniece of Ole*

1904 Postcard

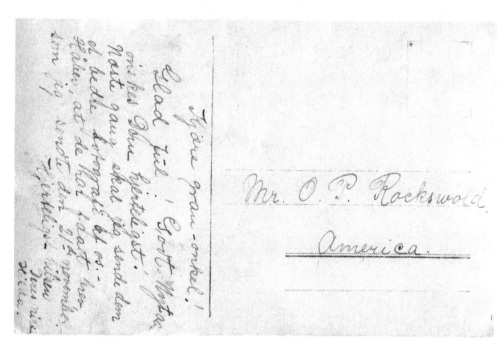

Postcard - date unknown

Translation

Hamar
27 February 1921

Dear Great-Uncle!

Today I wish to write a few lines to you and thank you so much for the issues of Decorah Posten that you send me. It is so very nice that you send them to me. Your warm-hearted feelings for my mother spill over to me.

May God bless you, kind gentleman, you who are about to turn 89 …

[second page]

… on the 30th of March. Mother said that your birthday and mother's are on the same day.

I hope you are doing well and are in good health. I wish you all the best from the bottom of my heart for today and always.

We are in good health and doing well. I hear from Laura rather often and all's well with them. Her son was confirmed in May 1920. Mother's brother, Peter Dahl in Kristiania [Oslo], sends greetings to you. He writes to me often.

[third page]

He says he would like to write a letter to you.

Life is not as expensive as before, prices have fallen in many places, less expensive for food, clothing, firewood, don't have to pay as much. And house prices are very low. One hectoliter [100 liters] of coke *[Translator: coal residue used for fuel]* cost 18½ Norwegian crowns last winter, but now costs 6 crowns.

In two days it will be 9 months since the death of my dear mother. I miss her terribly.

I don't know …

[fourth page]

… what else I might write today, so I'll close this poor letter. My husband sends greetings to you.

Fond greetings to you from

Your niece

Hilda Garaas

Translation by Jim Skurdall

Peter Dahl, *Ole's nephew*

Translation

Kristiania [Oslo], the 4th of November 1921

Most esteemed Uncle!

Some weeks ago I had the pleasure of receiving a letter from you, for which I express my heartfelt gratitude. It is true that it was not written in the same hand that left such an indelible impression on my memory some decades ago. The hand that once wielded a firearm in the historic struggle for freedom and humanity — that same hand also wielded the pen in its captivating descriptions that still grace the faded yellow sheets of stationery, conjuring up events of yore as vividly as when they happened. Yes, dear Uncle, there were at that time many eyes reading those lines with great interest just a few weeks after they were written. And for a long time now most of those eyes have been closed forever,

[second page]

I am no doubt the only one left on whom your powerful descriptions left such an indelible impression.

I wrote my first letter to you on the 6th of March, and my hope that it might reach you is confirmed now by this letter from you. On the 5th of June I wrote to you again expressing heartfelt gratitude for having received so unexpectedly both "Decorah Posten" and "Ved Arnen", which, I assumed, had been sent by you. I described in that letter the wide-ranging reading matter that "Decorah Posten" contains and the remarkable moods that come over me when reading these reports of family life and the organizational activities of Norwegian Americans. I reiterate my sincerest appreciation for "Decorah Posten" as the valuable gift that it is, and all the more inasmuch as you intend to send it to me for as long as you count yourself among the living, as you yourself put it.

It is most agreeable to see that you are, in your advanced age, as healthy as ever, and it is, quite truthfully, a delightful surprise to hear that your sight seems to be improving somewhat. And you inferred that you might be traveling quite some distance to a specialist this fall in the hope of even greater improvement. It is thus possible …

[third page]

… that you will in fact be far from Decorah when this letter arrives. In that case I hope that it will be forwarded to you, or that you will find it when you return. Just imagine if your eyesight had improved so much that you could read the letter! But I imagine that is too much to expect.

I see from your letter and from the newspapers, especially "Decorah Posten", that times are hard in America as well. The farmers especially complain, and with good reason, that they receive so little for what they produce, when, at the same time, prices are so high for all other goods.

And what are the circumstances in Norway? Here the high cost of living has become worse than it was three years ago, when war was still raging. And imported products are the most expensive of all. I can remember as a boy that Mother received 2 "daler" for a "bismerpund" of high-quality butter. Now a "bismerpund" of the same quality butter costs around 12 "daler", reckoning in the old currency. (As you perhaps remember, one "daler" is today equal to 4 "kroner", one "bismerpund" equals 6 "kilogram", or, put another way, one "kilogram" is equivalent to 2 "skaalpund" or 4 "mærker").

In my youth, one could buy a pair of good …

[fourth page]

… boots for 8 "kroner" (2 "daler"), or in any case order a pair of women's boots at that price from the shoemaker here in town. Today one must pay 100 "kroner" or 25 "daler" for the same kind of all-purpose handsewn women's boots. If I wish to have new half soles put on a pair of my shoes, or repair the heels, I have to pay 14 "kroner" or 3½ "daler". And the same is true for clothing, which now costs 4 times, and, in some cases, even 6 times as much as it did 8 years ago. And the same for food items such as fish, of which Norway has an abundant supply. One example: Today here in town simple salted herring costs 1 "krone" and 70 "øre" per kilogram, the equivalent of 2 "daler", 2 "mark" and 18 "skilling" per "bismerpund" in the old currency, making it more expensive than the best-quality dairy butter of earlier times. The price of herring is 8 times as high as it was just a few years ago. The price of all of the necessities of life here in Norway has increased drastically, and now three years after the end of the war there seems to be no perceptible improvement.

Sweden and Denmark also experienced a high cost of living during the war, though significantly lower than here in Norway, and in these two countries it has diminished appreciably.

[fifth page]

And now you will, with good reason, wish to ask:

Why has this extremely high cost of living persisted in Norway?

I shall answer this question by presenting a few facts:

1.) Norway is teeming with ruthless and unscrupulous speculators within the business community.

One example: a few days after the war broke out, a large number of wholesale merchants here in Kristiania believed that it soon would be difficult to import foodstuffs from abroad. So they decided to exploit this opportunity. They had significant stocks of imported rye flour, for which they had paid around 16 "kroner" or 4 "daler" per bag (1 bag contained 100 kilogram or around 220 American pounds). Now they decided to charge 60 to 80 "kroner" per bag, or, in other words, 4 to 5 times as much as they had paid. But these noble gentlemen were not able to execute their plan. The government banned all overcharging of this kind and set fixed prices as well as penalties for exceeding them. But the greed of the business community had grown at a rapid pace; meetings were held and associations established in order to appropriate as much as possible from the rest of society.

[sixth page]

By virtue of these associations — one could just as well call them conspiracies on the part of the business community — virtually all competition has been eliminated. They intend to use force to maintain the exorbitant prices. Any merchant who wishes to try to lower his prices is to be boycotted. Wholesalers will refuse to supply him with goods. The government has empowered certain authorities to monitor the activities of the business community and various trades, among others, and punish the worst instances of price-gouging with a paltry fine. Such fines are seldom imposed, and the names of offenders are never made public. If they were, it would help somewhat. But as things stand now, these folks can continue to brazenly fleece their customers and only risk a fine that is hardly one tenth of one percent of the profits that they rake in over the course of a year.

2.) Labor leaders are another type of speculator. For a long time now all branches of trade and industry, transport, longshoremen and shipping, the streetcar corporation and private railway, even the state-owned railway and the postal service — they are all organized into labor unions.

[seventh page]

Of all the sharp minds among tens of thousands of the aforementioned, it is the most cunning and greedy who maneuver their way into positions of leadership in each of these organizations. Each receives a large salary paid by member dues, and each conducts himself like a tribal chieftain bent on acquiring whatever is needed for his own personal comfort. And these labor leaders are allied throughout the country through their own federation and they have, so to speak, Parliament and the Government in their pocket serving their own needs. A public investigation has proven that during the year 1920 alone 12 million "kroner" have flowed from the workers into their common treasury. A portion of these funds are to be used to pay striking workers. And it is here we have the labor leaders' immense source of power: the threat of a strike.

Whenever they find that the time is right to increase their income, the union members are summoned to assemble at night for a so-called mass meeting, where they resolve to go on strike. Then negotiations begin with the employers, who in the beginning are unwilling to approve an increase in wages, which are already very high. The government then intervenes in the form of a public arbitrator.

[eighth page]

He will as a rule go a long way in support of the demands of the labor leaders. But not far enough. The negotiations break down. The private government in the "People's House" resolves to begin a sympathy strike by as many unions as deemed necessary to force their will on the employers, who must yield in the end. And the demands of the labor leaders have been met. But the ordinary workers have seen an increase in their wages and they are greatly indebted to their leaders, who have gained for them an increase in their annual income of 500 to 1,000 "kroner". And the labor leaders, who are now praised to high heaven, have for sure seen a many-fold increase in their own incomes.

These leaders have in this manner over many years managed with no constraints to solidify the power they have today. Now, with the enormously high cost of living, they can use it to justify a new increase in wages, again and again. Then the clever merchants point to the higher wages to justify a new increase in prices. The leaders on either side compete to push up the prices. Now, finally, all Norwegian products …

[ninth page]

… have become so expensive that those meant for export cannot find buyers abroad without the producers absorbing a huge loss. Thus production in Norway must cease. Tens of thousands of workers are unemployed. And on account of this situation in the country, the last two strikes, that of the railway workers and the general strike last spring and summer did not succeed.

Another factor contributing to the high cost of living in Norway is the unfortunate circumstance that the value of Norwegian currency has fallen in relationship to the currency of the countries from which we must buy many of our basic necessities. We are worst off in relationship to your second fatherland, dear Uncle, the powerful United States of America, whose almighty dollar has brought the entire Old World to its knees. Before the war, the value of the dollar was around 3,75 "kroner", while today the dollar costs about 8 "kroner". In England, Sweden, and Denmark Norwegian currency is not so weak, but in these countries as well it has lost at least a third of its value.

[tenth page]

All goods that Norway must import from these countries become of course much more expensive as soon as they enter the country. And when all the greedy middlemen of the business community have taken their share, one can understand why the regular consumer must pay a price many times higher than before.

It is so very lamentable that Norwegian currency should have been ruined in this way, knowing that during the war Norwegian shipping brought thousands of millions of "kroner" into the country. But immediately after the war those influential gentlemen of the business community began to import all kinds of products, luxury goods in particular, on an unprecedented scale. Their intent was to earn hundreds of millions in a short time. And the big shipowners who had lost hundreds of steamships to German torpedos, had ordered a huge number of new ships abroad at exorbitant prices — ships costing altogether many hundreds of millions. And a large number of megalomaniacal rich men who had earned their millions so easily, ...

[eleventh page]

... took pleasure trips abroad especially to *["Krigslandene", not sure if he means countries now or formerly at war]*, where they *[cannot decipher]* numerous millions on these trips. Senseless speculation by wholesale dealers and shipowners and foolish extravagance on the part of self-indulgent, ever-traveling plutocrats has rapidly created a spacious grave for those millions so swiftly acquired. And yet another wound to the country's currency was inflicted by the Board of Directors of the Norwegian Bank. It issues all paper currency, administrates gold reserves, and determines the rate of interest. In order to earn large sums on its own behalf, the bank has lent enormous sums of money to big speculators and permitted huge amounts of paper money to be issued that is not backed by gold reserves. This has also had a considerable influence on the high cost of living in Norway.

Dear Uncle, I fear I may have wearied you; but I wanted to provide you with an overview of the economic situation for the citizens of this country who do not enrich themselves at the expense of the rest of society.

As for my own situation, there is not much to say. My wife and I have both worked here in the city, 40 years in my case, and she a couple of years longer, even though she is 4 years younger than me. We had saved up ...

[twelfth page]

... a little to support ourselves in old age. Events in the world together with the aforementioned corruption of some in our beloved Norway have produced this seemingly endless crisis. For my wife and me it means that we now have only about one quarter of what we have saved. We have no children. Were this not so, things would now be all the worse. We have been married for 34½ years. Our only child, a little girl, was born to us 30 years ago, but she died not long after birth. My wife has always been very diligent, frugal and prudent in everything she undertakes. But she has never been particularly robust, and now in her advanced age she is alas often ill with gout in her limbs, and her internal state of health is equally fragile. In this condition she is still has the household to look after. Here in the city it seems that only the wealthy and those who belong to trusts and the like are able to find domestic help.

As for my own health, I cannot complain. You may know that as a small boy I suffered a bone injury that developed into an infection in my left ankle when I was 15 years old so that I was not able to put weight on that foot from the time I was 15 until I was 20 years old. I have been weak in that foot ever since.

In closing, sincere greetings from my wife and from your humble and devoted nephew

Peter

Translation by Jim Skurdall

Translation

Kristiania [Oslo], the 5th of March 1922

Dear Uncle!

A couple of years ago I wrote my first letter to you. 3 months later I sent you a letter in heartfelt gratitude for the ever so valuable gift of "Decorah Posten" and "Ved Arnen", these most interesting and informative newspapers. In September I was surprised to also receive a letter from you. A few days later, I sent you a letter in appreciation for your letter and for the pledge it contained that you would continue to send me the newspaper "for as long as you could count yourself among the living". As Christmas approached, I sent you a card with Christmas greetings and best wishes from my wife and me.

Yes, dear Uncle, I must once again thank you for "Decorah Posten". So far it has arrived regularly and continues to bring me each time a direct greeting from you. I dare to hope that you are still enjoying good health and perhaps even a little better eyesight. And it is my most fervent wish as well that these lines may reach you and bring you my most cordial and sincere best wishes on the day that you reach a milestone that few have the good fortune of reaching, and here I speak of your 90th birthday. May our Heavenly Father grant you good health and happiness for years to come. I believe that in the distance I am able to catch a glimpse of yet another milestone, one towering above everything, and one that He in His omniscience has reserved just for you! But at the threshhold of this glimpse of the future may we kneel in deep reverence and gratitude for what it means to have reached 90 years of age. How many memories does a life of this length conceal when looking back over these 9 milestones as the appear …

[second page]

… ever lower on the horizon, where one's course of life began? Between nos. 2 and 3 of these milestones and about one degree after no. 2 comes a great divide. It is the Atlantic Ocean, not to mention the North Sea and quite a large swath of the North American continent. This one step was certainly immense, but for the clear vision of your spirit it presented no obstacle. I am quite sure that you harbor many memories from the course of your life between the milestones on the east side of the Atlantic, and that these memories are a mixture of melancholy and love.

At about milestone no. 3, with 30 years behind you, your destiny had led you into the big arena, where hostile and friendly fire, iron and blood were the agents in one of world history's greatest dramas. In the course of 24 performances of this mighty drama in which you played a role and in which your life could have been extinguished at any moment, there seems to have been an invisible hand shielding you, the same hand that no doubt already had set up at least 9 large milestones to mark your path.

Just having passed milestone no. 7, which with the number 70 is designated "the year of dust", you greeted surviving relatives and acquaintances in your fatherland, where you also ventured into parts unknown. As agile as a youngster — it is said, even with unblemished teeth — those 70 years did not appear to weigh on you.

Of course I have only known your life from a distance, from the reports of others. I know that at your advanced age you are an independent spirit and have no doubt been for a long period of time. You are a "self-made man", a real veteran and a man of honor par excellence.

In this my special acknowledgement I send in closing a mutual greeting from my wife and from your humble and most grateful nephew

Peter

P. S. I so fervently wish, at your convenience, to receive a few lines informing me of your vision and otherwise your state of health — to the extent possible.

P.

Translation by Jim Skurdall

Translation

Kristiania [Oslo], 3 February 1924

Dear [first] Cousin!

It has been over 3 weeks since I received your letter and the pretty Christmas card with the familiar verse from Grundtvig's morning hymn. Thank you so much for this.

Over the past 2 to 3 years I have written several letters to your father. Before that, my sister had exchanged letters with him over a number of years, and during that time I was, on a regular basis, kept generally informed about his family. In the summer of 1902, when your father was 70 years old, he visited the fatherland, and, of course, his sister — my mother — at the Roksvold farm, his childhood home, to which he and his parents and two siblings bade farewell on 16 April 1853.

Following my sister's death in the spring of 1920, I decided — one year later — to send a letter to your father. It was a greeting to him on his 89th birthday, on March 30th, 1921. Your father was blind and could no longer write himself. But he surprised me when he sent me "Decorah Posten" and "Ved Arnen". And I also received a letter from him, written by someone else, but surely dictated by him. In the letter he said that he would continue to send me the newspaper [written singular] as long as "he could be counted among the living". I sent him several letters, among others, a greeting on his 90th birthday. But then sometime later I read in the Decorah Posten a report of the death of cousin Norman, and some weeks later I read, with an even greater feeling of melancholy, the headline: PIONEER LAID TO REST, the report of Uncle's passing and his memorable funeral. I have, my dear cousin [that written in English], read through your letter several times, and I am astonished at how well you write Norwegian. Your grammar is impeccable and your style exemplary. You must have your sense of language from the cradle, certainly developed through good schooling and reading of Norwegian literature. — —

But now to the point:

What I know about your parents' families is scarcely more than you know yourself, in fact, it may be less. I knew your father's paternal uncle, Ole Hansen, well. He was from the farm Sivesindhagen and died in January 1881. But I have never heard <u>where</u> he nor our grandfather were born. Great-Uncle was born in 1800. His son <u>Hans</u> is, as far as I know, living at Sivesindhagen and is over 80 years old. And a son of the aforemention Hans, whose name is Hans Peter, is also living at Sivesindhagen, and is presumably around 50 years old. I really don't know to what extent these two might be able to provide information about the family.

[second page]

As concerns <u>Grandmother Kjersti Roksvold's</u> family prior to her time, I know that her father's name was Ole Kjos and that he was from Hadeland. But Hadeland encompasses five clerical districts: <u>Jevnaker</u>, <u>Vestre Lunner</u>, <u>Østre Lunner</u>, <u>Gran</u>, and <u>Brandbu</u>. In Brandbu we find the farm called Molstadkværn, which indeed does have a gristmill *[Translator: "kvern/kværn" means mill, or, in this case, gristmill, in Norwegian]*. About 50 years ago the owner, John Molstadkværn, was living here. He was a brother of Grandmother Kjersti. I never did see him. Around the same time, my parents had a visit from two of his children, daughter Marthe and son Erik Johnsen. He had been in America for awhile and had returned to Norway. I've heard nothing about them since then. Grandmother also had another brother, Erik Preskværn, who lived in Hadeland, but I don't know anything about him.

Grandmother had three sisters in West Toten: <u>One</u>, whose first name I cannot remember, lived on the Søndre [South] Drager farm. I cannot remember her; she surely died before I was born. A <u>second</u> sister was named Marthe Hagesveen, and a <u>third</u> was Mari Rensvoldbrug. The last mentioned had no children and took my mother in at the age of two. She grew up there, and continued living there after marrying father until they moved to Roksvold, when our grandparents and three of their children emigrated to America in the spring of 1853. — I was born on the 22nd of May of the same year.

I know nothing about your mother's family. I have seen a photo of her and of your father side by side in an album my parents received from all of Mother's relatives in America in the spring of 1866 — that is to say, one year before I was born. That makes me an old man, and indeed it is 45 years since I left my home in West Toten. And it has been 17½ years since I visited my childhood home Roksvold. That was the last year that Mother lived there.

In conclusion, a couple of other remarks:

1.) I do <u>not</u> know whether our great-grandfather, Ole Kjos, lived in Brandbu (which, at that time, was an annex parish of <u>Gran</u>). <u>If</u> this was the case, you could write a letter to: Parish Pastor of Brandbu, Brandbu Parsonage, Norway.

2.) Or you could write to other neighboring clerical districts of Gran in Hadeland.

3.) Likewise, whether Grandfather was been born in West or East Toten, you need not include the name of the pastor in your written inquiry.

[the rest written in English]

My best greetings to yourself, Your husband and Children, from your cousin

Peter Dahl

Translation by Jim Skurdall

William Rasmussen, *Ole's pastor*

Translation

Waukon, Iowa, 8th of August 1922

My dear friend, O. P. Rocksvold!

I just received a letter from A. O. Anderson, writing to me for you. It was so nice to hear from you. I have thought of you so often and have spoken to Mrs. Norman Rocksvold about you on a number of occasions. I have hoped I would see you again, but we cannot steer God's will.

I'll not likely forget the conversation you and I had at your nursing home some time after Norman's funeral. You were so joyful and content in your strong faith and trust in the Lord. You said that you had never …

[second page]

… in your life had so much confidence in your own salvation as you did then. And one could see the joy, contentment, and bliss your faith gave you.

I hope, my faithful friend and brother, that your joy in the Lord is equally strong today. "Rejoice in the Lord always" *[Philippians 4:4 KJV]* — I assume you read what I wrote about Norman in "Decorah Posten".

"I am ready — <u>when</u> God calls me", was his reply to you. And that is surely <u>your</u> reply as well. I am certain of that. And then one can confidently put everything in God's hands and say: "May Your will be done."

"The Lord is my shepherd, I shall not want." *[Psalm 23:1]*

"For me to live is Christ, and to die is gain." *[Philippians 1:21 KJV]*

[third page]

"Blessed are the dead which die in the Lord". *[Revelations 14:13 KJV]*

"It was so much better for me to leave here and be with Christ." *[No source found; my translation.]*

"Bedre kan jeg ikke fare end at fare til min Gud" *[These are the opening two lines of the first verse of hymn no. 836 in the old Norwegian hymnal — Norsk Salmebok. They were written by Lauritz Beich in 1726. I'll not try to find an English translation. My own straightforward translation is: Nothing better can I have than to go to my God.]*

"I know of a sleep in Jesus' name,

it refreshes my weary limbs.

A bed is prepared in the earth's embrace,

how motherly it shelters me.

My soul is with God in Paradise

and all sorrows forgotten."

[Pastor Rasmussen quotes a well-known Norwegian hymn, here in my English translation, written by M. B. Landstad. It is hymn no. 856 in the Norwegian hymnal — Norsk Salmebok.]

May the dear Savior Jesus — your savior and best friend — be with you, my dear friend, and lead you according to His will! "All things work together for good to them that love God." *[Romans 8:28 KJV]*

How fervently I wish to be able to see you again here …

[fourth page]

… and speak with you again. You always gave me so much help and encouragement — in every way.

May God reward you for that!

Both pastor and congregation will sorely miss not having you in our midst. But as you are doing, so shall we do the same: "We shall submit to and accept the will of the Lord." *[Source not found; my translation.]*

My dear Rocksvold, should we not meet again here on Earth, I wish to express my heartfelt gratitude — for your prayers, for your love, for your generosity, and for your good example. And, above all, for your <u>Christian</u> example. God bless you — and may God give you courage …

[fifth page]

… when your hour draws nigh and may He grant you a blissful and easy journey to your heavenly home.

Should we not meet here again — may we meet in the presence of God and in the bliss and eternal happiness of Heaven.

"Gid jeg var der og mine med

Og alle Guds børn kjære."

[I assume the pastor is quoting a hymn, but I cannot find the text online. My straightforward translation reads: "Oh that I were there with my loved ones / And all God's beloved children."]

So long, Rocksvold, and may we meet again soon — either here on Earth or on High with Jesus. *[NB! Norwegians still use the surname in this way today.]*

Your devoted pastor,

Wilhelm Rasmussen

[He wrote "prest og sjælesorger", with "sjælesorger" literally meaning "spiritual adviser", but it usually simply means "pastor".]

Translation by Jim Skurdall

~ APPENDIX 4 ~

OTHER DOCUMENTS

B. Konfir. m

Nr.	Konfirmationsdag.	Konfirmandens fulde Navn.	Alder.	Fødested.	Forældre.	
6	1846 18 Octb:	Hans Hansen Abrengsrud	15½	Brellein	Hans Hansen og Maria Knuds datter egtf.	
7	"	Ole Olsen Ettero	15½	Skovhøftlie	Ole Pedersen og Kari Nilsdatter Jus?.	
8	"	Fredrik Olsen Kleivehaug	15½	Korteruid	Ole Fredriksen og Anne Laes datter egtf.	
9	"	Ole Pedersen Rokksvold	14½	Rogvolden	Peder Hansen og Kristi Ols datter egtf.	
10	"	Hans Andersen Mørenes	14¾	Mørenes	Anders Rasmussen og Sigrid Gulbrands d: egtf.	
11	"	Lars Olsen Ettero	14¾	Etton	Ole Larsen og Oline Johannes datter egtf.	
12	"	Peder Jensen Aarendalen	14¾	Aarendalen	Jens Johannesen og Marie Olsdatter egtf.	
13	"	Christian Johannesen Indal	15	Indal	Johannes Christiansen og Marie Christiansd: egtf.	
14	"	Hans Thomasen Gertaas	14¾	Rønaas	Thomas Tottersen og Marie Nilsdatter Jus?.	
15	"	Anders Johannesen Søaten	15	Søaten	Johannes Jensen og Eline Andersdatter egtf.	
16	"	Andreas Hansen Risetbruget	14¾	Risetbruget	Hans Olsen og Signette Johansrudatter egtf.	
17	"	Hans Olsen Rouseruid	14	Rouseruid	Ole Hansen og Marthe Arsd:? egtf.	
18	"	Johannes Johannesen Matteruid	14¾	Matteruid	Johannes Olsen og Christine Hansdatter egtf.	
19	"	Andreas Evensen Rønaas	14¾	Klavesbøle	Even Hansen og Maria Jacobsdatter egtf.	
20	"	Johannes Christiansen Rosit	15¾	Rosit	Christian Johannesen og Martha Larsdatter egtf.	
21	"	Ole Olsen Blaavarp	13	Blaavarp	Ole Nilsen og Berthe Christians datter egtf.	
22	"	Andreas Larsen Am?en	16¼	Bjørnrudengen	Lars Nilsen og Kirstine Hans datter Jus?	
23	"	Johannes Martinsen Eikruid	15½	Eikruid	Martin Davidsen og Johanne Johannesd: egtf.	
24	"	Ole Hansen Morteruid	15	Rijset	Hans Olsen og Anne Hansdatter egtf.	

Ole Rocksvold birth, baptism record Nor. archives pg 1

Ole Rocksvold birth, baptism record Nor. archives pg 2

Ole Rocksvold confirm. record Nor. archives pg 1

Ole Rocksvold confirm. record Nor. archives pg 2

51		Bramine	3	
52		Emma	1.	
53	1ᵐ	Peder Hansen Stas- volden og Hustruu	55	
54		Kirstie Olsdatter	54	
		samt deres Børn		til America. anm. H. 12ᵗᵉ Aprie 1853. —
55		Ole	21	
56		Anne Mathea	21	
57	1ᵐ	Agnethe Schmidts- datter Rosenberg	26.	
58		Pernille Johannes- datter Gamme	27	til America. anm. H. 12ᵗᵉ Aprie 1853

1853 Vestre Toten Emigration to America Rocksvold Family

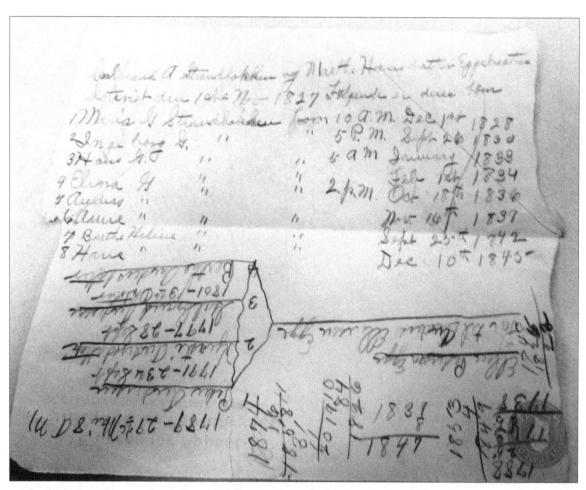

Genealogy data on Anne Strandbakken Rocksvold's family. Perhaps written as part of Ernest Anderson's request for information for his college writing assignment on family history.

Iowa Hornet's Nest Brigade

ATTENTION,

Comrades of the Iowa Hornet's Nest Brigade—the 2nd, 7th, 8th, 12th and 14th Iowa Infantry:

The Ninth Reunion of the Brigade will be held at Pittsburg Landing, Tennessee, on the battlefield of Shiloh, April 6th and 7th, 1912.

We enclose Program of Exercises, also full and complete instructions from the Committee on Transportation, as to rates, and securing tickets, etc., for the trip.

We have only a few of the metal badges left. Should you desire one for yourself and family, enclose fifty cents to R. L. Turner, Secretary, Oskaloosa, Iowa, so that, if necessary, we can order a new supply. Please act promptly.

We hope that each comrade and wife and as many of their family and friends as possible will meet with us.

Notify the Regimental Secretaries as soon as possible whether you will be present.

Please read carefully above instructions.

(Signed)

MAJ. SAMUEL MAHON, Pres.

R. L. TURNER, Sec'y

For further information as to rates, etc., address V. P. TWOMBLY, East Des Moines, Iowa. All other Brigade matters to R. L. TURNER, Secretary, Oskaloosa, Iowa.

Shiloh 9th reunion invitation.

Shiloh 50th reunion program.

THE BATTLE CRY OF FREEDOM

Yes we'll rally round the flag, boys, we'll rally once again,
Shouting the battle-cry of freedom;
We will rally from the hillside, we'll gather from the plain,
Shouting the battle-cry of freedom.

Chorus.

The Union forever! hurrah! boys, hurrah!
Down with the traitors, up with the stars;
While we rally round the flag, boys, rally once again,
Shouting the battle cry of freedom!

We are springing to the call of our brothers gone before,
Shouting the battle-cry of freedom;
And we'll fill the vacant ranks with a million freemen more,
Shouting the battle-cry of freedom.

Chorus—The Union forever, etc.

We will welcome to our numbers the loyal, true and brave,
Shouting the battle-cry of freedom;
And although he may be poor, he shall never be a slave,
Shouting the battle-cry of freedom.

Chorus—The Union forever, etc.

So, we're springing to the call from the East and from the West,
Shouting the battle-cry of freedom;
And we'll hurl the rebel crew from the land we love the best,
Shouting the battle-cry of freedom!

Chorus—The Union forever! etc.

AMERICA.

My country, 'tis of thee,
Sweet land of liberty,
Of thee I sing;
Land where our fathers died,
Land of the Pilgrim's Pride,
From every mountain side
Let freedom ring.

My native country, thee,
Land of the noble free—
Thy name I love;
I love thy rocks and rills,
Thy woods and templed hills,
My heart with rapture thrills
Like that above.

Our father's God to thee,
Author of liberty,
To thee I sing;
Long may our land be bright
With freedom's holy light,
Protect us by thy might;
Great God, our king.

WHEN JOHNNY COMES MARCHING HOME.

When Johnny comes marching home again, hurrah! hurrah!
We'll give him a hearty welcome then, hurrah! hurrah!
The men will cheer, the boys will shout,
The ladies, they will all turn out,
And we'll all feel gay,
When Johnny comes marching home.

The old church bell will peal with joy, hurrah! hurrah!
To welcome home our darling boy, hurrah! hurrah!
The village lads and lassies say,
With roses they will strew the way,
And we'll all feel gay,
When Johnny comes marching home.

Get ready for the jubilee, hurrah! hurrah!
We'll give the hero three times three, hurrah! hurrah!
The laurel wreath is ready now,
To place upon his loyal brow,
And we'll all feel gay,
When Johnny comes marching home.

Let love and friendship, on that day, hurrah! hurrah!
Their choicest treasures then display, hurrah! hurrah!
And let each one perform some part,
To fill with joy the warrior's heart,
And we'll all feel gay,
When Johnny comes marching home.

TRAMP! TRAMP! TRAMP!

In the prison cell I sit,
Thinking mother dear, of you,
And our bright and happy home so far away,
And the tears they fill my eyes,
spite of all that I can do,
Tho' I try to cheer my comrades and be gay.

Chorus.

Tramp, tramp, tramp, the boys are marching,
Cheer up, comrades, they will come,
And beneath the starry flag
We shall breathe the air again,
Of the free land in our own beloved home.

In the battle front we stood,
When their fiercest charge they made,
And they swept us off a hundred men or more,
But before we reached their lines,
They were beaten back dismayed,
And we heard the cry of victory o'er and o'er.

Chorus—Tramp, tramp, etc.

So, within the prison cell,
We are waiting for the day,
That shall come to open wide the iron door.
And the hollow eyes grow bright,
And the poor heart almost gay,
As we think of seeing home and friends once more.

Chorus—Tramp, tramp, etc.

MARCHING THROUGH GEORGIA.

Bring the good old bugle, boys, we'll sing another song—
Sing it with the spirit that will start the world along—
Sing it as we used to sing it, fifty thousand strong,
While we were marching through Georgia.

Hurrah! hurrah! we bring the Jubilee!
Hurrah! hurrah! the flag that makes you free!
So we sang the chorus from Atlanta to the sea,
While we were marching through Georgia.

How the darkies shouted when they heard the joyful sound!
How the turkeys gobbled which the commissary found!
How the sweet potatoes even started from the ground,
While we were marching through Georgia.

Chorus.—Hurrah! hurrah! etc.

Yes, and there were Union boys who wept with joyful tears,
When they saw the honored flag they had not seen for years;
Hardly could they be restrained from breaking off in cheers,
While we were marching through Georgia.

Chorus.—Hurrah! hurrah! etc.

"Sherman's dashing Yankee boys will never reach the coast!"
So the saucy rebels said, and 'twas a handsome boast,
Had they not forgot, alas! to reckon with the host,
While we were marching through Georgia.

Chorus.—Hurrah! hurrah! etc.

So we made a thoroughfare for freedom and her train,
Sixty miles in latitude—three hundred to the main;
Treason fled before us, for resistance was in vain,
While we were marching through Georgia.
Chorus.—Hurrah! hurrah, etc.

FUNERAL HYMN.

Air—"Shall we Gather at the River."

Shall we gather at the river,
Where bright angels feet have trod;
With its crystal tide forever
Flowing by the throne of God.

Chorus.

Yes we'll gather at the river,
The beautiful, the beautiful river;
Gather with the saints at the river,
That flows by the throne of God.

On the margin of the river,
Washing up its silver spray,
We will walk and worship ever,
All the happy, golden day.

Chorus.—Yes we'll gather, etc.

Soon we'll gather at the river,
Soon our pilgrimage will cease;
Soon our happy hearts will quiver
With the melody of peace.

Chorus.—Yes we'll gather, etc.

12th Iowa's Fifth Reunion song sheet page 2

S. K. HOOPER, Commander
    Late 1st Lt. and Adjt. 23d Ind. Infty.
        Denver, Colo.

E. H. COOPER, Sr. Vice-Commander
    Late Maj. 1st Ill. Light Artillery, Chicago, Ill.

WM. P. DAVIS, Jr. Vice-Commander
    Late Lt. Col. 23d Infty., Washington, D.C.

REV. R. M. BARNES, Chaplain
    Late Chaplain 6th Ind. Infty., Denver, Colo.

S. M. FRENCH, Adjutant and Q. M.
    Late 12th Iowa Infantry
        3205 W. 26th Ave., Denver, Colo.

National Association
Battle of Shiloh
Survivors

HEADQUARTERS
318 EQUITABLE BUILDING

Denver, Colorado

SEPT. 15, 1905.

CIRCULAR LETTER NO. 1

TO THE SURVIVORS OF THE BATTLE OF SHILOH.

Sirs and Comrades:

It is with much gratification that I am enabled to announce as the result of a mass meeting held by the survivors of the Battle of Shiloh on September 5th, 1905, during the 39th National Encampment of the G. A. R. at Denver, the formation of a National Association of the comrades who participated in that ever-memorable engagement.

There were approximately three hundred comrades at the meeting, which was enthusiastic indeed, and the proceedings most harmonious. The proposition to form a National Association was adopted without a dissenting voice, as was also the constitution, which you will find printed in full on a following page, and from which you will learn that the name adopted for our organization is "The National Association of the Battle of Shiloh Survivors."

The election of national officers resulted in the selection of Comrades S. K. Hooper, of Denver, Colo., as Commander; E. H. Cooper, of Chicago, Ill., as Senior Vice-Commander; W. P. Davis, of Washington, D. C., as Junior Vice-Commander; S. M. French, of Denver, Colo., as Adjutant and Quartermaster, and R. M. Barnes, of Denver, Colo., as Chaplain.

It may be of interest to you to know that we have now enrolled the names of some 900 Shiloh veterans who have thus expressed a desire to become members, about 230 of whom have paid the admission fee and received the certificate, thereby completing their membership, while the number is increasing rapidly. As the simple enrollment does not constitute membership, it is respectfully requested that those who have enrolled and not remitted the fee for certificate of membership do so at once; and all others who participated in this eventful battle are urgently solicited to forward their names with the admission fee of fifty cents, upon receipt of which a certificate of life membership will be forwarded, and, as you will note by the constitution, no other fees or dues of any character will thereafter be required.

It is also the earnest desire of the Commander and the unanimously expressed wish of the Association, at its first meeting, that in every locality where there is any considerable number of comrades who participated in the Battle of Shiloh that they form themselves into local associations, and that each State or each Department of the G. A. R. have its State or Department Association of the Battle of Shiloh Survivors, to be conducted as suggested in the constitution. I am advised that there are a number of these local associations already formed in different localities, and it is urgently requested that all such organizations become members of and attach themselves to the national organization, and with this end in view communicate directly with the Adjutant and Quartermaster of the National Association, whose address is given above. Each

Shiloh Battle Survivors organization letter 1905 pg 1

State or Department Association should forward at once to the Adjutant and Quartermaster the name of one comrade from such association, who will be enrolled as a member of the Executive Committee, as provided by the constitution.

This communication will be sent to comrades in the various localities that have not as yet formed local associations, as well as to those who have, with the hope that all who receive it will interest themselves in forming such local associations and push along the good work, or at least that comrades within the locality forward their names to the Adjutant and Quartermaster for direct membership in the National Association, although to add interest it is preferable that all comrades have membership in a local as well as the National Association.

While there are no fees or dues required, other than that provided by the constitution, yet with the idea that all members of our organization would be desirous of having a distinguishing badge to be worn during G. A. R. functions, the Association adopted a very handsome gold-plated metal badge, which will be furnished members and forwarded by mail on the payment of $1.00. There were two hundred of these badges manufactured and all of them have been disposed of, but another order has been placed and the badges will be forwarded without additional expense on receipt of the price. While it is not obligatory that any member of the Association shall be the possessor of this badge, yet it is desirable that every member, as nearly as possible, be provided therewith.

At the Encampment in Denver the Commander-in-Chief of the G. A. R. entered cordially into the idea of the formation of an Association of the Survivors of the Battle of Shiloh, and in furtherance of that end, in advance of our having perfected an organization, assigned us a prominent place in the first day's parade, on which occasion we turned out 504 strong, being a larger number than of any other similar organization in the parade, bearing aloft a most magnificent banner which had been presented by patriotic citizens of Denver.

With a membership such as we should be able to enroll within the next twelve months, we should go to the Encampment at Minneapolis in 1906 with an attendance in line sufficiently great to make it one of the principal features of the occasion. To accomplish this it is only necessary for each comrade to whom this circular is sent to complete his own membership and to do a little missionary work in having other comrades make the proper application for membership certificate.

Forty-three years have passed since this memorable battle, where thousands of our comrades laid down their lives, and an army of them have gone maimed through life as a result of wounds received there, and as each year passes the number of its survivors is gradually growing less, and it certainly seems meet that we who survived the terrible slaughter should keep alive the memory of the eventful occasion which more than any other decided the issues in favor of the Union army. That the glory of our victory may be handed down to future generations, there is no more appropriate or fitting way to perpetuate the memory of this historic event than that its survivors should band themselves together in this fraternal way and continue the organization as long as there are any yet left who participated in the engagement. The day is not far distant when there will be but one remaining to recount the glory of it. Who will it be?

Sincerely yours, in F., C. and L.,

S. K. Hooper
Commander.

J. W. French
Adjutant and Quartermaster.

Shiloh Battle Survivors organization letter 1905 pg 2

CONSTITUTION

of the

National Association of Battle of Shiloh Survivors

NAME.

The name of this organization shall be "National Association of Battle of Shiloh Survivors."

OBJECT.

The object of the Association is to perpetuate the memories, collect data of that historical engagement, and to nurture fraternal feeling among those who participated, through meetings, discussions, relating of personal incident, and social functions.

MEMBERSHIP.

All Union Soldiers, Sailors and Marines who participated in the Battle of Shiloh on the 6th or 7th day of April, 1862, may become members, and the members of their immediate families honorary members.

OFFICERS.

The officers of this Association shall be a Commander, Senior and Junior Vice-Commander, Chaplain, Adjutant, and Quartermaster, to be elected and installed at each annual meeting.

MEETINGS.

The meetings of this Association shall be held at the times and places of the meetings of the National Encampment G. A. R.

In each Department of the G. A. R. local associations may be formed.

It is suggested that local associations hold annual meetings on the date of the battle, and forward to the National Adjutant, immediately thereafter, copies of the programs and historical data of such meetings.

Special meetings, national or local, may be held at any time, on call of the Commander.

EXECUTIVE COMMITTEE.

The Executive Committee shall be the officers of the Association, and one member from each organized department association to be elected at the annual meeting. They shall transact all business pertaining to the welfare of the Association, and report to the annual meeting.

EXPENSES.

A nominal admission fee of fifty cents shall be paid by, and a certificate of membership be issued to each member on entering the Association, and no other fees or dues shall be required.

Shiloh Battle Survivors organization letter 1905 pg 3

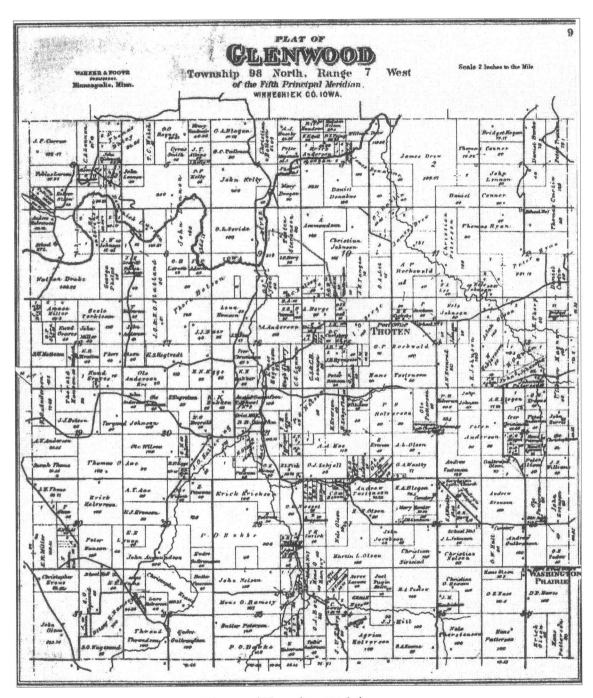

Glenwood Township 1886 close up.

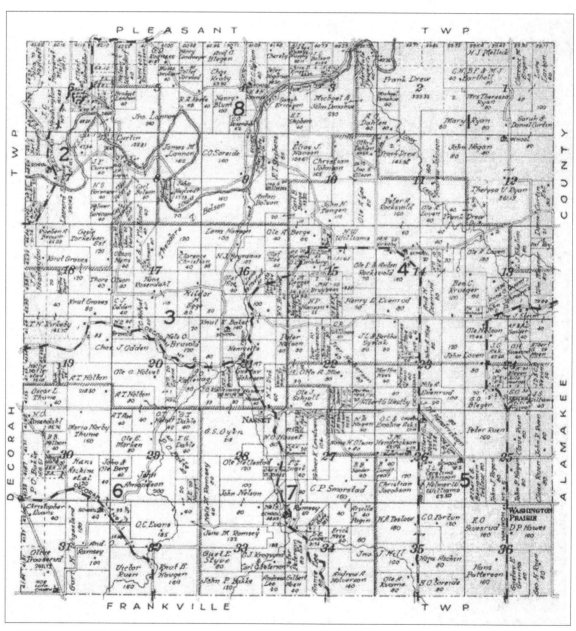

Glenwood Township 1915 close up.

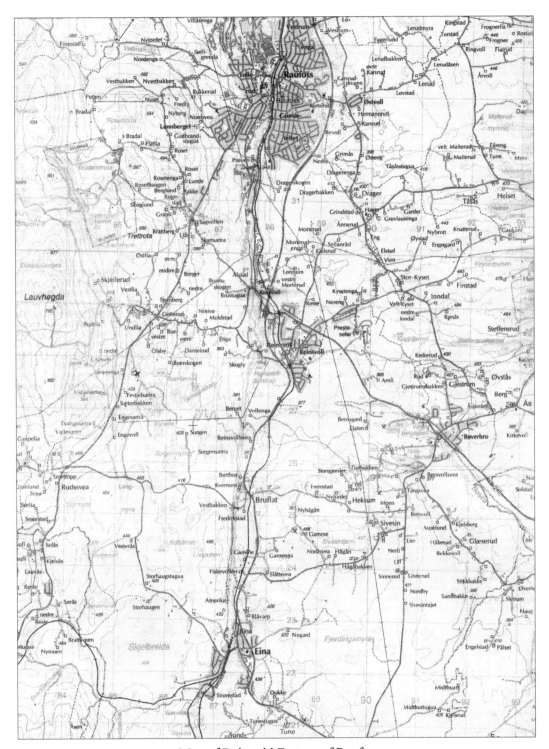

Map of Roksvold Farm s. of Raufoss

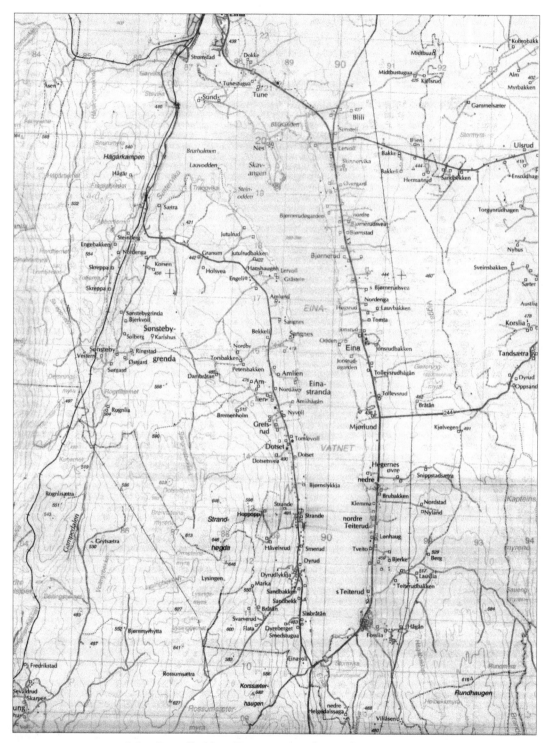

Map Strandbakken Farm near w. shore of Eina-Vatnet

Ole's ledger book.

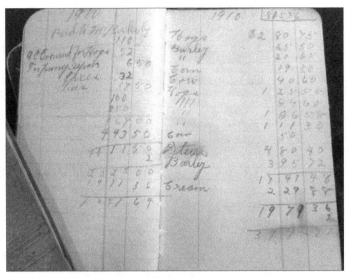

Interior page of a ledger book of Ole's.

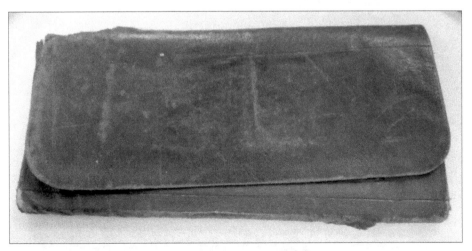

Another ledger book of Ole's.

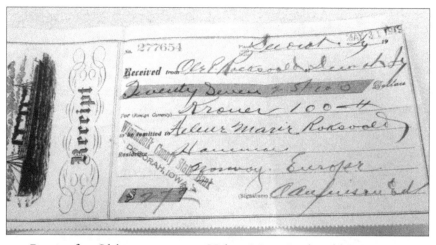

Receipt for Ole's money sent to Helene Marie Rocksvold in Norway

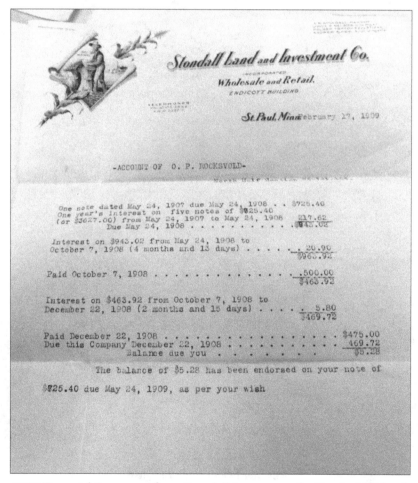

1909 Financial Statement from Stondall Investment for Beach, ND land.

FOR THE RECORDS OF **Totenlaget.**

Of the following questions answer such as you can or will; or give the information in any way you may find convenient. Use English or Norwegian. Where the spaces are too small use additional sheets of any suitable paper. If preferred or more convenient, all information may be given on other paper, without reference to this blank. Write all names of persons in full, giving first the form used here; then the full Norwegian form, with "farsnavn" and "gaardsnavn" or "pladsnavn". With the name of "gaard" or "plads" indicate divisions, as "nørre-", "sørre-", "uppi (gaarden)", etc., and the "bygd" or annex should be stated. Return the blanks as soon as filled.

Use two of these blanks for husband and wife.

1. Your name / Dit navn — *Ole P Rocksvold*

2. Address / Adresse — *Decorah Iowa R # D # 6*

3. Original Norwegian form of name if any change has been made / Den oprindelige norske form, hvis navnet er forandret — ....

4. Date of birth / Fødselsdato — *30te Marsi 1832*

5. Place of birth / Fødested — *paa gaarden Rocksvold Vsten*

6. Time of emigration of self or family...... / Hvad tid reiste De eller familie fra Norge — *Vaaren 1853*

7. Name of ship in which you or family sailed / Navn paa det skib De eller familie kom med — *Seils Skib Deodata*

8. Place and date of landing / Naar og hvor kom De iland — *i Juuni 1853*

9. Places of residence and time in each / Deres bosteder i Amerika og hvorlængepaa hvert sted — *at Quebec in Canada County Wiconsis 2 Maaneder, resten av tid høet til Winneshiek County Iowa*

10. Occupation or profession / Beskjæftigelse eller profession — *farming*

11. Public offices filled and dates / Offentlige tillidshverv indehaft og hvilken tid — ....

12. Military service and rank / Krigstjeneste og rang — ....

13. Church connection / Kirkelig forbindelse — ....

Ole P. Rocksvold Totenlaget application

Ole's Tax receipt for land 1887

12th Iowa's Fifth Reunion program book from Oct. 10-12, 1894

On the left, a ribbon from a Democratic convention Ole attended as a delegate in Cedar Rapids, IA, Aug. 6, 1890. In the middle, the 12th Iowa, company G Infantry pin given out for a Civil War reunion. On the right, Ole's Totenlaget pin for the Syttende Mai (May 17, Norwegian Independence Day) celebration in 1914 in Minneapolis. Totenlaget is a Norwegian-American organization promoting goodwill and contact between immigrants and their descendants who are in the U.S. This organization also helps preserve history and helps people searching for family history.

Postcard of Hotel Maristuen at which Ole stayed on his return trip to Norway, in July, 1902. The hotel is near Laerdal and Vang, in western Norway near the Sognefjord and the Borgund Stave Church.

Boat transport document related to Ole's 1902 trip to Norway.

Deed from 1877 for land in Winneshiek County, IA of Ole and Anne Rocksvold.

Translation

Decorah Posten 10-3-1893

The Democratic County Convention met at the courthouse on Saturday, the 30th of September, with A. Bernass presiding.

Upon completion of the necessary preparations, nominations were opened for a representative to the legislature. The nominees were O. P. Rocksvold, Dan Shea, M. J. Volland, Dessow and I. Zuckmeyer.

In the first round of voting, Rocksvold received 54 votes, Shea 9, Volland 32, Adams 2, Dessow 6, Zuckmeyer 6.

In the final round, Rocksvold received 75 and Volland 40 votes, after which Mr. Rocksvold was declared to be the party's nominated candidate.

[The rest of the article that you have included has to do with voting for candidates for county treasurer and school superintendant. No mention of Ole.]

Translated by Jim Skurdall

Den demkratiske County Convention møbte i Courthuset Lørdag den 30te September. A Bernay presiderede.

Saasnart man blev færdig med de nødvendige Forberedelser, skred man til-værks med at nominere Repræsentant for Legislaturen. Nominerede blev O P Rockswold, Dan Shea, M J Bol-land, DeCow og J Zuckmeyer.

Ved første Prøve-Afstemning fik Rockswold 54 Stemmer, Shea 9, Bol-land 32, Adams 2, DeCow 6, Zuck-meyer 6.

Ved den endelige Afstemning fik Rockswold 75 og Bolland 40 Stemmer, hvorpaa Mr. Rockswold erklæredes at være Partiets nominerede Kandidat.

Det næste paa Listen var Kandidat for County-Kasserer-Embedet. Den al-mindelige Mening var, at den nuvæ-rende Kasserer Hr. Jæger var beretti-get til en Termin til, og han blev no-mineret ved Akklamation.

N. Norgard blev ved anden Stem-meafgivning nomineret med 66 over 48 for H. B. Corlett.

Til Skolesuperintendent-Embedet nævntes C. H. Balder, M. Foss og J. C. Clark. Ved første Afstemning fik Balder 60 Stemmer, Foss 14 og Clark 41 St.

Ved den endelige Afstemning fik Bal-der 63 og Clark 43 Stemmer, og Hr. Balder erklæredes nomineret.

Hr. Balders Navn bragtes for Kon-ventionen uden hans Vidende og Billie, og da han paa ingen Maade kan over-tage Embedet, om han skulde blive valgt, har han underrettet rette Ved-kommende om, at han ikke er Kandidat.

Translation

Decorah Posten 10-3-1893

The Democratic County Convention met at the courthouse on Saturday, the 30th of September, with A. Bernass presiding.

Upon completion of the necessary preparations, nominations were opened for a representative to the legislature. The nominees were O. P. Rocksvold, Dan Shea, M. J. Volland, Dessow and I. Zuckmeyer.

In the first round of voting, Rocksvold received 54 votes, Shea 9, Volland 32, Adams 2, Dessow 6, Zuckmeyer 6.

In the final round, Rocksvold received 75 and Volland 40 votes, after which Mr. Rocksvold was declared to be the party's nominated candidate.

[The rest of the article that you have included has to do with voting for candidates for county treasurer and school superintendant. No mention of Ole.]

Translated by Jim Skurdall

Decorah Posten 10-3-1893 Ole R. assembly run.

George P Rocksvold in household of Ole P Rocksvold, "United States Census, 1870"

Name:	George P Rocksvold
Event Type:	Census
Event Year:	1870
Event Place:	Iowa, United States
Gender:	Male
Age:	5
Race:	White
Race (Original):	W
Birth Year (Estimated):	1864-1865
Birthplace:	Iowa
Page Number:	22
Household ID:	152
Line Number:	28
Affiliate Name:	The U.S. National Archives and Records Administration (NARA)
Affiliate Publication Number:	M593
GS Film number:	000545925
Digital Folder Number:	004263731
Image Number:	00360

Household	Gender	Age	Birthplace
Ole P Rocksvold	M	38	Norway
Ann Rocksvold	F	30	Norway
George P Rocksvold	M	5	Iowa

Ole Rocksvold Family 1870 census pg 1

Matilda Rocksvold		F	3	Iowa
Charle O Rocksvold	*Carl Oscar*	M	1	Iowa
John Johnson		M	12	Norway

Sources

View document

Citing this Record

"United States Census, 1870," index and images, *FamilySearch* (https://familysearch.org/pal:/MM9.1.1/MDKQ-S8G : accessed 28 Nov 2013), George P Rocksvold in household of Ole P Rocksvold, Iowa, United States; citing p. , family 152, NARA microfilm publication M593, FHL microfilm 000545925.

Ole Rocksvold Family 1870 census pg 2

⇥ancestry library edition

Iowa, State Census Collection, 1836-1925

Name:	**Hilda O Rocksvold**
Birth Year:	abt 1879
Birth Place:	Winneshiek
Gender:	Female
Race:	White
Census Date:	1895
Residence State:	Iowa
Residence County:	Winneshiek
Locality:	Glenwood
Roll:	IA1885_413
Line:	27
Family Number:	14
Neighbors:	

Household Members:	Name	Age
	Ole P Rocksvold	62
	Anne O Rocksvold	54
	Carl O Rocksvold	26
	Amanda O Rocksvold	21
	Hilda O Rocksvold	16
	Anton O Rocksvold	14
	William O Rocksvold	12

Source Information:
Ancestry.com. *Iowa, State Census Collection, 1836-1925* [database on-line]. Provo, UT, USA: Ancestry.com
Operations Inc, 2007.
Original data: Microfilm of Iowa State Censuses, 1856, 1885, 1895, 1905, 1915, 1925 as well various special censuses
from 1836-1897 obtained from the State Historical Society of Iowa via Heritage Quest.

Description:
This database contains Iowa state censuses for the following years: 1856, 1885, 1895, 1905, 1915, and 1925. It also
includes some head of household censuses and other special censuses from 1836-1897. Information available for an
individual will vary according to the census year and the information requested on the census form. Some of the
information contained in this database though includes: name, age, gender, race, birthplace, marital status, and
place of enumeration.

Hilda Rocksvold 1895 census

Decorah Posten, Aug. 25, 1922

Pioneer laid to rest

O.P. Rocksvold, which as mentioned, MN, died in a daughter's home in Invood, Iowa, the 20th ds., becomes today Thursday buried at home and from Glenwood Church. At death, he was the oldest member of Pontoppidan congregation, and the Pastor Wm. Rasmussen officiated at the funeral, but Glenwood Church was kindly left to the occasion, having larger and more spacious room than Pontoppidan's. Ole P. Rocksvold was born at Toten, Norway, the 30th of March1832 and came with his parents, a Twin sister and a younger Brother to America in 1853. After only a month stay in Yorkville, WI, joined the family directly to Glenwood Township, where they bought the farm, which has since without interruption remained the Home of the deceased.

Rocksvold enlisted in 1861 in Co. B. of Iowa volunteer infantry and served for three years and two months, was at the Battle of Shiloh together with others of his Company taken prisoner and remained captured about five months in captivity, resulting in a short time in the notorious Libby Prison. Exchanged and again the final tender for the reorganized Regiment he was in February 1863 at the Battle of Vicksburg and later with Sherman and Grant's Army under these generals' affluent Campaigns. He was wounded at Pleasant Hill in Louisiana, and he has to sit out the rest Life a cargo of "buckshot" in his one hip, like he was during the Battle of Shiloh got a ramrod through his hand - something he did not intend worth mentioning. He mustered out in Rathville, Tenn., the 7th of December 1864 and came back to Glenwood for an immediate start as a farmer.

Rocksvold was married 12th February 1865 to Anna Gilbertson, who bore him three sons and four daughters. The mother died July 4, 1895th. One son died in an infant age, three sons and one daughter, named George, Theodore, Norman, and Mrs.. A. Amundrud, having reached mature age. The surviving Born is Mrs.. A.O.Anderson, of Inwood, Iowa, Charles of Oakwood, ND; Miss Manda Rocksvold, Mrs. Ed Onstad of Argusville, ND and of William Beach, ND.

Five years ago began ... that fail old Rocksvold, and the last three years, he was completely blind. He was, as I said, the oldest member of Pontoppidan congregation, and so longstanding forces allowed his place in the Church never to be empty during church service. It was last May 30th end of which that he followed his daughter out of her Home in Inwood, where he shut his eyes Sunday 20th August. He obtained the old age of 90 years, 4 months and 21days.

Pioneer lagt tilhvile

O. P. Rocksvold, der som for naevnet afgik ved Doden i en Datters Hjem i Invood, Iowa, den 20de ds., bliver i dag Torsdag begravet fra Hjemmet og fra Glenwood Kirke. Af dode var aeldste Medlem af Pontoppidan Menighed, og Past., Wm. Rasmussen forrettede ved begravelesen, men Glenwood Kirke blev velvillig overladt for Anledningen, da den, der storre og mer rummelig en Pontoppdans. Ole P. Rocksvold var fodt paa Toten, Norge, den 30te Marts 1832 og kom med sine Foraeldre, en Tvillingsoster og en yngre Broder til Amerika i 1853. Efter kun Maaneder Ophold i Yorkville, Wis., kom Familien direkte til Glenwood Township, hvor de kjobte den Farm som siden uden Afbrydelse blev Afdodes Hjem.

Rocksvold hvervede sig i 1861 i Co. B. af Iowa frivillige Infanteri og tjente i tre Aar og to Maaneder, blev under Slaget ved Chiloh sammen med andre af sit Kmopani tagen til fange og forblev omkring fem Maaneder i dette Fangenskab, deraf en kort Tid i det beryktede Libby Faengselet. Udvexlet og igjen sluttender sig til det reorganiserede Regiment var han i Februar 1863 med Kampen ved Vicksburg og senere med Sherman og Grants Arme under disse Generales afluttende Felttog. Han blev saaret ved Plesant Hill i Louisiana, og han har for Resten af sit Liv en Ladning "buck shot" i sin ene Hofte, ligesom han under Slaget ved Chiloh fik en Ladestok gjennem sin ene Haand - noget han dog ikke agtede vaerd at naevne. Han afmonstredes i Rathville, Tenn., den 7de Dec 1864 og kom tilbage til Glenwood for strax at begynde som farmer.

Rocksvold blev 12te Februar 1865 gift med Anna Gilbertson, som fodte ham tre Sonner og fire Dotre. Moderen dode 4de Juli 1895. En Son dode i en spaed Alder, tre Sonner og en Datter, nemlig George, Theodore, Norman, og Mrs. A. Amundrud, efter at have opnaaet moden Alder. De gienlevende Born er Mrs. A.O. Anderson af Inwood, Iowa, Carl af Oakwood, N. Dak.: Miss Manda Rocksvold, Mrs. Ed Onstad af Argusville, N. Dak., og William af Beach, N. Dak.

For fem Aar siden begyndte Sy net at svigte gamle Rocksvold, og de sidste tre Aare var han fuldstaendig blind. Han var, som sagt, det aeldste Medlem af Pontoppidan Menighed, og saalenge Kraefterne tillod det var hans Plads i Kirken aldrig tom under Gudstjenesten. Det var sistleden 30te Mai at han fulgte sin Datter ud til hendes Hjem ved Inwood, og der fik han lukke sine Oine Sondag den 20de Aug. Han opnaaede den hoye Alder af 90 Aar, 4 Maaneder og 21 Dage.

From Winneshiek County Biographies

Ole P. Ruksvold. farmer and postmaster, Thoton P. 0.; owns 160 acres in Sec. 14, and 100 acres in Sec. 15; was born in Norway in 1832; was reared on a farm; came to the U.S. in 1853 and located in Wis., but only remained there two months; then came to Winneshiek Co., and bought a farm in Sec. 11, on which he lived several years, which he since sold to his brother in 1860, and then bought where he now resides. In 1861 he enlisted in Co. G, 12th lo. Inf., and served three years and two months. He received promotion to corporal at Pittsburg Landing, two days before he was taken prisoner at Shiloh. The rebels took him with other prisoners to Mobile, Cahaba, and then to Macon, Ga., where he was kept about five months, and then to Libby Prison, where he was confined ten days and exchanged at Aiken's Landing, on the James River. He was then taken to Annapolis and afterwards to St. Louis, where the regiment was reorganized, and then went to Vicksburg in Feb., 1863, and went through the campaign with Sherman and Grant. He was wounded at Pleasant Hill, on the Red River, La., being shot in the thigh with buck shot, which he still carries with him as an unpleasant reminder of those interest ing days. He was disharged at Nashville, Tenn., Dec. 7, 1864, and returned to lo. and resumed farming. He is one of the oldest settlers and prominent citizens, and has been a member of the board of county supervisors two terms, besides having held many township offices; is a republican in politics. Mr. R. was married in 1865 in this tp., to Miss Anna Gilbertson; they have eight children. During the war his farm was carried on by his younger brother, Anton P. Rucksvold, who now owns the farm in Sec. 11. He is a prominent citizen and has filled every office in the tp.; was married in 1873 in this tp., to Miss Anna Amundson.

WINNESHIEK COUNTY BIOGRAPHIES. 637

[This article, sent to the author from Winneshiek County Historical Society, is printed as it was originally written. It contains some information and alternate spellings that differ from some of the sources in this book and didn't contain a date when it was written.]

Winneshiek County Atlas book 1905, page with Ole's chapter on
Glenwood Township

The Vote for Winnesheik for 1893.

TOWNSHIPS	GOVERNOR				SENATOR		REPTIVE			TREAS'R			SHERIFF			SUPT		
	Frank D. Jackson, rep	Horace Boies, dem	Bennett Mitchell, prohib	J. M. Joseph, people's	Clark C. Upton, rep	Geo. W. Adams, dem	W. H. Klemme, rep	O. F. Rockävold, dem	Geo. O. Thomas, prohib	Lew R. Whitney, rep	Henry Yager, dem	Elijah Johnson, prohib	Clarence Christian, rep	O. N. Norgard, dem	E. T. Gibbs, prohib	H. L. Godsen, rep	J. H. Hoye, dem	

Vote totals when Ole ran unsuccessfully for Iowa Assembly in 1893.

1893

O. P. Rocksvold, democratic candidate for representative, was in the city Saturday. All who met him were free to say he was a pleasant and good hearted man. There are very few men in the county who have a more thorough knowledge of public affairs than Mr. Rocksvold. A constant student of political issues, and a thoroughly honest and consciencious man, which qualifies him for the position the democracy of Winnesheik county has nominated him. He has resided near Thoten in Glenwood township for over forty years; is an old soldier, and Norwegian by birth. A vote for Rocksvold is a vote for honest government.

Article about Ole Rocksvold, endorsing him in his unsuccessful run for Iowa state assembly in 1893. Source of the article is unknown and was found as a clipping in a letter his daughter Matilda, wrote.

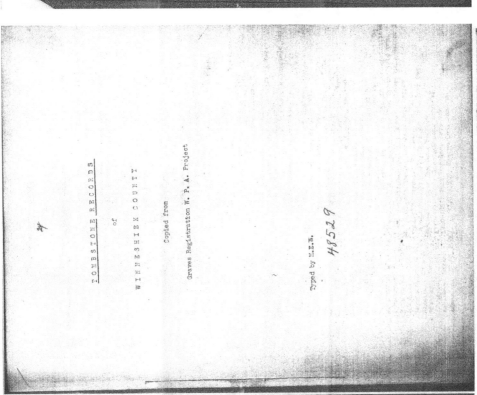

TOMBSTONE RECORDS

of

WINNESHIEK COUNTY

Copied from

Graves Registration W. P. A. Project

Typed by M.E.W.

48529

Robert, Hans E. 57, 1825-1882; Lutheran Cem. Decorah
Roberg, Jorgine, 85, 12/12/1848-7/12/1925; Lutheran Cem. Decorah
Robertson, Guy, 62, 1804-1866; Pagen Cem Frankville Twp.
Robinson, Claude A. died 10/3/1932; Burr Oak Cem. Burr Oak;
    Pvt. 117th Inf. 30th Div.
Robinson, Cynthia J. 86, 1835-1921; Freeport Cem. Freeport
Robinson, Heber, died 1998; Freeport Cem. Freeport;
    Pvt. Co. "B" 5th Minn. Inf. G.A.R.
Robinson, Janet, 38, 1837-1875; Hesper Cem. Hesper
Robinson, John, 20, 1870-1890; Hesper Cem. Hesper
Robinson, Inna F. 76, 1853-1929; Phelps Cem. Decorah
Robinson, Marietta, 52, 1852-1904; Freeport Cem. Freeport
Robinson, Sarah, 68, 1868-1936; Ridgeway Cem. Ridgeway
Robinson, Thomas, 46, 1854-1900; Burr Oak Cem. Burr Oak
Robinson, William, 76, 1823-1899; Hesper Cem. Hesper
Robinson, Mrs. William, 64, 1839-1903; Hesper Cem. Hesper
Roch, Elizabeth 67, 1834-1901; St. Agnes Cem. Burr Oak Twp.
Roch, Ellen A. 33, 6/24/1860-7/10/1893; Kierans Cem. Fremont Twp.
Roche, Margaret, 34, 3/17/1863-10/17/1897; Kierans Cem. Fremont Twp
Roche, Mary, 60, 1862-1922; Kierans Cem. Fremont Twp.
Roche, Lather, 46, 1827-1873; St. Agnes Cem. Burr Oak Twp.
Roche, Patrick, 46, 1859-1905; St. Agnes Cem. Burr Oak Twp.
Rocksvold, Anna, 56, 11/16/1839-7/4/1895; Glenwood Cem. Glenwood Twp.
Rocksvold, Anna, 69, 1848-1917; Glenwood Cem. Glenwood Twp.
Rocksvold, Anton P. 47, 3/17/1839-6/29/1886; Glenwood Cem. Glenwood Twp.
Rocksvold, Christian, 56, 1859-1915; Glenwood Cem. Glenwood Twp.
Rocksvold, George Paulus, 25, 11/14/1865-3/3/1890; Glenwood Cem. Glenwood Twp.
Rocksvold, Kirst, 96, 7/4/1799-3/9/1895; Glenwood Cem. Glenwood Twp.
Rocksvold, Norman A. 42, 1880-1922; Pontoppidan Cem. Glenwood Twp.
Rocksvold, Ole P. 90, 3/30/1832-8/20/1922; Glenwood Cem. Glenwood Twp.
    Pvt/ Co. "G" 12th Ia. Inf.
Rocksvold, Peder H. 87, 5/1/1798-3/12/1885; Glenwood Cem. Glenwood Twp.
Rocksvold, Peder H. no dates; Glenwood Cem. Glenwood Twp.
Rocksvold, Theodor, 18, 2/27/1876-3/17/1894; Glenwood Cem. Glenwood Twp.
Rodenkirck, Mathias, 74, 1858-1932; St. Francis Cem. Ossian
Rodenkirck, Rosa, 62, 1865-1927; St. Francis Cem. Ossian
Rodland, Anna, 70, 1832-1902; Stone Church Cem. Milton Twp.
Rodland, Christian J. 56, 1/16/1829-7/7/1885; Stone Church Cem. Military Twp.
Rodland, Elling, 83, 1831-1914; Stone Church Cem. Military Twp.
Rodlene, Elisabeth, 69, 1846-1915; Stanager Cem. Military Twp.
Rodline, Jens, 38, 1865-1903; Stanager Cem. Military Twp.
Rodvaang, Marit, 89, 4/25/1813-6/4/1902; Washington P-airie Cem. Springfield Twp.
Rodvaang, Ole A. 66, 11/18/1818-1/5/1884; Washington Prairie Cem. Springfield Twp.
Rogers, Francis, 74, 1804-5/23/1877; Young Farm Cem. Washington Twp.
Rognlien, Bertha, 62, 1821-1883; Washington Prairie Cem. Springfield Twp.
Ragnlein, Marie, 63, 10/1/1866-2/27/1929; Washington Prairie Cem. Springfield Twp.
Ragnelein, Nels H. 75, 2/4/1858-8/27/1933; Washington Prairie Cem. Springfield Twp.
Roinestal, Anna S. 63, 4/6/1825-2/18/1888; Stone Church Cem. Military Twp.
Rolfshus, Adelia, 17, 1891-1911; Hesper Lutheran Cem. Hesper
Rolfshus, Bennett G. 32, 1875-1907; Hesper Lutheran Cem. Hesper
Rolfshus, Christina, 21, 11/28/1877-8/20/1898; Hesper Lutheran Cem. Hesper
Rolfsus, Mrs. O. K. 82, 1811-1893; HesperLutheran Cem. Hesper
Rolfsus, O. K. 8/1/1816-6/25/1906; Hesper Lutheran Cem. Hesper
Rollins, Alvin, 65, 1855-1920; Burr Oak Cem. Burr Oak
Rollins, Charles, died Dec. 25, 1870-Decorah, Phelps Cem.
Rollins, Clayton E. 49, 1850-1899; Burr Oak Cem. Burr Oak

Winneshiek County Iowa Cemetery

1854 Bible of Anne Strandbakken Rocksvold,
Ole's wife.

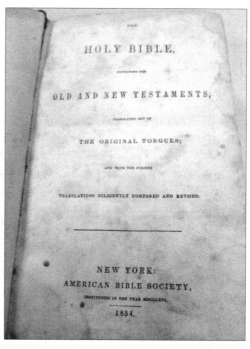

1854 Bible Title page from Anne
Rocksvold's Bible.

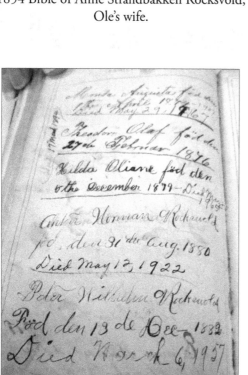

Interior Page of Anne Rocksvold's Bible
showing some genealogical information.

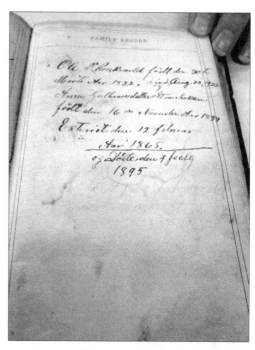

1854 Bible interior page with Ole
and Anne's dates written in.

Willie Rocksvold's Farm near Beach, ND

93

Parties	Date	By whom
Jacob Nilson Betsey Erickson	Nov. 5. 1863	P. Koren Minister
Knud Torguson Ingeborg Alfsdatter	Dec. 7. 1863	Rev. P. Koren
Erick Bendixon Sigbjornsdatter Gullong	Jany. 15. 1864	Rev. P. Koren
Ola Bjornson Löken Ingeborg Peterson	Jany 18, 1864	Rev. P. Koren
Gunnar Helgison Gunhild Evensdatter	May 28. 1864	Rev. P. Koren
Orm Osmundson Ellen Peterson	May 24, 1864	Rev. P. Koren
Christffer Knudson Ostram Anna Olesen	July 12. 1864	Rev. P. Koren
Mons Hanson Anna Pederson	Dec. 31, 1864	Rev. P. Koren
Ola H. Olesen Kristi Monsen	Jany 1st 1865	Rev. P. Koren
Ole P. Rockswold Anna Gulbranson	Feby 12. 1865	Rev. P. Koren

Marriage Record of Ole Rockswold, Anne Gulbrandson Strandbakken 1865

PICTURES
OLE, ANNE, CHILDREN

Matilda Anderson and Hilda Ohnstad, daughters of Ole and Anne Rocksvold taken in 1950, location unknown

From left: Matilda, Hilda, Peter William (Willie), and Anton Norman (Norman) Rocksvold, Ole and Anne's children, in Decorah, IA, 1892

Ole Rocksvold, probably at the occasion of a Civil War reunion, date
unknown, probably 1870-1880, Location unknown, likely IA

From left: Matilda Rocksvold Anderson, her husband Andrew (A.O.) Anderson, and Hilda Rocksvold Ohnstad, Matilda and Hilda were daughters of Ole and Anne Rocksvold. Picture likely taken 1940's-1951

Ole Rocksvold home, 1911, Beach, ND

Intersection of 258th St. and Glenville Road, Glenwood township,
Winneshiek County, IA
Glenville Road near here is where Ole and Anne Rocksvold's farm was.

Matilda Rocksvold, left, with students, and possibly friends.
Location likely near Decorah, IA. Probably taken in the late 1880's or early
1890's. Matilda was the daughter of Ole and Anne Rocksvold.

Ole Rocksvold's casket, taken by Decorah, IA, photographer.
Ole died Aug. 20, 1922 in Inwood, IA, at Matilda and A.O. Anderson's farm.
Portraits of Anne and Ole are on the walls.

Peter William Rocksvold, Ole and Anne Rocksvold's son.
Date probably early 1900's, location unknown, possibly near Decorah, IA, or Beach, ND.

Peter William (Willie) Rocksvold, son of Ole and Anne Rocksvold.
Date probably 1895-1900. Location, likely Decorah, IA.

Rocksvold family gravestone, Glenwood Lutheran Church cemetery,
Glenwood township, Winnishiek County, Iowa.

Author, Sharon Bowen, at Rocksvold family gravestone,
Glenwood Lutheran Church in background.
Location: Glenwood Church cemetery, Glenwood township,
Winneshiek County, IA, 2013

Ole Rocksvold in a horse-drawn buggy, 1915. Location unknown.

The watch Ole Rockvold gave his granddaughter, Irene Anderson (daughter of Matilda Rocksvold and A.O. Anderson), 1910. He also sent similar watches to granddaughters, Alberta and Olive Amunrud, (daughters of Emma Rockvold and Oscar Amunrud),the same year, as described in his letter to Irene Dec. 22, 1910.

Photos of Anne Strandbakken Rocksvold, left, and Ole Rocksvold, right
These pictures were visible in his home above Ole's casket upon his death
Aug. 20, 1922

Hilda Rocksvold Ohnstad, Ole and Anne Rocksvold's daughter
Date likely early 1900's

The current buildings on the property where Ole and Anne Rocksvold had their farm, Glenwood Township, Winneshiek County, IA, near the intersection of Glenville Road and 258th St., address: 1233 258th St., Decorah, IA 52101, picture taken in 2013. The small white building third from the left, was the original "Rocksvold School" which was moved from its original location that was further north on the same property many years ago. We know Ole's daughter, Matilda, became a teacher, but we aren't positive she taught in that specific school.

Ole's brother, Anton, lived near by at 1268 Coon Creek Road, Decorah, IA 52101.

From left, Carl Rocksvold (Ole's son), Ole, unknown friend?, Anton
Norman (Ole's son), unknown friend?, Andrew (A.O.) Anderson (Matilda's
husband and Ole's son-in-law)
Picture probably in the 1910's up to 1922, based the aged appearance of
Ole. Both Ole and Norman died in 1922

From left, Edward Ohnstad, Ole Rocksvold, Hilda Rocksvold Ohnstad
Location unknown, possibly the farm near Beach, ND where Ole, Willie,
and Hilda lived for a few years, or the Ohnstad farm near Argusville, ND.
Picture taken probably 1910-1913

Anne Guldbrandsdatter Strandbakken Rocksvold, Ole's future wife, in bunad, probably when she was in her teens, 1853-59?

PICTURES
OLE'S GRANDCHILDREN AND BEYOND

Laura Øistad Roseth. Taken in Montevideo, MN likely about 1898.

Laura was the daughter of Helene Marie Dahl and Bernt Øistad, and granddaughter of Helene Roksvold and Lar Dahl. She was the grandniece of Ole Rocksvold.

Laura Øistad Roseth and Hilda Roksvold Dahl Garaas, sisters.

Location and date unknown. Based on appearance/age, possibly in the 1890's. Laura and Hilda were the daughters of Helene Marie Dahl and Bernt Øistad, and granddaughter of Helene Roksvold and Lar Dahl. They were the grandnieces of Ole Rocksvold.

Hilda Roksvold Øistad Garaas, date unknown.
Location somewhere in Norway, likely near Hamar. Hilda is the daughter of Helene Marie Roksvold Dahl and Bernt Øistad, granddaughter of Helene Roksvold and Lars Dahl and grandniece of Ole and Anne Rocksvold. Helene was Ole's sister.

(BL) Hilman Roseth, son of Laura Øistad and Anton Roseth, grandson of Helene Marie Dahl and Bernt Øistad, great grandson of Helene Roksvold and Lars Dahl, grandnephew of Ole and Anne Rocksvold. Date - likely about 1912-14, location, Boyd, MN

(BR) Hilman and Maybelle Meade Rosseth
Hilman was the son of Laura Øistad and Anton Roseth. He was the grandson of Helene Marie Dahl and Bernt Øistad. He was the great grandson of Helene Roksvold and Lars Dahl. Taken at Cleveland, OH, 1979.

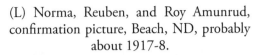

(L) Norma, Reuben, and Roy Amunrud, confirmation picture, Beach, ND, probably about 1917-8.

Norma, Reuben, and Roy were the children of Oscar and Emma Rocksvold Amunrud, grandchildren of Ole and Anne Rocksvold.

(BL) Genevieve and Owen Rocksvold

Children of Peter William (Willie) and Helen Bengtson Rocksvold, taken probably about 1922-23. They are the grandchildren of Ole and Anne Rocksvold.

(BR) Genevieve Rocksvold and Williard Asch, daughter of Peter Willie and Helen Rocksvold

Owen and Dorothy Carlson Rocksvold.
Son of Willie and Helen Rocksvold

Owen Rocksvold and Dorothy Carlson Rocksvold
during WW II.
Owen was the son Willie and Helen Bengtson Rocksvold,
grandson of Ole and Anne Rocksvold.

Pauline Evenrud and Paul Mickelson farm, Twin Valley, MN
Pauline was the daughter of Anne Mathea Rocksvold and Hans Evenrud, niece of Ole Rocksvold.

Pauline Evenrud and Paul Mickelson's wedding.
March 2, 1887, Decorah, IA.

Pauline is the daughter of Hans Evenrud and Anne Mathea Rocksvold Evenrud, Ole Rocksvold's twin.

Willis, Olive, Roy Milliron, A.O. Anderson, Alice Anderson. 1952, probably IA.

Willis is the son of Olive and Roy. Olive is the daughter of Oscar Amunrud and Emma Rocksvold and the granddaughter of Ole and Anne Rocksvold. A.O. is the husband of Mathilda Rocksvold, Ole's daughter. Alice is the granddaughter of A.O. and Mathilda Anderson and the daughter of George Anderson and Minnie Munson.

Rocksvold cousins group shot about 1912, likely near Decorah, IA

From left in back row: six from the left is Irene Anderson, seventh from left, her father, A.O. Anderson, husband of Matilda Rocksvold, Ole's daughter. In second row of adults from the front: second person from right is Matilda Rocksvold Anderson, Ole's daughter.

Johanne Sonsteby Grefsrud
with her children

Johanne is the daughter of Pernille Sonsteby, granddaughter of Iver Hansen, who was the maternal uncle of Anne Standbakken's Ole Rocksvold's wife.

Hans Sonsteby Grefsrud and Johanne Karine Sonsteby, with son Per.

Johanne is the daughter of Pernille Sonsteby, granddaughter of Iver Hansen, who was the maternal uncle of Anne Standbakken's Ole Rocksvold's wife.

Johanna Sonsteby Grefsrud relatives, from cousin Hans Gresfrud's photos in Hadeland, Norway
Johanna is descended from Iver Hansen Sonsteby, brother of Marthe Eggebraaten. Marthe was the
sister of Anne Strandbakken, Ole Rocksvold's wife.

Pernille and Paul Grefsrud Jacobson, likely near West Moe, MN, near Alexandria.

Pernille is the daughter of Kari Egge and Iver Hanson Eggebraaten Sonsteby. Iver was maternal uncle of Anne Strandbakken Rocksvold, Ole Rocksvold's wife.

Wedding picture of Ernest and Bernice Anderson, IA
From left: Ernest Anderson, Bernice Yost, with attendants Laura Sauke, George Anderson (brother of Ernest)
Ernest, George, and Irene Anderson were the children of Matilda Rocksvold and A.O. Anderson, and grandchildren of Ole and Anne Rocksvold.

Edward and Hilda Rocksvold Ohnstad Family
L-R, back; Vernon, Esther, Norman, Olive. L-R, front: Edward, Florence, Hilda
Hilda is the daughter of Ole and Anne Rocksvold.
Taken probably about 1939-42, location probably Fargo, ND or Moorhead, MN
Last formal picture of this family before Vernon was killed as a soldier in a vehicular
accident in OK in WWII 2-26-42. His father, Edward, died 3-31-43.

Roy Rocksvold and Joanne Criss, 1947
Roy was the son of A. Norman and Tilda Foss
Rocksvold, grandson of Ole and Anne Rocksvold.

Oscar Amunrud, with twin children Ruben, Roy, and daughter Magdalene (Mother was Emma Rocksvold, Ole and Anne Rocksvold's daughter)
Location near Beach, ND, date probably about 1910-11

Ida Kirkeby and Olaf Crogan, about 1890's. Ida is daughter of Anton Kirkeby and Mathilda (Tilla) Evenrud, granddaughter, great granddaughter of Anne Mathea Rocksvold and Hans Evenrud. Anne Mathea was the twin sister of Ole Rocksvold.

John Trollope and Alberta Amunrud Trollope, probably taken in about 1950's,
perhaps in western ND or eastern MT.
Alberta was the daughter of Emma Rocksvold and Oscar Amunrud,
granddaughter of Ole and Anne Rocksvold.

Russel Rocksvold with his sons in 1977, Iowa
Russel Rocksvold is the son of Peter Rocksvold, grandson of Anton Rocksvold
(the brother of Ole Rocksvold)
Left to right: Edsel, Craig, Russel, Peter, and Kersten Rocksvold

Rocksvold brothers with some of their sons, Oct. 3, 2015, Iowa

Craig, Peter, and Kersten are sons of Russel Rocksvold, grandsons of Peter Rocksvold, and great grandsons of Anton Rocksvold (brother of Ole Rocksvold).

Front from left to right: Craig, Peter, Kersten

Back from left to right: Jeff (son of Edsel-not pictured), Andy (son of Peter), Luke (son of Craig), Matt (son of Edsel)

Robert and Judy Rosseth.

Bob's parents were Hilman and Maybelle Meade Rosseth (originally Roseth). His grandparents were Laura Øistad and Anton Roseth. His great grandparents were Helene Marie Dahl and Bernt Øistad. His great great grandparents were Helene Roksvold and Lars Dahl. Taken in New Bern, NC., 2016. Helene was Ole Rocksvold's older sister.

Channey (Chandler), Rome, Colleen, David Mickelson

Children of Roy Mickelson. Another sibling, Paul, is deceased. Grandchildren of Pauline Evenrud and Paul Mickelson, great grandchildren of Anne Mathea Rocksvold and Hans Evenrud, grandniece and nephews of Ole Rocksvold.

Rocksvold cousins with the author, Sharon Bowen, in 2012, Decorah, IA:

Back from left: Darrel Crawford, Sharon Bowen, Craig Rocksvold, Peter Rocksvold, Kersten (Kert) Rocksvold. Front: Ione Rocksvold Crawford

Iona is the daughter of Peter and Ida Berge Rocksvold, granddaughter of Anton Rocksvold, Ole's brother. Darrel is Iona's son. Kert, Craig, and Peter are the sons of Russel Rocksvold and Emma Swehla, grandchildren of Peter and Ida Berge Rocksvold, great grandsons of Anton and Anne Elvestuen Rocksvold, great grandnephews of Ole Rocksvold. Not pictured is Russel and Emma's son, Edsel.

The wedding day of Olive Ohnstad and Phillip Timmer, June 22, 1946, Moorhead, MN
Olive was the daughter of Hilda and Ed Ohnstad, and the granddaughter of Ole and Anne Rocksvold.

Skylar, Steve and Sheila Holm Timmer, 2012, Moorhead, MN
Steve is the son of Phil and Olive Ohnstad Timmer, grandson of Hilda and Ed Ohnstad, and great grandson of Ole and Anne Rocksvold.

Don Erstad and Donnie Ueckert Erstad
2014, Fargo, ND

Donnie is the daughter of Marilyn Trollope and Ervin Ueckert, granddaughter of Alberta Amunrud and John Trollope, greatdaughter of Emma Rocksvold and Oscar Amunrud, great great granddaughter of Ole and Anne Rocksvold.

Donie Ueckert Erstad and Don Erstad Family, April 2017, Fargo, ND.
Back row, from left: Donie Ueckert Erstad, Don Erstad, their son, Shane Erstad, holding his son, Adam. Front row, from left: Tricia Erstad, Shane's wife, their daughter Chelsea Erstad, Ashley Jenniges, Tyler Jenniges, and Don and Donie's daughter, Sheila Erstad Jenniges, Tony Jenniges.
Donie Ueckert Erstad is the daughter of Marilyn Trollope Ueckert and Ervin Ueckert, granddaughter of Alberta Amunrud Trollope, great granddaughter of Emma Rocksvold Amunrud and Oscar Amunrud, great great granddaughter of Ole and Anne Rocksvold.

Edward and Esther Ohnstad Randash in the 1960's, Great Falls, Montana
Esther was the daughter of Hilda and Ed Ohnstad, and the granddaughter of Ole and Anne Rocksvold.

From left: Five Cousins: Norrine Amunrud Lunde, Marlene Amunrud Welliever, Dorothy Forder, Sharon Bowen, Dee Seay Taken July, 2015, Wibaux, MT.

Norrine and Marlene are sisters, daughters of Roy and Norma Stockwell Amunrud, granddaughters of Emma Rocksvold and Oscar Amunrud, great granddaughters of Ole and Anne Rocksvold. Dorothy and Dee are sisters, daughters of Esther Ohnstad and Ed Randash, granddaughters of Hilda Rocksvold and Ed Ohnstad, great granddaughters of Ole and Anne Rocksvold. Sharon Bowen is the daughter of Florence Ohnstad and Ed Smith, granddaughter of Hilda and Ed Ohnstad, great granddaughter of Ole and Anne Rocksvold.

Ed and Florence Ohnstad Smith Family Reunion, Christmas, 2014, New Brighton, MN.
Florence was the daughter of Hilda Rocksvold and Ed Ohnstad, and granddaughter of Ole and Anne Rocksvold.
From left back row: Sharon Smith Bowen, Joel Chitwood, Katie Will, Nathan Kalmoe, Ryan Smith Sherman Smith, Stan Smith, Max Bowen
From left front row: Nancy Hann Smith, Summer Smith Chitwood, Vincent Smith, baby Theo Smith, Elizabeth Carter Smith. Children of Ed and Florence: Stan, Sharon, Sherman.
Spouses: Sharon with Max, Nancy with Stan, Katie with Nathan, Elizabeth with Ryan, Summer with Joel. The little ones, Vincent and Theo, are those of Ryan and Elizabeth Smith.

Wedding picture of Florence Ohnstad and Edward Smith, 7-24-1945, Moorhead, MN

Florence was the granddaughter of Ole and Anne Rocksvold, daughter of Hilda and Ed Ohnstad, and Florence and Ed were the parents of the author, Sharon Smith Bowen, plus sons Stan and Sherman Smith.

Florence and Ed Smith Family, 2000, New Brighton, MN

Florence was the daughter of Hilda and Ed Ohnstad, and granddaughter of Ole and Anne Rocksvold.
From left front: Sherman Smith, Florence Ohnstad Smith, Cowboy her dog, Ryan Smith, Nathan Kalmoe
From left back: Stan Smith, Nancy Hann Smith, Summer Smith, Sharon Smith Bowen, Max Bowen.
Summer and Ryan are Stan and Nancy Hann Smith's children. Nathan is the son of Sharon Bowen.
Max is Sharon's husband.

Fred and Gale Hagen Family
From left: Nate, Gale, Fred, Eric, Aaron
Fred is descended from Ole Sivesind Hagen, brother of Peder Hanson Rocksvold, Ole's father.

From left: Dorothy Randash Forder, Sharon Smith Bowen, Dee Randash Seay, and Dean Randash, July, 2015, Helena, MT.

Quadruplets Dorothy, Dee, Dean, and Donna were born to Ed and Esther Ohnstad Randash. Sadly, Donna died shortly after birth. These surviving triplets are the grandchildren of Hilda Rocksvold and Ed Ohnstad, and great grandchildren of Ole and Anne Rocksvold. The triplets are first cousins of Sharon since Sharon's mother, Florence Ohnstad Smith, was Esther's sister.

Siblings: Dorothy Forder, Ed Randash, and Delores (Dee) Seay, with author Sharon Bowen, in Billings, MT, July, 2015. Sadly, Ed died Oct. 2, 2015.

Dorothy, Ed, and Dee (along with Dean, not pictured), are the children of Ed and Esther Ohnstad Randash, grandchildren of Hilda Rocksvold and Ed Ohnstad, great grandchildren of Ole and Anne Rocksvold. Sharon is first cousin of these Randashes, since they share the same grandparents, Hilda and Ed Ohnstad.

∽ APPENDIX 7 ∾

TRIP TO NORWAY
PICTURES OF AUTHOR AND HUSBAND

Norlien School, where Helene Rocksvold Dahl's son, Karl, and grandson, Lars, taught. Vestre Toten, Oppland, Norway. Photo 2014. Helene was Ole Rocksvold's older sister who didn't emigrate with the rest of the family to the U.S.

Toten specialty rolls at Rocksvold-Strandbakken cousin party, 2014, Vestre Toten, Oppland, Norway

Amazing Toten specialities at the Rocksvold-Strandbakken cousin party, 2014,
Vestre Toten, Oppland, Norway

Toten Almond Cake Tower, at Rocksvold-Strandbakken cousin party,
Vestre Toten, Oppland, Norway

Raddum cousins at Rockvold-Strandbakken cousin party. 2014,
Vestre Toten, Oppland, Norway.

Cousins at Rocksvold-Strandbakken party, Vestre Toten, Oppland, Norway 2014.
Max Bowen, Sharon's husband, in center back of picture.

Raddum Cousins at Rocksvold-Strandbakken cousin party 2014

Party for Rocksvold cousins (Raddum family members) and Strandbakken cousins (Gresfrud family members) to meet Sharon and Max Bowen. Also pictured are Rune Nedrud and Mette Nordengen, genealogists, on the left.

Liv and Håkon Raddum, of Skreia, Vestre Toten, Oppland, Norway.
He is a Rocksvold cousin. 2014.
They very generously hosted a big party of Rocksvold and Strandbakken cousins when we visited, uniting both sides of the author's ancestors, some of whom had never met.

Valg Church inscription, church built in 1814, where Anne Strandbakken's (Ole's wife), family were members while living on the Eggebraaten/Egge farmland.

Aas Church inscription. The latest building of the church was built in 1921. The original building, the one Ole Rocksvold's family were members, was built in 1789. It burnt in 1915.

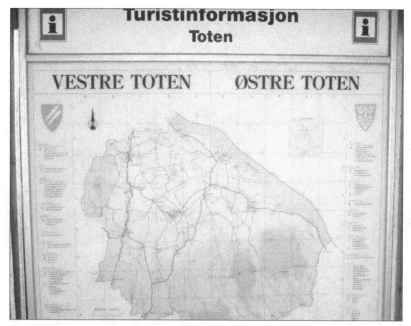

Toten area map. Ole Rocksvold's farm was in Vestre Toten on the Roksvoll farm. There have been a variety of spellings for Rocksvold through the years.

Sharon Bowen, Håkon and Sveinung Raddum, Mette Nordengen, 2014, Vestre Toten, Oppland, Norway

The Raddum brothers are cousins of Sharon's on the Rocksvold side. They are descended from Ole's sister, Helene, who was the only member of Ole's nuclear family growing up that didn't emigrate with them to the U.S. Mette Nordengen's research made it possible for us to meet.

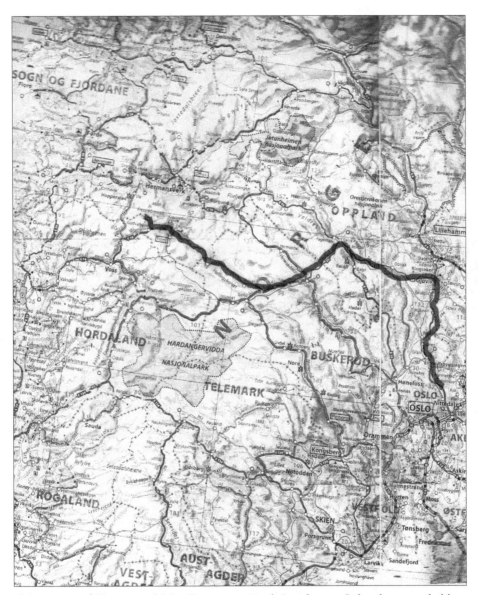

Trip route of Sharon and Max Bowen in 2014. Landing is Oslo, they traveled by car to visit relatives in the Hadeland area, Vestre Toten, Oppland region, then to Aurland, Vestland, Sogne Fjordane region on the west coast.

Sharon Bowen, Hans and Inger Guro Gresfrud, June, 2014,
at their home in Brandbu, Hadeland, Norway
Hans is descended from Marthe Eggebraaten's brother Iver Hansen Sonsteby. Marthe
was the mother of Anne Strandbakken, Ole Rocksvold's wife.

All cousins at Andreas' and Anders Markus' confirmation, Sept 1. 2013: Anders Markus, Andreas, Lene Christine, Hilde Karine, Elle Marit, Anne Therese, Maren Helen, Silje Agnethe and Juliane.

Sept. 1. 2013. Hans Grefsrud, Per Fossheim, Elle Marit Grefsrud, Eli Grefsrud (Hans' siste), Andreas Fossheim, Anders Grefsrud, Inger Guro M. Grefsrud, Juliane Fossheim, Anders Markus and Maren Helen Grefsrud. (The two smallest boys are friends of us).

Råssum - farm where we live.

Hans Grefsrud Family. Hans is related to Ole Rocksvold's wife, Anne's side. Hans is a descendant of Iver Hansen Sonsteby, the brother of Anne's mother, Marthe Eggebraaten.

Bibliography

Chapter 1

Anderson, Ernest R. "Autobiography of Ernest R. Anderson." unpublished, submitted as an assignment to St. Olaf College, Northfield, MN, 1923.

Ruen, Lyla. Kjøs-Eggebraaten Family History. Decorah, IA: Amundsen Publishing Co., 1982.

Standard Historical Atlas of Winneshiek County, Iowa. Davenport, IA: Anderson and Goodwin Co., 1905.

Chapter 2

Anderson, Ernest R. "Autobiography of Ernest R. Anderson." unpublished, submitted as an assignment to St. Olaf College, Northfield, MN, 1923.

Benedictow, Ole J. "The Black Death: The Greatest Catastrophe Ever." History Today. http://www.historytoday.com/ole-j-benedictow/black-death-greatest-catastrophe-ever. March 2005

Bygeboks (church records), Ås Church, Toten, Norway. www.arkivverket.no and www.disnorge.no

Christianson, John Robert. "Why Christian Glasrud Immigrated to America." Decorah, IA: Luther College, 2002.

Christianson, Karen. "100th Anniversary of Toten Lag in American 1910-2010." Rogers Publishing Company, 2010. p. 69-70.

Deodata ship photograph source at Larvik Museum, Norway: https://digitaltmuseum.no/021015650266/fartoy-seilskip-bark-deodata.

Gesme, Ann Urness. Between Rocks and Hard Places. Hastings, MN: Caragana Press, 1993.

"How the Potato Came to Norway." http://www.sciencenordic.com. 1 June, 2014.

Linnevold, William. "Toten Settlement in Glenwood Township, Winneshiek County, Iowa." unpublished, about 1930, obtained from Winneshiek County Historical Society.

Norton, W.H. Et all. "Underground Water Resources of Iowa." Washingon, D.C. Government Printing Office, 1912.

Ole Rocksvold Obituary. Decorah Journal. 23 Aug., 1922.

Ole Rocksvold Obituary. Decorah Posten. 25 Aug., 1922.

Rosholt, Jerry. Ole Goes to War: Men From Norway Who Fought in America's Civil War. Decorah, IA: Vesterheim Norwegian-American Museum, 2003.

Ruen, Lyla. Kjøs-Eggebraaten Family History. Decorah, IA: Amundsen Publishing Co., 1982.

"Things to Know About Ships."http://www.norwayheritage.com/articles/templates/ships. 1997.

Totenlagets Aarbook 1929. http://www.worldcat.org/title/totenlagets-yearbook-collection-1911-1929/oclc/32482409

Ulvestad, Martin. Norwegians in America (Nordmaendene i Amerika), Vol 2. Minneapolis, MN: Astri My Astri Publishing, 2011.

Chapter 3 and 4

Abernethy. Byron, (editor). Private Elisha Stockwell, Jr. See the Civil War. Norman, Oklahoma: University of Oklahoma Press, 1958.

Billings, John. Hard Tack and Coffee-The Unwritten Story of Army Life. Boston, MA: George M. Smith and Company, 1887. Reprinted by Konecky and Konecky, Old Saybrook, CT.(Year not given).

Blaton, Deanna, and Lauren Cook. The Fought Like Demons: Women Soldiers in the Civil War. New York: Vintage Books, A Division of Random House, Inc., 2002.

"First Reunion of the Hornets' Nest Brigade, 2nd, 7th, 8th, 12th, and 14th Infantry." DesMoines, IA, Oct. 12 and 13, 1887." Oskaloosa, IA: Globe Printing Company, 1888.

Goodwill, Doris Kearns. Team of Rivals. New York, NY: Simon and Schuster,. 2005.

Groom, Winston. Shiloh 1862. Washington, D.C.: National Geography, 2012.

Groom, Winston. Vicksburg 1863. New York, N.Y.: Alfred A. Knopf, 2009.

Johnston, William Preston. The Life of Albert Sidney Johnston. Buffalo Gap, TX: State House Press. 1997 (reprinted)

Kalmoe, Nathan. "Our Civil War Ancestors." unpublished document. 2011.

McPherson, James M. For Cause and Comrades. New York: Oxford University Press, 1997.

Ole Rocksvold Obituary. Decorah Posten. 25 Aug., 1922.

Reardon, Carol and Tom Vossler. "The Battle of Gettysburg Campaign." www.history.military/gettysburg/statistics. Washington, D.C. : U.S. Army Center of Military History. 2013.

Reed, David W. Campaigns and Battles of the Twelfth Regiment Iowa Veteran Volunteer Infantry. Evanston, IL: National Park Service, 1903. (Reprinted in 2015 by ULAN Press, Lexington, KY.)

"Reunion of the Twelfth Iowa Veteran Volunteer Infantry." Dubuque, IA, 1880. https://archive.org/details/reunionoftwelfth00iowa

Rocksvold, Ole, Letters to Anne Guldbrandsdatter Strandbakken (aka Gilbertson) and to Hans Ruen, Jan. 5, 1863-April 18, 1864. Private Collection of Bev Anderson Swenson, Hutchinson, MN, copies shared with Sharon Bowen, Neenah, WI.

Rosholt, Jerry. Ole Goes to War: Men From Norway Who Fought in America's Civil War. Decorah, IA: Vesterheim Norwegian-American Museum, 2003.

Straubing, Harold Elk. Civil War Eyewitness Reports. Hamden, CT: Archon Books, 1985.

"Twelfth Iowa Volunteer Infantry Regiment." http://www.wikipedia.org/wiki/12th_Iowa_Volunteer_Infantry_Regiment . 2014.

U.S. National Archives and Records Administration. Washington, D.C. Federal Military Civil War Pension Records of Ole Rocksvold.http://www.archives.gov/research/military/civil-war/resources.html .

Vesterheim Museum Civil War Records. Decorah, IA. http://vesterheim.org/CivilWar/d/b/r/roc/009199.html.

Wiley, Bell I. The Common Soldier of the Civil War. New York, New York: Charles Scribner's Sons, 1973.

Chapter 5

Anderson, Ernest R. "Autobiography of Ernest R. Anderson." unpublished, submitted as an assignment to St. Olaf College, Northfield, MN, 1923.

Berg, Don. "Glenwood-Hadeland." Unpublished, 1982. Provided by Winneshiek County Historical Society.

Bryan, Joyce. "Immigration in the United States." http://teachersinstitute.yale.edu/curriculum/units/1999/3/99.03.01.x.html . 1999.

Fevold, Eugene. The Norwegian Immigrant and His Church, summarized at: https://www.naha.stolaf.edu/pubs/nas/volume23/vol23_1.html. May, 1966.

Gesme, Ann Urness. Between Rocks and Hard Places. Hastings, MN: Caragana Press, 1993.

Glenwood Lutheran Church. www.glenwoodlutheran.org/history

"Honored by Iowa Democrats." New York, New York: New York Times, Sept. 5, 1893.

Jacobson, Charlotte. "Minutes of the Congregational Proceedings in Little Iowa Norwegian-Evangelical Lutheran Congregation and the Glenwood Congregation Begun 1-12-1854-1-1934." Unpublished (translated by Charlotte Jacobson 6-1981). Glenwood, IA: Glenwood Lutheran Church, 1981.

Kelley, Bruce Gunn. "Ethnocultural Voting Trends in Rural Iowa, 1890-1898." Des Moines, IA: State Historical Society of Iowa, 44.6 (1978): 441-461.

Nelson, David T. The Diary of Elisabeth Koren 1853-55. Northfield, MN: Norwegian-American Historical Association, 1955.

Nelson, E. Clifford et al. The Lutherans in North American. Philadelphia: Fortress Press. 1975.

Norton, W. H., et al. Underground Water Resources of Iowa. Washingon, D.C.: Government Printing Office, 1912.

Ruen, Lyla. Kjøs-Eggebraaten Family History. Decorah, IA: Amundsen Publishing Co., 1982.

Wikipedia. Horace Boies. https://en.wikipedia.org/wiki/Horace_Boies 2015.

Appendix: Glenwood Church and Ole's Participation There

Fevold, Eugene. The Norwegian Immigrant and His Church, summarized at: http://www.naha.stolaf.edu/pubs/nas/volume23/vol23_1.html. May, 1966.

Glenwood Lutheran Church. www.glenwoodlutheran.org/history

Hansen, Karen. Encounter on the Great Plains:Scandinavian Settlers and the Dispossession of Dakota Indians. New York, New York: Oxford University Press. 2013

Iverson, Jeffrey. Lutheran Understanding of the Chosen: Election Controversy in Midwestern Lutheranism and Its Lasting Ramifications. Chetek, WI: 2013 (self-published.) www.imsus.org/lutheranunderstandingofchosen.pdf.

Jacobson, Charlotte. "Minutes of the Congregational Proceedings in Little Iowa Norwegian-Evangelical Lutheran Congregation and the Glenwood Congregation Begun 1-12-1854-1-1934." Unpublished (translated by Charlotte Jacobson 6-1981). Glenwood, IA: Glenwood Lutheran Church, 1981.

Nelson, E. Clifford et al. The Lutherans in North American. Philadelphia: Fortress Press. 1975.

Scheie, David L. The Predestination Controversy. http://scheie.homedns.org/AppendixA-Predest.htm. 2006.